cognitive science

a philosophical introduction

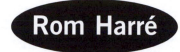

Rom Harré

cognitive science

a philosophical introduction

SAGE Publications
London • Thousand Oaks • New Delhi

First published 2002

Apart from any fair dealing for the purposes of research or
private study, or criticism or review, as permitted under the
Copyright, Designs and Patents Act, 1988, this publication
may be reproduced, stored or transmitted in any form, or by
any means, only with the prior permission in writing of the
publishers, or in the case of reprographic reproduction, in
accordance with the terms of licences issued by the Copyright
Licensing Agency. Inquiries concerning reproduction outside
those terms should be sent to the publishers.

SAGE Publications Ltd
6 Bonhill Street
London EC2A 4PU

SAGE Publications Inc
2455 Teller Road
Thousand Oaks, California 91320

SAGE Publications India PVT Ltd
32, M-Block Market
Greater Kailash – 1
New Delhi 110 048

British Library Cataloguing in Publication data

A catalogue record for this book is available from
the British Library

ISBN 0 7619 6807 5
ISBN 0 7619 6808 3 (pbk)

Library of Congress Control Number: 2001132950

Typest by Photoprint, Torquay, Devon
Printed in Great Britain by The Cromwell Press,
Trowbridge, Wiltshire

Contents

List of illustrations   xiv
List of abbreviations   xv
Preface   xvii
Acknowledgements   xviii
How to use this book in the classroom   xix

part one

The nature and methods of science   1

chapter one

A science for psychology   5

What is the domain of cognitive science?   5
What makes a study program scientific?   8
Learning Point: What is Science?   9

Philosophy in the context of science   9
Some other terms for presuppositions   11
Learning Point: What is Philosophy?   12

Ontology: presuppositions as to what there is   12
Learning Point: Ontology   15

Science, philosophy and psychology in history   15
The project of a scientific psychology in full   16
Conclusion   17

chapter two

The natural sciences   19

The world of the natural sciences   20
Learning Point: The World of the Natural Sciences   23

Rival interpretations of science   24
Learning Point: Positivism and Realism   29

Indirect experiments: testing hypotheses about the unobservable   30
Learning Point: Experimenting in Region Three   32

Conclusion   33

chapter three

Understanding scientific method   35

section one

Describing and Classifying   36

The role of concepts in classification   36
Hierarchical classification systems   37
The bases of type distinctions   38
Learning Point: 1: Describing and classifying   41

section two

Explaining   42

Models   42
Analytical and explanatory uses of models   44
The cognitive foundations of model building   48
Assessing the worth of models   50
Experimental apparatus as model worlds   51
Further uses of modeling   52
Learning Point: 2: Model making   54

Conclusion   54

part two

The search for a science of human behavior   59

chapter four

Psychology as the science of mental substances   65

Descartes's psychology   65
The psychology of John Locke   68
The realist psychology of David Hartley   71
The positivist psychology of David Hume   72
Causes and agents: the transcendental solution   73
Learning Point: The Search for a Scientific Psychology 1:
   Mental substances   **75**

Conclusion   76

chapter five

Psychology as a science of material substances   79

section one

Ontological materialism   81

section two

Methodological materialism   83

section three

Conceptual materialism   85

The arguments for eliminative materialism   86
The arguments against eliminative materialism   87
Psychology cannot do without the person   89
Learning Point: The Search for a Scientific Psychology 2:
   Materialism   **90**

section four

Psychology as a branch of biology   91

Aristotelian beginnings: psychology as the science of
  goal-directed action   92
The modern Aristotelians   95
Evolutionary psychology   96
Learning Point: The Search for a Scientific Psychology 3: Biologism 100

Conclusion   101

chapter six

The beginnings of cognitive science   103

section one

The First Cognitive Revolution   105

Early attempts at devising a cognitive machine   106
Learning Point: Sources of the First Cognitive Revolution   109

The second attempt: computing machines   109
Using artificial intelligence models in psychology   112
Sources of artificial intelligence models   113
Learning Point: The Projects of Artificial Intelligence   115

section two

Strengths and weaknesses of the First Cognitive
Revolution   116

The troubling questions   117
The representation of intentionality   118
Global aspects of linguistic meaning   123
Learning Point: The Problem of Intentionality   124

The representation of normativity   125
Problems with a rule-based psychology   125
Learning Point: Can Normativity be Represented?   129

Conclusion   130

part three

Towards a scientific psychology 137

chapter seven

Grammar and cognition 141

Symbols and their meanings 142
The central role of language 143
The domain of psychology: the act–action distinction 146
The grammars of everyday life 147
The intentional stance 150
Skill 151
Meta-discourses or 'human sciences' 152
Positioning: the moral dimension 154
The ontology of persons 154
'Mind–body' ties: three links between P, O and M discourses 156
Psychology as a hybrid science 162
Learning Point: Discursive Psychology: The Presuppositions 165

Conclusion 166

chapter eight

Cognitive science: the analytical phase 169

Cognitive tasks and symbolic tools 169
Reinterpreting experiments 170
Two worked examples 176
Grammar as a research tool 181
Learning Point: From a Causal to a Normative Metaphysics 186

Conclusion 187

chapter nine

Connectionism and the brain   189

section one

What is a connectionist system?   191

Neurons and nets   191
Model nets as research tools   197
Strokes and other lesions   200
Problems with the brain structure :: model net analogy   200
**Learning Point: Connectionism and Parallel Distributed
    Processing**   **202**

section two

The brain as an organ for performing cognitive tasks   203

The anatomy of the human brain   204
The physiology of the human brain   204
Negative correlations: aphasias and brain damage   206
Positive correlations: scanning technology   207
Learning Point: Artificial Nets and Real Brains   **209**

Conclusion   210

part four

Cognitive science in action   215

chapter ten

The memory machine   221

section one

The vernacular vocabulary of remembering   222

What can be remembered?   223
The problem of authentication   225

section two

Remembering as a topic for cognitive psychology   226

Neisser's paradox and the Ebbinghaus paradigm   227
The problem of the workings of memory machines   229
Generic models: representation and retention   229
The research program summarized   230

section three

Cognitive psychology of remembering, phase one: a descriptive taxonomy   232

Collective remembering   233
Individual remembering   234
Learning Point: Remembering: Vocabularies and Classifications   **237**

section four

Cognitive psychology of remembering, phase two: explanation   238

Some important metaphors   238
Models for the psychology of remembering   239
Transforming a cognitive model into an artificial intelligence
    simulation   244
Worked example: the hippocampus   246
Learning Point: Models for Remembering   **251**

Conclusion   252

chapter eleven

The psychology of classifying   255

The Aristotelian logic of classification   255
The expression and representation of bodies of knowledge   258
Learning Point: Basic Principles of Knowledge Representation   **260**

Alternative conceptions of a knowledge base   261
Problems common to all approaches to knowledge engineering   264
Limitations of the project so far   265

Cognitive psychology of classifying: take one   266
Cognitive psychology of classifying: take two   268
Learning Point: Alternative Methods of Classification   **270**

Connectionism: the way forward?   270
Exercise: extracting a prototype   271
Disadvantages with connectionist models   272
Neuropsychology of classifying   273
Learning Point: Connectionist Models of Classifying   **274**

Conclusion   274

chapter twelve

Cognitive disorders   277

section one

Presuppositions of psychiatry and clinical psychology   278

The expansion of the domain of psychopathology   280
Bizarre thought patterns and disordered brains   282
The presupposition of psychotherapy   283
Classifying phenomena and modeling the unobservable   285
**Learning Point: Sources of Concepts of Psychopathology:
Deviance and Unacceptability**   **286**

section two

Defects of discourse   287

Non-standard story lines using standard syntax   287
Non-standard syntax and standard narrative conventions   288
Learning Point: Psychopathology as Improper Narration   **291**

section three

Psychopathology and brain malfunction   291

The insertion of an old trouble into the Hybrid Psychology
    framework   292
The creation of a new mental illness: the case of attention
    deficit hyperactivity disorder   294

Contesting a grammar: the case of chronic fatigue syndrome   296
**Learning Point: The Transformation, Invention and Contesting
    of Mental Illnesses**   **297**

Conclusion   298

Epilog   303
References   305
Name index   311
Subject index   312

List of illustrations

3.1 Tree representation of a classificatory system 38
3.2 Taxonomic hierarchy 41
3.3 Type hierarchy of material things 50
6.1 TOTE machine for hammering home nails 107
9.1 Basic structure of real nerve cell 192
9.2 Synapse in detail 192
9.3 Migration of sodium and potassium ions 193
9.4 Structure of an artificial neuron 194
9.5 Threshold function 194
9.6 Sigmoid function 194
9.7 Connectionist neural net 195
9.8 From real net to model net 196
9.9 Hinton diagram of the pattern associator 197
9.10 Untrained net 199
9.11 Untrained weight matrix 199
9.12 Weights in a trained net 200
9.13 A median section of the brain showing the location of the
 hippocampus 205
10.1 Summary taxonomy of 'remembering' concepts 237
10.2 Connections with the hippocampus 247
10.3 Forward connections from areas of cerebral association neocortex
 to the hippocampus 249
10.4 A neural network simulation of the hippocampus 250
10.5 An eight-unit auto-associator 250
11.1 A Porphyry Tree 256
12.1 Boundary fixing 281

List of abbreviations

ADHD	attention deficit hyperactivity disorder
AI	artificial intelligence
ASCII	American Standard Code for Information Interchange
CFS	chronic fatigue syndrome
CNS	central nervous system
EEG	electroencephalograph
GOFAI	good old-fashioned artificial intelligence
IPS	information-processing system
PDP	parallel distributed processing
PET	positron emission tomography
SSH	symbol system hypothesis
T/T	task/tool
TOTE	test/operate/test/exit
TPP	Taxonomic Priority Principle

Preface

This book is based on the Machette Lectures, delivered at the University of Ohio, Athens OH in March 1998. It gives me great pleasure to acknowledge the generous support of the Machette Foundation for the lecture series and its subsequent publication. I am particularly grateful to the Philosophy Department of Ohio University at Athens OH for inviting me and for providing such a rewarding and stimulating environment in which to do philosophy. My special thanks to James Petrik, Donald Borchert and Albert Mosley for managing the executive side of the visit so efficiently.

The basic work on preparing the lectures and the text that accompanies them was carried out when I was Guest Professor at the Philosophy Institute, Aarhus University, Aarhus, Denmark. I am very grateful for the opportunity. I owe special thanks to Uffe Juul Jensen, Chairman of the Philosophy Institute, both for the original invitation and for the many ways in which he made my stay both profitable and agreeable. I am immensely grateful to friends and colleagues with whom I had many discussions around the topics of these lectures, in particular Hans Fink and Steen Brock, as well as friends and colleagues at Aalborg and Copenhagen Universities.

The final form of this text owes much to the feedback from three generations of students at Georgetown University, Washington DC, and to the students of the Honors Program at American University in that same great city.

I am particularly grateful to my friends and colleagues Ali Moghaddam and Darlene Howard for their invaluable advice and comments.

Rom Harré
Oxford and Washington DC

Acknowledgements

I am grateful to the publishers of the following books for kind permission to reproduce various diagrams.

McLeod, P., Plunkett, K. and Rolls, E.T. (1998) *Introduction to Connectionist Modelling of Cognitive Processes*, Oxford: Oxford University Press.

Miller, G.A., Galanter, G. and Pribram, K.H. (1967) *Plans and the Structure of Behavior*, New York: Holt Rinehart & Winston.

Restak, R.M. (1995) *Brainscapes*, New York: Hyperion Press.

How to use this book in the classroom

Increasingly, over the last decade, many psychology departments are including required courses in philosophy of psychology in their curricula. The content and level of such courses vary widely. Some have been devoted exclusively to philosophy of science. Others have covered topics in philosophy of mind. The course on which this text is based deals with philosophical questions raised by the project of developing psychology as a science.

Psychology students have usually had little exposure to criticial reflections on the concepts employed in their courses on standard psychological topics. Nor are critical discussions of standard methods of research at all common in the methodology courses offered in most universities. Experience in teaching the philosophy of physics has shown that students studying a science gain most from a course which introduces philosophical issues in discussions of specific topics drawn from the science in question. This text is aimed at introducing the practice of philosophical reflection in relation to examples drawn from branches of psychology that are already covered in the usual curriculum. These are presented in a way that highlights aspects of scientific psychology of particular philosophical interest.

What is philosophy of science? The contents of courses range from studies of the logic of scientific enquiry to the sociology of scientific institutions. For the most part, the available textbooks in philosophy of science are not easy to adapt for use by psychology students. They seem increasingly to reflect the way that philosophy of science has become a specialist field detached from the sciences themselves. The tendency to confine discussion to rather abstract debates concerning topics of interest to logicians and other scholars of a formal bent has left a gap when one is looking for a text that will have some immediacy of impact on psychology students. To some extent, philosophy of mind has followed the same path, into an increasingly esoteric and specialized pattern of debate around topics that have become difficult to reintegrate into psychology courses proper. This text is an attempt to remedy the situation. The need for courses that stand back from the routine presentation of 'results' and 'theories' is felt in many departments. The courses on which this text is based have been built up on the basis of the principle that one can be philosophical, that is one can stand back and reflect on the onto-logical, epistemological and methodological presuppositions of psychological practice – while remaining in close touch with that practice.

Increasingly, psychology is becoming polarized around two seemingly irreconcilable schools of thought. There are those who see, rightly, that the phe-nomena that psychologists study are discursive, that is, consist largely of mean-ings and the means by which people manage them. There are also those who see, rightly, that the instruments of cognition are material, the brain and nervous sys-tem. These positions can and should be reconciled. Courses such as those for which this book has been written could serve, one hopes, as part of a long-term project to integrate the seemingly diverse directions of cutting-edge research into a unified though hybrid discipline.

This is intended as a teaching text. Though it presents a certain point of view on controversial matters it is not intended as a treatise or monograph either in discursive psychology or artificial intelligence. I hope that enough detail has been provided as a general groundwork to the more technical aspects of contem-porary cognitive psychology without the risk of intimidating undergraduates. In some universities, undergraduates may be taking as many as four other courses in the semester in which they are advised to take a philosophy course. It is essential, therefore, that examples are drawn, at least in part, from standard topics in psy-chology with which most will have become acquainted.

University libraries are rich in detailed studies and telling discussions of many of the topics treated here. I very much hope that students will be encour-aged to pursue their own interests by consulting some of this literature. To that end, I have offered some suggestions for further reading beyond the supplemen-tary excerpts following each Self-test section. These are only suggestions. They should not be regarded as in any way definitive of what is worth serious study.

The level of exposition presumes that classes will be attended mainly by students in their Junior or Senior years, who have already taken some psychology or philosophy courses. Specific psychological content has been presented in a simplified way, but without, I hope, becoming so schematized as to lead to misunderstandings.

The structure is keyed in to a twelve-week teaching term or semester, assuming classroom time set aside for tests and quizzes. Each 'Learning Point' is meant to summarize the material that would roughly comprise a single lecture. It is good pedagogical practice to maintain continuity in the course by using the Learning Point of one lecture to introduce the next. Each part or module is more or less self-contained, with sets of study questions appended for revision and self-testing. The study questions for each chapter are followed by suggested chapter-length readings from a list of co-texts which would be on library reserve. In practice each module fits a six-lecture pattern of teaching, completed by a review session and a test.

There is sufficient material in each part to allow different course patterns to be created by selection of particular topics. For example in Part I, Chapter 2 could be omitted or, in Part II, Chapter 4. In Part III, Chapter 8 could be left out, while in Part IV, any one of Chapters 10, 11 or 12 could be used as an example of an integrated research program. Other patterns have been found to be workable, depending on departmental interests and requirements.

Co-textbooks

These should be on reserve in the library. Chapter-length readings are suggested for each self-test section at the end of each part. The books below have been selected not only on their intrinsic merits but also because they are believed to be in print. ISBNs have been included for the convenience of librarians.

Part One The nature and methods of science

Harré, R. (2000) *One Thousand Years of Philosophy*, Oxford: Blackwell (ISBN 0 631 21901 3).
McErlean, J. (2000) *Philosophies of Science: From Foundations to Contemporary Issues*, Belmont CA: Wadsworth (ISBN 0 534 55163 7).
Morgan, M. and Morrison, M.S. (1999) *Models as Mediators*, Cambridge: Cambridge University Press (ISBN 0 52 165571 4).

Part Two The search for a science of human behavior

Robinson, D.N. (1995) *An Intellectual History of Psychology*, third edition, London: Arnold (ISBN 0 340 66212 3).
Copeland, J. (1998) *Artificial Intelligence*, Oxford: Blackwell (ISBN 0 19 852313 0).

Part Three Towards a scientific psychology

Edwards, D. (1997) *Discourse and Cognition*, London: Sage (ISBN 0 80 397697 6).
Dennett, D. (1987) *The Intentional Stance*, Cambridge MA: MIT Press (ISBN 0 262 04093 X).
Copeland, J. (1998) *Artificial Intelligence*, Oxford: Blackwell (ISBN 0 19 852313 0).

Part Four Cognitive science in action

Cohen, G., Kiss, G. and Le Voi, M. (1993) *Memory: Current Issues*, Buckingham and Philadelphia: Open University Press (ISBN 0 335 19079 0).
Way, E.C. (1992) *Knowledge Representation and Metaphor*, Dordrecht: Kluwer (ISBN 1851516390).
Gillett, Grant (1999) *The Mind and its Discontents: an Essay in Discursive Psychiatry*, Oxford: Oxford University Press (ISBN 0 19 852313 0).

Additional readings

There are many useful publications covering aspects of the topics covered in this text. The following are recommended for supplementary reference.

Boden, M.A. (1988) *Artificial Intelligence in Psychology*, Cambridge MA: MIT Press.

Button, G., Coulter, J., Lee, J.R.E. and Sharrock, W. (1995) *Computers, Minds and Conduct*, Cambridge: Polity Press.

Dreyfus, H.L. (1972) *What Computers Can't Do: a Critique of Artificial Reason*, New York: Harper & Row.

Engel, S. (1999) *Context is Everything: The Nature of Memory*, New York: Freeman

Fulford, K.W.M. (1998) *The Philosophical Basis of Ethics: Standards in Psychiatry*, Preston: University of Lancaster Press.

Giere, R.N. (1988) *Explaining Science: a Cognitive Approach*, Chicago: University of Chicago Press.

Gigenrenzer, G. and Goldstein, D.G. (1996) 'Mind as computer: birth of a metaphor', *Creativity Research Journal* 9: 131–44.

Gillies, A. (1996) *Artificial Intelligence and Scientific Method*, Oxford: Oxford University Press, chapter 2.

Luria, A.R. (1981) *Language and Cognition*, New York: Wiley.

Sobel, C.P. (2001) *The Cognitive Sciences*, Mountain View CA: Mayfield.

The nature and methods of science

Psychology is the study of thinking, feeling (emotions), perceiving and acting. The field of cognitive psychology has traditionally been concerned with just one of the four kinds of psychological phenomena: namely, thinking or cognition. What do we mean by 'cognition'? In scientific matters it is unwise to set up hard-and-fast definitions. It is best to list some examples of what a general concept covers, and to add an etcetera! Among the psychological phenomena in the field of cognition are remembering, reasoning, calculating, classifying, deciding, etc.

In recent years it has become increasingly clear that neither the psychology of the emotions, nor the psychology of perception, nor social psychology can be studied without considerable attention being paid to the role of the processes listed above as the topics of cognitive psychology. In this text we shall be concerned only with the principles and methods of the scientific study of cognition.

Cognitive science is the attempt to study cognitive phenomena in a way not unlike the way the physical sciences study material phenomena. Physics includes mechanics, the study of the laws of motion of elementary material things. Chemistry includes the study of the synthesis of material substances from other material substances in the light of knowledge of their atomic constituents and internal structures. In recent years the field of cognitive science has been taken to include the study of the relevant aspects of the neuroanatomy and neurophysiology of the brain and nervous system.

The history of attempts to create a cognitive *science* which includes both naturalistic studies of thinking and technically sophisticated studies of the relevant brain activities, reveals many false starts. For the most part the failure of these programs of research can be accounted for by the philosophical presuppositions that their progenitors took for granted. Science is a human practice. Like tennis, the law, politics and other human practices, science has its presuppositions. Some presuppositions of past attempts to create a science of the cognitive activities of human beings were metaphysical, such as the presupposition that the domain of cognition involves non-material entities, ideas in the mind. Some were methodological, such as the presupposition that the work of cognitive

1

psychologists can be reduced to a study of the material aspects of thinking alone, psychology as neuroscience. In studying a scientific project philosophically we bring out taken for granted presuppositions and subject them to critical scrutiny. To do well in the practices of some domain it is desirable to have a clear idea of what is presupposed in what one does. Philosophical studies of presuppositions have a practical role.

Not only are there philosophical presuppositions involved in the practice of the sciences, but there are highly influential philosophical theories of the very nature of science itself. These too we must scrutinize. Taking the sciences to be the disciplined searching for indubitable truths, philosophers have demanded that only what can be perceived by the senses should be admitted to the domain of the sciences. This is the philosophical position of positivism. The contrasting position is realism. The physical sciences, from their beginnings in the ancient world, have been based on hypotheses about processes that cannot be readily perceived. Astronomers imagined various heavenly architectures. Chemists and physicists imagined a realm of minute, invisible atoms, the motions and rearrangements of which accounted for the phenomena human beings could perceive. Realists argue that we have good reason for preferring some pictures of the invisible regions of nature to others. The history of the physical sciences shows a pattern of back and forth between positivistic reactions to unsupported speculations about the causes of what can be observed and realist developments of more disciplined and plausible hypotheses about the world beyond the limits of the senses. At the turn of the third millennium the physical sciences are in a strongly realist phase of this cycle. Physicists are happy with quarks. Chemists have no trouble with atomic structures. Biologists are comfortable with genes. Geologists talk freely about tectonic plates, and so on. We will follow the fashion. The program for cognitive science presented here will be realist, using techniques like those well established in physics, chemistry, biology and the earth sciences, to pass beyond what can be perceived by the senses, into the deeper realms of material reality.

As we look into the philosophy of the natural sciences for guidelines to be followed in developing a scientific psychology of cognition, we find two main aspects of scientific work. There is the complex task of classifying the phenomena of the field of interest. This requires not only that they be found places in a classificatory scheme, but also that such a scheme be well founded, free of contradictions and linked with theories about the nature of what it is we are classifying.

Then there is the task of building explanations of the phenomena of interest. For the most part the processes that produce phenomena are not observable in the same way as the phenomena, if they are observable at all. Chemical reactions can be seen, heard and sometimes smelled. The molecular processes by which they are explained cannot be. Molecules and their behavior are works of the human imagination, representing, one hopes, real productive processes. The techniques by which this phase of scientific work is done are well understood.

However, the insights that have come from a close study of the physical sciences have yet to be fully integrated into the methods of cognitive science. In our course we shall be at the 'cutting edge', learning the very latest techniques for creating explanations of psychological phenomena that can stand alongside those of physics, chemistry and biology.

Part I introduces two main themes. We shall be learning how philosophers delve into the presuppositions of human practices. Then we will look closely into the two main phases of a scientific research program, classifying and explaining. Bringing the two themes together will introduce us to the philosophy of science. We shall then be ready to follow the history of attempts to found and develop psychology as cognitive science.

A science for psychology

There are two aims in the course. One is to gain a command of what it takes to make a philosophical approach to a human practice, unearthing the presuppositions upon which a way of thinking and acting depends. The other is to achieve some mastery of the basic principles of a unified cognitive science. We shall take for granted that both projects are worth undertaking. Philosophy is a long-standing way of taking up a critical attitude to human practices. Cognitive science, in the hybrid form we will develop it in this course, is, one might say, the best shot yet at achieving a genuinely scientific psychology. There have been many such attempts in the past, but all have so far fallen by the wayside for one reason or another. We will pay some attention to the debris of past enthusiasms that litters the path of history. From each false start we can gain a better view of what it would take to get it right eventually.

We begin with an overview of two aspects of our topic, first sketching the way scientific knowledge is produced and presented. Then we turn to examine what is involved in doing philosophy. We shall then be in a position to understand what it is to do philosophy of science, bringing the two disciplines into fruitful conjunction. It will then be an easy step to the constructive phase of the course – coming to a philosophical understanding of what is required for there to be a science of cognition – a genuinely scientific psychology.

What is the domain of cognitive science?

There is a range of human activities – remembering, deciding, reasoning, classifying, planning and so on – that have traditionally been thought to belong to a group of mental processes, generally falling under the label 'cognition'. We can think of cognitive activities in terms of tasks. We use our cognitive powers and capacities to carry out all sorts of projects, from deciding what to wear to a party to 'keeping tabs' on a bank account. We may use our cognitive powers to solve problems – for example, to find the shortest way home. Tasks can be performed well or ill, carefully or carelessly, correctly or incorrectly, with many intermediate possibilities. Solutions can be more or less adequate, more or less cleverly arrived at, and so on.

The study of these activities, and the standards to which they are taken to conform, is *cognitive psychology,* the descriptive phase of a psychological science. However, what about the explanatory phase? What must be invoked to account for a person's ability to make choices, to do sums and to solve problems? The principal thesis of what has come to be called 'cognitive science' is that there are neural mechanisms by which cognitive tasks are performed.

The course for which this textbook has been written is based on the conviction that cognitive science should cover a broader field than just the neuro-psychology of cognition. It is based on the principle that any branch of psychology, be it the study of cognition, emotions, social action or any other aspect of human mental life, is necessarily a hybrid. It must encompass the naturalistic study of psychological phenomena as they are manifested in what people do. It must also include an empirical and theoretical investigation of the neural mechanisms by which people act and think as they do. Both types of research, however different the natures of the phenomena they study, can be carried out in conformity with the standards and methods of *scientific* investigations. We will develop our understanding of the nature of scientific as opposed to other kinds of research by attending to how research is actually conducted in the realm of the natural sciences.

Why should it be necessary to take time out to establish what is needed to make a method of enquiry 'scientific', in the sense that chemistry and physics are scientific? In the not so recent past psychologists slipped into following mistaken or partial interpretations of the natural sciences. This was particularly true in the days of the dominance of behaviorism. We shall follow the rise and fall of behaviorism as a case study. It illustrates very well how mistaken philosophical views on the nature of science can exert a malign influence on the development of a new science. Even now, a good deal of the misleading terminology of behaviorism and the simplistic empiricism of which it was a part survives among the presuppositions of some contemporary psychology. Fortunately, philosophers of science now offer us a much more satisfactory and plausible account of the natural sciences than heretofore. This will be our guide in following the way that a true cognitive science can be developed.

Our studies in this course will begin with a thorough analysis of the natural sciences. This will provide a methodological springboard from which we will build our understanding of the actual and possible achievements of cognitive psychology and its relation to neuroscience. It will also give us the ability to identify and understand some of its current shortcomings and to appreciate the ways we may overcome them in fruitful programs of research. Some of the practical exercises suggested in the text could become contributions to the growth of cognitive psychology itself.

This course is demanding. We shall be dealing with four disciplines: philosophy of science, discursive or naturalistic psychology, cognitive psychology and the modeling of thought by the use of techniques from artificial intelligence. Finally, to complete the progression, some basic brain chemistry, anatomy and physiology will be required to understand how some and only some forms of computer modeling can be fruitful sources of deep theories in cognitive science. Inevitably, none of these disciplines can be studied in real depth, but that does not mean that the aspects selected in this treatment will be superficial. Readings in supplementary specialist textbooks will, therefore, be of great importance. They will be given in detail as our studies progress.

When we carry out cognitive tasks such as calculating or classifying we use systems of symbols, *meaningful* shapes, marks, patterns, real and imaginary, sounds and so on. One major problem, to which we will frequently return, is how to give a plausible account of what it is that makes a mark a meaningful mark. This is the problem of *intentionality*. No serious efforts at creating a cognitive science can pass it by.

There are right and wrong ways of using symbols which are meaningful for us. One useful metaphor for discussing the standards of their correct uses is to think of manipulating them as if we were consciously paying attention to rules and instructions for so doing. A key field of investigation in the philosophy of cognitive science is how to express the norms that are evidently at work in much that we do but that we are not consciously following. If norms are not expressed as explicit rules and conventions how can they be so efficacious? This is the problem of *normativity*. This problem too must be tackled as we try to build a science of cognition.

Among the symbols and symbol systems we use are words, gestures, signs, diagrams, models, drawings and so on. Cognitive psychology must start with studies of activities such as classifying or remembering, as they are performed by people using the symbol systems available to them in their own cultures. A dancer thinks of a routine in the form of a flow of bodily movements. A student remembers the theme of a lecture in the form of words, propositions. A chemist may think about a chemical reaction in the form of a model or picture of the flux and reflux of ions in a solution.

How are these cognitive tasks performed? By the use of organs in the brain and nervous system, 'cerebral tools'. Cognitive science must include an essential neuro-anatomical and neuro-physiological dimension. We must not forget that most of us possess a supplementary kit of prosthetic devices, such as electronic organizers, which can take over some of the functions of the tools we are endowed with naturally. One can use one's brain to remember an appointment, one's hippocampus to find one's way home and so on. However, one can also use a diary for keeping track of personal commitments in time and a map to manage one's movements in space. Nowadays each of these devices is readily available in electronic form. One of the major questions we will be asking is how much can we learn about how the natural tools work from understanding how the artificial ones do their version of the job. This will take us into the field of artificial intelligence and computational models of the mind.

Our first acquaintance with cognitive activities comes very early in life, much earlier we now believe than had hitherto been thought. Under the influence of the recently rediscovered developmental studies of L.S. Vygotsky (1978), we no longer think of ourselves as maturing cognitively as isolated individuals according to some predetermined schedule, step by step. Our cognitive skills have their beginnings in the flow of symbolic activity of ordinary life in co-operative activities with other people, particularly in the family. Vygotsky's importance for cognitive psychology comes from his work in unraveling the complex processes by which the cognitive and practical skills of adults are acquired by infants and young children in social interactions. Higher order cognitive functions, he said, appear first in the relations between people and only later as part of an individual's mental endowment. First of all we think publicly and collectively with the assistance of others. Only later do we get the knack of thinking privately.

What makes a study program scientific?

In a scientific treatment of some domain, for example the surface of the earth, we make use of a classification system to identify, describe and categorize the main features of geography. We use such categories as 'islands'. 'continents', 'oceans', 'seas', 'estuaries' and so on. In most sciences, intermediate or borderline cases soon appear, and boundary disputes take place. Is Australia a large island or a small continent? Questions like this can never be settled by observation or experiment. It is not a matter of fact until we have settled on how we will use the concept of 'continent'. Adherents of one way of drawing a boundary around the domain of a classificatory concept offer their reasons and their opponents offer theirs. Issues of convenience, consistency and so on are used to bring agreement on a working convention for settling the scope of application of a category.

A scientific treatment of the surface of the earth would be incomplete without an explanation of how the observable features and their patterns of distribution came about. Why does South America seem to fit so snugly into the curve of Africa, if we imagine them juxtaposed? Scientific explanations typically postulate unobservable entities and processes which bring about the geographical features we can observe. In the case of the earth, geologists nowadays invoke the existence of tectonic plates, slowly moving across the semi-liquid magma in the interior of the earth, and carrying the observable features of the surface with them.

How could we possibly know what these plates are like? We cannot observe them as they are in themselves. Beliefs about the unobservable entities and processes that account for observable states of affairs are usually arrived at by the use of powerful, plausible and fruitful analogies. Instead of trying to think about the real but inaccessible deep structures of earth's crust, we think about Wegener's tectonic plates. How we do that? The plates are a model, that is, a pictorial representation of the real structures. We imagine what they are like by drawing an analogy with something we already know. Perhaps Wegener, the man who first proposed the theory of tectonic plates, saw a similarity between the behavior of icefloes grinding against one another as they are driven by currents in the water and tectonic plates grinding against one another as they are driven by the circulation currents of the molten iron that forms the core of the earth.

Thus a complete earth science must be a hybrid of geography, playing the descriptive role, and geology or plate tectonics, playing the explanatory role.

Here we have a simple example of one of the major techniques of theory building in science. This is model making, using analogies with discretion. Understanding the role of models in science leads to an understanding of the main research methods and procedures by means of which human beings, limited in space, time and resources have gained an understanding of the forces of nature. This has enhanced the human capacity to manage and manipulate them. Most philosophers of science now believe that the basis of our understanding of nature is our capacity to create and manipulate analogs and models of those aspects of the material world that interest us.

Giving written or discursive form to the insights we thus acquire, that is, presenting our scientific knowledge in books and articles, is a secondary matter when compared with the primacy of model making.

---

learning point   **What is science?**

1   A science consists of:

  a)   An ordered catalog of phenomena.
  b)   A system of models representing the unobservable mechanisms by which observable phenomena are produced.

2   A scientist therefore needs to have:

  a)   A system of concepts for classifying phenomena. These will define types and kinds, and so create a taxonomy.
  b)   An accepted source of concepts as a means of controling the making of models, representing the unobservable processes by which phenomena are produced.

Ideally the classification system and the repertoire of explanatory models should be linked in a coherent overall system. There are various ways that this can be achieved.

Philosophy in the context of science

Philosophers try to bring to light and critically examine some, at least, of the presuppositions upon which the effectiveness, intelligibility and so on of human practices depend. This involves making a preliminary distinction between factual presuppositions and presuppositions concerning the relations between concepts. Conceptual presuppositions are evident in the meanings we give to our concepts and the ways that we take them to be interrelated.

The realization of the great importance of this basic distinction has been one of the major philosophical contributions to our ability to interpret the sciences and to our sensitivity in detecting deep-lying fallacies and muddles. We have learned from Wittgenstein how easy it is to fall into treating an issue about concepts or the uses of words as if it were an issue about matters of fact. Is it just a matter of fact that I cannot feel your pain, or is it a matter of how the word 'pain' is to be used in everyday language? If it is a matter of fact, it could have been otherwise. If it is a matter of the uses of words, we ought not even to make sense of the alternative.

Matters of fact are adjudicated by observation and experiment. Nevertheless, conceptual presuppositions are always involved. To rely on observation and experiment we must presuppose that there are no paradoxes, contradictions or other faults in the system of concepts we use to describe our factual discoveries. Philosophical investigations sometimes involve asking how well a factual presupposition of one aspect of a practice fits with one or more conceptual presuppositions of some other aspect. For example, the practice of finding people guilty of breaking the law presupposes that as a matter of fact someone could have done otherwise than he or she did. However, this clashes with the presupposition of much of psychiatric medicine that in fact aberrant social behavior is fully explicable in terms of neurophysiology and genetics.

Matters of the rules for the correct use of words and other symbols are adjudicated by an analysis of meanings. Sometimes such an analysis reveals unnoticed confusions, contradictions and other faults in a seemingly coherent conceptual system. These can be revealed by studying the interrelations among the meanings of the words that are the verbal expression of a conceptual system. For example, if it is a matter of the meanings of words that people are active agents purposefully finding their way through the problems of living, how can that be reconciled with the use of the concept of unconscious wishes driving a person to behave in ways that are contrary to a long-standing pattern of life?

This kind of critical analysis of large-scale conceptual systems often involves making connections with presuppositions of adjoining practices. For instance, legal philosophy and medical ethics involve cross-connections and comparisons between medical and legal uses of what seem to be the same concepts. In both practices, important parts are played by concepts such as 'death', 'madness' and so on. The *concepts* of 'life' and 'death' have changed in recent years, and this has had its effect on how the law interprets such controversial practices as abortion and euthanasia. To illustrate the fundamental distinction between the two main kinds of presuppositions let us examine a simple, everyday practice. What is presupposed in ordinary commercial transactions where money is used in exchange for goods and services?

An elderly philosopher approaches the ticket office at Jefferson's mansion at Monticello. The clerk says, 'The entrance tickets cost $20.' The philosopher proffers $15 and his Golden Age card. He receives an entrance ticket. What has been presupposed in this not untypical human practice? First of all, here are some *factual presuppositions*:

1   Hidden from view there is a mansion.
2   There was such a person as Thomas Jefferson, who ordered the construction of the mansion in accordance with his plans.

3   There is a discount for senior citizens.
4   The philosopher is a senior citizen and the Golden Age card is his.
5   This is Monticello, Charlottesville, Virginia.
6   The dollar is the local unit of currency.

Here are some *conceptual or philosophical presuppositions*:

1   Dollars are fungible, that is, the $5 bills the philosopher received in change
     elsewhere are still, in this new context, worth $5. It would not make sense
     for the philosopher to ask the cashier, 'Which $5 do you want?'
2   The mansion, being a material thing, will still be there when the visitor has
     ascended the hill.

Since the philosophical presuppositions do not involve matters of fact, they can
be brought into question only by discussion and analysis. For example, one could
get into a discussion about the concept of 'money'. The concept has changed
since the days when Hamilton settled on the Maria Theresa thalers, the original
silver dollars, as the federal unit of currency. Now dollars are more often than
not electronic somethings in cyberspace. Our visitor could have paid by debit
card. One could get into a discussion about the concept of a material object. For
example, is the mansion that is eventually visited by the philosopher the same
mansion that is being visited by each person in the group, if, as some philosophers
have maintained, the mansion exists for each visitor only as patterns of colored
patches in their personal and private visual fields?
       Philosophy of science is a study of the non-factual presuppositions of the
practices of the natural and the human sciences. In short, it is a study of the systems of concepts that are put to work in scientific research and theorizing.

Some other terms for presuppositions

Thomas Reid (1788), writing towards the end of the eighteenth century, called the
presuppositions of the human way of life 'the principles of common sense'. By
'common sense' he did not mean everyday wisdom but rather principles that
formed a shared background for everyone capable of rational thought.
       In the same period Immanuel Kant (1787) coined the phrase 'synthetic *a
priori* propositions' to identify the working presuppositions of perception, thought
and action. He meant by this to draw attention to the fact that, as he thought, we
did not arrive at these principles by the analysis of our experiences. Rather they
were what made orderly experience possible. By calling them *a priori* he wanted
to emphasize that they were *not arrived at from experience*. By calling them *synthetic*
he wanted to emphasize their role in the processes by which our minds synthesize
the raw data of the senses into the material world as we know it and, at the same
time, into our thoughts about that world. Somehow each person comes into the
world equipped with the same basic system of schemata. Though we perform our
syntheses of sensations individually to reciprocally create our worlds and our
minds, the worlds we create are more or less the same.

In modern times Wittgenstein (1953) expressed the same general idea in his image of the frame and the picture. Our systems of concepts form the frame in which we paint pictures of the world. The frame is not part of the picture. An even more striking and apposite image was his way of referring to the rules for the correct use of words as a 'grammar', extending the idea of correctness beyond the bounds of our ordinary school grammars of nouns, verbs, adjectives and the like. Throughout this course we will use the word 'grammar' for the systems of concepts and their symbolic bearers by means of which we categorize and make sense of our experiences. A grammar, then, can be expressed as *an open set of malleable rules for using various symbol systems correctly.* From time to time old grammars are dropped or modified, and new grammars grow up. Our typewriting concepts have given way to a completely new grammar for managing computing and cyberspace communication.

These three ways of describing some important aspects of the presuppositions of human practices draw our attention to three aspects of the background to what we think, feel and do. It is shared. It is involved in shaping what we experience. It maintains local standards of correctness.

(learning point)   **What is philosophy?**

1   The project of philosophy is to bring to light and critically discuss the presuppositions of human practices, for instance the law, music and the sciences, even sports. Presuppositions are of two kinds:

   a)   *Factual*, which can be tested by observation and experiment.
   b)   *Conceptual*, which can be tested only by discussion as to their plausibility, utility and coherence.

2   Three ways of presenting the nature of conceptual presuppositions:

   a)   *Thomas Reid.* Principles of common sense: shared by all, used to make sense of experience.
   b)   *Immanuel Kant.* Synthetic *a priori* propositions: express the schemata by which we synthesize an orderly world and tidy minds (synthetic). They are not learned from experience (*a priori*). The list of synthetic *a priori* propositions is limited and fixed.
   c)   *Ludwig Wittgenstein.* Grammars: rules for the correct use of symbols. Grammars can change, usually at different rates under various circumstances.

Ontology: presuppositions as to what there is

Scientific realists feel free to speculate in disciplined ways about the state of the world beyond the limits of perception. To do so rationally they must have in mind certain ideas about what kinds of things, properties, processes, qualities and so on the world may contain. A catalog of what is taken to be really real in some domain of enquiry is its *ontology*. This takes us back to the discussion of presuppositions. An ontology will be among the presuppositions of a science at each moment in its development. Therefore philosophy of science must include discussions of ontology, the general assumptions about the presumed nature of the entities, structures, properties and processes both observable and unobservable characteristic of the relevant domain of enquiry.

Two versions of a materialist ontology

For four centuries the natural sciences have balanced uneasily between two major and very different materialist ontologies. Their indirect influence on psychology has been profound. We must pause to look at them rather closely.

Atomists imagined the world to be a swarm of solid, material particles, moving randomly in an empty void, occasionally making contact by colliding with one another. When not in immediate contact these fundamental bodies were thought to behave quite independently of one another. Atomic particles were passive except in so far as they were in motion. Gravity, magnetism and electricity posed great difficulties for mechanical atomism, since each of these types of interaction seemed to work without a material link from body to body. The attempts by such scientific geniuses as Isaac Newton to accommodate action at a distance, as it was called, into the atomistic ontology were ingenious but ultimately unconvincing. The force of gravity remained a great mystery for Newton and his successors. They could describe how it manifested itself, but its real nature remained quite unknown. A universal medium, the ether, was postulated to explain all non-mechanical phenomena, even the processes of thought.

Dynamism expressed an opposite standpoint in almost every respect. Everything was actively involved with everything else. Space was filled with fields of force: described in terms of potentials for action at every point, ready to bring about effects whenever some suitably sensitive test body was brought under their influences. The phenomena of magnetism, the study of which had begun in the sixteenth century by William Gilbert, were taken up again by another scientific genius in the nineteenth century with a radically different ontology from that of the atomists. In the work of Michael Faraday we have the beginnings of the modern ideas of forces, charges and fields, typical dynamicist concepts, defining an interlinked world of active beings.

While the adoption of atomism by the physicists of the seventeenth century opened up a wealth of research possibilities, it eventually became a burden, since it required all action to be mediated by direct contact between material corpuscles. The shift to dynamicist ideas, allowing natural scientists to picture a world of active beings interacting with one another across the whole of time and space, ushered in the modern era. Instead of atoms wandering in the void, we now have charges and fields interacting through the whole universe.

Table 1.1   Atomism versus dynamism

Atomism	Dynamism
1 Multitude of beings in a void, or empty space. (Newtonian mechanics)	1 Multitude of centers, but influence occupies the whole of space. (Charges and fields)
2 React only when in actual contact	2 In continuous interaction even at a distance
3 Logically independent: deleting one does not affect others. (Selling one sheep from a large flock does not affect the remainder)	3 Logically dependent. (All members of a soccer team affected when one player sent off)
4 Atoms are passive: react only when acted upon	4 Dynamic entities are active: act unless action blocked
5 Generally deterministic: future and past both actual. Possibilities not real. Properties occurrent	5 Generally indeterminstic: past actual but future open. Possibilities real. Properties dispositional

We can appreciate the contrasts between these points of view most easily in a comparative table setting out their main characteristics (Table 1.1). Which ontology shall we take as our model in setting up psychology? Behaviorism was not only positivistic but also tended to treat human beings as the passive sites of responses to stimuli, much as the atomists of the seventeenth century had thought of material particles as responding to action only by contact with another such particle. Moreover, there was a tendency to divide stimulus conditions and responses into atom-like units, the independent and dependent variables of behaviorist psychology. However, in our era, one can chart the growing influence in psychology of dynamicist ideas. One can see psychologists taking up and developing the idea of people as agents, actively trying to realize their projects, plans and intentions, rather than simply passively responding in well conditioned ways to environmental stimuli.

Ontological presuppositions in psychology

The breadth and depth of these contrasting ontologies suggest that there are better and worse general conceptions of the nature of the world and of the domain of each science at each stage of the development of the sciences. The history of science illustrates very clearly that assessments of the ultimate value of this or that ontology may not be wise until it has been tried out in many ways and in many contexts. We can judge a set of foundational principles only in the long run and by hindsight. 'Doing justice to our life experiences' in a manner that is recognizably scientific is what we want from a successful cognitive science.

How is that worthy sentiment to be given teeth? It will not be achieved without careful attention to the ontology implicit in our attempts to realize our scientific ambitions. We will find that the domain of psychology includes not one but two ontologies, neither reducible to the other. One of the great achievements of theoretical psychology in recent years has been to offer a sketch of how unification is to be achieved. The two ontologies that seem at first sight to be rivals are *mentalism,* the view that the domain of psychology ought to be confined to thoughts, feelings and meaningful actions, and *materialism*, the view that the domain of psychology ought to be confined to material states of the body, in particular of the brain and nervous system.

 Ontology

Presuppositions about what there is in the domain of a science. Two major variants:

1 *Classical atomism.* Logically independent passive Newtonian particles in the void, defined by occurrent properties, acting only by contact, in a deterministic closed future.
2 *Modern dynamism.* Logically dependent agents in continuous interaction, in an open future, defined by dispositional properties, for example charges and fields.

In psychology many of the leading ideas of classical atomism reappeared in behaviorism. In treating people as active agents we see the beginnings of a dynamical point of view in psychology.

Science, philosophy and psychology in history

The project of creating a scientific psychology has made several false starts. The first of the modern attempts to create such a psychology must surely have been the efforts in the seventeenth century to study the world of ideas in the same manner as the physicists of the era were studying the world of matter. Most of the issues that have troubled contemporary efforts to create a scientific psychology, beginning with Wundt's laboratory for psychophysics in the nineteenth century, were already well understood in the seventeenth and were discussed in depth in the eighteenth. In this book we shall be looking at the most recent attempt to achieve the laudable aim of a science of cognition. It will be necessary to survey some of the older and unsatisfactory attempts in order to get a feel for the problems that have led to so many failures to create a scientific psychology that can stand alongside physics and chemistry, the sciences of material things and substances. There are excellent histories of psychology in which the story of the psychologies of the post-Renaissance era can be followed in greater detail. Our task will be to understand, in the light of some significant past failures, the most recent and the most promising start yet.

Psychologists neglect philosophy at their peril. The interplay between philosophy and psychology will be as much a feature of twenty-first-century psychology as it has been part of the formation of all the sciences since the days of Aristotle. However, the penetration of science by philosophy, evident as it is in physics no less than in psychology, has to be viewed critically. The insidious effect of positivism is perhaps the most striking example of the kind of psychology that has proven to be so disappointing as a pointer to a future science. To get the presuppositions of the natural sciences wrong was indeed a terrible legacy of the positivistic era in philosophy. The positivist/realist distinction will occupy us in Chapter 2.

The project of a scientific psychology in full

Inevitably, psychology will be a hybrid science. This was foretold by Wilhelm Wundt a century and a half ago. Naturalistic studies of ordinary ways of thinking that make use of language and other symbolic systems will give us an insight into the culturally and historically diverse phenomena of thinking, acting and feeling. Neurological studies will give us insights into the cerebral tools we use to accomplish the cognitive tasks contemporary life presents us with. How do we bridge the gap between naturalistic studies of meaningful actions by active people and neurological research programs studying material processes, so that the latter are relevant to the former? We need some technique by which we can abstract important patterns from the concrete reality of everyday cognitive processes and phenomena. Such a technique must also allow the abstract processes so discerned to be given a concrete interpretation in neurological terms. The answer is to be found in developments in artificial intelligence, with the help of which we can build effective and abstract models of the *possible* mechanisms of cognition, based on abstract models of processes of cognition.

We shall be treating the project of developing a scientific psychology as a progression through four stages, each of which depends on successful undertakings in that which precedes it.

1   To record, analyse and understand the public and private processes and procedures by which competent people use the available symbolic resources and techniques to accomplish cognitive tasks. We shall be alert to identify the standards by which such tasks are assessed, formally and informally in different cultures (Cole, 1996).

2   To develop abstract analytical or descriptive models of the ways people accomplish these tasks, based on abstractions from the task descriptions themselves. Such 'models of mental processes' have no existential implications. They are pragmatically helpful ways of presenting what we know of the phenomena in question (Baddeley, 1998).

3   To develop abstract artificial intelligence models of the processes that may be involved in actually performing the cognitive and practical tasks described in the first stage of a research program (Copeland, 1998).

4   To use the models developed in Stage 3 to control neuroscience research programs on the look out for cellular structures as real analogs of the abstract structures presented in good working artificial intelligence models (McLeod et al., 1998).

In the successful accomplishment of such a program for at least some of the major cognitive skills displayed by human beings we will have finally overcome the legacy of behaviorism and broken the ties with the positivist myth.

Conclusion

A scientific research program comprises two main projects. There must be a way of identifying and classifying the phenomena to be studied. There must also be a way of thinking about the processes by which those phenomena come into being, and so explaining them. The classifying job needs a system of categories and kinds, expressed in the concepts of a taxonomy. The explaining job needs a picture or model of the mechanisms involved. At the beginning of a research project the real mechanisms cannot usually be observed. As the project unfolds methods of extending the resources of experimental and observational techniques into previously hidden regions of the world are developed.

Much is presupposed in the initiation and development of research programs. Philosophers specialize in bringing at least some of the presuppositions of human practices to light. These fall into two main groups. There are factual presuppositions, which can be tested like any factual claims. There are also conceptual presuppositions, expressing the way the components of conceptual systems are interrelated. Conceptual presuppositions can be examined for consistency, plausibility and so on. It is important to realize that there is no hard-and-fast line to be drawn between factual and conceptual presuppositions. Any particular proposition may drift from one category to the other as our knowledge and techniques of enquiry change and develop.

Framing the whole of a program of scientific research are ontological presuppositions, presumptions as to what sorts of beings there are in the domain of research. The history of science discloses two main ways in which the beings of the material world have been taken to be. The atomistic ontology is based on the principle that the material world consists of a swarm of minute material particles. They interact only when they come into contact. The only source of activity is motion. The dynamicist ontology is based on the principle that the material world is a field of continuously interacting centers of activity. Each such center is an active agent, exerting its influence on all around it. Newtonian mechanics is the scientific basis of the atomistic ontology. The physics of electromagentism of Faraday is the scientific basis of the dynamicist ontology.

The study of thinking, feeling, perceiving and acting, the field of the human sciences, must take account of the mental lives of human beings. They seem to involve non-material phenomena. Yet human beings are embodied, living in a material world of causal processes. Focusing only on the immaterial aspects of human experience leads to mentalism, while focusing only on bodily processes leads to materialism. The aim of this course is show how it is possible to unify the two main trends in contemporary, twenty-first-century psychology, to create a scientific psychology powerful enough to include minds and bodies in a common research program.

The natural sciences

The natural sciences have given us insights into and mastery of much of the material universe, including our own bodies. The ultimate value of this fount of knowledge has often been questioned, when set against that which gives quality to human lives. However, there can be no question of the magnitude of the achievement. The idea that the methods of the natural sciences might be applied to our mental and social lives is not new. It was very much on the agenda in the seventeenth century. For example, John Locke (1690) sketched a science of ideas to parallel the science of material particles. In 1748 La Mettrie laid down some comprehensive working principles for providing neuro-physiological answers to psychological questions. These and other beginnings did not burgeon into a systematic science in the way that the chemistry of Boyle and the physics of Newton were taken up by many talented successors and developed at an ever increasing rate into the well established disciplines we are familiar with and increasingly rely upon today.

Psychology, as a possible science, has begun again and again. Each beginning has faded away. A new wave of enthusiasts has started again from a new point of view. In the twentieth century some of the reasons for some of the false starts were philosophical, deep conceptual confusions. However, from our point of view by far the most important influence clogging the stream of scientific development was a misinterpretation of the natural sciences. This led to the adoption of inadequate conceptions on which to model a science of mind. In learning about the origin and development of cognitive science, the topic of our studies, we shall trace some of the failed attempts at getting going a science of cognition. In many cases these have their origins in mistaken philosophical conceptions of the natural sciences.

To guard against falling once again into some of the old traps set by faulty conceptions of science, our first task will be to get a clear grasp of the way that the natural sciences actually work. In doing this we can begin to appreciate the reasons for their immense successes. At the same time, it will help us to gain some mastery of a model on which to base a genuine science of human thought and action.

The world of the natural sciences

Considered in relation to the perceptual powers of human beings, the material world appears to fall into three distinct regions, between which are rather fuzzy and historically variable boundaries. I shall be using the biologists' term 'umwelt' to refer to those regions of the material universe to which human beings have access at some definite historical moment. In biology the umwelt of a species is the region of the world available to it, given the perceptual and motor resources that the members of the species possess. Not every species inhabits the same world, in the sense of umwelt, since some have access to the air, others to water, some to trees and others to decaying vegetation and so on. Worms cannot see, so their world is bounded by what can be heard, touched and tasted. Most fish cannot fly. Their world ends at the surface of seas, lakes and rivers. The umwelt of the adult tapeworm is the gut of a host organism. The umwelt of the condor is the upper air of the Andes, and so on. The natural sciences have developed as techniques for exploring the human umwelt. As they have become increasingly sophisticated, so our human umwelt has opened out into new regions we could once hardly have imagined. For example, we are now all so familiar with the idea that our world is shot through with a flux of electromagnetic radiation that we do not think it at all odd to debate the possible effects on the human brain of the fields generated by mobile phones. Aristotle had not the faintest glimmer of this extension of the domain of human existence.

The natural sciences have given us an umwelt, that part of the completely material universe that is currently available to human beings. It includes three distinct but fuzzily bounded regions, which differ in the way in which we have access to them.

Region One: what we can perceive

I shall refer to those aspects of the material world that are available to the unaided senses of human beings and their limited bodily powers as Region One. The boundaries of this region are indefinite along several dimensions. For instance, some people will have a larger umwelt than others, just because they are more adventurous in their exploration of their environment. Others will occupy a wider world because they have equipment with which to enter new regions, such as ships to cross oceans, lamps and ropes to explore caves, spacecraft to cross the interplanetary void and so on. Others will enjoy a richer world because they have more elaborate conceptual systems with which to recognize and classify the things, properties and relations available to their unaided senses than others who are less sophisticated. How many species of trees can you pick out? How many kinds of rock can you recognize? The more kinds of insects one can distinguish the richer is the world in which one lives.

Region Two: what we can visualize

Since the seventeenth century the aeons-long limitations of perception that set rough boundaries to the human umwelt as more or less those of Region One have been breached by the invention of sense-extending instruments of all kinds. These open new features of the world to sight, hearing and the other senses. They extend our umwelt by adding new regions, hitherto unknown or at best only imagined. Along with this achievement has gone a different conception of the material world. Since the era of such inventions as the telescope and the micro-scope, philosophers and scientists have taken seriously the idea of a region of the universe beyond the domain of the unaided senses. We could have access to this domain were the appropriate sense-extending instrument to be made available. For example, John Locke, living in the age of the microscope, remarked that had we microscopical eyes the fine structure of the surfaces of things would be avail-able to us. Galileo's use of the telescope to observe the moons of Jupiter was at least as important a break with an Earth-centered universe as the Copernican theory of the solar system. This region, which would be available to the senses were the equipment available, I shall call Region Two.

The bounds of Region Two depend not only on the instruments actually available but also on what instruments we think could be constructed. New instruments made the contents of at least some of the previously hidden popula-tions of Region Two available to perception. The boundary between Regions One and Two is historically variable. It changes with the available instrumentation. Furthermore, since it is revealed by instruments which extend the existing senses, as far as the general character of its inhabitants goes it must be thought of as an extension of Region One. The natural kinds that are first imagined and then revealed by sense-extending instruments must, in a general way, conform to those already accepted. Thus we classify bacteria as micro-organisms. Fine-tuning of new versions of old natural kind concepts will surely occur. The concept of 'organism' has changed as the attributes of bacteria and viruses have become better known. However, the broad structure of the natural kinds of the organic and inorganic beings of Region One is conserved in Region Two.

The concept of material thing must play a central role in our conception of the inhabitants of Region Two. It follows that the criteria for identifying and indi-viduating them must be broadly the same as those of Region One. These criteria are intimately interwoven with concepts of space and time. For example, one of the ways we determine how many entities we have in some region is by taking notice of the principle that nothing can be in two places at the same time. Regions One and Two share a spatio-temporal framework. The ways we describe and theorize about the inhabitants of these Regions must share a common grammar of spatial and temporal terms.

Finally, and importantly, our explorations of Region Two are guided by the work of the disciplined imagination. Driven by the need to explain phenomena not explicable by reference to processes readily observable in Region One, we imagine currently unobservable and perhaps imperceptible mechanisms that would do the job. We immerse a piece of copper and a piece of silver in a mildly acidic solution, making sure the copper is connected to the negative pole of a battery and the silver to the positive pole. After a while, a thin layer of silver is deposited on the copper. Chemists, led by Humphrey Davy, imagined that a stream of imperceptible, positively charged silver atoms, ions, had passed through the solution from the anode to the cathode. Medical scientists, led by Louis Pasteur, imagined that micro-organisms infecting the human body caused the symptoms of anthrax. In this case the imagined beings were perceptible, thanks to the development of the optical microscope.

There are interesting philosophical problems about the status of what is made available to the senses by the use of instruments. For example, how do we tell artifacts of the equipment from genuine observations, given that we do not have independent access to Region Two, with which to check whether our instruments are revealing it as it is? These problems have mainly been put to rest with various practical solutions. They will recur in the relevant form when we begin to look at ways in which cognitive science may parallel the natural sciences in extending cognition beyond the bounds of consciousness.

Region Three: what we can imagine

From its earliest beginnings in the dawn of antiquity the scientific approach to the understanding of the world has made use of a further extension of the imagined umwelt, into a region beyond any possibility of observation. It reaches beyond our existing perceptual capacities, and even beyond their extension through instrumentation. I shall call this Region Three. At some periods Region Three has been thought of as a mere extension of Regions One and Two. Yet it is an extension from which we are for ever excluded by ubiquitous features of human existence, such as our limited perceptual capacity. In the seventeenth century the world was thought of as a swarm of moving particles, like but not just like ordinary chunks of matter. However, the fundamental particles of the material universe were imagined to be much too small to be perceivable by the senses, aided or unaided. For the most part physicists of the seventeenth century thought that the fundamental material beings shared only some of the attributes that their perceptible counterparts possessed.

At other periods the inhabitants of Region Three have been conceivable only with the help of metaphors. By pushing our imaginative powers beyond the limits of the perceptible we can sometimes catch a glimpse of something quite alien to our ordinary everyday experience. How could we conceive of a being that is neither wave nor particle? Certainly not in pictorial terms! How would the pattern of forces that seem to be operative when material things go into free fall near a planetary surface be conceivable? Nothing tangible is pushing or pulling the falling apple. What, then, is the gravitational field? We do have concepts of power and energy which can be pressed into service to give us a sense of what it is we are referring to when we invoke Region Three in explanations of the most fundamental processes in the material world. Realists want to claim Region Three as a part of the human umwelt, albeit at the very edge of intelligibility. Positivists are happy to see it lapse into the realm of the dispensable, contenting themselves with the laws of observable phenomena alone. The gravitational law, $s = \frac{1}{2} g t^2$, is useful to calculate where something will be after falling for a certain time. Should we or should we not try to give some more substantial sense to the mysterious constant g than just 9·80 m/s/s?

Human access to the material world

The human umwelt, the world to which we have some measure of access, consists of these three regions carved out of the indeterminate background that is the material universe as a whole. In our physical embodiment we inhabit Region One. However, in our imagination we conceive ourselves also to be inhabitants of Regions Two and Three. A main and perennial concern of the philosophy of science is a systematic attempt to critically assess and, for some philosophers, to justify our belief in the reality of regions to which we have access only in thought.

Could there be indirect means of access, achieved perhaps through the manipulation of some of the imperceptible beings of Regions Two and Three – for instance, molecules and magnetic fields – by the use of apparatus that is part of Region One? By heating a liquid we make its imperceptible molecules move sufficiently quickly to escape the forces holding them inside the surface of the liquid. Their escaping is what we perceive as boiling. By passing a current through a coil we shape a magnetic field, the structure of which becomes visible when we scatter iron filings on a nearby sheet of paper. I shall try to show that there is indeed good reason to think that we do have the power to manipulate at least some of the inhabitants of Regions Two and Three in ways which have observable consequences in Region One, the perceptible states of our experimental equipment. Most people would accept the examples just sketched as manipulations of imperceptible but real beings. However, is this acceptance rational? Would it stand up to tough philosophical scrutiny?

learning point   ## The world of the natural sciences

1   *The human* umwelt. The biological concept of *Umwelt*, the environment available to a particular species of organism, includes, for human beings, the regions the sciences open up.

   a)   *Region One*. The world as we perceive it with our normal sense organs.
   b)   *Region Two*. The world as we would and sometimes do experience it with sense-extending instruments.
   c)   *Region Three*. The world as we imagine it to be beyond the reach of all our powers of perception, aided or unaided by instruments.

(continued)

2 *Access.* Natural scientists presuppose all three regions can be explored by appropriate techniques.

    a) Sense-extending instruments give us access to Regions One and Two.

    b) Successful theory-controlled manipulation of Region Three entities as imagined or modeled gives us access to unobservables.

Rival interpretations of science

The seventeenth century saw the development of a particular way of investigating the natural world that, for many people of that time and thereafter, defined the province of reliable knowledge. For the most part the scientists of the sixteenth and seventeenth centuries took the realist stance for granted. Few doubted the possibility of using scientific method – theoretical insights combined with experimental and observation techniques – to explore all three regions of the human umwelt.

Astronomy emerged from astrology, dynamics and statics from ballistics, military engineering and architecture, chemistry from alchemy and medicine, botany and zoology from practical interest in the nature and uses of plants and animals. It must not be supposed that the early moments in the development of these scientific fields were primitive. The seventeenth century began with one of the greatest of all works of experimental physics, William Gilbert's *De Magnete*, published in 1600. It ended with one of the greatest works of theoretical physics, Isaac Newton's *Principia Mathematica,* published in 1687. How should the extraordinary power of this cluster of methods, analyses and techniques to bring forth reliable knowledge be accounted for? What was special about it? How could its pretensions to supersede all other methods of enquiry into the natures of things be justified? The question was not new in the seventeenth century. Intimations of the 'scientific method' and discussions of its powers and limitations can be found in the ancient world in plenty, and in the medieval era, though somewhat more rarely. However, the dominance of this cluster of procedures by the end of the seventeenth century was unprecedented. Efforts to analyse the methodology of science, to justify the claims of 'natural philosophers' to be in possession of knowledge superior to all others, and to account for both the successes and the failures of 'science', have continued to be at the forefront of philosophy since that time.

The seeds of positivism were already sown in the seventeenth century in the priority that philosophers such as Locke gave to knowledge obtained through the senses. It was through seeing, hearing, touching and tasting that we made contact with the material world. The senses, it seemed, gave us indubitable knowledge. Yet the sciences had already begun to make claims about states and conditions of the material world that were beyond the limits of what any human being could perceive. By the eighteenth century this paradox had become a central preoccupation of the most thoughtful philosophers.

The debates between positivism and realism are not just intellectual exercises for philosophers to entertain themselves with. How a new science of a hitherto neglected field of natural phenomena will be developed depends in large part on which account of science the progenitors and pioneers have adopted. This is particularly true of efforts to build psychology as a science of mind.

To look more deeply into the contrasts between positivism and realism we can begin by reflecting on two main interrelated questions to which philosophies of science are directed.

1   The first broad question can be posed in several ways. It runs something like this. What is the content and standing of the knowledge claims of the natural sciences? How general and how deep can they be?
2   The second question concerns the meaning of the vocabulary developed by various scientific communities. How are meanings established? Is there a distinct way in which explanatory terminology gets its meaning?

These two broad questions are related. Answers to the second influence answers to the first. Positivism and realism can be thought of as distinct ways of answering the two sets of questions posed above.

Positivism

The positivist philosophy of science was often motivated by religious scepticism. By setting a very stringent standard for legitimate knowledge claims, it was felt that theology could be set aside as a source of knowledge superior to all others. In time this sceptical attitude modulated into an attack on all metaphysics, legitimate or speculative. Science was to be pruned of all claims to knowledge that went beyond those that could be verified by the use of the human senses alone.

How was this discipline to be achieved? In the eighteenth and nineteenth centuries the *content* of knowledge claims was the focus of positivistic stringency. David Hume ends his *Enquiry Concerning Human Understanding* of 1777, with the following dramatic advice (section xii, Part III):

> When we run over libraries, persuaded of these [positivistic] principles, what havoc must we make? If we take in our hand any volume; of divinity or school metaphysics for instance [and we must add theoretical physics]; let us ask, *Does it contain any abstract reasoning concerning quantity or number?* No. *Does it contain any experimental reasoning concerning matter of fact or existence?* No. Commit it then to the flames: for it can contain nothing but sophistry and illusion.
>
> (Hume, 1777 [1951]: 165)

Hume's reasons for this amazing metaphor were philosophical, that is, based on the analysis of concepts. Of most relevance to science was his analysis of the content of the concept of causality. According to Hume the concept of causality involves two main root ideas: that there is a regular pattern of correlation between events of the cause type and those of the effect type, and that there is a necessary connection between pairs of events exemplifying such regularity. The pattern of events is perceptible, but Hume insisted that:

> When we look about us towards external objects, and consider the operation of causes, we are never able in a single instance, to discover any power or necessary connexion; any quality, which binds the effect to the cause, and renders the one an infallible consequence of the other.
>
> (Hume, 1777 [1951]: 63)

This clearly depends on the positivist principle that only what is perceptible counts as real. How are we to account for our conviction that causes necessitate their effects, all else being equal? Hume's answer was ingenious. We acquired the habit of expecting an event of the type of the effect subsequent to the occurrence of an event of the type of the cause, just because we had experienced similar sequences regularly in the past. In reality, the conviction of necessity in the causal relation was just a psychological consequence of the regularity. Hume had cleverly folded back the sense of a necessitating power in the cause on to the observed regularity.

Half a century later Auguste Comte had this to say:

> [In the] theological state of mind [a person looks for explanations in terms of the] continuous and arbitrary actions of supernatural agents. [The next, more advanced, state of mind is only a modification of the first, replacing supernatural agents by] abstract forces ... capable of giving rise by themselves to all the phenomena observed. [In the third or positive state the human mind] endeavours now to discover by a well-combined use of reasoning and observation, the actual *laws* of phenomena ... that is to say, their invariable relations of succession and likeness.
>
> (Comte, 1830–42: 5)

The same point can be made in terms of meanings. Hume himself argued that the 'real' meaning of an 'idea' was the sense impression from which it was derived. Since, according to Hume, our idea of causation came directly and indirectly from regular patterns of correlations between pairs of instances of kinds of impressions, the real meaning of 'causation' was an experienced regularity. Traditional aspects of causality such as agency, efficacy and necessity were to be traced back to psychological effects of such sensory regularities. For example, we come to expect a certain kind of experience to follow one of a kind that has been long associated with it in our experience. Our idea of necessity comes from the psychological state of expectation.

Frequently experiencing a feeling of warmth in proximity to a fire, one acquires the habit of expecting that feeling when approaching a fire. That is all there is to the causal relation between fires and feelings of warmth. Introducing anything like infra-red radiation to account for the regularity would have seemed wildly speculative to Hume.

In the early decades of the twentieth century positivism became linked with logicism, the principle that the rationality of science amounts to adherence to the laws of logic alone. Logicism and positivism came together in the 'covering law' account of explanation. A scientific explanation seems to be a story that describes the processes that bring some phenomenon into being whether they can be perceived or not. But positivism rules out reference to unobservables. Logicism provided an account of explanation that was in keeping with the stringent restrictions on the content of explanations that was imposed by positivism.

According to the logical positivist account, explanations and predictions are of the same logical form. The account goes like this. To explain something, we deduce a description of what is to be explained from a law of nature and the conditions of its application. This is just what we do to make a prediction. The only difference between the two procedures is the time at which the deduction is made. If it is before we observe the event a description of which has been deduced from the law it is a prediction. If it is after the event has been observed it is an explanation. According to the positivist point of view laws of nature are nothing but statements of the correlations of observable states of affairs, as we have perceived them.

There is now no problem about the legitimacy of referring in explanations to states of affairs, kinds of things and natural processes that we cannot observe. We are not really doing that. To interpret explanations as descriptions of the workings of imperceptible causal mechanisms is a misunderstanding of their true import. Expressions like 'infra-red radiation', 'gas molecule', 'gravitational field' and so on seem to refer only to processes 'behind the scenes'. Using Hume's stringent principle of meaning, such expressions can really refer only to the sensory impression from which they were derived. In the case of explanations in terms of chemical atoms, the true content of such a theory could be nothing else but the regularities in the relative weights of the reagents in a reaction. The expression 'gravitational field' can mean nothing more than a summary of the accelerations undergone by falling bodies near the surface of a planet. At best, such notions as 'atom' or 'field' are psychological devices assisting the more formal processes of thinking that are at the heart of science.

Many – indeed, most – scientific explanations seem to refer to entities, properties and processes that could not be observed even in principle. For example, we explain many diseases by reference to imperceptible viruses, television pictures by reference to beams of imperceptible electrons and so on. So, according to the general proscription of imperceptibles by positivism, the entities we imagine must either be eliminated or the concepts that refer to them be shown to mean something other than they seem to mean, something a human being can perceive. What could be made of explanations that cited gas molecules, genetic codes, magnetic fields, photons and the like? Human beings can perceive none of these 'things' even with microscopes, telescopes and other hi-tech equipment.

According to positivism, only the beings we find in Region One are acceptable *epistemologically*, that is, as something of which can claim to have knowledge. For instance, Ernst Mach (1894), one of the fathers of modern positivism, laid down a strict relation between claims to knowledge and the possibility of perceiving what one claims to know. However, positivism is not only a doctrine about the limits of claims to have knowledge. It is also a doctrine about the limits of claims about what there is. It is also an *ontological* doctrine. We can easily see that these doctrines are closely linked. We can have genuine knowledge only about what we believe really exists. Hypotheses about entities and processes in Regions Two and Three, populated only by the exercise of the imagination, cannot be used to make genuine knowledge claims. At best, they are of psychological value only, useful fictions enabling scientists to get on with the task of generalizing observations of regularities into laws of nature, and testing them by predicting yet more observable correlations.

The positivist point of view has had an enormous and largely malign influence in psychology. If the domain of legitimate objects of knowledge is restricted to what can be publicly observed, psychology must be restricted to a science of public behavioral responses to stimuli imposed from the external environment. This was the ontological basis of the classical behaviorism advocated by Watson (1930). It followed that the only legitimate results of psychological research would be correlations between types of stimuli and types of responses. B.F. Skinner (1974) widened the ontology of psychology to include private, subjective experiences. Thoughts could be admitted as response correlates of stimuli. However, his radical behaviorism retained one of the main principles of positivism. Neither unobservable mental processes nor neural processes of any kind were to be introduced in an explanatory role into scientific psychology.

Realism

Realists hold that human beings have access to the world not only through their senses, the world as perceived, but also through the use of the imagination, the world as conceived. The mature natural sciences are directed to bringing as much of the world as conceived or imagined within the reach of experiment. However, that need not be confined to revealing something perceptible. We have already come upon the idea of an umwelt, that portion of the material world that is available as a living space to this or that species. The boundaries that define the extent of an umwelt are related to the biological and perception capacities of the species in question. The umwelt for earthworms is different from the umwelt for sparrows. The growth of science and technology has greatly enlarged the human umwelt in some directions, outward to the galaxies and inward to the realm of subatomic particles. It has also diminished it in other directions, excising demons, witches and other malevolent beings from the world as most people assume it to be. Which ontological presuppositions and which associated experimental techniques are privileged for a certain field of interest is relative to the task set to the scientists and to their degree of success in fulfilling it. Thus, if the task is explaining the diversity of organic life and its seeming adaptation to environments, we might say that Darwinian concepts and techniques do better than creationist or Lamarckian or Lysenkian.

It has so turned out that people have developed new modes of access to the material world, not provided by nature, thus enlarging their umwelt in different ways.

Region Two is accessible through the development of experimental and observational techniques that open up previously imperceptible aspects of the material world.

Region Three is accessible through the controlled exercise of the imagination, associated with techniques of indirect experimentation, which we will describe in some detail below.

In thinking about the unobserved or unobservable causes of what we can perceive, we frequently use analogies. Thus we imagine the electrical 'flow' in a circuit as like the flow of liquid in a network of pipes. Thus we construct a hydro-dynamic *model* of electricity that accounts for the behavior of ammeters and voltmeters and resistances in electrical circuits. In constructing the model, some of the attributes of its originating source are ignored or deliberately deleted. This kind of model building is typical of the devices we use to think about the sorts of beings and the kinds of processes that we would expect to find in Region Two. Models of this ontologically conservative kind are also to be observed in patterns of thinking about Region Three. Gas molecules are minute material bodies but will probably remain for ever beyond the reach of the most sophisticated sense-extending instruments.

However, there is a more radical ontology to which physicists have had recourse in thinking beyond the limits of possible observation. This is the ontology of dispositions and powers, realized in such concepts as 'field of potential' and 'kinetic energy'. These concepts will play a big part in our construction of a scientific psychology, and we will return to spell them out more thoroughly.

 Positivism and realism

1   *Philosophical preliminaries.* The study of the presuppositions of the sciences leads into two branches of philosophy, epistemology and ontology.

    a)   *Epistemology.* The study of the nature and limits of claims to know.

    b)   *Ontology.* The catalogue of types of beings believed to exist in a certain domain. Each of the major interpretations of the sciences involves claims both about what can be known and about what can be taken to exist.

2   *Positivism*

    a)   *Epistemology.* We can legitimately claim to have knowledge only about what we can perceive.

    b)   *Ontology.* We can legitimately believe to exist only those beings we can perceive.

(continued)

3 *Realism*

a) *Epistemology*. We have reliable knowledge about things, structures, processes and so on that we cannot perceive.

b) *Ontology*. We can legitimately presume the existence not only of what we can perceive but also of what we can conceive, within the constraints of the methods of theoretical science.

Indirect experiments: testing hypotheses about the unobservable

Two main ways have been developed in the physical sciences for testing hypotheses about Region Three. The first is exemplified by a huge number of experimental programs in physics and chemistry in which we use our imaginations to set up instructions for manipulating unobservable states of the world indirectly. Experiments of this sort were well understood and well described by Robert Boyle (1688). The second is exemplified in thought experiments. Galileo and Einstein were both great practitioners of this subtle art. We can use imagined experiments to justify deleting something from or add something to what we believe exists in the third Region of the natural world relevant to our explanations.

Boyle-type manipulation experiments

For Boyle and the scientific establishment of the seventeenth and eighteenth centuries the most fundamental explanations of observable phenomena were couched in terms of the atomic (or corpuscularian) theory and the laws of mechanics, finally successfully formulated by Newton. Robert Boyle developed a research program to investigate the corpuscularian hypothesis empirically. Reconstructing his reasoning in our terms, we could say that he begins with the general presupposition that mechanical causes have mechanical effects. A manipulation that involves mechanical operations such as changes in motion and decomposition into parts and their recombination into new wholes should have effects of the same sort, new states of motion and new combinations of corpuscles. When we perform an experiment in which the manipulations are all mechanical and the observed effect is non-mechanical, say a change in the color or the taste of the stuff we have acted upon, we must conclude that this change is an observed effect of an *unobserved* mechanical change. In Boyle's terminology, the real change is in the bulk, figure, motion or texture (that is, arrangement) of the insensible parts. In this way Boyle thought we would be testing an ontology, in so far as we accomplished reliable and testable results with our manipulations, and never found ourselves with a contradiction or incompatibility in the formulation of a program of manipulations. Boyle offered dozens of experiments in his *The Origin of Forms and Qualities* (1688) to support the general ontological thesis that animated the work of nearly all the physicists and chemists of the period. They thought that Region Three consisted of structured ensembles of corpuscles. Each type of structure was the grounding of a particular power to act on other such structures and on human beings, particularly their sense organs, causing them to experience the appropriate qualities – color, warmth, taste and so on.

There are plenty of examples of the use of the same technique to be culled from contemporary experimental physics and chemistry. Of course, the repertoire of concepts available for creating a Region Three story has been transformed by the advent of electromagnetism and quantum mechanics. In the Stern–Gerlach experiment, for instance, observations of the changing shapes of images on a screen produced by switching on a magnetic field are linked with the unobservable quantum states of the particles projected through the apparatus. The linkage is suggested by electromagnetic theory, that electromagnetic manipulations have electromagnetic effects.

The strength of this type of move is that the linking principle, that extends the application of what we know from studies of perceptible phenomena to imperceptible states of affairs – for example the mechanical properties of material things too small, fast or remote to be studied directly – can be treated as a testable empirical generalization. We can experiment to see whether mechanical causes have mechanical effects in Region One, and we can and have done the same for electromagnetic operations with magnets, coils and batteries.

Galileo-style thought experiments

There is another way in which we can discipline the work of the imagination in building conceptions of what must exist in Region Three, the technique of thought *experiments*. We imagine a situation that exemplifies the basic model that underlies some important theory, and imagine how things would happen in the imagined circumstances. A most striking and historically influential example of this occurs in Galileo's discussion of relative motion in his great book *Dialogue Concerning the Two Chief World Systems* of 1632. He imagines a number of experiments being carried out in the cabin of a ship.

> Shut yourself up with some friend in the main cabin below decks of some large ship, and have with you some flies, butterflies and other small flying animals. Have a large bowl of water with some fish in it; hang up a bottle that empties drop by drop into a wide vessel beneath it. With the ship standing still, observe carefully how the little animals fly with equal speeds to all sides of the cabin. The fish swim indifferently in all directions; the drops of water fall into the vessel underneath; and in throwing anything to your friend, you need throw it no more strongly in one direction than in another, the distances being equal; jumping up with your feet together, you pass equal spaces in every direction. When you have observed all these things carefully (though there is no doubt that when the ship is standing still everything must happen in this way), have

the ship proceed with any speed you like, so long as the motion is uniform and not fluctuating this way and that. YOU WILL DISCOVER NOT THE LEAST CHANGE IN THE EFFECTS NAMED, NOR COULD YOU TELL FROM ANY OF THEM WHETHER THE SHIP IS MOVING OR STANDING STILL.

(Galileo, 1632 [1953: 186–7])

This was the beginning of the theory of relativity. Galileo shows, by an act of the imagination alone, that there is no possibility of determining whether we are in absolute motion. We can only compare the motion of one thing with the motion of another. The notion of absolute motion has no place in the world as it is presented in the science of mechanics.

Einstein was unrivaled in the art of invoking telling images to convey deep intuitions about the nature of the material world, especially those aspects we have been calling Region Three. One of his most powerful thought experiments was aimed at disposing of a long-standing Region Three concept, the ether. It was supposed to be a mysterious but ubiquitous stuff that carried the wave trains of electromagnetic radiation, in a way somewhat analogous to the way the air carries the wave trains of sound. He asked his readers to compare two familiar experiments. In one, a coil of wire is moved over a magnet, generating a current in the wire. In the other, a magnet is inserted into a stationary coil. Again, a current is generated in the wire. One of these effects is explained by reference to the ether, but the other is not. Surely, says Einstein, the experiments are perfectly symmetrical. If we have no need of the ether hypothesis for one, we have no need of it for the other. The concept of the ether can be dropped from our Region Three ontology.

 Experimenting in Region Three

1   A Boyle manipulation experiment:

   a)   Testing hypotheses about imperceptible states of the world by manipulating them indirectly to produce a perceptible effect.

   b)   This requires a strong hypothesis linking mechanical (or electrical) manipulations with mechanical (or electrical) effects.

2   A Galileo thought experiment:

   a)   Imagining the carrying out of an experiment to test hypotheses about Region Three entities and processes.

   b)   In important cases the 'experiment' shows that some seemingly important concept is dispensable and that what it refers to need not be presupposed to exist.

Conclusion

The argument of this chapter is directed to justifying the claim of scientific Realism that we do have access to those regions of the world that are imperceptible. Only within this philosophy of science can we make sense of the project of cognitive psychology to explain psychological phenomena by hypotheses about cognitive processes of most of which we are unaware. We have distinguished between those which are imperceptible in fact (Region Two) and those which are imperceptible in principle (Region Three). Physics, in particular, seems to extend the human umwelt through Region Two into Region Three. However, if this extension is to be something other than 'just another story' there must be a set of procedures for assessing and distinguishing between better and worse stories with respect to the scientific task of acquiring knowledge and developing techniques of manipulative efficacy. There are at least two possibilities for justifying extensions of the human umwelt beyond the boundaries of the perceptible. One was originated by Boyle, and depended on experimental manipulations of unobservable states of affairs. The other was exploited with great finesse by Galileo and Einstein, and depended on the use of thought experiments, coupled with intuitions in favor of symmetry and simplicity, to delete or add concepts to our deepest conceptions of the material world.

What sort of phenomena comprises the domain that we want to explore and understand? How are we to think in a disciplined way about regions of the world we cannot perceive? Answering these questions takes us to the heart of scientific method. It involves the development of systems of concepts for classifying phenomena, and so of managing a growing body of knowledge. It also involves the construction and manipulation of models, simplified representations of phenomena and imaginary representations of what there is in regions of the world we cannot perceive. The study of scientific method will occupy us in the next chapter.

Understanding scientific method

In Chapter 2, we learned how a science is built on two main pillars, its founding presuppositions. There is its *ontology*, the catalog of beings the existence of which is presupposed in every aspect of the way a science develops. If *these* are the kinds of beings we are studying, *this* is the sort of thing we can come to know about them. The means by which we are to obtain such knowledge is the *methodology* of the science in question. For example, meteorology is concerned with the movements of air masses, identified by their temperature, pressure, humidity and patterns of circulation. Meteorological knowledge is obtained from carefully sited thermometers, barometers and hygrometers, and from observations from satellites and so on. Philosophers reflect upon the value and status of the claims to knowledge made by those who make use of this or that methodology. The upshot of these reflections is the *epistemology* of the science.

In this chapter we will undertake a more thorough and detailed investigation of the way ontological, methodological and epistemological presuppositions are actually manifested in the practices of a scientific community. The ontology of a science is revealed in the systems of concepts that are used for classifying the beings that the science is concerned with. Classifying is based on a *taxonomy*, an organized system of concepts by which kinds, types, groups and sorts are defined. The ontology of a science is also revealed in the ways that theories are created and tested. Theory building and hypothesis testing are based on a system of *models and metaphors*, patterns of analogy through which concepts are modified and extended into new domains. The choice of models and metaphors involves presuppositions about what sorts of beings exist in the domain of the science.

We will make a close study of the underlying logic in the way that kinds and types are used in classifying. This will be followed up by a similarly detailed study of the principles that underlie the uses of models in constructing and testing theories. These studies will give us a grasp of scientific method. At the same time, we will get to grips with the problem of the status of the knowledge we have obtained. How general is it? How secure from revision is it? And so on.

Knowing how the prestigious and successful natural sciences have developed we will be able to suggest how the new field of cognitive science could be further developed from its first beginnings in the mid-twentieth century. We will be able to use our understanding of scientific method to identify dead ends in research, as well as fruitful ways forward.

(section one)

Describing and classifying

All thinking and acting makes use of general concepts, expressed in the words we use in assigning individual things and events to kinds and types. Classification is fundamental to everything we do. We could hardly manage to make our way through the everyday world without being able to take account of whatever we encounter *as a something*, that is, as an instance of type, sort or kind.

Perceiving a black furry organism as a cat will direct our actions towards it and our thoughts about it in quite different ways from those we would adopt were we perceiving it as a chinchilla. Thinking of Joe as a friend serves to support very different ways of interacting with him from thinking of him as an enemy. And so on. Concepts like 'cat', 'chinchilla', 'friend' and 'enemy' are general concepts usually comprehending many individuals. The same is true of events. Concepts like 'lightning strike', 'sunrise', 'surprise', 'outcome' and so on are general concepts comprehending many individual events. The use of general concepts establishes a framework for managing experience.

Logicians take account of classes, which, though well defined, have no members. A class word like 'unicorn' comprehends nothing in a domain in which there are such beings as cows and donkeys. We shall not be concerned with empty classes in this brief introduction to classificatory procedures.

The role of concepts in classification

The great eighteenth-century philosopher Immanuel Kant once said, 'Concepts without percepts are empty: percepts without concepts are blind.' To perceive anything *as* something having a definite character our bodily sensations must be interpreted by the application of systems of concepts. A concept which cannot find any realization in human experience is worthless. At the cutting edge of scientific research, the process of 'perceiving as' may be quite conscious. For example, one has to learn how to make sense of what one sees with the help of a microscope. It requires training to be able to see colored patches as microorganisms. Bodily sensations alone, be they visual, auditory, tactile or in the other sensory modalities, do not suffice for bringing us a world of natural phenomena.

Once a perceptual realm has been established by the general adoption of a working system of concepts – for example, the living world of plants and animals, of vertebrates and invertebrates and so on – the relevant scientific community generally takes that way of classifying its subject matter for granted. We need reminding that what we ordinarily perceive is also a product of the organizing power of concepts.

In the beginnings of scientific research programs in psychology this point is of great importance. For example, when we are mere infants, we must have learned how to apply the concepts 'remembering' and 'imagining' to our thoughts in order for the psychological phenomenon of *memory* as a true representation of the past to be established. As adults we simply take the distinction for granted, even perhaps slipping into the presupposition that it is somehow 'natural' to distinguish what we imagine happened in the past from what we remember. Psychiatry now deploys a system of concepts for classifying mental disorders that is different in important ways from that which was in common use in the seventeenth century. Moreover, everyone in our Western culture has picked up some of the vocabulary, and thinks of unusual ways of thinking and acting in terms of not very accurate renditions of technical psychiatric concepts like 'manic', 'schizophrenic', 'chronic fatigue syndrome', 'Alzheimer's disease' and so on. At the same time, these coexist with such expressions as 'worn out', 'Granny is losing her marbles' and so on. This linguistic phenomenon is of importance, and we will return to it in later chapters.

At least we can say that scientific taxonomies evolve out of and interact with folk taxonomies, traditional and commonsense ways of bringing order to the multitude of things, events and processes we encounter in everyday life.

Hierarchical classification systems

Each natural science has developed a taxonomy, a system of concepts for classifying the items in its particular domain in an orderly fashion. Botanical and zoological classifications are based on the binary scheme of Linnaeus. Animals, for example, are grouped into kinds by genus and species. Thus the common rabbit is *Lepus cuniculus*. Genera are ordered hierarchically into higher groups called 'orders', which, in turn, are grouped into 'classes'. Linnaeus himself proposed six classes of animals: Mammals, Birds, Reptiles, Fishes, Insects, and Vermes [worm-like beings]. Chemical classification is based on the broad distinction between elements and compounds, while the elements are classified by their physical and chemical properties in the famous periodic table, using groupings like 'halogen', which includes 'fluorine', 'chlorine' and 'iodine'. In physics, fundamental particles are classified according to various properties such as charge, mass, spin and so on. One and all, and in various ways, these classification systems fix the range of phenomena that define the research domain of each of the sciences. They express ontologies. We should bear in mind that these systems are hierarchical. Expressed diagrammatically they appear as 'trees' (Figure 3.1). Each branch point we will call a 'node'. This is a mere crude and obsolete fragment of the vast

Figure 3.1

Tree representation
of a classificatory
system

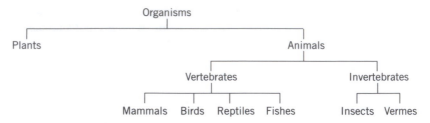

edifice of zoological and botanical categories that is currently in use. However, it illustrates the hierarchical structure of classification systems.

Once established, the taxonomies of the domains of the natural sciences seem entirely natural and inevitable. But that is an illusion. Much debate was required and much controversy endured before the kinds and categories of beings that we take for granted were stabilized.

How is the knowledge that is encapsulated in a type hierarchy organized? One way of presenting this is in terms of the 'inheritance relation'. If we pick some subtype and run always up the hierarchy, we pass from the more specific category at the point we started to the most general supertype at the apex. The lowest subtype in this exercise inherits all the properties of those above it in the hierarchy. Thus a mammal is a vertebrate, an animal and an organism, while a worm is an invertebrate, an animal and an organism.

Reading such a table vertically gives us supertypes and their dependent subtypes. Reading the table horizontally, we see that each row in the hierarchy comprehends 'all creatures great and small'. The type concepts in each row represent a finer and finer demarcation of the total population into subtypes.

Nowhere in this scheme do we find individual creatures. It is a hierarchy of types. The study of individuals is also part of science. An idiographic study is an investigation into single individuals taken one by one. For example, the study of the planets of the solar system is largely idiographic, since each has its characteristic and individual composition, structure and so on. Nevertheless each individual, in any domain, has characteristics that are, in some degree, like those of other individuals. It is both an individual and exemplifies a type.

In each domain, we must strike a balance between attention to the unique characters of individuals and to the general characteristics of types. In microbiology the unique attributes of individual bacteria play almost no role. How should the balance be struck in psychology? There is no general answer. It depends on the matter of interest. In cognitive psychology we assume that most people remember things in the same way, while allowing that what each person remembers is sure to be different, even if the same historical event is in question.

The bases of type distinctions

In using type distinctions we can attend to various aspects of what it is to be a representative of a type. Two fundamental distinctions are implicit in our everyday use of typologies. There is the distinction between the intension and the extension of a class or group. There is also the distinction between the real and the nominal essences of types or kinds.

The intension/extension distinction

The intension of a class comprises the attributes that each member shares with every other. Among them are the defining characteristics of class membership, the necessary and sufficient conditions that must be satisfied for some individual to count as a member of a class or an instance of a kind. Thus every sheep is woolly, cloven-hoofed and so on. The extension of a class is the actual members of some class, the sheep of the flock of Polyphemus, the one-eyed giant encountered by Ulysses and his men.

It is important for methodological purposes to realize that the intension and the extension of a class are in reciprocal relation to one another. Roughly, *intension varies inversely as extension*. The more detailed we make the intension of a class the fewer individuals will be found to fall within it. There are fewer black merinos than there are merinos.

The intension of a class, type or group consists of the attributes a candidate must have to be counted as a member. It follows that every member will display those characteristics. However, in real cases there may be other characteristics which every member displays but which have not been made use of for setting up a taxonomy. Characteristics that are common to all members but not criterial for membership are called 'propria'. Every merino sheep goes 'Baa', but we do not identify a merino by its bleat.

However, circumstances may change. More may be learned about the nature of the beings in question. It can happen that a characteristic that is criterial loses that role, while one which was not so used migrates from the propria to the essence. Color and metallic qualities were once enough to identify 'gold'. However, the King of Syracuse became suspicious of the court jeweler, and Archimedes was called in to the check whether the king had been defrauded, and the gold of his crown alloyed with silver. The great scientist changed the criteria. The test for gold he adopted was based on specific gravity. Indeed, the king had been the victim of a swindle.

Nominal and real essences

In making use of any type description, be it 'gold' as a kind of metal, 'horse' as a kind of animal or 'quasar' as a kind of stellar object, we presume some criteria by which we determine whether a candidate object belongs or does not belong to that kind. To be admitted as gold a sample of metal *must* be yellow, malleable, ductile, of specific gravity 19·6 g/cc and so on. The sample will not properly be called 'gold' or classified as an instance of the gold type without these essential properties.

As long ago as the seventeenth century this seemingly simple and uncontroversial way of managing admission to kinds was brought into question, or at least the presuppositions of making use of it were brought to light. The key distinction was that between the nominal essence and real essence of a substance, species, type and so on. The nominal essence includes the properties that would be required for a candidate animal to be properly *called* 'Equus' and assigned to the species *horse*. The real essence includes the inner nature of the members of the kind, species or type that accounts for the range and stability of the properties that were chosen as the nominal essence. It was realized that, while the properties that make up nominal essences must all be observable, the properties that make up real essences will usually be theoretical and imperceptible. Thus it is correct to call a certain piece of metal 'gold' if it has all the above list of observable properties. Chemistry and physics inform us that the reason why these are the characteristic properties of this stuff is that it has a certain atomic structure of protons, neutrons and electrons. However, this aspect of metallic gold is not perceptible. It is a hypothesis based on a chain of inferences, none of which is secure.

While the nominal essence, the properties used by practical people to pick out examples of kinds and types, may change, there is usually a clear continuity between the old criteria and the new. However, there may be great changes in what people take the real essences of kinds to be. This is particularly noticeable as science broadens and deepens our knowledge of the imperceptible aspects of nature, known to us only through our theories. The real essences of metals were once supposed to be distinctive ratios of the four principles, the Hot, the Cold, the Wet and the Dry. Now we use atomic structure for the same purpose.

We are now well acquainted with the broad distinction between the positivistic recipe for science and the realist one. It is easy to see that positivists would be inclined to admit only nominal essences as the basis of classification systems, while realists would be ready to admit both real and nominal essences, giving priority to the real essences. Furthermore, since there are indefinitely many ways that things are similar to and different from one another, all classificatory criteria are ultimately arbitrary for those of a positivist persuasion.

Realists are quite happy with well supported hypotheses about the real essences of those types of beings that could legitimately claim to possess them. Thus the classifications of chemical elements, animal and plant species, the geological classifications of rocks, taxonomies of subatomic particles and so on, carried out by reference to some of their observable properties, are justified and supported by theoretically validated hypotheses concerning the real essences of these natural kinds. Indeed that is what makes them natural kinds. All red things, everything of volume greater than 2 litres and so on are not natural kinds, just because there is no way in our current science to find corresponding real essences. However, such scientifically arbitrary kinds could be used in classification systems for some purpose or other. The category of red things of volume greater than 2 litres may have a use for the store-man in a paint warehouse.

How do we know what the real essences of natural kinds we suspect to have them may be? To understand how we pass beyond the limits of the perceptible in a scientifically disciplined way we must turn to a study of the main instrument of scientific thought, models. Here we begin to develop our understanding of scientific methodology according to the realist point of view. Models play a central role in theorizing and experimenting, the two main procedures in scientific method.

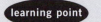 **1 Describing and classifying**

We must bring to light the presuppositions involved in these tasks by laying out the classificatory system or taxonomy in use in this or that domain.

1   Classificatory systems:

   a)   A taxonomy is a hierarchical lay out of classes, types and kinds (Figure 3.2). Each level comprises all living beings, and partitions them into types more and more finely.

   b)   A type hierarchy stores knowledge vertically, in the inheritance relation. To discover what is presupposed about a lower type one runs up the hierarchy through the nodes to the apex. Thus the species 'cat' is vertebrate, animal, living thing.

2   Features of types:

   a)   Membership requires meeting necessary and sufficient conditions. Properties can change places between definitions and accidental attributes.

   b)   Intension/Extension:

   i)   Cluster of common properties of members is the class intension.

   ii)   Membership is the class extension.

   iii)   Intension varies inversely as extension.

   (c)   Nominal and real essence:

   i)   Criteria for assigning a particular to a type according to observable characteristics make up the nominal essence.

   ii)   The real nature of the particular that accounts for its possessing the nominal essence attributes is the real essence (known only from theory).

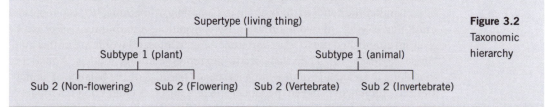

Figure 3.2
Taxonomic hierarchy

Explaining

The positivists advocated a very simple pattern of explanation, one that gave fewest 'hostages to fortune'. The 'covering law' pattern went as follows.

1   Establish an exceptionless correlation between the occurrence of one phenomenon and the subsequent occurrence of another. This is the simplest basis possible for a scientific law. It takes its strength from the absence of any counter-instances. Thus we might have 'Drinking red wine is correlated with having a healthy heart'.

2   Identify an instance of the consequent phenomenon; let us say the healthy hearts of the French.

3   Apply the law in the following pattern:

All who drink red wine have healthy hearts
↓
The French drink red wine
↓
so
↓
The French have healthy hearts.

The conclusion of this simple pattern of deductive reasoning is the very phenomenon we wanted to explain. Nothing but observable states of affairs has gone into the explanatory propositions.

Yet, for most scientists, this stripped down explanation format leaves everything yet to play for. To give an adequate explanation we would want to know *how* red wine does the trick. That would involve indirect study of unobservables, such as molecular structures, processes of free radical elimination and so on. By what cognitive processes could anyone, scientist or lay person, come to well grounded conjectures about what cannot be observed? This is the art of model making.

Models

A model is a tool for thinking, one of the ways we make representations of some subject matter the better to think about it. Generally, something, 'R', can represent something else, 'T' in two main ways. By convention, an arbitrary *symbol* can be given an established use to represent something. Almost all words are of this kind. 'Smile' represents ☺. Then there are iconic representations, models. A model of something is an analog, representing its subject because of the balance of similarities and differences between the model and its subject. A child's doll is a model of a human being. It has the necessary superficial features of a human body.

In mathematics and logic, abstract systems of signs are developed for various purposes. Systems of objects can be associated with these signs to give them a meaning. Such systems of objects are also called 'models'. The word 'model', as currently used, covers systems of objects that are used for meaning making, that is, for interpreting, as well as for representing. Fortunately, the main categories of modeling relations are expressed with different prepositions. Thus we have a toy car as a model *of* a real car. We have Niels Bohr's atom modeled *on* the solar system. In addition, we have the natural numbers as a model *for* the basic logical calculus. Part of our task in this section of our studies is to acquire a clear grasp of the different kinds and uses of models in science, so that we do not lose our way when we turn to the kind of model making that is needed to build a cognitive *science*.

Models in science: a checkered history

Before we can make sense of how theories, which refer to unobservable states of affairs, are constructed and experimental projects to investigate them are planned, we need to go somewhat further into the nature, uses and sources of models. The use of models was a central focus of study in the philosophy of science in the late 1950s and early 1960s. It was relegated to the margins with the advent of logicism by a new generation of philosophers of science, influenced by the dominance of logicism in general philosophy. For example, Hempel (1953) explicitly consigned models to a secondary and merely heuristic role, while Popper (1961), though he did not discuss models explicitly in his main work on the philosophy of science, implicitly relegated them to mere psychological aspects of scientific thinking. However, in recent years the topic of models in science has once again moved to center place.

The variety of uses of the word 'model'

The concept of 'model' is very widely used in everyday life in a wide variety of contexts. For example, there are model cars and other realistic toys. A model car shares some key features with a real car, for instance it usually has four wheels, while there are obvious differences, such as size and interior furnishings. Both the toy car and the real car are material things. Then there are model or ideal procedures that we copy to learn how something is best to be done. For example, a professor might provide a class with model answers to examination questions. There are men and women who earn a living as models, playing the role of idealized human figures. We have models as representations and models as idealizations.

The root ideas in current usage seem to be model as representation and model as ideal. Both these uses of the word 'model' for things, real or imagined, which are either analogs of something else or idealized forms of some type of thing, can be found in the sciences. Once we have learned to see scientific thinking and experimenting as model building and model using, we shall be well on the way to resolving the seemingly intractable problem of justifying claims to have reliable though in principle revisable knowledge about regions of the world we cannot observe.

Analytical and explanatory uses of models

Subjects and sources

Another distinction is of help in understanding how models are used in the natural sciences. In the examples so far discussed both the model and its subject have been available for inspection. Indeed, the subject of the model is none other than its source. The real Bugatti Type 33 serves as the source of the attributes of a 1/72 scale model of that very car. The degree of abstraction and idealization in building the model based on its subject can easily be ascertained. In science, models that are based on the identity of subject and source are extremely common, serving to bring out salient features of some system that is under investigation. For example, an anatomical model of the brain is based upon the discernible attributes of the brain. An orrery, a scale model of our planetary system, is based on the known sizes, orbits and speeds of the planets. I shall refer to this kind of construction as an analytical model. It represents the result of an analysis and ranking of the attributes of some natural system that is both the source and the subject of the model.

However, of even greater importance for science, and especially for the realist program in science, are models that have as subjects systems and structures that are as yet unobserved. How do we know what attributes to give to a model of that which we cannot perceive? The technique is to abstract from and idealize a plausible source. For example, no one has ever been able directly to observe the real constituents of a gas. The molecular model represents those unknown constituents. The concept of a molecule is arrived at by abstraction from and idealization of the properties of perceptible material things. Molecules have mass, they have shape and volume, they move with a certain velocity along well defined trajectories and so on. Models of this kind must play a predominant role in the building up of scientific explanations. They are the key to realism, since they are the main devices by which the disciplined imagination of scientists moves beyond the boundaries of what is perceptible. I shall refer to this kind of construction as an explanatory model.

In terms of the distinction between subject and source, the difference between the two basic kinds of models is easily expressed. For analytical models, source and subject are the same, while for explanatory models they are generally different.

Models as idealizations of their subjects: the analytical role

Let us look in a little more detail into the way that analytical models are arrived at from their source subjects, the making of the kind of model that is very common in biology, in geology and in engineering. A model as a version of some complex natural entity is created by abstraction, that is, ignoring some of its aspects, and by idealization, that is, smoothing out and simplifying others. Natural history museums sometimes have models showing a cross-section of the local landscape, displaying the geological strata below the surface, separated by nice smooth edges with each stratum uniformly colored. Taken together, abstraction (not every detail in a stratum need be reproduced in the geological model) and idealization (not every kink and break in the strata boundaries need be reproduced in the model) lead to a simplification of the natural state of affairs in the model representing it. This may have great practical value, both in teaching people geology and in developing experimental programs, theoretical explanations and so on in geological science. Patterns emerge when the obscuring details are washed out.

Using the terminology from the last section, we can characterize these models by the fact that their sources are the same as their subject. In the above case, the geological strata below a landscape are the source and the subject of the model. Such models are useful representations of the known, even though they are, in a sense, conservative in not going beyond the rim of the observable. Nevertheless, they do throw up new insights. They may even play a role in explanations of the character of the landscape as we observe it.

Some analytical models are such that their source and subject are the same, and we have discussed some examples above. However, it is also the case that sometimes a powerful analytical model may be devised by drawing on a source different from its subject. For example, one of the most powerful analytical models in use in social psychology is the dramaturgical model revived by Erving Goffman (1969). In using that model the source, a staged drama, is not the same social set-up as the subject of Goffman's analysis, a restaurant, a doctor's clinic or a banking hall. In this case, concepts from the drama are taken across, so to speak, to illuminate aspects of these familiar scenes.

Models as representations of the unknown: the explanatory role

How, asks the positivist, could we ever create a representation of aspects of regions of the world to which we have no access by means of observations and direct experimentation of the entities themselves? We can feel warmth but we cannot observe, even with the most powerful microscopes, the molecular motions that cause that feeling. At best, we can observe the random Brownian motion of visible particles suspended in a liquid. This phenomenon is most convincingly explained as the effect on the visible particles of being struck by invisible moving particles. Where does the idea of such particles come from? The realist responds to the claim that molecules are inadmissible because imperceptible by pointing out that though we cannot perceive such states of the world we can imagine them. However, not any fantasy of the imperceptibly small will do. Imagining must be constrained by what is taken in scientific circles to be plausible as a candidate being for that domain. What better way of constraining the imagination than by building models to represent that which we cannot yet perceive?

Just how can a scientist build a model of something hitherto unknown? The possibility of this feat follows from the way that a model of an unknown subject can be constructed by drawing on some source other than that subject. Suppose I imagine myself in the place of Benjamin Franklin. I do not know how electricity is propagated in a conductor, though I do know from the readings of my instruments that it is. I do know that water passes through pipes, and I have meters that register the rate of flow and the pressure. I invent a model of the propagation of electricity *imagined as a fluid*. I devise my conception of the electric fluid, not by abstracting from electrical phenomena, but by drawing on the flow of water in a pipe as a process analogous to the flow of electricity in a conductor. This leap of the imagination was expressed by the use of the metaphor 'Electricity is a fluid'. Here is the very heart of scientific creativity, the furnace in which theories are forged.

The working schema is something like this:

1   *Observed*. Unknown process, P produces a certain kind of observable phenomenon, O.
2   *Imagined*. An iconic model, M, of P 'produces' a certain kind of 'observable phenomenon', 'O'.
3   If 'O' is a good likeness of O, and M is ontologically plausible as a possible existent if it were realized in the location of P, we can say that M more or less faithfully represents P.

Models evolve and develop as research programs are pursued. Sometimes theoretical considerations lead to changes in the working models at the heart of a sequence of theories, sometimes a model is changed to accommodate new experimental results. These, in their turn, are made sense of in the newly evolved model. A splendid example of such an evolution is the sequence of progressively more refined formulations of the general gas law that 'track', so to say, the evolving conception of the gas molecule as a model of the unknown constituents of gases. It begins with the simple form we learn at school: $PV = RT$. This simple law is represented by a simple model of the molecule, as a mere point particle. Enriching the model by giving the 'molecules' volume ('b' in the revised formula) and we get $P(V - b) = RT$. Further enrichments took place, leading to more complex, but more observationally accurate, formulations of the law.

However, when we turn to examine real scientific thinking we find that models in science are constrained not only by reference to the phenomena they help to explain, but also by reference to the source from which they are drawn. Thus the molecular model gives meaning to formulas such as $PV = RT$ as a law of the behavior of gases, since it can be matched by a 'law' describing the imagined behavior of gas molecules, conceived as minute material things. The law of molecules is $pv = 1/3 \ nmc^2$. The model gains its plausibility as a good representation of the unknown constituents of gases, not just from the accuracy of its representation of the experimental results, but also from the fact that molecules are modeled on the known properties of moving 'Newtonian particles'. We already know that instances of this general type of thing exist.

A scientific model provides a resource for a certain prescription to which an object, attribute, state, substance or structure must more or less conform. If we have developed a microbiological model for understanding non-microbial diseases such as influenza, then that model will serve as a resource for prescribing the criteria for claiming to have successfully discovered the material cause of influenza, namely *this* virus.

Theories and models

Let us begin with some examples to illustrate how models have been used as the core of theories. Darwin's exposition of his theory of natural selection can be looked upon both as a prescription of a model for understanding the history of living things, and also as a hypothesis about the main process by which that history was brought about.

Darwin (1859) describes his reasoning in the first few chapters of *On the Origin of Species*. He begins with a discussion of the concepts of 'species' and 'varieties'. This is directed to breaking down the traditional differences in the way these concepts have been used. Species were supposed to be unchanging, so that all changes in organic forms were minimized as mere varieties. Then he describes how farmers and gardeners produce new breeds of plants and animals. They use selective breeding, so that only those specimens that exhibit the attribute the stockbreeder wants are allowed to reproduce. In that way, new animal and plant forms are produced. Perhaps these are only varieties within species. However, if the distinction between species and varieties is not absolute it is possible that enough small changes could lead, after many generations, to a population that would be a new species.

That is domestic selection. What happens in nature? Just as there are variations in each generation on the farm and in the garden that are exploited by the stockbreeder, so too there are variations in nature. If these are to lead to changes in the attributes of subsequent generations there must be differences in rates of reproduction between individuals having favored and less favored characteristics. There must be natural selection. The model for nature is the farm. Better-adapted animals and plants breed more freely, and more of their offspring survive. This mechanism matches the farmer's or gardener's way of producing new breeds by controlling the reproduction of organisms. By building a model we have managed to create a picture of a process that, because of its vast scale in time and space, we could never observe in a hundred human lifetimes. To complete the theory Darwin showed how natural forces could play the role of the stockbreeder in controlling reproduction rates, though without any intention to do so.

When Niels Bohr was trying to picture the inner structure of atoms, a structure that would enable him to account for the way atoms of different elements emitted different patterns of spectral lines, he began to think of the pattern of heavy nucleus and light electrons as if the electrons orbited the atomic nucleus as planets orbit the sun. He even called them 'planetary' electrons. Just as Darwin had to freely invent some aspects of his mechanism not available in the core model, so too did Bohr. He thought of the electrons as jumping from orbit to orbit as they absorbed and emitted energy in definite amounts, the quanta. These jumps were discontinuous, so that the spectrum of the light emitted was also discontinuous, conforming to the known character of the spectra of the elements. The core model had further useful features. For instance, it could be imagined that the electrons spun on their axes, some in one sense and some in another.

Theoretical discourse is not, in the first instance, an attempt (hazardous and underdetermined) to describe aspects of the natural world that we cannot perceive, such as the dance of the molecules or the interior of black holes and so on, but as instructions for making models of them. The kinetic theory of gases, thus read, appears as a set of instructions for making a progressive sequence of models of gases such that the behavior of samples of gas is simulated by the behavior of the model.

The cognitive foundations of model building

What is the underlying cognitive process upon which these examples of model building as concrete reasoning depend? Do they have a common general form? In the 1950s the favored account was based on the relation of analogy, between a model and its source and a model and its subject. Models were assessed by making a balanced comparison between similarities and differences in the range of properties assigned to the model and those that were ascribed to source and subject.

There are two main problems with this proposal. Since any two entities differ in indefinitely many ways and are similar in indefinitely many ways, how do we choose which of these ways are relevant to the assessment of a model as a representation of its subject? Even having done that there is still the question of how models should be ranked in degree of verisimilitude. Two models may bear very similar levels or degrees of relationship to a common subject. How is a choice to be made between them? It has been suggested that we adopt a deeper conception of the underlying cognitive processes of model building and model use. This is the idea of the type hierarchy. We shall see that this proposal avoids the difficulties that the simple analogy account falls into. At the same time it accounts for the fact that models, once constructed, are analogs of the sources and subjects.

Cognitive processes of model making

As we learned in Section 1 of this chapter, a taxonomy, or classification *system*, consists of a hierarchy of types, related 'vertically' as subtypes and supertypes. Thus 'feline' is a supertype relative to 'cat', 'lion' and 'tiger', which are among its subtypes.

Aronson (1991), Way (1992) and others have taken up the idea that model building is based on finding subtypes, within an existing type hierarchy, one of which is the source of the model and another its subject. Creating the model by abstraction and idealization of attributes from the source creates another subtype at the same level in the type hierarchy. Similarly, the subject of the model falls into place as another subtype in the same set of places in the type hierarchy.

It is because the molecular model of the constituents of gases is conceived as exemplifying a subtype of the supertype <Newtonian particle> that there is a similarity relation between the molecule type and the billiard ball type, since the latter is also a subtype of the same supertype. That molecules and billiard balls are analogous in certain respects is a consequence of their location in the type hierarchy in use for this bit of physics. Relative to another type hierarchy, say that of materials for sport, they might not be thought analogous at all. In Darwin's world, 'nature' is a subtype of the same supertype as 'farm'. The relevant similarities include 'being a breeding ground'.

This insight has a profound consequence for how we think of analogy in general. It is not that one type of entity is seen to be analogous to another and then both are seen as exemplifying the same supertype. Rather it is because they exemplify the same supertype that they are analogous. Why is this? Because it is the structure of the type hierarchy that fixes the relevance and irrelevance of the attributes of real or imagined beings that they should stand in analogy relations. There is no relevance problem.

The origins of type hierarchies

The second point of substance concerns the origins of type hierarchies. I believe that were we to trace the development of any one hierarchy that is of importance in the work of model construction we would find an initially rough and tentative classification system. This would be gradually firmed up as it was put to use, undergoing all sorts of transformations as new items were discovered and worked into the structure. Provided we were not tempted to crystallize relations in the working hierarchy too soon into a rigid logic of necessary and sufficient conditions, it would retain its fluidity and dynamic character.[1]

The problem of the salience or relevance of similarities and differences in presenting analogical reasoning is solved by attending to 'vertical' relations in the relevant type hierarchy with the 'horizontal' comparison relations dominated by inheritance from supertypes. This does not mean that comparisons by similarity and difference play no role in the cognitive development of the sciences. Indeed, in the early stages of the formation of a type hierarchy it is only because similarities and differences are noticed relative to some project then being undertaken that type relations are created in the first place. Indeed, even in the most sophisticated uses of such hierarchies, the point of the supertype–subtype relation is to fix which similarities and differences should be attended to in building and assessing models.

Figure 3.3
Type hierarchy of
material things

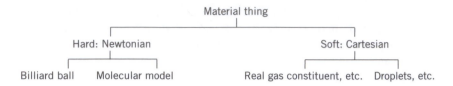

Type hierarchies and models

In order that a model can stand in a representational relation to that of which it is a model, both model and subject must be members of the same type hierarchy. Their relationship – for example, that the model is an analog of its subject – will be determined by what they each inherit from the lowest common supertype they fall under in the type hierarchy. For example, Figure 3.3 is a type hierarchy of material things. If we wish to construct a model for a new type of material entity, we shall have to find a place for it in this hierarchy. Once that place has been settled, all else will follow, since the model will inherit all the properties of the supertype it falls under, and so will all the other entity types that also fall under it.

Assessing the worth of models

We can now say something about the basis of judgments of the scientific worth of this or that model.

For analysing observable states and processes

In using analytical models to reveal the structures and processes in observable phenomena that would otherwise be too obscure, too complex or too fleeting to allow scientific work to be done on them we make use of certain standards to assess the value of the model that is being employed. The two of most importance are clarity and fruitfulness. These are so commonsensical that we need only look at some examples to understand them. Clarity must not be confused with simplicity. The use of the staging and performing of a play is a well known analytical model in social psychology. It is not simple, but it allows aspects of social episodes to be clearly identified, such as roles, costumes, settings and scenes. Fruitfulness is just the power of the analytical model to enable the user to see relationships that might have been obscured by too much detail in the original phenomenon. For instance, a model of the hippocampus as a three-layered neural net allows the neuropsychologist to see relationships between the layers that are not clearly visible even to the most detailed anatomical studies, unanalysed with the help of connectionist or neural net models. Analytic models have no pretensions to independent powers of representation. They are one kind of heuristic model, useful but not scientifically creative.

As providing plausible representations of possible realities

This quality of a model can be assessed by looking at its relationship with exemplifications of other subtypes that are instantiated in the world accessible to human beings. Molecules are minimally ontologically plausible as a representation of the real constituents of gases because billiard balls are exemplifications of a subtype of the same common supertype in the common world of ordinary experience. In addition, not only billiard balls but dust motes, cannon balls, grains of sand and other such things have places under the Newtonian supertype in the general material type hierarchy. So located they exemplify a variety of similarity relations to each other and to the molecule. Since we know billiard balls and dust motes exist, molecules that are like them in several ways are plausible candidates for good representations of the real constituents of gases.

This opens up the possibility of a different concept of truth for scientific theories, based on the plausibility of the relevant models. We could call it 'iconic truth', the truth of pictures as opposed to the truth of statements, verbal presentations of fact.

Iconic truth naturally admits of degrees. Within the frame of some agreed standard of likeness or similarity, the question of a better or worse representation can be made sense of. The question is multi-layered. Is the picture P a good portrait of A? That is, given the person, how well does the picture catch a likeness? In the case of pictures of a person created by identikit or fotofit techniques we have to find a subject to which it stands as a portrait does to its sitter. That is, given the picture, can we find a person to fit it? We have the idea of being 'true to the subject' in both cases. Iconic truth in science is like that.

Iconic truth is context-sensitive. Only in relation to particular applications does the question of degrees of likeness arise. A police artist may be so taken with the aesthetic qualities of an identikit picture that he or she takes it home and frames it on the sitting room wall. How like it is to the villain the original sketch was meant to represent is now irrelevant.

If a model's behavior simulates the behavior of the process or mechanism it is meant to represent, but it is ontologically implausible, the wrong kind of thing if imagined to have been imported into the place of the real process, then we say we have a merely heuristic model.

Experimental apparatus as model worlds

The second major application of the newly revived notion of model has to do with the role and nature of experiments as a source of knowledge. In the discussion so far we have been thinking of models mainly as the work of the disciplined imagination. However, if we turn back to the way the concept of a model was introduced, several of the examples were of models as real things themselves. Models can also be the work of engineers, laboratory technicians or instrument makers. Playing with such devices is experimenting on a model world.

Pieces of apparatus can be looked on as models of natural mechanisms or processes or environments: Nature domesticated. In the laboratory context we create a stripped-down version of a natural set-up. The apparatus is a model of that set-up because both the apparatus and the natural site of the process being investigated are subtypes of the same supertype. This is ensured by following the instructions for building the apparatus as an analog of the natural setting. Thereby apparatus and natural setting share whatever they have inherited from the common supertype. Running the experiment is creating a model of the natural process.

Let us take two simple cases to illustrate this 'domestication' thesis. Two parts of hydrogen and one part of oxygen are mixed in a strong glass tube, with electrodes embedded in the glass. When a spark is passed, there is a small explosion and water droplets appear on the inside of the tube. Here we could say that we have a domesticated version of the mixing of primeval gas clouds in the atmosphere of a planet in the early stages of its development, and the effect of a flash of lightning. Alternatively, we could take a simple experiment in calorimetry. We cool a water-filled calorimeter to $0°$ C. The water begins to freeze. We cool another calorimeter containing an ice and salt solution which at $-4°$ C has still not frozen. Here we might say we have domesticated a little bit of the sea. We can now understand how icefloes form. The eudiometer is a model of some aspect of the primeval state of the universe, while the calorimeter is a model of the sea. As subtypes of the relevant supertypes the model and its subject inherit the same properties. What we learn from manipulating the model we can feed back into our knowledge of its subject. We shall be returning to this conception of experiments as running model worlds when we turn to psychology. It will provide an important insight into the right way to interpret psychological experiments.

Further uses of modeling

Existence proofs: models as guides to explorations of the world

Science can open out or cut back the boundaries of the human umwelt. Since models are often created to represent that which we cannot perceive, how may we assess whether such a representation is up to the standards of iconic truth, a good likeness? What does it take to justify a scientific picture or model constructed by following the prescriptions of theory as an instruction manual?

Obviously, the public display of that which the model purports to represent, if it can be accomplished, will allow anyone who cares to look to see how good or bad the likeness is. Displays of this sort are existence proofs. They may be introduced by a gesture drawing attention to something to be taken note of with cries of 'Behold!' or '*Voilà!*' Let us look at some examples of existence proofs.

1   Where the entity looked for would, if it existed, be perceivable without any special equipment. At the moment our confidence in the existence

of planets around other stars rests on quite recondite methods of model making by inferences from the effect of the alleged planets on the motion of the star. Send out the *Enterprise* with Jim and Spock, and there it is, the earth-like planet of Alpha Centaurus.

2   We learn in our school texts to think with the model of electricity as electrons. The model becomes very much more plausible, at least to me, by such experiments as Wilson's cloud chamber. In that apparatus, moving electrons leave visible tracks as they ionize the vapor in the chamber. Electrons are claimed to be responsible for the concentric rings that appear on photographic plates exposed to electron beams. In this and other ways, electrons were brought forth. How did Wilson know that what he had brought forth were electrons? The Thomson model provided the criteria for recognizing them. At that time the model for whatever an electron was, was a charged material particle. This was just the right sort of thing to ionize the vapor in a cloud chamber and so to leave a track.

Manipulative efficacy: models as guides to practice

The experimental techniques described above depend on the models prescribed by theories. If theories are taken as instructions for constructing models, then the standing of theories is just the standing of the models they can be used to create. We have seen the key role of type hierarchies in assessments of the plausibility of models as simulacra of real things. The type hierarchy within which the core model of theory finds a place is the most powerful device by which ontological plausibility can be assessed and the value of the theory (model) in the control of research confirmed. For example, finding that the hypothesis that the natural process of speciation by selection could be found a place in a type hierarchy of ways of selective breeding gave it immediate plausibility, sufficient to guarantee its role as the foundation of the very latest theories of the origin of species.

Closely tied to ontological plausibility is manipulative efficacy. If a model is sufficiently similar to its subject that manipulations of the real world analog worked out by reference to the model are successful, then so much the more does the model commend itself as a representation of something real. In Chapter 2 we made much of the importance of Boyle-type experiments. We recollect that Boyle made use of the principle that mechanical causes can have only mechanical effects. If mechanical manipulation brings about a change in an observable non-mechanical property of something, say its color, then in fact an unobservable mechanical property has been changed. An unobservable mechanical effect causes us to experience a different observable property from that which we observed before. However, why is this the least degree plausible? It is because the manipulation was designed and its execution planned in accordance with a corpuscular model of the inner constitution of matter. That the manipulation has a better than chance likelihood of success is surely support for the technique of picturing the structure of matter in accordance with the corpuscularian model.

2 Model making

General principle: scientific thinking is model making and model using

1   A model is a real or imaginary representation of a real system, for some purpose.
2   Basic distinctions:

   a) Subject of model is what M is a model *of*.
   b) Source of model is what M is modeled *on*.

      i) For analytic or descriptive models, source R is the same as subject S.
      ii) For explanatory models, source R is different from subject S.

   NB. Thus, an explanatory model can reach beyond what is already observable to represent what cannot yet be observed.
3   Basic functions:

   a) Descriptive models permit the study of complex or remote processes and structures in an accessible form.
   b) Explanatory models permit the construction of hypotheses about unobservable processes and structures that can be used to explain observable phenomena.

   For example, Darwin used farming, domestic selection to create new breeds, as a source to develop his theoretical concept of natural selection to explain the emergence of new species.
4   The working logic of model using is analogy: patterns of likenesses and differences between model and source/subject.
5   The use of analogy presupposes that model, source and subject are subtypes of the same supertype within a type hierarchy. They are related to one another via the inheritance relation. Thus domestic selection and natural selection are subtypes of the supertype selective breeding.

Conclusion

Only in the model-to-world relation do we have a confrontation between two entities that share the same mode of being, namely things or pictures of things. This is why existence proofs are of such importance in science. They confront a model with that which it represents. They are like that moment when the police pick up a suspect whose appearance matches the identikit picture. The construction of a model permits the working out of a cluster of procedures for 'bringing forth' some hitherto unobserved aspect of Nature.

It seems that at the heart of the scientific enterprise there is a shifting repertoire of practices, ways of doing things, through which the world is made manifest to human beings. We have called that region of the world that is available to us our 'umwelt', borrowing a useful expression from biology. There is indeed a human umwelt, but it is for ever changing its boundaries as new ways of acting in the world are invented, and new ways of thinking about the world are developed.

We may be tempted to think that those regions of the world that are currently outside the umwelt are concrete and determinate, just waiting to be found, like the phenomena which we encounter within it. The old idea of the experiment took the apparatus as if it were transparent, revealing Nature as it is. Indeed, the microscope is a type of apparatus more or less of this sort, though we need to learn to interpret what we see. However, when we penetrate more deeply into Nature experiments take on a different cast.

In the light of this analysis what can be said about the world beyond the boundaries of the umwelt? It can be thought of only as a field of indeterminate possibilities. Indeterminate because without a specification of the apparatus or the kind of observational techniques with which we human beings force the world to manifest itself in displays of phenomena we can give it no determinate character. Penetrating the world as we enlarge our umwelt is not like mining for gold that is already there in the earth, waiting to be found. It is more like draining a marsh. Before draining, it cannot be said to have already been a field. It was not that the possibility of a field existed, either. Rather, only when bound into a drainage system, and only then, does a marsh afford a field.

Natural science is based on two main principles. The phenomena in a domain of interest do fall into groupings as *natural* types and kinds. This claim is justified by the way theoretically grounded postulations of real essences can be used to bolster the claims of nominal essences to represent real distinctions in nature. Analytical models, some of which may even be built on the laboratory bench as apparatus, accomplish the extraction of patterns from a messy field of phenomena. The construction of working models of aspects of unobservable aspects of the world not only provides well founded conjectures as to real essences but also gives insights into the kinds of unobservable causal mechanisms that produce the phenomena of some domain that has caught the attention of scientists. The underlying cognitive structure that supports both claims about essences and the procedures of model building is a network of ever-changing type hierarchies.

Philosophy is the study of presuppositions. In reflecting on the uses of models and models in use we bring out the *sources* that are presupposed in scientific theorizing.

Can we so develop cognitive psychology that it can meet the challenge of matching up to the requirements of a science as they have become established for the natural sciences?

What has happened to the laws of Nature? They were once thought to be the very heart of scientific achievement. We can now see how superficial a role they play. Laws of Nature are sometimes no more than records of conceptual relations involved in classificatory systems. Sometimes they are descriptions of the workings of models, analytic or explanatory.

Here are two examples of the first sort, one from natural science and one from psychology:

All halogen atoms have seven electrons in the outer electronic shell.

All deliberate human actions are accompanied by an intention.

Here are two examples of the second sort, one from natural science and one from psychology:

The distribution of molecular velocities in an enclosed sample of gas accords with a root mean square law.

Information is first retained in the short-term memory store.

It should be easy to see that each example is accompanied in thought by the ghostly presence of its sense-making model!

Note

1   Both these points are drawn from Way (1992).

---

self-test   Study questions

Chapter 1 A science for psychology

1   Name four cognitive activities studied in cognitive psychology.
2   What are the two main aspects of a scientific treatment of a domain?
3   What is required to unify a science?
4   What is the 'project of philosophy' for any field of interest?
5   What are the two main kinds of presuppositions?
6   How is each kind tested?
7   What was Reid's conception of presuppositions?
8   What was Kant's conception of presuppositions?

9   What was Wittgenstein's conception of presuppositions?

10   According to which of these is change possible?

11   What is an ontology?

12   List three main features of the atomist ontology.

13   List three main features of the dynamist ontology.

14   How do they differ in their analysis of causality?

15   What are the four main stages of a scientific research project?

Reading

Harré (2000), chapter 1

Chapter 2 The natural sciences

1   What is an 'umwelt'?

2   Describe the three regions explored by the natural sciences.

3   How is work in Region Two guided and bounded?

4   How is work in Region Three guided?

5   What is positivism?

6   What is the positivist conception of knowledge?

7   What is the positivist conception of meaning?

8   What is the positivist conception of rationality?

9   What is realism?

10   What is the realist account of knowledge?

11   What is the realist account of meaning?

12   What does the realist add to the positivist account of rationality?

13   What drove most of the positivists to their 'stringent' viewpoint?

14   What is the principle behind Boyle-type manipulation experiments?

15   What is the principle behind Galileo-type thought experiments?

Reading

McErlean (2000), pp. 88–95, 108–13.

(study questions continued overleaf)

Study questions continued

Chapter 3 Understanding scientific method

1   Describe the role of concepts in identifying and classifying phenomena.
2   What is a taxonomy?
3   What are the organizing principles of a type hierarchy?
4   What is the intension of a class?
5   What is extension of a class?
6   How are they related?
7   What is the nominal essence of a kind?
8   What is the real essence of a kind?
9   What are the two main uses of models in science?
10 Distinguish subjects and sources of modeling.
11 Describe the uses of models as idealizations.
12 Describe the uses of models as representations.
13 How is model making managed and controlled?
14 What is the relation between theories and models?
15 What role do type hierarchies play in model making?
16 How is the value of a model assessed?
17 How can an apparatus be a model?
18 What kind of truth is involved in assessing models?
19 How do models guide experimental manipulations?

Reading

Morgan and Morrison (1999).

The search for a science of human behavior

'The proper study of mankind is man'. It is all very well giving that advice to one's fellow human beings, but how should this desirable undertaking be carried on? A huge variety of enterprises already exist of which humankind is the target. There is history, there is literature in many forms, jurisprudence, there are all sorts of religions, philosophy in many styles, sports coaching, pedagogy and so on. What else do we need? It is difficult enough to scrape acquaintance with even a fragment of the good things to be found in the works of those who have given us so many insights into life. What advance could be made on the character studies by Shakespeare or Tolstoy, on the subtleties of the common law, and so on? Could or should some development or extension of the natural sciences find a place in this catalog of reflections on the lives of human beings?

The word 'psychology' is used to cover a diverse cluster of practices engaged in by a goodly number of people for a great many different reasons. In this course we are studying the ways that psychology has been proposed as a possible science. What would be needed for studies of thinking, feeling, perceiving and acting to be accepted as sources of reliable knowledge on an equal footing with physics, chemistry, biology, geology as sources of knowledge about the non-human world? It is not easy to answer this question. The task is made difficult by the fact that there are three dimensions along which natural sciences as possible exemplars for a scientific psychology have varied.

1   When the modern era began in the seventeenth century, physics was based on the presupposition that the world was a swarming mass of material corpuscles, acting on each other only when in contact. Scientific instrumentation was primitive. By the mid-nineteenth century, physics was grounded in energetics and field theories, presupposing charges as active agents in continuous mutual interaction. Should psychology emulate corpuscularian physics or field physics?

2   Positivist interpretations of the physical sciences laid great stress on the priority of what could be observed, and downplayed the

importance of theory. Realist interpretations emphasized the role of hypotheses concerning unobservable processes in explaining the observable phenomena. Should psychology follow the positivist or the realist ideal of science?

3   The earliest attempts to devise scientific psychologies drew on physics, the most impressive science of the seventeenth and eighteenth centuries. In the twentieth century the rapid rise of the life sciences has provided another ideal, thought by many to fit the needs of nascent scientific psychology better than physics could.

Part II is concerned with some of the ways that the established sciences have served as exemplars for a possible scientific psychology, a science of thoughts, feelings, perceptions and actions, over the last four centuries.

From the beginning of the seventeenth century, physics played an important role as an ideal of science. There are three main ways that physics has served in this role:

1   Like all the sciences, physics deploys an ever-changing and developing *way of classifying* relevant phenomena, a taxonomy of the kinds of beings that make up the domain of this science. At the heart of physical theorizing is a well established technique for representing aspects of the material world that we are currently unable to observe directly, the *technique of model making*. Any discipline with pretensions to the status of a science must incorporate both these aspects.

2   In physics, phenomena are represented by clusters of numerical measurements, using instruments that are affected causally by the state of the properties of the phenomenon to be represented. Laws of nature and the theories in which they are embedded are expressed algebraically. Psychologists have used the terminology of physics. Descriptions of phenomena are often called 'measurements' and the means of achieving them called 'instruments'. One sees the point of the metaphor. However, it is a moot point how far this feature of physics should be literally transposed to psychology. This issue will be postponed until Part III.

3   The third way that physics has influenced psychology is ontological. We have looked at the two main ontological foundations on which physics has been based, atoms in the void and charges and their fields. These were set out in Part I in Table 1.1. In the seventeenth century a psychology of mental 'atoms' was inaugurated. In the twentieth century a psychology of active agents has been advocated. Though it would not be right to say that psychologists borrowed directly and knowingly from physics, it is quite evident that there have been common frames of thought occupying a dominant position at different times.

The idea of passive atoms reacting to external stimuli, even if paradoxically the external stimuli are atoms in motion, is surely an ancestor of behaviorism. The behaviorist paradigm involved reducing human psychology to the statistics of responses to stimuli. Charges actively engaging with other charges which act on them can be recruited as a source of general ideas for a very different paradigm. Nowadays there is growing interest in devising a psychology of active agents co-ordinatively, even if sometimes hostilely, carrying through their projects. We co-operate by informally assigning tasks to move a piano. We fight in accordance with rules and conventions in a boxing bout. In modern war not anything goes. A leader who ignores moral standards can find himself arraigned in the dock at The Hague for crimes against humanity. Whether we act co-operatively or in opposition to one another, psychologists need to treat the people involved as actively engaged in projects.

The second theme running through these attempts has been the question of the status of persons in psychology. Must this concept be preserved in a psychological science? Are there persons *and* thoughts, feelings, perceptions and actions? Alternatively, are persons *nothing but* collocated and enduring patterns of thoughts, feelings, perceptions and actions? This issue is tied up with several of the other issues just sketched. In particular, is psychology necessarily committed to the existence of active agents as an ineliminable ontological category?

The first main topic of Part II is the status of thoughts, feelings, perceptions and actions in two major attempts to create a scientific psychology along the lines of the sciences of matter.

Do thoughts, feelings, perceptions and actions exist as properties of something? Alternatively, do they exist as individual entities in their own realm? If they are properties, are they properties of a mental substance or of a material substance? If properties of material substance, are they simply material properties seen from a certain point of view or do they represent certain non-material properties that some material things, structured in certain ways, can display?

Descartes and Locke were mentalists. However, while Descartes assumed that thoughts were properties of a mental substance, Locke gave them an entity-like status in the mind. For Descartes the mind was a substance, and thinking was its characteristic attribute. For Locke the mind was a container of ideas of several kinds, correlated in various ways. These proposals led to a general psychology based on the thesis that the observable patterns of the phenomena of thinking, feeling, perceiving and acting were caused by habit, or the 'association of ideas'. Hartley suggested a dualism of associations. The association of ideas was exactly mirrored in and ultimately caused by associations among the invisible 'vibrations' of Newton's material ether in the corpuscularian system of the human body. Hume refined associationist psychology into just two basic processes in terms of which all else could be explained.

In the same era a vigorous materialism was also inaugurated. It has persisted to the present day. Hobbes, writing in the middle of the seventeenth century, was an *ontological materialist*, like some psychologists in the twenty-first century. An ontological materialist holds that there are only material substances. Mental states and processes, whatever they may seem, are really nothing but mechanical (or, in modern times, electrical) properties of matter.

La Mettrie was a *methodological materialist*, also anticipating views held today. He seems to have held that thoughts were not material attributes of the material nervous system but were causally produced by and exceptionlessly cor-related with states of the material body. The mind could be studied by studying the correlative bodily phenomena.

We will also explore the most recent, twentieth-century proposals for *conceptual materialism*. According the proponents of this view mentalistic con-cepts, with their allegedly misleading presuppositions of the existence of mental entities, should be replaced by neurophysiological concepts presupposing the existence of nothing but material entities, states and processes. This proposal turns out to be fraught with all sorts of difficulties and confusions of thought which it would be instructive to explore.

Biology has also provided a model for a scientific psychology. This was Aristotle's way, and it was echoed in the twentieth century by various attempts to generalize the psychology of the higher primates to include human beings. We will study Aristotle's bio-psychology in some detail.

Both Descartes and Locke seem to have presumed the existence of an immaterial being that perceived and reflected on ideas and could act in the mental *and* the material realm. Hume explicitly denied the existence of any such being. When a person pays attention to his or her own mental states, he insisted, noth-ing but patterns of mental states and processes can be discerned. No *entity* comes into view. The need to incorporate the notion of person as a basic concept will come back into prominence in Parts III and IV as we chart the emergence of a deeper and more subtle scientific psychology that emphasizes human activity.

In this century, there are clear signs of the emergence of a scientific psychology that escapes the criticisms to which previous nascent sciences of the mind have been subjected. In part, this is due to the revival of realism in the philosophy of science in general and in the philosophy of physics in particular. Taking the natural sciences as they really are as our guide, we are offered a paradigm rich in possibilities for the development of a truly scientific psychology.

A psychology that took over many of the principles of scientific realism came on the scene in the First Cognitive Revolution, inaugurated by Jerome Bruner and George Miller. Bruner (1983), in particular, offered experimental demonstrations of the need for hypotheses that referred to imperceptible cogni-tive processes. Without them, the results of his experiments were inexplicable. These hypotheses were quickly given further and thrilling content by the compu-tational model of the mind, the brain as a computer. This development was driven on by the work of Alan Turing. Not only did he provide the technical foundations of the idea of a universal computing machine, but he vigorously promoted the computing machine as a prime model of the human brain.

Much in the program of the First Cognitive Revolution has turned out to be simplistic. The experimental refutation of behaviorism was followed by a vigorous but ultimately unsatisfactory attempt to recruit the growing technical successes of machine computation to the task of explaining the basis of human cognitive skills. Part of the problem was the survival into mainstream experi-mental psychology of some basic features of behaviorism. The persistence of causal analyses of psychological phenomena has proved particularly problematic. The advent of discursive psychology has brought a more subtle analytical technique and more sophisticated concepts to bear on the analysis of psychological phenomena. Psychological phenomena must preserve their meaningful and normative character in a scientific psychology.

Bruner himself, one of the architects of the First Revolution, inaugurated the Second Revolution. The causal analysis of phenomena was replaced by interpretations of the meanings of actions and the rules and norms that explained the observable patterns. While building on a critical selection of the advances made in the First Cognitive Revolution, the Second Revolution has turned to a more advanced computational model, connectionism, to link psychological phenomena with their neural groundings. The first attempt to spell out the equation of brains thinking to computers running programs was a heroic failure. However, as a thoroughgoing realist program it did point the way ahead. It led to more fruitful developments to which we will turn in Parts III and IV. There we explore the nature and consequences of the Second Cognitive Revolution.

There is a deep metaphysical chasm separating contemporary psychologists into two camps. This rift was visible even in antiquity. Are human beings active agents or are they passive media of extrinsic and intrinsic forces? Aristotle argued for the former view, while the psychology displayed in the Homeric epics depicted human beings as subject to the capricious will of the Olympian gods. The sources of the passive and, in our day, mechanistic view of human beings are many. There are historical and metaphysical roots, but above all, and least easily acknowledged, these positions represent moral and political stances to human nature and the problems of living.

The aim of this course is positive, establishing the outlines of a forward-looking cognitive science. We will not spend more time critically examining either mentalism or materialism beyond what is needed to understand their limitations as programs for a scientific psychology. They have both been bypassed by the commonsense insight that the rigid distinction once drawn between public behavior, to be described in material terms, and private experience, to be described in mentalistic terms, can be discarded. Once we acknowledge the role of symbolic systems, and especially language, in both the formulation and the expressions of our thoughts we can see that there is a common realm, the realm of symbols and their manipulation according to rule. In the demise of behaviorism the domain of a scientific psychology has been enlarged to include many kinds of private experiences, such as bodily feelings, mental images and thoughts of all kinds, including private rehearsals for public acts. The alleged gap between the subjective and the objective has dissolved. Many psychologists have come to realize that public actions are reliable expressions of private thoughts and feelings. Moreover, on the 'flip side' of this intuition we must acknowledge that the domain of psychology also includes public performances in so far as they are taken to be expressions of the intentions of the actors and constrained by local customs and conventions.

A useful way to introduce the deep differences between the First Cognitive Revolution and the Second is to contrast causal explanations with normative.

The causal picture: the First Cognitive Revolution. Psychological phenomena are linked by cause–effect relations, presupposing the existence of (unobservable) causal mechanisms. A one-dimensional version of this picture, such as Hume's associationist psychology, has cognitive states, or ideas, causing subsequent cognitive states with which they have been associated. La Mettrie's proposal and its descendants presuppose a linear causal sequence of bodily states, each of which causes a correlative mental state, a two-dimensional version of the Causal Picture. In the first version, it is presupposed that thoughts can cause thoughts. In the second version, it is presupposed that neural states can cause other neural states and thoughts and feelings as well. We will examine several examples of research based on each of these versions of the Causal Picture in Part III. In the Causal Picture, a person is just a place where causal processes occur, a site for one psychological event to cause another.

The agentive picture: the Second Cognitive Revolution. Psychological phenomena are attributes of the flow of public and private actions by means of which persons are actively engaged, usually with real or imagined others, in carrying through various cognitive and practical projects. The flow of actions is orderly because actions are linked into sequences by the demands of meaning, and by the local standards of correctness to which people generally try to conform. In the agentive picture a person is the prime inaugurator of meaningful actions. Psychological phenomena are the products of human beings actively engaged in carrying through, or trying to carry through, their projects.

The rival pictures will dominate our discussions. In much the same way the two great world systems, earth-centered geocentrism and sun-centered heliocentrism, dominated the discussion of the material universe in the sixteenth and seventeenth centuries. However, the upshot will be different. In the end the sun-centered system prevailed. In the case of psychology there are excellent reasons for making use of both pictures. In Parts III and IV we shall be learning how to use them in a complementary fashion, creating a hybrid psychology in which neither eliminates the other.

There are intimations of the possibility of a hybrid psychology in the eighteenth century in the writings of the great philosopher Immanuel Kant. We will visit them briefly. There are also intimations of a complementarity between causal and agentive pictures in the twentieth century. The discovery of the genetic origins of many human capacities led some biologists to make extravagant claims for the reduction of psychology to genetics. Criticisms of these claims turned on the ineliminable role of culture in the way that our genetic inheritance is developed and used in different epochs and in different cultures. Neither genetics nor cultural history and anthropology can give a complete account of how we think, feel, perceive and act. Taken together they are a powerful hybrid.

The historical material to come is very selective. My aim in this survey is not so much historical as to demonstrate how philosophical accounts of the physical sciences have been the vehicle by which these sciences have influenced the development of psychologies.

Psychology as the science of mental substances

In the seventeenth century Descartes, Locke and many others began the development of a mental science based on the presupposition that the character of psychological phenomena required the existence of a mental substance, a kind of mind stuff. The repertoires of mental realities set out in the great majority of the psychologically oriented writings of the period were based on a sharp distinction between the material and mental aspects of a human being. I will discuss three variants of seventeenth and eighteenth-century mentalism, that of Descartes, that of Locke and that of Hume. As this program developed a common thesis about the mechanism of cognition emerged, the association of ideas. Mentalism became increasingly positivistic. However, the principle of association was taken up by Hartley, and used to sketch a realist psychology. In Hartley's scheme, unobservable brain processes explained observable associations of ideas, the association of material 'vibrations' exactly matching the associations of ideas.

Seventeenth-century science was dominated by the work of Galileo and later Newton on the mechanics of moving material bodies, and the results of collisions between them. Gradually the laws of motion were systematized, including motion under the influence of gravity. The pioneering work of William Gilbert, which laid down the basic principles of magnetism, lay dormant until the mid-nineteenth century. Though many doubted the existence of an empty space or void in which the material constituents of the universe were free to move, almost all scientists of the period accepted the principle that material stuff was divided into particles or corpuscles. It was in this intellectual environment that Descartes and Locke developed their attempts at a science of human thought.

Descartes's psychology

In the Cartesian ontology (Descartes, 1641) there is taken to be a unique and distinct mental substance in each person, intimately interwoven with the material stuff of the body. It is endowed with distinctively mental properties. These are different in every respect from the material properties that characterize the material substance constitutive of human bodies. Thoughts are *attributes* of mental substances. While each person's body is made of the same stuff, each mind is constituted of a different and unique mental stuff.

Descartes's project fell into two phases. In the first phase he tried to show by an analysis of common experience that the mental aspects of each person must be attributed to a mental substance. In the second phase he followed this up with a study of the nature of and relations among mental attributes.

The existence of mental substances

Descartes's analysis is made more complicated by the fact that he was attempting to reach two major conclusions by means of it. He wanted, first, to establish the indubitable existence of mental states and processes. He argued that, since mental states and processes had nothing in common with the properties of material stuff, there must be a mental substance to which they could properly be attributed. At the same time he wanted to establish that he, Descartes, was to be identified with the mental substance that he believed he had shown to be an essential constituent of his individual being.

His route to this thesis was to follow a systematic program of doubting the verisimilitude of all his thoughts. This is Descartes's 'method of doubt'. The program is not directed to establishing a thoroughgoing skepticism about the scope of human knowledge. Rather it is intended as a way of ranking beliefs in order of their plausibility and certain truth. He asks himself: what can I be sure of? I cannot be sure beyond all possible doubt that there is a material world beyond the curtain of my sensations. I can even doubt the existence of my own body. Carrying through the program as far as it is possible to go leaves Descartes apparently doubting everything. However, that establishes that a certain cognitive phenomenon, namely doubting, exists. Even to doubt that doubting exists is to exemplify it. Doubting is a species of thinking. So the existence of thought in general is proved.

Nevertheless, Descartes wants more. He wants to establish that *he* exists as a thinking being. The route by which he tries to establish his existence as a thinking *thing*, a *res cogitans*, notoriously begs the question. The famous argument *cogito ergo sum* (I think, therefore I am) presumes an 'I' and thus already involves the presupposition that Descartes as thinker exists, since it begins with a statement in the first person. All that Descartes can legitimately draw from the argument is the existence of *cogitans*, thinking. That has already been established as the upshot of the use of the method of doubt. So the existence of persons as embodied *immaterial substances* has not been shown by this argument. Descartes's methodological doubt yields the certainty only of the existence of the phenomenon of thinking, not that thinking must be an attribute of a mental *substance*.

Is this mental stuff the essence of personhood? If *I* can perceive the attributes of my body and *I* can be aware of my thoughts as attributes of my mind, even as *I* doubt their verisimilitude, it would seem that I cannot be either my body or my mind. How can a person know what they are thinking or experience a private feeling if they are the sum of their thoughts and feelings? It seems as if there must be another 'something', neither mental nor material, implicit in this scheme. Surely there must be the inward eye of an internal observer who perceives these private states. Is it the very same being who perceives the things of the material world? The Cartesian answer ought to have been 'Yes'.

Cartesian psychology seems to presuppose an active, knowing self as well as a mental substance the properties of which are thoughts and feelings.

The Cartesian typology of psychological phenomena

In order to show that the mind as mental substance is quite unlike the body as material substance Descartes sets out to show that the mind is neither extended in space nor divisible into parts. The essence of matter is extension, he declares. The essence of mind is thought, which has no extension.

Having established to his own satisfaction that the mind has no parts, nor is it extended, Descartes offered a comprehensive typology for the operations of the mind. Note well that this is not a typology of the parts of the mind. There are none, according to Descartes. However, when we come to study Descartes's psychology in detail we find that he draws on hypotheses concerning the material realm of animal spirits and on others concerning the mental realm of the 'soul', equally freely.

Thoughts fall into two main groups or types:

> After having thus taken into consideration all the functions that belong to the body alone, it is easy to understand that there remains nothing in us that we should attribute to our soul but our thoughts, which are principally of two genera – the first, namely, are the actions of the soul, the other are its passions. The ones I call its actions are all of our volitions, because we find by experience that they come directly from our soul and seem to depend only on it; as, on the other hand, all the sorts of cases of perfection or knowledge to be found in us can generally be called its passions, because it is often not our soul that makes them such as they are, and because it always receives them from things that are presented by them.
>
> (Descartes, 1649 [1989]: Article 17)

There are two subtypes of volitions, those that terminate in the soul, such as willing oneself to believe in God, and those that terminate in the body, such as willing oneself to get up in the morning.

There are again two subtypes of the passions of the soul, that is, of *perceptions*. There are those which are caused by the soul itself, for example perceiving an act of volition, such as being aware of trying to do something. Then there are those which are caused by the body. The psychological treatise that contains Descartes's most detailed development of his dualism is devoted to the passions, with a few brief mentions of volitions or actions of the soul.

Hybrid patterns of explanation

At the heart of Descartes's psychology is his attempt to unite the actions of the animal spirits in the nerves and brain, and the actions of the soul, a wholly mental being. The body's spirits and the soul's actions come together in the pineal gland, so he believes. Here is a typical Cartesian account of a psychological phenomenon of some importance in everyday life:

> And all the struggles that people customarily imagine between the lower part of the soul, which is called sensitive, and the higher, which is rational, or between the natural appetites and the will, consist only in the opposition between the movements of the body by its spirits and the soul by its will tend to excite simultaneously in the gland. For there is only a single soul in us, and this soul has within itself no diversity of parts; the very one that is sensitive is rational, and all its appetites are volitions.
>
> (Descartes, 1649 [1989]: Article 47)

Let me illustrate the intimate interaction Descartes postulates between body and soul with a very different example.

> As for Desire, it is plain that, when it proceeds from true knowledge, it cannot be bad, provided that it is not immoderate, and this knowledge regulates it. It is plain too that Joy cannot fail to be good or Sadness bad with respect to the soul, because all the distress the soul receives from evil consists in the latter; and all the enjoyment of the good that belongs to it consists in the former, so that, if we had no body, I should be so bold as to say that we could not abandon ourselves too much to Love and to Joy, or shun Hatred and Sadness too much. But all of the bodily movements that accompany them can be harmful to health, when they are extremely vigorous, and can on the other hand be useful to it when they are moderate.
>
> (Descartes, 1649 [1989]: Article 141)

Though there is little in the details that we would subscribe to these days it is noteworthy that Descartes's postulation of an immaterial mind/soul does not lead him into a psychology of a wholly idealist cast. The body plays an indispensable role in these explanations. In short, Descartes has attempted to create a *hybrid* psychology, giving space both to immaterial and to material aspects of the 'mechanism' of cognition and emotion. This is not the problem with Descartes's attempt at a scientific psychology. The problem is the use of the category of 'substance' to give an account of the ontology of thoughts, feelings and at least some actions. He sets a mental stuff alongside the material stuff of the body and the animal spirits.

The psychology of John Locke

In Locke's psychology the mind is pictured more as a container than as a substance. Its contents, however, are mental, ideas. Thoughts, sensations, concepts, acts of will and so on are all treated as ideas, that is, as *entities* within the mind. ''tis past doubt', says Locke (1690: Book II, chapter 1), 'that men have in their minds several ideas ...'. He asks how the mind is 'furnished' with ideas. Then he asks, 'Whence comes it by that vast store, which the busy and boundless fancy of man has painted on it, with an almost endless variety.' In section 3 of that chapter he says, 'our senses ... convey into the mind several distinct perceptions of things'. These are ideas. The dominant metaphor in Locke's account of cognition is the mind as container with ideas as its contents.

> Our observations, employed either about external sensible objects, or about the internal operations of our minds perceived and reflected upon by ourselves, is that which supplies our understanding with all the materials of thinking.
>
> (Locke, 1690: Book 2, chapter 1, section 2)

Lockean ideas are somewhat like mental atoms. They cluster into complex ideas according to principles of association analogous to the Newtonian laws which describe the way material atoms cluster into molecules. There is an inner observer who perceives these ideas, since, according to Locke, ideas are the exclusive content of the mind. That inner eye can attend to first order ideas and form ideas about them, the ideas of reflection, which are also entities within the mind.

In terms of the philosophy of science, Locke was trying to construct a model to represent mental processes. The source of the model seems to have been Newtonian ontology of atoms in motion, associating with or dissociating from one another when they come into contact. Material corpuscles are one subtype in this type hierarchy, and Lockean ideas are another.

The quotations above make it abundantly clear that Locke thinks of the person as being other than the totality of the ideas which it contemplates and, to some extent, manages. So in Locke's psychology we have an example of a scheme which incorporates a source of activity exercised on the contents of the mind. Do simple ideas associate themselves or does a person do the associating? Locke thought that simple ideas were experienced in clusters. This was why they came to be associated in the mind. No personal synthetic activity was required. However, the mind did have the power to form complex ideas and to create its own associations. It is unclear to me whether Locke meant this for the mind-as-person or whether the mind was a causally active mental machine.

Locke's system of classifying ideas

Let us look at Locke's mentalistic taxonomy in more detail.

Ideas fall into two types: There are those derived from the senses, ideas of sensation, such as 'yellow, ... heat, ... soft, ... bitter'. Then there are those derived from 'the perception of the operations of our own minds', such as 'perception, thinking, doubting, believing, reasoning, knowing, willing'. These are ideas of reflection. Again, we note that Locke presumes that there is a something which performs these second order acts of perceptions.

In each category there are simple and complex ideas. Locke introduces this important distinction as follows:

> We have hitherto considered those *ideas*, in the reception of which the mind is only passive, which are those simple ones received from *sensation* and *reflection* … whereof the mind cannot make any one to itself, nor have any *idea* which does not wholly consist of them. But as the mind is wholly passive in the reception of all its simple *ideas*, so it exerts several acts of its own, whereby out of its simple *ideas*, as the materials and foundations of the rest, the other are framed.
>
> (Locke, 1690: chapter XII: para. 1)

Thus complex ideas are created by an active psychological process. This process is the basis of Locke's psychology. There are several ways that 'the mind exerts its power over simple ideas':

1   Combining simple *ideas* into one compound one, and thus all complex *ideas* are made.
2   … bring two *ideas*, whether simple or complex, together; and setting them by one another, so as to take a view of them at once, without uniting them into one; by which way it gets all its *ideas* of relations.
3   … separating them from all other *ideas* that accompany them in their real existence; this is called *abstraction*: and thus are all general *ideas* made.

(Locke, 1690: chapter XII: para. 1)

Locke remarks that 'this shows a man's power and its ways of operation to be much the same in the material and intellectual world' (Locke, 1690: chapter XII: para. 1). This underlines the tacit assimilation that Locke makes between persons and their minds.

Ideas are further subdivided by reference to their content. Do they concern attributes of substances? These are 'ideas of modes'. Do they concern that which can subsist by itself? These are 'ideas of substances'. Do they consist in the comparing of one idea with another? These are 'ideas of relation'. Within this scheme, there are subtypes of ideas of sensation: those of one sense only, such as ideas of colors, noises, tastes, etc. Then there are those of more than one sense: ideas of square, swift, etc. Similarly, there are subtypes of ideas of reflection. These are Perception, Thinking, and Volition or willing. Locke allows for a fourth major type that covers ideas that can fall either into ideas of sensation or of reflection. These are a rather heterogeneous lot, including 'ideas of pleasure' and 'ideas of pain'. This pair can derive either from sensation or from reflection on the operations of our own minds. This type also includes 'ideas of existence', which can have a place either among ideas of sensation or among ideas of reflection.

Ideas of primary and of secondary qualities

This paradigm for psychology has its own special load of difficulties, not least when Locke tries to use it to develop a psychology of perception. His strategy is to claim that some ideas, for example the idea of shape, resemble their material causes, the real qualities of material things, and so offer a direct entry into a non-mental world. Other ideas, for example the idea of warmth, do not resemble their material causes, for example molecular motions, and we can say only that things in the world have the power to induce such ideas in us. How a being whose knowledge consists only of ideas and their relations one to another could ever find support for such a claim is a mystery Locke never resolves. In order to know that some ideas resemble their causes and some do not a psychologist would need to observe both ideas and material qualities and to study their correlations. However, according to Locke, one can never have anything in mind except ideas. So the test could never be applied.

Locke can hardly be said to have any explanatory model for representing the mechanisms of cognition and perception. At best, he suggests that the mind actively combines simple ideas into complex ones. Though it does so on the basis of patterned ways simple ideas are presented, he does not adopt this as the explanation of their continued association in complex ideas. There is activity of the mind in the formation of complex ideas.

The realist psychology of David Hartley

Locke does not relate associated ideas with acquired properties of the brain and nervous system. The domain of psychology, of the human understanding, consists only of ideas. Earlier in the seventeenth century Hobbes had pointed to the possibility of a one-to-one correlation between ideas and the motion of material corpuscles in the brain and nervous system (see Chapter 5). However, his system was materialist, in that only the corpuscular domain was real. Hartley's innovation was to propose a psychology based on a hybrid ontology. Both ideas and states of the brain and nervous system were real, each in its own domain.

That there is always some state of the brain and nervous system when someone is thinking does not strike one as particularly significant. However, if the same type of brain state is usually found with the same type of thinking or feeling one is much more inclined to posit at least a causal relation between trains of ideas and trains of brain states. One might even toy with the suggestion that the correlation may signal identity beneath a superficial difference. The project of a unified psychology, linking laws of association of ideas with laws of psychophysics as applied to the nervous system, was set out in detail by David Hartley in his massive treatise of 1749. Hartley's psychology was realist. The associations of ideas observable to a human being attending to his or her own mental processes was to be explained by an association of elementary but unobservable physical states in that person's brain and nervous system.

Hartley held to the general principle that ideas, the beings that populated the realm of human experience, were caused by corresponding minute 'vibrations' in the brain and nervous system. He drew his account of the nervous system from a generalization of Newton's theory of the ether as the sustainer of material existence and causality. He turned to physics as a source for his model of cognition. However, he turned to a different part of physics from the atomism which Locke seems to have drawn on for his theory of simple and complex ideas. But it is his unifying thesis that is of most interest to us. Just as ideas cluster because of associations formed by repeated experience of their appearing together either simultaneously or sequentially in our experience, so there must be associated vibrations in our nervous systems.

Hartley introduces the notion of 'idea' as follows: '[Sensations are] internal feelings of the mind, which arise from the impressions made upon the several parts of our bodies. All our other internal feelings may be called *ideas*' (Hartley, 1749: ii). Ideas of sensation are simple. All other ideas are complex. Finding a place among both sensations and ideas are pleasure and pain. Here we have the Lockean psychology. Hartley describes the association of ideas in experiential terms, as the result of a 'sufficient repetition of a sensation' (Hartley, 1749: 57). Once established, associations among ideas allow the whole complex from which they were drawn to be recalled when only a part is presented. We shall find a modern version of this observation and its neurophysiological explanation in Chapter 10.

The corresponding neural association is described as follows: 'we are to suppose, that the simple miniature vibrations, corresponding to these simple ideas, are, in like manner, [associated] into a complex miniature vibration, corresponding to the resulting complex idea' (Hartley, 1749: 790). Words, too, are associated with ideas by a similar simple mechanism. The experiential pattern of words and ideas is matched by a similar pattern of vibrations.

Despite the many examples of hybrid associations Hartley offers he did not try to abstract the basic laws of association. Therefore the full parallel between Newton's mechanics and a psychology of ideas was still to be worked out.

With a little updating on the neural side, versions of this general account can be found even in the twenty-first century. It represents with great clarity the general standpoint that comes from maintaining a strict tie between a phenomenological analysis of the structure and components of conscious experience and the pattern of causal processes in the nervous system.

The positivist psychology of David Hume

Newton's three laws cover all possible interactions by contact between moving material bodies. Galileo and Boyle had begun the study of the laws by which the corpuscles of matter clustered into larger units. Inspired by physics, the psychologists of the seventeenth and eighteenth centuries sought the laws of the association of ideas. However, Hartley does not offer any specific laws of association as such. Locke's proposals are rather sketchy. It was left to Hume to present three laws of association that may be compared for the ambition of their scope with Newton's three laws of motion.

Hume's influence can still be felt in the positivistic wraiths that haunt mainstream psychology laboratories. Like Locke, he sets out a taxonomy of 'perceptions of the mind'. There are 'thoughts or ideas' and 'impressions'. The former are less lively than the latter but have the same content. For instance, there are impressions that derive from hearing, seeing, feeling, loving, hating, desiring and willing. The creative power of the mind is exercised on these elementary units of cognition, in 'compounding, transposing, augmenting, and diminishing the materials afforded by the senses and experience' (Hume, 1777 [1963]: pp. 18–19).

Hume reduces the principles or laws of association to just three. Ideas tend to cluster if they resemble one another, if they are contiguous and if they are related by cause and effect. The repeated appearance of ideas clustered in any of these manners in the experience of a human being leads to their being thought and recalled together, that is, associated. In a famous *tour de force* Hume offers an analysis of the relation of cause and effect that reduces it to the upshot of repeated pairings of contiguous events. For example, why do we think that scraping the bow over the strings of a violin *causes* a listener to hear a sound? Having experienced the regular sequence of a visual impression of bowing followed by an auditory impression of sound, the idea of bowing becomes associated with the idea of sound. A person who sees someone moving the bow over the strings expects to hear a sound. That is all there is to it. In the end, then, there are only two laws of association, and one essential process, the ingraining of mental habits by repetition of pairs of impressions that resemble one another. In this way, types of ideas are paired. Ideas are the mental remnants of impressions. When an impression of one type occurs the idea of the associated impression occurs.

Hume does not speculate on what may be the unobservable domain of material causes of the trains and clusters of ideas a person experiences. In his general philosophy he allowed neither unobservable causal powers nor unobservable material substances any place. His psychology is strictly positivistic.

Causes and agents: the transcendental solution

In 1781 Immanuel Kant published his great work the *Critique of Pure Reason*, followed by a second, revised edition in 1787. All human experience, he argued, is shaped by twelve schemata, reflecting twelve forms of judgment. Rational beings, he tried to show, can think and perceive only in accordance with these principles. According to Kant, this is because we synthesize the content of our experience by means of these schemata out of a stream of inchoate impressions. Thus it comes about that we perceive an orderly world of stable things and sequences of events as causes and their effects. At the same time we synthesize a mental realm of conscious and orderly thoughts. It follows that everything rational beings can think or perceive will display characteristics conforming to the twelve schemata.

Here is how he puts the point: 'But though all our knowledge begins with experience, it does not follow that it all arises out of experience. For it may well be that even our empirical knowledge is made up of what we receive through impressions and of what our own faculty of knowledge (sensible impressions serving merely as the occasion) supplies from itself' (Kant, 1787 [1996]: B1).

Among the twelve schemata is causality. It is related to the conditional form of judgment 'If A, then B.' Thus one might say, 'If one strikes the bell with a hammer, the bell will ring.' This judgment expresses a causal relation between hammer blow and bell ringing. Why can we make such judgments? It is because in our experience of the world events are perceived in such pairs. However, we might ask: why does the world, as we experience it, display cause–effect sequences everywhere? It follows, according to Kant, because the world as we perceive it, and our thoughts as we experience them, are synthesized from a primitive flux of sensations. The 'empirical world' conforms to the Causal Picture, as it was described in the introduction to Part II. Everything we can experience will appear to us as sequences of causally related events.

However, Kant was struck by what he took to be the fact that human beings live according to moral principles, at least sometimes. We do not always follow instinctive promptings or indulge our wants. Human life is not wholly explicable in terms of causal laws. We do try to conform to moral laws. In so doing we are not moved by causes but are self-active beings following the dictates of reason. How could that be possible in a world that was dominated by causality? There must be another aspect of human existence.

How do I know that I am a being that has the power to act according to reason? It is not because I can turn my attention to my active self. That would require me to have an experience of the very self that is doing the experiencing. As Kant says, 'I cannot determine my existence as a self-active being; all I can do is to represent to myself the spontaneity of my thought … my existence is still only determined sensibly, that is, as the existence of an *appearance*. But it is owing to this spontaneity that I entitle myself an intelligence' (Kant: 1787 [1996]: B156, footnote b).

In the empirical world, he thought, there were no agents. One cannot experience oneself as an agent. Sometimes one does act spontaneously, that is, contrary to the flow of cause and effect. In some cases at least one's actions are explicable by reasons rather than by causes. Human beings exist in the world of cause and effect, the world that is revealed by the senses, both external and internal. They must also exist in a world of reason. In the world of cause and effect there are empirical selves. In the world of reason a human being is an active agent. We cannot know that world empirically, that is, by observation. We know it by reason, not by the senses. It is transcendental. Kant calls our mode of being in the world of reason a *noumenal* self.

Human life must therefore be treated as a hybrid of the play of causality and the uses of reason. Though Kant does not express the matter that way, it is not hard to draw this conclusion from his analysis of what it is to be a human being. We exist in a material world, synthesized in accordance with the schemata embedded in our faculty of knowledge. However, we also exist in a moral world, a world of norms, standards to which reason requires that each of us should conform.

Here we have an attempt to make use of *both* the Causal Picture and the Agentive Picture as they were set out in the introduction to Part II. Kant convinced himself that both pictures are required and that neither can be used to eliminate the other.

The Search for a Scientific Psychology 1: Mental substances

1   Project:

  a)   To create a scientific psychology by conforming to the general style of Newtonian physics. Material atomism will serve as the source model or common supertype for both ideas, as a model for the mind and corpuscles as a model for the world.

  b)   A science requires an ontology, a taxonomy, and an explanatory format. The metaphysics of ideas provided a basis for all three.

2   Descartes and the dual ontology: matter and *mind stuff*, a *res cogitans*, constituted a unified thinking thing:

  a)   There are two groups of personal attributes:

   i)   Extension, (material) occupying space and time.
   ii)   Thought, (immaterial) confined neither by space nor by time.

  b)   Each person is a combination of a mind and a body. The person is identical only with the mind = soul. (*Cogito, ergo sum.*)

  c)   Psychology is the study of the actions of the soul, what one does, acting on the mind or the body; and the passions of the soul, what happens to the soul acted on by the mind or the body.

  d)   In his detailed analyses and theoretical discussions Descartes employs a hybrid psychology using both mentalistic and material concepts.

3   Locke and an ontology of ideas:

  a)   The mind is a container of mental atoms, 'ideas'. (Whatever is in a man's mind when he thinks.)

  b)   These include:

   i)   Simple ideas, like 'white' or 'cold', and complex ideas, like 'snow'.
   ii)   Ideas of sensation, like 'red', 'round', 'apple', and ideas of reflection like 'perception', 'knowing', 'willing'.

4   Hartley's realist hybrid psychology:

  a)   Observable associations of ideas are caused by unobservable associations of 'vibrations' in the brain and nervous system.

  b)   Both domains are real.

5   Hume's positivistic psychology:

  a)   From the same starting point of observed correlations of ideas Hume's three laws of association of ideas seem to echo the Newtonian three laws of motion.

  b)   Hume's laws of association are based on resemblance, contiguity, and cause and effect, effective through repetition.

(continued)

6 Kant's transcendental ego:

    a) Human experience is ordered according to twelve schemata, among which is the schema of cause and effect.

    b) However, human beings can also act in accordance with reason, against the flow of cause and effect.

    c) People must exist in two realms, one empirical and one transcendental.

Conclusion

Neither the Cartesian nor the Lockean picture is fully consistent, but each marks one main way that thoughts and feelings have been classified – as mental attributes and as mental entities. In neither case is direct public access to the thoughts and feelings of another sentient being possible.

Starting with observational knowledge of association of ideas, Hartley followed the realist paradigm to propose hypotheses about unobservable 'vibrations' in the brain and nervous system. These could be used to explain the way ideas were associated in human experience. This step was explicitly based on the ether hypothesis of Newtonian physics. Ether vibrations were the unobservable causes of such phenomena as the visible spectrum of colors. Could they play a similar role in psychology?

Hume's principles of association seemed to offer a powerful basis for understanding how patterns of thought are formed. It is not hard to see how the psychologies of Hume and Hartley could be welded into one. Analysis of associated ideas provides the observational and factual dimension. Hypotheses about vibrations provide the explanatory dimension. Technical breakthroughs might have led to hitherto unobservable ether vibrations becoming observable. Why, then, did associationism drop out of favor? In the late nineteenth century a wave of positivist stringency swept across the scientific world. It seemed to many as if one fundamental criterion for scientific knowledge could not be met by any of these versions of a psychology of ideas: namely that hypotheses must be capable of intersubjective, public tests of correctness. Neither Cartesian reports of the properties of a mental substance nor reports of the behavior of ideas as mental 'atoms' could be the subject of publicly testable hypotheses. At best, one could test behavioral predictions drawn from Cartesian or Lockean hypotheses. Studies of one's own mind, which had been offered as a perfectly legitimate field of scientific knowledge, were ruled out of court. Hume's principles of association of privately experienced ideas disappeared along with everything else that could not be publicly observed.

Ironically, the principle that the clustering of ideas in the individual consciousness is brought about by repetition of like pairs of impressions, according to the associationists, was picked up and transposed by behaviorists. Behaviorism takes the same principle of association by repetition and simply changes the context from the private to the public domain, from ideas to behavior. Association of ideas is transposed into conditioning of responses to stimuli.

Psychology as a science of material substances

In psychology, materialism has been explicitly advocated in various forms and has been implicit in the presuppositions of research programs and proposals. We shall see that the different forms of materialism are interconnected in important ways. We can be *ontological* materialists, building our science on the explicit principle that only the material attributes of the human organism that can be ultimately accounted for in terms of the concepts of physics, are of relevance to the task of developing a science of thinking, feeling, perceiving and acting. Or we can be *methodological* materialists, allowing that there may be a realm of immaterial beings, thoughts, feelings and so on, but that the methods of psychological research need take no account of it. Each of these 'materialisms' depends on deep but disputable presuppositions implicit in certain methods of studying and explaining human ways of thinking, feeling, perceiving and acting. They have often, but not always, been brought to light and critically assessed by philosophers. Psychologists, following their intuitions, need to be reminded about the presuppositions of their approaches to human life. That is a job for philosophers. Thirdly, we can be *conceptual* materialists, bringing the presuppositions of folk and 'scientific psychology' to light, and proposing the elimination from psychological science of all expressions that do not have a reference to material things, states and processes. This way of advocating materialism has been pioneered by philosophers explicitly debating the standing of presuppositions of the uses of different vocabularies for describing and explaining human life.

Presented baldly, materialism sounds simple. We must just accept that our intuitions in favor of a richer universe than the material world are illusory. However, there are at least three different ways that the materialist conception of scientific psychology has been taken.

1   *Physicalism* expresses the presupposition that the only attributes required to describe and account for human thought, feeling, perception and action are those that the human body shares with non-human organisms and with inorganic beings. From a scientific point of view, these are the properties and processes of material

things in general that are studied by physicists and chemists. They include the masses and motions of atomic particles. In the end, only the concepts of physics should have a place. Following this line would reduce psychology to physics, step by step: psychology to neurology, neurology to biochemistry and biophysics, and chemistry to physics.

2   It is fairly obvious that human capacities for thinking, feeling, perceiving and acting depend on properties and processes of the brain and nervous system, though the heart and the liver have also been implicated. *Neural* materialism presupposes that the attributes sufficient to account for human thinking, feeling, perceiving and acting, though including those that are presupposed by simple materialism, also include distinctive attributes of the brain and nervous system. These include electrical discharges in nerve fibers, the electrical field of an active brain, oxidation of visual purple in the retina and so on. Following this line would reduce psychology to the study of the brain and nervous system. There are structural properties of the organism that cannot be accounted for by physics.

3   Biology covers not only the anatomy and physiology of the whole organism and its functionally distinct parts but also ethology, the study of patterns of life of whole organisms. *Ethological* materialism presupposes that all-important psychological phenomena are, in one way or another, human versions of patterns of behavior common to the higher primates. The explanation of a psychological capacity should be Darwinian, that is, it should be by reference to the way the existence and exercise of the capacity facilitates gene selection. Following this line would reduce psychology to a branch of evolutionary biology.

These 'materialisms', tied respectively to physics, to neuroscience and to ethology, overlap with the distinctions we have drawn between ontological, methodological and conceptual materialisms. Ethological materialism, with its link to genetics and Darwinian selection, deserves a separate section. It involves all three basic issues: ontology, methodology and conceptual revision.

Let us remind ourselves that a science of psychology must enable its practitioners to identify and classify psychological phenomena *and* to explain the contemporaneous and sequential patterns to be observed among the phenomena. This makes two demands on materialism in psychology. Can those phenomena we ordinarily take to be psychological be shown actually to be material? Alternatively, can they be exceptionlessly correlated with material phenomena? The second demand concerns the means by which psychological phenomena are brought into existence, whatever their ontological standing. In a thoroughgoing materialist psychology we would expect psychologists to be working with the presupposition that psychological phenomena are produced exclusively by the workings of material 'mechanisms'.

section one

Ontological materialism

Ontological materialism is the thesis that there are really only material entities, states and processes. Psychological capacities and processes must, therefore, be described and explained in terms of material entities, states and processes. Our ordinary ways of describing and explaining what people think, feel, perceive and do make use of all sorts of non-material concepts, like 'correct' and 'incorrect', 'pains and pleasures' and many others. It seems likely that some revision of our systems of concepts would follow from the adoption of materialism as an onto-logical thesis, a thesis about what really exists. To understand what materialists are claiming we must first settle on what is meant by 'material' in this context. A useful working definition might run as follows: *the domain of the material is defined as those categories of entities, properties and processes that are common to both organic and inorganic substances*. A materialist psychological science might take its start from the principle that what seem to be mental attributes and processes are, when seen aright, nothing but material attributes and processes of and in the human organ-ism. The mind is just one aspect of the material processes in the human body. Such processes could as easily take place in inorganic as in organic bodies. In many works, and particularly in *Leviathan* (1651 [1953]), Hobbes worked out a detailed psychology, including the psychology of perception, on a strictly material-ist basis, reducing the mental realm to nothing but 'matter in motion'.

Here is how he explains the seeming subjective qualities of sense experi-ence: though the sense organs lead moving atoms *into* the brain we perceive things *outside* our bodies, in the opposite direction, so to say. According to Hobbes, this must be because the incoming atoms cause a reaction in the material of the inner parts of the body, for instance visual cortex, that is directed outwards, contrary to the flow of sensory atoms inwards.

> The cause of sense, is the external body, or object, which presseth the organ proper to each sense, either immediately, as in taste and touch; or mediately, as in seeing, hearing and smelling; which pressure, by the mediation of the nerves, and other strings and membranes of the body, continued inwards to the brain and heart, causeth there a resistance, or counter-pressure, or endeavour of the heart to deliver itself, which endeavour, because *outward*, seemeth to be some matter without. And this *seeming* or *fancy*, is that which men call *sense* ... All which qualities, called sensible, are in the object, which causeth them, but so many several motions of the matter, by which it presseth our organs diversely. Neither in us that are pressed, are they any thing else but divers motions; for motion produceth nothing but motion.
>
> (Hobbes, 1651 [1953]: pp. 22–3)

This is an application of the principle that later became Newton's third law of motion, that action and reaction are equal and opposite. The principle is applied literally, to the motion of material corpuscles. The only concepts that Hobbes uses in his account of perception and in his other treatments of psychological phenomena are 'matter' and 'motion', the leading concepts of the physics of his day.

There are surely some profound problems with this bold reduction of the mental to the material. It seems obvious that thoughts and feelings are not entities common to both the organic and the inorganic domains, nor are their properties, either. For example, a thought could be illogical. No inorganic entity could have such a property. However, there may be ways in which this seeming impasse could be circumvented. Here are two ways in which a simple materialist psychology might make sense.

1   Thoughts and feelings only seem to be non-material. Much as perceived warmth does not resemble the molecular motions that cause the feelings of heat and cold, so a feeling of pain does not resemble the material neural processes that cause it. Thoughts and feelings, as experienced, have much the same status as Locke's ideas of secondary qualities.

However, there is a huge problem with this. By what or by whom are thoughts and feelings experienced? If we are to carry through the parallel between mental states and processes and ideas of secondary qualities we will need to supply an analog of the person as perceiver, presumed in Locke's account of perception. To make sense it would require the postulation of a homunculus, a person inside the person. Therefore, as psychologists, we would be no further forward. We would still need to explain the powers of the homunculus. If they could be explained materially we would have no need of the homunculus. We could simply apply the explanation to the person. If they could not be so explained, we would need a second order homunculus, opening up the possibility of a debilitating regress.

2   Thoughts and feelings are emergent properties of material structures and processes. In addition to their molecular constituents, beings with mental capacities are structured in quite particular ways. The structures of brains and nervous systems engender properties that are not shared by any of the material constituents of these structures. Brains can think when embodied as persons. However, brain cells cannot think. This is not because it is too hard for them. It is because the concept 'thinks' is meaningful only as referring to a capacity of whole human beings. The concept of 'emergent property' has a wide range of useful applications. For example, a melody is not a property of any one of the notes that are its constituents. Yet it exists only in the structure of those notes.

The properties of the human organism that are relevant to psychology seem to be just those we would see as emergent.

Methodological materialism

Methodological materialism trades on the observation that there may well be a thoroughgoing parallel between the flow of thoughts and feelings, perceptions and actions, as they are experienced by this or that human being, and the stream of material states of the person as an organism. Thoughts and feelings, it may be argued, though they are not material, are caused by material states of the human organism in perfect synchrony. Research projects into what people will think, feel, perceive and do under well defined conditions can be carried through by studying the flow of material states alone.

About the same time that Hartley was proposing his dualistic association-ist psychology, the French physiologist, G.O. de La Mettrie was putting forward a project for a scientific psychology very like the Methodological Materialism we have just sketched. Recall that in Hartley's scheme, associations of ideas were observable and associations of micro-vibrations in the nervous system were un-observable. Empirical research must, therefore, be based on studies of the flux of immaterial ideas. However, unlike Hartley, La Mettrie, in his *L'Homme Machine* (1749), argued for a methodologically materialist psychology. While leaving open the question of whether mental states and processes were or were not identical with physical states and processes, particularly in the brain and nervous system, he proposed that a scientific psychology should be built around their uniform and exceptionless correlation.

He offers a great variety of examples to show that in general 'The various states of the soul are always correlated with those of the body' (La Mettrie, 1749). He presents this as a matter of fact, established by observation and experiment. Let us suppose that the perfect correlation of types of mental states with types of material states of the brain and nervous system has been accomplished. If we are interested only in predicting the way that patterns of thought and feeling will develop we can study either the sequence of types of mental states or the sequence of types of material states. By passing back and forth, we can accomplish whatever predictive and retrodictive tasks we like.

On this basis, La Mettrie could have argued that it is indifferent whether one studies the flow of thoughts and feelings or the flow of material states of the brain and nervous system. If they are perfectly correlated, then, at every point, a thoroughgoing cross-inference can be made from the one to the other. However, he used the thesis of the perfect correlation between mental and bodily states as the working basis for a scientific research program into human psychology that is methodologically materialist. Only neurophysiology and anatomy need to be taken into account.

La Mettrie is careful to draw back from any claims about the essence of humankind. 'Man [in the species sense] is a Machine so organized that it is impossible to arrive at a clear idea of it, and consequently at a definition.' At best, we can arrive at the highest state of probability for the presupposition on which the rationality of a materialist research project depends, namely that every mental state is correlated with a material state. The failure to specify exactly in what a human being consists is not because there is a mysterious ingredient, the soul, but because the mechanism is so subtle, refined and complex.

The way La Mettrie presented his materialism needs to be carefully qualified. If, as a matter of fact, there is always some brain state correlated with any given mental state, this may be of little interest. We all acknowledge that human beings are embodied. However, if each time a mental state of a certain *kind* occurs a brain state of a certain *kind* occurs this seems a much more telling correlation in support of La Mettrie's methodological materialism. A random distribution of kinds of mental states correlated with kinds of bodily states, even though every mental state was correlated with some bodily state, would not support La Mettrie's program.

La Mettrie was inclined to interpret the correlation between mental and material states as if it were clearly causal, but in a very narrow sense. 'Our feeble understanding,' he says, 'derived from very crude observations, cannot show us the relations that obtain between cause and effect.' Physiology cannot explain *how* consciousness arises from matter, it demonstrates only *that* it does. The scientific program of neuropsychology was to be based on taking the observable correlations between mental states and material states of a human being to be without exception, but without an explanation either.

In discussing the two great world systems in Chapter 2, atomism and dynamism, I pointed out how strongly material atomism is tied up with a presupposition of the passivity of material things. Could a wholly mechanical device be an agent? La Mettrie claimed to be taking the animal/machine concept from Descartes and to have extended it to human beings, but he did not leave it unmodified. Material mechanisms we may be but, according to La Mettrie, we are capable of native and originating activity. Organisms have active powers. 'Living bodies have all that is needed for self-movement, feeling, thought ... and to conduct themselves, in a word, in the physical and the moral world' (La Mettrie, 1749). They are quite unlike material corpuscles that remain quiescent until acted upon by other corpuscles the only relevant property of which is their motion. They acquired this from contact with yet another moving particle, and so on back to the Divine creation of the world.

Like Locke, La Mettrie thought that matter could have mental powers. However, unlike Locke, who drew back from asserting that the possibility was true as a matter of fact, La Mettrie affirmed it. This boldness was not appreciated by many of his contemporaries. Church and lay folk alike roundly criticized him for his materialist stance. Surely our agentic powers spoke for a soul? La Mettrie was not alone in thinking that matter could have all sorts of powers, including mental capacities and skills. Joseph Priestley (1777) was similarly convinced that there was a common material basis for both physical and cognitive powers. Priestley too was anathematized. He was suspected of radical politics as well as radical interpretations of the soul! His house was burned by a mob and not long afterwards he made his way to America.

Methodological materialism does not claim that mental states and processes are nothing but states and processes of the material human body. Rather it is based on the thesis that there is a perfect or near-perfect synchrony between mental states and their temporal development and certain states of the body and their sequential evolution as material processes. This holds whatever may be the nature of mental states and processes, that is, of thoughts and feelings. If this is indeed true then all one needs to know about the *patterns* of thought, feeling and action can be discovered by studying the material side of the equation alone. One may remain ignorant of the nature of thoughts, feelings and actions while understanding their relationships very well. If the goal of a scientific psychology is no more than the prediction and retrodiction of psychological phenomena, the study of the relevant processes in the body will be sufficient. Relevance is determined by looking for correlations from mental states to bodily states, since there are many states of a human body that have no mental counterpart. This means that the mentalistic vocabulary and concepts cannot be dispensed with in setting up and interpreting the results of scientific research programs. They determine what are to be picked out of the huge range of possible material states of a human body to play a part in a materialist system of prediction, retrodiction and explanation.

section three

Conceptual materialism

The foundational proposals sketched above have seemed to some philosophers to be insufficiently robust as the basis for a materialist psychology. It leaves an autonomous domain of psychological concepts intact, even if ignored in research programs. Conceptual materialism asserts that psychology needs only material concepts to describe and explain the totality of psychological phenomena. Ontological debates are inconclusive and interminable. The elimination of mentalistic concepts from our discursive repertoire would remove the threat of immaterialism at one stroke. Furthermore, there would be only one way of designing research projects, since there would be only a materialist vocabulary with which to do so. Adopting conceptual materialism would lead to ontological and methodological materialism at a stroke.

The collapse of behaviorism encouraged many philosophers and philosophically minded psychologists to try to develop a realist psychology, giving due weight even to unobservable cognitive phenomena, thoughts and feelings as such. This was ontologically pluralistic. Others, impressed by the modest but exciting successes of investigations of the neural basis of human thought and action, advocated methodological materialism not unlike that of La Mettrie. However, it was proposed to base it on twentieth-century neuroscience rather than on eighteenth-century mechanics of material particles in motion. Both responses to the demise of behaviorism left the ontological question unsettled. Given the emphasis that philosophers in the twentieth century had placed on matters of language, it is not surprising that a new range of supporting considerations favoring a strong materialism were based on the analysis of the presuppositions of lay and professional uses of language.

Arguments in support of conceptual materialism take their stand on questions of the presuppositions of the uses of certain vocabularies. Could we dispense with mentalistic words in favor of a materialist vocabulary? Since our mentalistic vocabulary mostly comes from the vernacular, ordinary everyday use of words, the proposal amounts to the proposal that the ordinary language of thoughts and feelings, presupposing the existence of an immaterial mental realm, should be replaced by a vocabulary of expressions drawn from neurophysiology and anatomy, presupposing only material states and processes. The new vocabulary would be drawn from the sciences that are most obviously relevant to those activities we take to be the domain of psychology: namely, thinking, feeling, perceiving and acting.

We learned in Part I to look closely at the status of presuppositions of human practices. Are they factual? Or are they conceptual? Or are they conceptual but presented as if they expressed matters of fact? Conceptual materialism, in its twentieth-century guise as eliminative materialism, concerns the presuppositions of the vocabularies of two discourse genres, ways of describing and explaining human affairs. What is presupposed by the uses of ordinary everyday terminology to describe and explain our thoughts, feelings, perceptions and actions is critically juxtaposed with what is presupposed by the uses of the vocabulary of neuroscience in carrying out the same tasks. The discussion is meant to show that we should prefer the vocabulary of neuroscience to the vernacular because the presuppositions of the former are preferable to those of the latter.

The arguments for eliminative materialism

Drawing on the long established principle of the theory-ladenness of observations (or observation descriptions) Churchland (1981, 1984) has developed a philosophical argument in favor of the claim that all mental state references can be removed from psychology in favor of expressions referring only to physical or material properties and things with no loss of substantive content. Nothing would be lost in the change-over. Whatever we could say in the vernacular, we would be able to say in the new language.

The idea of theory-ladenness is simply stated. The meaning people take a word to have depends in part on the theory they share concerning the nature of the beings in the domain in which the word is to be used. Even if we use the same sound or written sign, if we do not share a theory relevant to the topic under discussion, the meanings of our words are not the same. Tycho Brahe, believing the sun circles the earth, and Johannes Kepler, believing the earth orbits the sun, may both have used the word *Sonnenuntergang* (sunset). However, according to the principle of the theory-ladenness of descriptive vocabularies, each meant something different by it.

To understand how the program of eliminative materialism would work, we can begin with a thought experiment. Churchland imagines a culture in which, instead of learning words like 'red apple', 'pain', 'hope' and so on, children would learn expressions like 'a matrix of molecules reflecting photons at certain critical wavelengths', 'the c-fibers of this body are firing', 'the cerebral cortex of this brain is in a certain n state' and so on (Churchland, 1984: 15). Though he concedes that this is not how apples look, or pain feels, or hopes introspectively seem, that is nevertheless what these experiences are 'really ... in their innermost depth'. Things would be much better, Churchland advises, if we too adopted this vocabulary.

What would we gain? We would have no temptation to believe in such non-existent mental entities as beliefs, feelings and so on. Why might we be so tempted? Because, Churchland thought, the English language incorporates a folk psychology presupposing a mentalistic ontology. Among the kinds of items in the ontology would be mental states such as being in pain, mental entities such as beliefs and desires, mental events such as remembering the name of an acquaintance. According to Churchland, the words of English are loaded with this theory, just as the words used by astronomers once were loaded with the false geocentric theory, when they were used in such vernacular expressions as 'sunrise'. Modern astronomy uses a different vocabulary that is 'loaded' with the true, heliocentric theory.

Churchland thinks that, in interacting with other people and reflecting on our experience, we form hypotheses about cognition, emotion, perception and action, the implicit psychology of everyday English, which refer to mental entities, properties and processes. Why? Because our everyday language is loaded with a theory that is based on assumptions about the existence of such mental beings. He says, 'an introspective judgement is just an instance of an acquired habit of conceptual response to one's internal states, and the integrity of any particular response is always contingent on the integrity of the acquired conceptual framework (theory) in which the response is framed' (Churchland, 1981: 70).

According to Churchland, the presuppositions revealed by philosophical analysis of ordinary English are factual. Moreover, they are false. There are no such *entities* as thoughts, feelings, perceptions and actions. Either our words do not mean what they seem to mean or they should be replaced by words the uses of which presuppose only material beings.

The arguments against eliminative materialism

1. The arguments for the program of eliminative materialism depend on a thesis about the ontology of ordinary English, and presumably other Indo-European

languages. The use of the words of these languages, such as 'belief', a noun, pre-suppose the existence of mental entities, that is, of beliefs. Churchland claims that this presupposition is factual and false. However, this claim depends on a philo-sophical analysis of the uses of words like 'belief'. In fact they do not presuppose the existence of a realm of mental entities. Indeed, on the contrary, it is wrong to interpret them so. Beliefs and most other mental beings are not entitative, that is, thing-like, nor are they the properties of mental substances. To ascribe a belief to someone else is to ascribe a broad disposition to speak and act in certain ways. To ascribe a belief to oneself is an indirect way of committing oneself to the truth of an assertion. That is how the Christian Creed begins: 'I believe in God the Father Almighty …'. Most of what the eliminative materialists say about the ontological presuppositions of Indo-European vernaculars is simply wrong. Ryle (1947) and Wittgenstein (1953), and many others, have brought out how complex and many-faceted is the cluster of ontological presuppositions in the use of the English and German vernaculars. Does every theory change create a new perceptual world? Churchland concedes that 'warmth … does not feel like the mean kinetic energy of millions of tiny molecules'. (I think he means their motion.) It seems to follow that, if the new vocabulary is used in the circumstances in which the old one was appropriate, the new words will be doing the same work as the old. In which case the old and the new words will be synonyms. Churchland might reply that while phenomenologically they mean the same their ontological presuppositions are different. If 'mean kinetic energy' comes to mean 'warmth' the scientistic vocabu-lary has changed its meaning, towards that of the traditional vocabulary. Why should it not take up the presuppositions of the old as well as its experiential import (Vollmer, 1990)?

2. It may be argued that the existence of scientifically authenticated beings, such as neural firings, is guaranteed by science, and there is no such guarantee of the existence of experienced sounds. However, existence claims are settled by an actual encounter with the being in question. Belief in scientific existents is surely less well authenticated than experiential ones. Neither micro-brain states nor molecular vibrations of the air are perceivable, but the sounds of music are. The experiential grounds for belief in the existence of colors, of hopes, of meanings and so on are better than those for theoretical entities, be they mental or material. We need to be skeptical about current scientific theories and their ontologies. It seems to me quite obvious that theory is less secure than experience as a guide to what there is is. What theory purports to tell us about the world changes more rapidly than what experience shows us about the world. So we are not justified in preferring neural to mental words as guides to what there really is. This point links back with the earlier objection that if experience is the common ground for claims about what exists, then feelings, beliefs and so on have a better claim to the accolade than any theoretical entities.

3. There is also an *ad hominem* objection.[1] How does this affect Church-land's case? On the one hand, as Vollmer points out, his theory of knowledge draws on notions like learning, perceiving, and understanding, since he wants our re-educated population to understand and explain their lives differently. However, these notions require the concept of a person and his or her mental states and dis-

positions. Yet Churchland's philosophy of psychology is based on the denial that any such things exist. His theory of knowledge is couched in the language of persons, and his theory of psychology in the language of molecules. If the latter were true, the former would be incoherent. If the former were coherent, the latter would be false.

4. While it may not be true that the world as perceived changes with change of vocabulary, the new words mean something different from the old in that they presuppose a different ontology. However, the experiential conditions under which the new words are to be learned are identical with those under which the old words were learned. And, at the time of learning them, infants know no bio-chemistry or physics. So the only sense they can give to them must be identical to that of the vocabulary the new words have displaced. Thus the phrase 'firing in my c-fibers' has exactly the same role in life as the word 'pain', namely to express a particular kind of discomfort for those who, like infants, do not know any neuroscience. Infants could not learn the meanings of their vocabulary that depended on materialist presuppositions if these are the presuppositions of some neurological theory. Hence 'firing in the body's c-fibers' must be an exact syn-onym for 'bring in pain'. The linguistic reforms of eliminative materialism amount to no more than a pseudo-transformation of meanings. In learning the new vocabulary the children have learned how the state they experience is caused: namely that the cause of the experience of warmth in me is the motion of molecules in the water. But even when this step is possible for them, when they have learned some biochemistry and physics, they will need both mental and neuroscience concepts to understand it. Someone will now have to teach them the word 'pain'!

The two aspects of materialism, its way of analysing psychological con-cepts and its way of explaining psychological phenomena by reference to pro-cesses describable in terms of physics and chemistry alone, are evident in the presuppositions of the eliminative program. Materialist forms of explanation are the only kind that is left if the concepts of psychology are wholly material.

Psychology cannot do without the person

Why have ontological, methodological and conceptual materialisms been aban-doned by many psychologists in favor of assumptions about the reality of cogni-tive processes? This includes favoring the ontologies of various folk psychologies. There seem to be two main reasons:

1   Eliminating all but biochemical and biophysical terminology seems to be eliminating the subject matter of psychology as well. Psychological phenomena are not given to people *as* material phenomena. Remembering is experienced in a quite different manner from the way one would experi-ence a chemical reaction or a burst of electrical current in a circuit.
2   To identify and individuate a relevant material state of the brain and nervous system of the thinking thing, be it person or machine, one must be

able to identify and individuate the psychological phenomenon in question. In addition, that requires one to draw on categories that are deeply embedded in the vernacular.

La Mettrie's thesis of exceptionless correlation between the flow of thought, feeling and action and the flow of processes in the body seems to be highly plausible as a starting point for creating a hybrid science. It would do justice both to human experience and to the discoveries that have been piling up about what is happening in the brain and nervous system when someone is thinking, feeling, perceiving and acting. However, at this point we are still far short of our goal of providing thorough and robust support for some version of his program.

Each version of materialism presupposes, at first sight paradoxically, an essential role for a center of consciousness, or point of vantage that is not itself one among the contents of consciousness. A person must be aware of what he or she is thinking, feeling, perceiving or doing in order for facts of that sort to be used in the project of setting a materialist psychology on the basis of exceptionless correlations between psychological and neural and cerebral phenomena. This is the very presupposition that we found to be common to the idea-based prescriptions for a scientific psychology.

Kant (1787 [1996]) called this the 'transcendental unity of apperception'. It is transcendental because it is not something anyone could be aware of directly. It is not a thought, a feeling, an object of perception or an action, or any combination of these. It is a unity because for each person there is just one field of thoughts, feelings, perceptions and actions of which he or she is conscious. There may be other ways that items like these could exist for someone. None of them could overlap with the domain of that of which a person is conscious.

Somehow our attempts at a scientific psychology must preserve this essential feature of human experience. Persons are necessarily embodied. Persons are neither thoughts nor feelings, nor can they be perceived, nor are they actions. They are the ontological basis of a scientific psychology, but they are neither material nor immaterial.

 The Search for a Scientific Psychology 2: Materialism

Lemma: A property of a complex entity or substance is emergent, if the components of that entity or substance do not have this property.

1   Ontological materialism. Hobbes simply replaces the concepts of psychology by those of mechanics. For example, perception is a motion of material particles in the 'brain and heart'.

(continued)

2 Methodological materialism:

   a) La Mettrie's thesis of perfect correlation: for every mental state or process of a certain type there is a state or process of a certain type in the brain or nervous system.

   b) Studying the laws of the sequence of brain states must be enough to account for the character and sequence of mental states.

3 Conceptual materialism:

   a) Every descriptive word is loaded with, *presupposes*, the theory that is presupposed by its user. For example, 'sunset' is loaded with geocentrism for some and heliocentrism for other astronomers, and so has different meanings for each group.

   b) It is claimed that ordinary language of the mental life is loaded with, or presupposes, an ontology of *mental beings*, such as 'beliefs'. This presupposition, folk psychology, is *factual and false*, according to Churchland.

   c) Mentalistic words should be replaced by a vocabulary which is loaded with a factually true theory, neurophysiology.

   d) Criticisms:

      i) The implicit psychology of European vernaculars does not presuppose immaterial beings. Beliefs, for example, are dispositions.

      ii) If the new words are used for the same communicative purposes as the old words, they are synonyms, and presuppose the ontology of subjective experience.

      iii) Infants would have to learn neurophysiology before they could understand the meanings of experiential words.

section four

Psychology as a branch of biology

The materialisms so far examined have presupposed that the study of psychology is the study of some aspects of human beings as isolated individuals. However, during the course of the last century biology was greatly enriched by increasing attention to animal–environment interactions, and particularly animal communication. Many animals seemed to have experiences rather like our own. The higher primates seemed to be capable of communication by the use of intentional signs and even of reflexive thought. At the beginning the trade ran from human to animal, in a kind of controlled anthropomorphism; it soon began to run the other way. Concepts originally developed in animal studies began to be applied to human beings. This was the ethological revolution in animal studies.

The leading principle is simple and powerful: *human beings and other animals perform essentially the same social acts and similar cognitive operations*. Ethology is the branch of biology that is concerned with the life forms of animals and birds in the wild. It includes the study of the creation and maintenance of social relations and the investigation of cognitive performances and skills. The study of the feral, unfettered lives of animals (including birds) shows that a good deal of their activity is goal-directed, involving higher order monitoring of performance as well as simple reactions to stimuli. According to the ethological point of view human activity does not differ in kind from the social and cognitive performances of animals, only in degree of complexity and sophistication. The same principles apply to both.

The ontology of the relevant aspects of this branch of biology as a home for a scientific psychology is different from that of the biophysics and biochemistry of Hobbesian ontological materialism and the methodological materialism of La Mettrie. The basic particulars for the great biologists such as Aristotle and Darwin were *organisms*. Organ structures and systems, and their constituent molecules, for example proteins and DNA sequences, are relevant just in so far as they contribute to the attributes of the basic particulars, that is, to powers and capacities of whole organisms.

Aristotelian beginnings: psychology as the science of goal-directed action

In many ways Aristotle's psychology remains among the most powerful and comprehensive ever proposed. Though it is set within a generally biological orientation to the problems of understanding human life, Aristotle uses the same broad system of concepts for the development of sciences of all kinds (Wallace, 1996). The two works in which these concepts are mainly set out are the *Metaphysics* and the *Posterior Analytics*. Many of the ideas deployed in his great psychological work *De anima* are to be found in contemporary psychology.

A hierarchy of animate forms

According to Aristotle, the attributes of all kinds of *individual* beings are to be explained by the particular ways in which the essential form or structure of the species to which they belong is realized in the particular matter of which they are made. The root idea is derived from the work of the sculptor, who moulds clay or chips away at marble, the *matter*, to bring a certain shape or *form* into being.

Differences between *kinds* of beings are to be accounted for predominantly by differences in their forms or essential organization. Each species of organic being has its proper or characteristic form. Each individual organism, as a member of the species, has a certain nature instantiating that form. Every bear is a chunk of matter, organized in more or less the same way as every other bear. However, the form of The Bear differs from the form of The Horse, of The Rat and so on. Therefore each bear differs from each horse and from each rat.

According to Aristotle, there are four levels of organic beings, according to their powers and capacities.

1   Plants are characterized by the capacity to absorb nourishment and to grow.
2   Lower animals are characterized by sensitivity to their environment as well as the capacity to absorb nourishment and to grow.
3   Higher animals have the capacity to move, as well as nutritive and sensitive capacities.
4   Human beings have all three lower capacities together with a pair of cognitive capacities characteristic of them alone. People can solve problems (the capacity the Greeks called *nous*) and they can abstract general ideas from a host of particulars (the capacity they called *epistemonikon*).

At each level of the hierarchy the capacities belonging to beings at that level derive from the form by which the matter of the animal or plant body is structured.

The root conception in this scheme applied as a psychology to both human beings and animals is that of a capacity or capacities to realize certain ends appropriate to the kind of being in question. There are two basic questions for research within this framework:

1   Which ends or goals are proper for a particular kind of being, and how are they related to its form of life?
2   What actualizes this or that capacity in concrete situations in the life of the animal?

Aristotle's account of animate behavior goes as follows. An animal is moved by objects in its environment. The bear approaches the tree when it sees bees flying in and out. Is that because bee movements cause bear movements, as a stimulus causes a response? Not according to the Aristotelian/ethological point of view. It is not behaviorism since the animal itself cannot be deleted from the story to be replaced by a mere conditioned reflex. Animals are self-movers. The bear breaks open a beehive to get at the honey because getting honey is a natural goal for bears. Bears are so constructed as to try to achieve goals that are good for bears. A stimulus is effective only when the animal takes it to be indicative of an object of desire. It has this power because it is in the nature of bears to perceive the whole set-up of bees, trees and honeycombs that way: namely as good for bears.

This analysis makes use of the idea of an action being directed towards some goal or desirable future state. Accounting for actions in terms of the *future* goals towards which they are directed is called 'teleological explanation'. Such an explanation is to be contrasted with efficient cause explanations. In these accounts a *past* stimulus is cited in explanation of a present action. An efficient cause account of a phenomenon involves four components.

1   The cause is a necessary and sufficient condition for the effect state or event to occur.
2   The causal conditions are either simultaneous with the effect or occur before it.
3   The effect must occur when or after the causal conditions occur, if nothing intervenes. This is sometimes called the *ceteris paribus* clause. The effect must occur, everything else being equal.
4   The effect is not represented in the stimulus conditions.

For example, heating a soufflé causes it to rise, *ceteris paribus*. If some yolk got into the separated whites they will not stiffen properly when beaten.

A teleological account of a phenomenon differs from the efficient cause account in conditions 2 and 4. In such an account, the future state or event is cited in explanation of the occurrence of the phenomenon. Typically, this is because the desired outcome is represented in the system on which the causal conditions act. A teleological account of someone driving up I-81 on a Sunday afternoon in order to have some Tin Roof Fudge Pie at the Victorian Restaurant in Montrose PA requires that the achievement of the goal is in the future, and that the driver has a mouth-watering image of this delectable dessert in mind during the drive.

In the case of the bear and the honey the Aristotelian scheme allows the ethologist to distinguish between a mere response to a sensation and an action as the outcome of the more complex cognitive phenomenon of perceiving something *as* something. A bear perceives a yellow patch as a beehive. It is in the nature of bears to take beehives as a source of what is good for beings of their kind: namely, bears. That is honey. According to Aristotle, this cognitive achievement is made possible by the cognitive faculty of fantasy, the capacity to see things as relevant to practical goals and so as objects of desire. Animals are self-movers. Bears go to beehives because the bear knows beehives contain honey, and honey is good for bears. The beehive is relevant to the explanation of why the bear goes that way through the forest only in so far as the bear takes it to be an object of desire. Bears are so built, that is, their form is such that they recognize beehives as a source of honey and so as a good for bears. Mice are recognized by cats as a good for cats, and so on. The capacity to recognize a complex goal, and to pursue it, is built into the animal's nature. The goal for human beings is the acquisition of knowledge, and the achievement of virtue. Therefore, according to Aristotle, the pursuit of knowledge realizes what is most characteristic of the nature of human beings.

The Aristotelian schema for a scientific enquiry

Any scientific enquiry, framed in the Aristotelian paradigm, must address four questions:

1   What is the material stuff of which the active being is made?
2   What is the form that, realized in the matter, endows the being with the necessary capacities to prosper as a being of that kind?
3   What are the proper goals for beings of that kind?
4   What kind of situation triggers the activity in question?

In this scheme we have an emphasis on deep similarities in the characters of the beings of the animate world, from plants to humans. The different natures of different kinds of creatures are explained by their different modes of organization, which endows each type of being with its proper capacities. The pattern of explanation is always teleological: namely, to what end is the activity of an animate being directed? Animals are self-movers, in that it is only because they are built to perceive things as good for beings of their own kind that they do the things they do.

Our understanding of the very important 'perceiving something as something' capacity is left to our commonsense intuitions in this context and for the moment. It introduces a concept into psychology that it is of outstanding importance. When a bear perceives a hive as a source of honey it is going beyond the observable material properties of the hive. Understanding or perceiving something *as* something is the phenomenon of intentionality. A 'stop' sign is not just a red octagon. A competent motorist perceives it as expressing an order or instruction. A thought is always a thought *of* something. Emotional displays and feeling also point beyond themselves. One is angry with someone, jealous of someone, ashamed of something, and so on. Some psychologists and philosophers have held that psychology is just the science of the phenomenon of intentionality. It will play a large part in our later explorations of our topic.

The modern Aristotelians

The ethological tradition was revived in the twentieth century by Nikko Tinbergen, Konrad Lorentz and von Frisch, among others (Tinbergen, 1968). They developed a non-behaviorist psychology of animals and birds that was generally Aristotelian rather than behaviorist in style, but included two new ideas.

1   There are fixed action patterns, extended routines through which various important aspects of the lives of these creatures are created and maintained. For instance, mate selection is accomplished through the performance of complex and extended routines. The mechanisms which produce these routines are derived from the genetic material inherited in Darwinian fashion generation by generation.
2   The target of the routines is not usually determined by inherited preferences, but is imprinted at an early age. The gosling, for example, attaches itself to the first other being it sees at a certain 'sensitive period' in its development.

There is nothing in the work of the great ethologists that precludes a large element of culture and tradition in the life form of any creature. It is said that some species of birds do not inherit their song patterns but learn them. Here were action patterns that were not fixed *a priori* by inherited genetic endowment shaping the structure of the nervous system.

The capacity of higher primates to act intelligently, that is, seemingly with a goal in mind, has been well nigh established by the work of Jane Goodall, Franz de Waal and Alan and Beatrice Gardner, and other primatologists. Here is an example from the observations made by Jane Goodall (1989). Every now and again a young male chimpanzee will challenge the dominant social position of the alpha chimp. Empty kerosene cans were stacked behind Goodall's camp. One day one of the younger chimps, Goliath, began to challenge the senior male, David. The challenger picked up some branches, fluffed out his hair and began to bound up and down, flourishing the branches and making a moderate amount of noise. David simply ignored the performance. Goliath looked around and spotted the kerosene cans. After a short pause he dropped the branches, picked up a can in each hand and began a new challenge. The noise was impressive, and the display formidable. This time David retreated, leaving the field and the alpha status to his young rival.

Though formulated more than 2,000 years ago the Aristotelian scheme seems as valuable a paradigm now as it was to Aristotle himself.

Evolutionary psychology

Whether we adopt Picture One, the old paradigm, causal account of psychological phenomena, or Picture Two, the new paradigm, agentive account, the same question appears. How did people come to acquire the mechanisms that are activated by psychologically relevant causes? Or how did people come to acquire the capacities and skills to perform intentional, normative actions?

Genetic endowment, cognitive capacities and emotional predisposition

In popular accounts, some of the discoveries that link aspects of the genetic code with specific cognitive skills and deficits have been presented as if they established a new and more sophisticated form of materialism than the ontological, methodological and conceptual theses we have already discussed. Here is an example of the sort of thing I am talking about. K-P. Lesch et al. (1996) claim to have shown that there is a gene on chromosome 17 that switches on a nearby gene that codes for a protein that transports the neurotransmitter, serotonin, into brain cells for reuse. There are two forms of the 'promoter gene', a short and a long form. This is a description of a neural process in which only chemical and biological terminology figures. It seems that a correlation can be established between people's tendency to worry a great deal and the possession of the short form of the gene. How are we to understand this correlation?

Biological interpretations of the psychology of human behavior along these lines have become very common these days. Scarcely a week goes by without another such report appearing in the quality press. How seriously should psychologists take these announcements? It can hardly be denied that genetics, as the source of important aspects of neural structures and the materials involved in neurological processes, must play an important part in a scientific cognitive psychology. Indeed, it fits snugly into the Aristotelian paradigm, serving to account for the way that animate beings come to have the structures that ground the capacity of animate beings to seek what is good for them.

When we attend to any cognitive capacity that can be plausibly argued to have a genetic origin, we see innumerable variations of the way the generic cognitive capacity appears in different cultural settings. The neural mechanisms by which people remember things are no doubt the product of gene-based developmental processes in the human organism. However, in predominantly pre-literate cultures the capacity to learn and recall vast amounts of material, such as sacred epics, bodies of law and genealogies, was highly developed. It is a capacity that has almost atrophied in contemporary Western cultures. It is very unlikely that a mere two thousand years are enough to transform the genetics of the hippocampus[2] and the frontal lobes.

As our studies develop we shall be increasingly concerned to balance the foundational role of human biology with the enormous influence of local cultural norms and practices on our psychologies. There will no longer be a psychology but a loose cluster of psychologies. Fortunately the concepts we have been mastering will allow us to lay out a chain of relationships that legitimately link aspects of the genome to high-grade human performances without slipping into an implausible attempt to reduce psychology to biology.

The complex path from genetic endowment to cognitive practice

It is often possible to identify a necessary condition for something to exist that leaves room for other factors to be involved. Each step in the four-stage sequence described below is a necessary condition for the subsequent step. What that means is simply that unless the prior condition, state, etc., existed the subsequent one would not be possible. However, I think it is now very clear that these are not sufficient conditions. This implies that at each stage there is an extrinsic, non-genetic condition or conditions that must also be realized before the subsequent stage can be actualized.

It is important to realize that the sequence to be described is usually taken to be applicable to a particular organism and, in the interesting cases for us, this organism is a member of the species *Homo sapiens*.

1   There exists a certain gene or pattern of genes in the genome of a certain organism.
2   The cerebral cortex of the organism has a certain character, perhaps a certain size or structure.

3   The organism, as an adult, has a certain skill or aptitude for a certain level
     of cognitive activity.
4   The organism exercises the skill in carrying out certain practices and bring-
     ing certain projects to fruition.

How is the possession of the gene in Stage 1 related to the practices in Stage 4?

From Stage 1 to Stage 2 there are all sorts of extra genetic influences.
'Epigenetic' processes affect the way that the gene sequence is expressed in the
characteristics of an organ such as the brain or one of its subsystems, at each
stage of development.

From Stage 2 to Stage 3 there are all sorts of influences from the socio-
discursive environment that are relevant to how the potential of the organism's
nervous system is realized in the possession of skills and capacities. Even the
simple matter of the quantity of talk that surrounds an infant has been shown to
have a decisive effect on cognitive development.

From Stage 3 to Stage 4 we also know that the character of particular
occasions and situations, material and symbolic, plays a vital role in the way a
skill is exercised by a particular person or particular persons in a performance.

In accordance with the methods we are following, we must now ask ourselves about the ontological presuppositions of the above stages. It is easy to see
that they do not share a common ontology. The gene story must make use of the
concept of 'molecule' as its fundamental type of powerful particular. The cortex
story requires the organism as its ontological basis. Stages 3 and 4 require the
linked ontologies of persons and their intentional actions. Thus, from the point of
view of how we express our knowledge of each of these domains, each stage
requires a different ontology.

There are two gaps to be bridged in this schema. There is that between
genes and brain structures. That there is a gap requiring biological forces other
than genes is evident from the relative paucity of genes in the human genome
compare with the huge variety of proteins that must be synthesized to create the
adult organism. There is a second gap between the paired Stages 1 and 2 and the
paired Stages 3 and 4. As we shall see in the examples that follow, this gap is to
be filled by reference to the contributions of culture and tradition.

In each of the examples we shall see that in drawing up a balance between
biological factors, presumably coded for by genes, and the purely cultural influences, there are no pure 'organismic' cases.

1   Dolan (1999) demonstrated that a certain region of the brain, the amygdala,
     is implicated in the way that people become fearful if they look at the face
     of someone displaying fear. He showed this by using a PET scan to identify
     the region of the brain that was active during the process. Dolan declares
     that the response 'is hard-wired' and built into the brain from birth. Its origin
     is lost deep in evolution. Here we have a plausible case of a phenomenon
     that owes little or nothing to culture. The phenomenon falls neatly into the
     causal paradigm of explanation.

2   Shammi and Stuss (1999), using a different methodology, claimed to have discovered the part of the brain, the right frontal lobe, involved in appreciating 'humour', presumably something we would call 'seeing the joke'. People with right frontal damage also showed less overt reaction to jokes. They smiled and laughed less than people usually do to similar funny situations and tales. Shammi and Stuss claim that this region is implicated in appreciating humor and understanding irony. We can easily see that this can, at best, be only part of the story. We know from cross-cultural studies that the expression of emotions – indeed, the actual repertoire of emotions any person has available – is highly culturally specific (Lutz, 1988; Wierzbicka, 1992). How people *show* their appreciation of jokes is also widely variable. Paul Theroux has pointed out how different is the role of laughter among Chinese people from its role among Europeans. Indeed, the forms of appreciative display also vary according to social class (Pocheptsov, 1990). Once again, we find the familiar conundrum for cognitive psychology. How are we to integrate the cultural and biological dimensions into a unified scientific paradigm?

3   The claim that there is a deterministic, culture-free genetic basis for an excitable personality has been exploded in a very instructive way. The claim was based on a correlation between the presence of a certain version of the dopamine receptor gene with a person's displaying an excitable personality. (Bowker, 1996). However, when the studies were expanded to cover many more people, for example Finnish men and groups from the Middle East, the results did not support the original claim. Personality is predominantly a cultural phenomenon, heavily influenced by local norms of propriety and the local code of manners.

Each of these studies involved very few subjects. Though the numbers for the first study are not reported they could not have exceeded fifty, and all were from Scotland. The humor appreciation research was done with the participation of patients with frontal lobe damage. Even in a large city like Toronto there cannot have been many. In general, experiments using brain scans and other high-tech equipment are expensive and time-consuming and must therefore be restricted to a rather small number of people conveniently situated close to the physical location of the equipment.

However, this need not be a flaw. The intensive design is based on a few *typical* instances, studied in depth. Small numbers also imply a rather restricted cultural setting. Jokes that appeal in Toronto may fall flat in Ulan Bator, and personalities that are acceptable in one place may be out of place in another.

Psychology as a hybrid science

Explaining what someone thinks, feels, perceives or does on some particular occasion may, at first sight, seem to be achieved by describing the conditions under which that person acts. However, any such explanation must presuppose that the person has the capacity or power to so act. The local scene calls for the exercise of this or that capacity. Negotiating a business deal successfully requires one to use one's capacity to pick up the emotional tone of the other people involved. Solving a pair of simultaneous equations requires the use of one's mathematical training. But that one can be trained in mathematics presupposes that one has a general capacity for abstract symbolic reasoning. Psychologists need to pay attention to three matters. How do life situations determine which skills and capacities a person brings to bear upon them? How did that person acquire those skills and capacities? With what potentialities and capacities to acquire capacities and skills was that person endowed genetically?

---

learning point   ## The Search for a Scientific Psychology 3: Biologism

Principle. Psychology is a part of biology: the basis of the ontology is 'organism'.

1   Two model sources:

   a)   Explanations of the existence of human capacities should be Darwinian.
   b)   Analyses of action patterns should be teleological, that is, goal-directed.

2   Aristotle's psychology:

   a)   Organisms have the capabilities they do because of their form or structure.
   b)   There are four levels of being:

      i)   Nutritive: to grow (plants).
      ii)   Nutritive + sensitive: to respond to stimuli (simple animals, e.g. anemone).
      iii)   Nutritive + sensitive + mobility: to move in search of nourishment (complex animals).
      iv)   Nutritive + sensitive + mobility + cognitive powers: to reason (human beings).

   c)   Human cognitive powers include *nous* (problem solving) and *epistemonikon* (forming general ideas).
   d)   An animal perceives something as affording what is good for animals of its sort, and seeks it.
   e)   What is good for people is the full development of all capacities.

3   Aristotle's scientific method. A scientific investigation of 'something' tries to answer four questions. What is it made of? What is its structure? What are its proper goals? What triggers off the pursuit of a proper goal?

4   Evolutionary psychology:

   a)   Human psychology is a development of ethology, based on genetically deter-mined fixed action patterns.

(continued)

b) Explanatory sequence:

  i) Gene in genome.
  ii) Determines structure in cortex or receptor or protein synthesis.
  iii) Confers a tendency to perform a fixed action pattern exercised in certain practical contexts.
  iv) Problem: how far must cultural explanations be called on?

c) Examples of biological and semi-cultural explanations of human capacities:

  i) Sight of fearful face causes fear.
  ii) 'Visual perception taking' associated with frontal lobe region (but emotions, humor, etc. are culturally differentiated).
  iii) Alleged genetic source of excitable personality disproved by wider range of people studied.

d) The wholesale reduction of psychology to biology cannot be achieved:

  i) The human genome contains too few genes for there to be a simple link from genes to actual cognitive capacities.
  ii) Cultural inventions and practices, such as deductive logic, emotion suppression and elaboration, reading and writing, and so on, must be included in a hybrid psychology.

Conclusion

The strong biologistic thesis, that human psychology is to be completely absorbed by the ethology of the human organism, needs a corrective. There is little doubt that cultural artifacts, human inventions and conventions, and customs, play a huge role in our psychology. For example, that there are different conventions for the display of feelings has been well authenticated. There is suppression of some emotions in some cultures, emphasis on and elaboration of emotions in others. People in some cultures reason in accordance with Western conceptions of logic. Others use patterns of metaphor, analogy and coincidence in ways we would regard as irrational. How can we build these facts into a general psychology while acknowledging the key role played by our brain and nervous system in whatever we do, be it in playing tennis or in solving problems in the differential calculus?

When the organism is embedded in genetics there is a subtle change of ontology. Some authors, for instance Richard Dawkins (1976), presents the gene itself as the basic particular. The organism is a product, the 'interactor', and the means by which genes are tested against the environment. Discoveries emerging from the human genome project have disclosed, to everyone's surprise, that there are many fewer genes than had been thought. Since the original estimates were based on the thesis that organismic characteristics were predominantly the product of genes, the discovery is damaging to simplistic versions of a biologically reductive psychology, such as that of E.O. Wilson (1998).

Craig Venter, the leader of one of the genome teams, has summed up the situation very well:

> There are two fallacies to be avoided. We must eschew determinism, the idea that all characteristics of a person are hard-wired by the genome. We must also avoid reductionism, that now the human genome is completely known it is just a matter of time before our understanding of gene functions and interactions will provide a complete causal description of human variability. There is no 'gene for this and a gene for that'.

Psychology cannot, it seems, be just a branch of biology.

Notes

1   This is when one objects to something about the person whose views one is criticizing rather then the views themselves.
2   The hippocampus is a complex structure involved in the formation of lasting memories. We shall be studying it closely in Part IV.

chapter six

The beginnings of cognitive science

In Chapter 2 we learned how behaviorism perfectly fulfilled the requirements of a strictly positivistic conception of science. The phenomena admitted into the domain of psychology were to be restricted to what could be perceived. While Skinner allowed both public and private perceptible states into the domain of scientific psychology, Watson restricted psychology to the study of objective phenomena only. Theoretical explanations referring to unobservable entities and processes were eliminated in favor of statistically analysed correlations between type of stimulus and type of response. The deathblow to behaviorism was finally given by the researches of J.S. Bruner (1973, 1983) into the role of cognitive factors in perception and in responses to perceptual stimuli. Let us remind ourselves briefly of his groundbreaking discoveries, the 'Judas eye' experiments. The metaphor points to how much more we can perceive than we can sense. We look out through the peephole or Judas eye set in the door to catch a glimpse of the person outside. On the basis of that limited information we have to decide whether or not to admit the visitor. Bruner's metaphor suggests that, if what we perceive goes beyond the information provided by the sensory stimulus alone, a person must have some prior knowledge of what is to be perceived. His experiments suggested that there must be prior cognitive schemas that are involved in perception and utilized in cognitive processes of which we are unaware.

Bruner's first telling experiment involved an interaction between perceptual recognition and the valuation of what is to be perceived. Ten-year-old schoolchildren were 'to adjust a patch of light to match the size of a nickel, a dime, a quarter and a half-dollar. … Half the kids were from schools in affluent parts of Boston; the others from the city's slums. … The more valuable the coin, the greater [was] the overestimation of its size. And the poorer children overestimated more than the affluent ones' (Bruner, 1983: 69–70). Evidently the difference in value of the coins played a role in the perceptual process. Again, a realist hypothesis of an actual unobserved cognitive process seems called for to account for the phenomenon. One may feel drawn to the inclusion of concepts of meaning into the hypotheses one offers. Value is not a material attribute of coins. Nickels, though larger than dimes, were underestimated.

In a later experiment, done with Leo Postman, Bruner carried the research into non-conscious cognitive processes much further. Each participant was briefly presented with a word from a list of eighteen pre-selected according to the relative speed of associative reactions, quick, slow or average. The participants had to say which word had been shown. In general, the time taken to recognize a word was related to the time to offer an association. However, when the words were threatening in some way, with slow associative reactions, they were recognized either more swiftly than average or more slowly (Bruner, 1983: 79–80).

In general, offensive and emotionally significant words were recognized either more quickly or more slowly than neutral and inoffensive words. How could this possibly be? It must be because the meaning of the word had been *grasped* and it had been categorized as emotionally significant or neutral before it was *consciously perceived*. If it had been categorized only after it had been perceived there should have been no difference in the time it took to recognize similar words, whatever the emotional load. If behaviorism had been true, a person would not be able to realize what sort of word was being presented until after it had been recognized.

In another experiment, people were shown playing cards on which the colors usually associated with the suits were reversed. The suits of playing cards had been printed in the opposite colors to their usual style, hearts black, clubs red and so on. 'Sensing a bit of red at fast exposure [in a tachistoscope, a device for presenting stimuli for short periods of time], they would try on subsequent ones to make a heart or a diamond of what they could see' (Bruner, 1983: 86). Of course, they had been shown a card with red clubs. Some participants persisted in misidentifying the suits on the basis of their prior knowledge of the color conventions longer than it would have taken them to recognize a card printed in the 'correct' color. Red clubs were 'seen' as hearts and black hearts as clubs, even when the participant had had a reasonable opportunity to look more closely at them.

Instead of the behaviorist pattern:

Stimulus (retinal sensation) → Response (perception of word)

we must have

Observable stimulus (retinal sensation) together with unobservable Cognitive process ('knowledge utilization') → Observable response (recognition of word)

Therefore, perception of something as something is not just a response to a stimulus. It is the upshot of a cognitive process, as yet only guessed at and so at best hypothetical. One hypothesis as to the nature of such a process may be that it involves classifying something as something. In the 'recognition of words' experiment it would require the use of appropriate general categories of words, such as 'offensive', 'inoffensive' and so on. The person who hesitates to report an offensive word, or reports seeing a red club as a heart, is unaware that any such 'thinking' is going on.

The First Cognitive Revolution

What pattern of scientific analysis and explanation do these results call for? In a radical break with the philosophical presuppositions of the immediate past Bruner saw that the new cognitive psychology must follow the realist pattern rather than the positivist. A new style of explanation was called for, involving hypotheses about unobserved processes, which are in part responsible for the character of the response to the stimulus. The process involves the use of linguistic *knowledge* in the 'loaded words' experiment, of *knowledge* about playing cards in the 'wrong spots' experiment. It involves *valuations* in the oblique coin experiment. The prior existence of this knowledge and these valuations is an essential part of the role they play in any explanation of the phenomenon. The psychology of 'Judas eye' phenomenon must be realist. It must postulate unobservable cognitive processes. To handle these in a proper scientific way we must devise iconic working models as plausible representations of cognitive processes that may exist and mechanisms, abstract or concrete, that would be engaged in the production of these phenomena.

Let us begin with a reminder as to what the realist shape for a science involves. The main thrust of this interpretation of science, particularly the development of hypotheses about and models of hypothetical generative mechanisms is that, though unobserved by investigators, such mechanisms are necessary for the production of the observed phenomena. Where do the hypotheses about unobserved generative mechanisms come from? In the physical sciences, as we have seen, they are not the result of blind guesswork or the unfettered imagination. They are created by the invention of models or hypothetical representations of what such mechanisms may plausibly be. The invention of adequate and plausible models is constrained by the requirement that the nature of what is proposed should conform to the basic type hierarchy that expresses the beliefs people have about the nature of the world.

In the First Cognitive Revolution Bruner and others interpreted their experimental results as showing that there were unobserved, in this case unconscious, *cognitive* processes going on which would explain what they had observed. There was something like reasoning, classifying and evaluating going on, but the perceiver was not aware of it. What sort of metaphysics does that presuppose? What kind of existence did these unobservable processes share? Could they be construed as wholly neuropsychological? Were they really processes in the brain and nervous system, fully describable in the language of biophysics and biochemistry? If we are disinclined to accept a simple materialist account of the required 'hidden' processes, because they seem to involve meanings, what should we conclude? This seemed to suggest a return to something like the Cartesian mind-stuff to provide a site for unconscious cognition. We thought we had left that idea behind for ever in untangling the muddled thinking that led Descartes to the false conclusion that thinking must be located in a mental substance. In fact the next step by cognitive psychologists was towards a different terminus.

Looking back half a century, it seems, in hindsight, that the architects of the First Cognitive Revolution very quickly used their cognitive hypotheses to devise models of *material* processes that could be imagined to produce the *cognitive* phenomena that they had observed. However, the material processes they described were not neurophysiological. They were the ancestors of what we now see as models in the domain of artificial intelligence, machines that would simulate what people can and do do. The use of cognitive categories to describe the first generation of working models was clearly metaphorical, since the machines were material. However, what those machines did was to fulfill certain abstract schemata that were neither material nor immaterial. This is the crucial insight, which we will develop much further in Part IV.

Early attempts at devising a cognitive machine

There is a long history of attempts to make machines that will do what people can do. The seventeenth century saw a proliferation of automata, from singing birds to mechanical and hydraulic orchestras that simulated the *behavior* of organisms, including human beings. In the nineteenth century Thomas Babbage built the first device that could simulate some rudimentary human *cognitive* performances. Babbage's machine, like a modern pocket calculator, could, when put into an initial state that *represented* an arithmetical problem, chunter away and come to a stop in a state which could be interpreted as a representation of the answer. However successful such a machine may be, it does not follow that the material process by which it goes from initial to final state is anything like the material process by which a human being gets the answer to an arithmetical problem. However, it may be that each material system, calculator or brain, realizes the same abstract pattern of symbol manipulation.

The twentieth century saw the rapid development of ideas about possible thinking machines. These would give representations of correct answers to problems that had been input, suitably represented in machine states. Ideally we might find a machine which would not only output representations of what human beings would interpret as correct answers to the questions that had been input, but would also work in ways similar to the way a human being accomplished a problem-solving task, be it practical or cognitive. Miller, Galanter and Pribram, in a very subtle and forward-looking publication of the 1960s, *Plans and the Structure of Behavior*, set out a program for a cognitive science that had much the same form as the programs of earlier centuries (Miller et al., 1967: 27–36). However, they made use of more sophisticated ideas about how to create a model of the relevant abstract cognitive process and of a material mechanism that might be able to perform it.

To see the importance of the mechanism they imagined we must return to look again, in a slightly different way, at the metaphysics of behaviorism. Buried in the foundations of that paradigm was Thorndike's law of effect, that the probability of the emission of a behavior was a function of the effect of emitting the same behavior in the past. This law was based on the metaphysical assumption that there were neural structures, reflex arcs, underlying the observed correlations. Since behaviorists were united in their rejection of any specific hypotheses about the neural mechanisms of behavior, the status of this presupposition was not at all clear. It was assumed that the neural structures that underlay behavioral correlations were either inborn or established as reflex arcs in the nervous system by conditioning, a conditioning made possible by the phenomenon described in the law of effect.

In a vital step that inaugurated the beginnings of cognitive science, Miller et al. pointed out that these imaginary arcs *did not include feedback loops*, on the occasions on which they were activated. The system was not self-adjusting. Instead of a theoretical model based implicitly on imagined reflex arcs, they based the models for their psychology on a different kind of imaginary mechanism, the TOTE unit. Remembering what we learned about model making in Chapter 3 Miller et al. were, in effect, proposing a new supertype on which the type hierarchy that included their working models of goal-directed action was to be based.

The general pattern of the structure of TOTE units can best be appreciated in a diagram (see Figure 6.1). In their example the task was hammering in a nail. It required that the head was finally flush with the surface into which the nail was hammered. If, at the Test stage, the nail is not flush then the hammer strikes again. This Operate cycle continues until the Test finds the head is flush with the surface of the floor, if that is what someone is nailing down. There is a means–end plan or project a person (or machine surrogate) is to accomplish. The

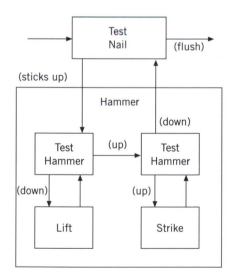

Figure 6.1 TOTE machine for hammering home nails. Reproduced, with kind permission, from Miller, G.A., Galanter, G. and Pribram, K.H. *Plans and the Structure of Behavior*, (1967) by courtesy of Rinehart & Winston.

overall pattern is Test/Operate/Test/Exit, or TOTE. We can see too that it incorporates norms of correctness. A nail has been driven in *properly* when its head is flush with the floor.

The importance of this device lay not so much in its role in analysing complex tasks as in the alternative interpretations of the schematic mechanisms offered by the authors. It is in these interpretations that we begin to see the crystallizing out of a possible cognitive science. It would link standards of correct hammering with material realizations of abstract mechanisms. These mechanisms would be capable, when realized in some material stuff, of maintaining such standards. A TOTE unit could be thought of in three ways.

1   Figure 6.1 could be interpreted as a real mechanism, for example the hydraulic circuits to operate a jackhammer or a pile driver. The arrows represent lines of energy flow through the system. It could also be a schematic diagram of the neural structure supporting the skill of a carpenter in driving a nail home. In that case too the arrows would represent lines of energy flow.

2   The diagram could be read more abstractly as an information system. Messages are transmitted along channels represented by the arrows. What information? Miller et al. suggest that it takes the form of representations of correlations in the appropriate medium, for example 'incongruity/operate' and 'congruity/exit'.

3   There is a yet more instructive level of abstraction for a possible cognitive science. A single TOTE unit, or a hierarchy of such units, could be thought of in terms of 'control'. A TOTE unit represents something which effects a certain *sequence* of actions, 'Do a test,' 'Do a test' … 'Stop.' A TOTE hierarchy, in which after exit another unit starts up, is a representation of control transfer.

It was at this point that Miller et al. saw the analogy with computing (1967: 49). A program is a sequence of instructions each of which executes an operation in turn. However, a system such as a TOTE hierarchy is a sequence of dedicated boxes, each of which executes a specific operation in turn. Instead of a sequence of instructions for one mechanism to do different things, a system is a sequence of different mechanisms each of which does something different. Running a program on the data in a single central processing unit and activating a system through which a stream of data flows are functionally equivalent. A program operating sequentially on the initial state of one device would perform the same task as a system in which each instruction was realized in its own dedicated module or box, activated sequentially. Programs include grouped instructions, while systems include groups of modules, and in each case there is a basic level of 'unit' computational instructions and a basic level of unit modules.

The TOTE idea takes the place of the rejected concept of the hypothetical reflex arc as the generic model or supertype for the invention of working models of cognitive mechanisms behind the actions that psychologists can observe.

---

learning point **Sources of the First Cognitive Revolution**

1 Bruner's experiments suggested that there were unobservable cognitive processes involved in all sorts of overt human activities:

   a) Obnoxious words are recognized either more quickly (vigilance) or more slowly (defense) than normal words: unconscious classification must have occurred before conscious recognition.

   b) Reversed colors on suits of playing cards led to red clubs being seen as hearts and black hearts being seen as spades. Prior knowledge must be being applied in the perceptual/classification task.

   c) Perceiving a coin at an oblique angle: rich children perceived the coin as a narrower ellipse than poor children did. Unconscious valuation must have occurred during the procedure.

   Conclusion: scientific realism suggests:

   a) There are hidden but real cognitive processes.

   b) Problem: with what ontology do we conceive them and hence how do we model them?

2 Between meaningful phenomena and neurophysical processes:

   a) Miller et al. proposed a system model, a device that would perform unobserved cognitive processes and preserve the normativity of real intentional action.

   b) For example, the TOTE machine, Test/Operate/Test/Exit, includes a criterion for correctness and hence a Stop rule.

   c) Any system as a sequence of boxes each performing one operation can be replaced by a single box performing a sequence of operations.

The second attempt: computing machines

The next major attempt to devise a cognitive machine, that is, a machine that could perform at least some of the cognitive operations performed by a human being, was the famous Turing Machine. It encapsulated the deep idea of 'thinking as computation'. I shall refer to this program generally as the implementation of the computational model. It marks a new phase in the development of the First Cognitive Revolution. At the heart of the computational model are two fundamental presuppositions or guiding principles.

The principle of cognition as computation

According to this principle, any cognitive *process* can be represented by a computable function. The result of a computation using such a function represents the outcome of the cognitive process the function represents. For example, if remembering is represented by a computable function or functions, the recollection that emerges from my racking my brains about what happened on Tuesday is represented by the result of a suitable computation using the relevant function or functions. This is in principle though not in practice no different from solving an arithmetical problem. The sum of 2 and 2 is 4 is represented by the computation '2 + 2 = 4'. Our first fundamental question, a question that homes in on the most powerful presupposition of the computational model, is this: *is it true that every cognitive process can be represented by a computable function?*

What is meant by 'computable function'? The basic idea is quite simple. Suppose we take the function:

$$x + 2y$$

The value of the function will depend on what is substituted for x and y. Suppose '$x = 2$' and '$y = 7$'. Substituting these values in the function gives:

$$2 + 2 \times 7$$

Applying the rules of arithmetic, we get:

$$16$$

There was no need to use our intelligence or to make use of clever mathematical insights. The procedure was 'mechanical'. Any function that can be evaluated in such a way, whatever numbers are substituted for the variables, is called a 'computable function'.

Let us take this idea one step nearer modeling thought processes. Is the following an example of valid reasoning? Either my cat has mange or your dog has fleas. My cat does not have mange. Therefore your dog must have fleas.

Quite early in the history of modern logic, a computable version of this sort of reasoning was developed by logicians. There are two alleged matters of fact involved, 'My cat has mange' and 'Your dog has fleas'. They can be represented by the letters p and q respectively. 'Either ... or ...' is represented by v, 'not' by $\neg$, 'and;' by & and 'if ... then ...' by $\rightarrow$. These symbols can be used to represent an abstract version of the above argument and all those that have the same form. Brackets help to keep track of the syntax.

$$\{(p \ v \ q) \ \& \ \neg p\} \rightarrow q$$

The logical signs could be interpreted as arithmetical operators. v becomes $+$, $\neg$ becomes '$1 -$', & becomes $\times$ and $\rightarrow$ becomes '$(1 - p) + q$'. True and False can be represented by 1 and 0. Here is the corresponding function:

$$[1 - \{(p + q) \times (1 - p)\}] + q$$

There are four possible cases: $p = 1$ and $q = 1$, $p = 1$ and $q = 0$, $p = 0$ and $q = 1$ and $p = 0$ and $q = 0$. If the complex sentence above expresses a valid argument the outcome of computing the value of the whole function for each of the possible assignments of True and False should be 1, that is, 'True'. There is one difference from ordinary arithmetic. Since 2 does not have a meaning in this system, $1 + 1 = 1$.

The calculations are very simple. Here is the line representing the first assignment of truth and falsity to the two basic sentences.

$$[1 - \{(1 + 1) \times (1 - 1)\}] + 1$$
$$[1 - \{1 \times 0\}] + 1$$
$$[1 - 0] + 1$$
$$1 + 1$$
$$1$$

By calculating the values of the function for the other three assignments of 0 and 1 students can verify that the outcome is always 1. That is, the argument is valid. It is true whatever the truth or falsity of the component clauses. We have performed a complex cognitive operation by evaluating a simple computable function. This is the deep idea behind the computational model for the psychology of cognition.

Cognitive computations can be performed on some actual machine

The second principle expresses the presupposition that there is or will be some hardware with which the alleged 'computations' can be performed. This hardware can be likened to a brain and central nervous system (CNS) in which the cognitive process we are tracking takes place. Our second fundamental question is this: *is it likely that any inorganic machine and the way it runs will be an adequate explanatory model of the brain and its workings?*

We must make sure that we keep in mind a fundamental distinction between artificial intelligence as a branch of engineering and artificial intelligence as a psychology. Engineers try to devise machines that will output useful answers to cognitive questions input to a machine in the proper code. There is no necessary relation between success in this project and support for the psychological thesis that brains are computing machines, albeit of a material quite other than that of which one's laptop is made. We need people to understand the question that is encoded for the machine to process. We need them no less to understand the output as an answer to that question. Psychologists, on the other hand, look to the computer as a model for understanding cognition rather than merely serving as a practical device for simulating input and output aspects of cognitive questions. Our two questions above are rather different when seen in the light of the uses to which scientific models can be put. The idea that we should try to represent cognitive processes in formal ways according to the requirements of computability is a proposal for creating analytical or heuristic models of psychological processes. The idea that we should try to represent the brain mechanisms by which these processes are realized is a proposal for creating an explanatory model of neurological processes relevant to cognition. We may well espouse the former while remaining skeptical about the latter.

The question as to which form of computational engine to choose as a model of the brain as the tool by which *we* carry out our cognitive tasks is rather like the legendary prosecutor's question 'Have you stopped beating your mother yet?' Whether the defendant says 'Yes' or 'No', he admits to having once beaten his mother. The question about how the hardware could serve as model of the brain presupposes that we are reasonably confident that thinking *is* a form of computation. If we devote ourselves only to the second question, as many do, we are assuming a positive answer to the first question.

Using artificial intelligence models in psychology

Simulating cognition: products and processes

The use of artificial intelligence models in psychology involves two steps. We need to make an abstract representation of a meaningful situation and of a meaningful product of thinking about, through, or in such a situation. Then we need to make an abstract representation of a machine capable of performing the thinking thereby presupposed. The computational thesis is simply an expression of the principles described above. Moreover, all this must be understood dynamically. The result of thinking cannot be simply the public display of an internal representation of whatever it is one has thought. Our aim is to model *thinking*.

Mental representations can, at best, be parts of abstract artificial intelligence *models* built up from a certain source. They cannot be projected on to reality as if they were like molecules in the kinetic model of gases. The only realities in psychology are people using symbols, publicly and privately for cognitive tasks, and the neurophysiological and other processes that occur in the tools and prostheses by which those tasks are accomplished.

We must beware of the product/process fallacy. It does not follow that the products of a process bear any resemblance to the process by which the product has been produced. To assume that there must be such a resemblance is to fall prey to the product/process fallacy. In psychology cognitive *products*, intentional entities and processes of many types, are characterized by the demands of public meaningfulness. However, cognitive *processes* are constrained by the architecture and neurophysiology of the cluster of cells we call the brain. Beware the product/process fallacy. The second 'cognitive' above, in the phrase 'cognitive process', is defined by picking out some relevant neural process that, meaningless in itself, has an outcome that displays intentionality and meaning. The generative process is not cognitive in that sense. This is a subtle point but of the greatest significance in understanding the strengths and the limits of cognitive 'science'. We will delve much more deeply into this key distinction later in the chapter.

Turing's conjecture

Alan Turing (1950) proposed that the answer to both questions must be 'Yes'. His basic principle for constructing models of mechanisms capable of cognition can be summed up in the analogical formula:

Brains : Thinking :: Computing machines : Computing.

We are presented with two deep questions:

1   Do computers think? Alternatively, more precisely, is computing a form of thinking?
2   Are brains computers? On the other hand, more precisely, is thinking a form of computing?

The basis of Turing's 'Yes' answers has been much debated in philosophy of psychology. He thought that if we could never tell whether we were interacting via a keyboard and a screen with a thinking machine or with a person, then we would be obliged to concede that the machine could think. The flip side of this claim is that in such circumstances we would be obliged to concede that people thinking *were* in effect computers computing. There is a huge literature related to the *Turing test*, its interpretation and its possible outcomes and consequences.

Does the Turing Conjecture raise a philosophical or an empirical question? Is it a matter of fact whether computers can think? Is it a question of how far we would be wise to extend the scope of the word 'think'? It seems fairly obvious that it is the latter. Should we enlarge the scope of the cognitive vocabulary to include certain humanoid activities of non-organic beings? In philosophy we weigh up the consequences for and against making such a change in our ways of thinking. Debates about whether this is a scientific or a philosophical question involve issues other than the scope of cognitive concepts. For example, there are moral issues involved. Recollect the question of the 'right to life' raised by the problem of what to do about HAL, the rogue computer, in *2001: a Space Odyssey*. The astronaut who survived the computer killing the rest of the crew removes more and more processing units as HAL pleads not be to be destroyed. This sequence raises moral issues only if the cognitive vocabulary is extended to cover such beings as HAL. In the movie we are persuaded not only that HAL can think but also that it has a sense of self and at least some moral standing.

Sources of artificial intelligence models

The Turing machine

In 1936 Turing demonstrated that there was a general design for a machine that would evaluate any computable function. This is the famous Turing machine. From the point of view of psychology, the question of the relevance of the machine turns on how far it is reasonable to analyse various forms of thinking as computation.

The generic or abstract Turing machine consists of an endless tape, marked off in squares. There is a device for reading what is on each square as it comes under the head, 0 or 1, in binary notation ('bit'). The head can erase what is there and write either 0 or 1 in that square. The 'head' can move the tape to the left or right, any number of squares. Turing showed that by acting in accordance a limited set of rules, around twenty in all, the machine could perform all possible computations. The details need not worry us in this discussion. They can be found in many places. An excellent account of computation and the Turing machine can be found in Copeland (1998: chapter 4). Any material realization of the Turing machine is a material model of an abstract set of procedures applied to certain strings of numbers.

Von Neumann architecture

In designing material realizations of Turing machines, actual gadgets capable of performing the tasks defined in the abstract mathematics of computing, the basic layout or architecture of the commonest breed of machines was devised by von Neumann. Thus, we have 'von' machines and 'non-von' machines. Nearly all real computers are von machines. In this design there is a single central processing unit, surrounded by 'memory' stores. Each item of data and each program instruction has a concrete representation in one of these stores, and a unique location or address. Every item of data and every instruction must be *represented* concretely and individually in some physical state of some part of the machine.

The computing procedure has to be understood in terms of operations on data, expressed as sequences of bit (bi[nary uni]t) strings. Each bit string is a sequence of 0s and 1s. In accordance with the ASCII code, each letter or other sign that can be activated by a keystroke or something similar is represented in the machine by a sequence of seven binary digits. For example the letter 'a' is represented by the sequence 100000.

In any concrete version of a Turing machine built according to the von Neumann architecture, data are represented by bit strings that are realized in the physical state of *registers*. Registers are material entities consisting of rows of 'flip-flops'. These can be thought of as switches that can be in either the 'off' or the 'on' position. The standard format is for 'off' to represent 0 and 'on' to represent 1. So the bit string for 'a', namely 100000, would be realized in a register as 'on, off, off, off, off, off, off'.

In a machine built according to the von Neumann architecture the 'instructions' that make up the program, or programs, are also realized as sequences of bit strings in registers. They can be taken from memory to the CPU, *to operate causally upon the switches in the registers* to which they have been directed. These directions are again causal actions upon the physical states of registers. Inside the machine there are nothing but physical states acting upon each other electrically. In the von Neumann type of machine, data are represented in physical states of registers, and rules of computation are represented in real material states. Rule following is represented by a real physical process occurring in the material structure and material states of the machine.

It has become customary to refer to the kind of artificial intelligence engineering based on the technology of the von Neumann-type machine as Good Old Fashioned Artificial Intelligence, or GOFAI for short.

The symbol system hypothesis

In 1961 Newell and Simon gave formal expression to the computational model of cognition in their 'symbol system hypothesis' (SSH). This hypothesis was spelled out in much greater detail in their massive textbook of 1972. The most general concept is that of an information-processing system (IPS). In such a system there are symbols and symbol structures, ordered sets of symbols. It is important to understand that symbols, for Newell and Simon, are actual material entities. They are said to be 'tokens', not 'types'. Symbols and symbol structures are meaningless states of a material system. Designating symbols point to objects. However, there is no necessary relation between the characteristics of the symbol and the characteristics of the object designated. As far as the information-processing system manipulates symbols, only their material properties are relevant. Symbol identity does not mean 'having the same meaning' but 'having the same material characteristics'. Thinking, according to the symbol system hypothesis, is the arrangement and rearrangement of symbols according to programs, that is, symbol structures that designate 'information processes'.

 The projects of artificial intelligence

1   Artificial intelligence as engineering. To construct a machine that when input with a formalized version of a human cognitive task will output a result interpretable as the completion or outcome of the task.

2   Artificial intelligence as psychology:

   a)   To create a working *analytical* model of the performance of some cognitive task, and to serve as an *explanatory* working model of the way the task is performed by a human being.

   b)   Turing's conjecture: Brain/Thinking as Computer/Computing.

   i)   Thinking *is* computing
   ii)   Brains *are* computers.

   Together these theses constitute *the computational model of mind*

   c)   The Turing test: if a person cannot tell whether he/she is interacting with another person or a computer then we *must* say that computers can think.

   i)   Is this an empirical or a philosophical question, that is, a question about the reach of concepts?
   ii)   Does the Turing test, if passed by a programmed machine, prove that brains, which can perform the same tasks, are computers?

   (continued)

Computation and computing machines

1   What are the basic principles of mechanical computation?

    a)   Computable functions. A relation between variables such that from substitution of numerical values the value of the function can be determined by a sequence of mechanical steps.

    b)   Binary representations. ASCII code assigns a binary representation (seven-digit 0s and 1s) to every input sign.

    c)   Computational operations are performed on the input, stored in registers (blocks of on/off switches, according to rule.

2   The structure of the basic Turing machine:

    a)   An endless tape marked in 0s and 1s.

    b)   A read/write/erase head that can move the tape through itself for so many steps, left or right.

3   The structure of the basic von Neumann machine:

    a)   All operations are carried out in a central processing unit.

    b)   Data and computational rules (programs) are stored in satellite memory sites.

4   Newell and Simon's symbol system hypothesis. Thinking is the manipulation of symbols, that is, signs bereft of intentionality, according to causal processes, representing rules bereft of normativity.

section two

Strengths and weaknesses of the First Cognitive Revolution

Let us remind ourselves how the modeling of cognition in GOFAI computers was to be achieved.

1   Meaningful signs are represented, one by one, as bit strings in registers, that is, as material states of the machine.

2.   Rules, norms, customs, conventions and instructions alike, whether explicit or tacit, are represented by commands in programs, which, in their turn, are realized as causal processes on bit strings, that is, as material processes in the machine.

3   Cognitive tasks are input, according to the procedure as in (1). Their accomplishment is assessed as output, interpreted in accordance with (1).

To investigate the strengths and weaknesses of this kind of modeling of cognitive processes as contributions to psychology we must bring out what is presupposed in the project. We have seen that cognitive phenomena are represented by bit strings in registers and that the norms of cognitive procedures, processes and practices are represented in programs. From the point of view of cognitive psychology these presuppositions can be summed up in two prescriptive statements:

1   The intentionality of meaningful signs is deemed irrelevant to modeling the content of cognitive phenomena, such as thoughts, decisions and so on, in models of material systems such as the brain.
2   The modality of norms as expressing standards of correctness is deemed irrelevant to the modeling of cognitive processes and procedures.

In being entered into the machine for processing, meaningful relations have been transformed into correlations between material states of the machine, in particular the states of some of its registers. Similarly, in being input as the steps in a program, rule conformity has been transformed into material causation, electrical impulses acting on the material states of registers.

The troubling questions

To assess the viability of computers based on the von Neumann architecture as models of psychological significance there are two important questions:

1   Human cognition involves the management of meaningful signs according to standards of correctness. In developing a computer model we lose the two main features of human cognition, intentionality, the meaningfulness of signs, and normativity, conformity to standards. Is this or is it not a fatal defect of this kind of modeling?
2   If we agree that the project of moving from abstract representations of patterns of thinking to computer simulations is, in principle, an acceptable way of developing psychological theories, are von Neumann-type machines adequate as the models of neural tools that people use in everyday cognitive tasks? Is it plausible to be committed to the principle that each item of data and each rule has a specific representation in the brain and nervous system, physically realized in something very like a register? If we think that GOFAI models are defective as models does it mean that all types of computation and all types of computing machine are debarred from serving as the source of models of neural functioning?

117

The representation of intentionality

Human cognitive practices depend on our ability to recognize the intentionality of signs. This property is not exhaustively describable in terms of the material properties of the sign as a physical thing or event. Is this property preserved through the steps that are required to transform a human practice into a computation in a GOFAI machine? Even if it is not, does that have any bearing on the value of computer modeling in general? We can get to grips with this important issue by a close examination of a thought experiment that was intended to show that no computational model could possibly be adequate. This is the 'Chinese room' argument, proposed many years ago by John Searle (1980).

The 'Chinese room' argument

His thought experiment was designed to show that there is no place for the use of mentalistic language in describing the performance of computing machines when running programs. Since it seems that mentalistic language is ineliminable from the description of human thought and action, the thought experiment should also bear upon the claim that human brains themselves are a species of computing machines. In short, the argument is intended to dispose of the symbol system hypothesis, in its most general form. To perform cognitive operations a material system need only operate according to certain rules on meaningless symbols, material states of that system. In less formal parlance the thought experiment is intended to prove that it is conceptually incoherent to declare that brains are a species of computer and that computers can understand what they do as uses of language and other cognitive systems. In this discussion we are addressing a philosophical presupposition of the uses of computer models in the study of thinking.

The argument can also be seen as a way of bringing out the emptiness of the Turing test, or any other *behavioral* comparison, as a way of deciding whether a being of a certain kind is carrying out cognitive tasks in the way people do. The assessment of the power of a material system to model human beings performing cognitive tasks in a psychologically relevant way depends on being able to make this comparison.

The original argument was set up in terms of the mentalistic concept, 'understanding what is written is some human language'. It sets up a contrast between someone who performs meaningless operations in the way a computer does and someone who understands the symbols presented to him as questions and the meaningless symbols he returns as answers. Symbols are merely distinctively shaped physical objects. Questions and answers are meaningful. To know their meaning is to understand them. Here is the thought experiment, elaborated somewhat from its original form.

Jim, who is not a competent speaker of Chinese, is confined in a room sealed except for an entry slot and an exit slot. Jim is equipped with a huge stock of manuals, with the help of which he can look up acceptable correlations and combinations of Chinese ideographs, though he does know the symbols he receives as such. In this way he can chose which symbol should be sent back in response to any given input. Perhaps he begins by converting the input symbols into the binary ASCII code for Chinese. Jim's symbols are understood as Chinese ideographs by those outside. As so read they turn out to be correct answers to the questions pushed through the inlet slot.

Searle points out that Jim gives correct answers without having any knowledge of Chinese. In particular, we cannot say that he understands the questions posed to him in Chinese. Nor does he understand the responses that he so has laboriously created as answers. He does not even know that the marks he is manipulating are a language. Jim is behaving just like a computer behaves. Indeed, Jim is serving as a computer, since he is doing exactly what a computer does.

'Successful performance of the task' means something different for Jim and for the Chinese people outside. For Jim it simply means 'conforming to the diagrams in the manual and the rules for manipulating and matching them'. For the Chinese it means 'giving a meaningful and correct answer to a meaningful question'. Thus far goes Searle's thought experiment.

To appreciate what this thought experiment does and does not establish we need to bring to light the implicit foil. With what are we implicitly contrasting Jim and his way of 'answering questions'? Is Jim performing as a computer to be contrasted with a person or with a person's brain?

Let us elaborate the story a little further. Wu, who is a competent speaker of Chinese, is also confined in an adjoining 'Chinese room'. He is presented with the same ideographs as Jim receives. He sends out ideographs in response, which are also correct answers according to the outsiders. However, Wu has chosen the ideographs to send back in a way quite different from the method Jim used. Wu understand the ideographs as questions. He knows that they mean. He answers according to this understanding. He does not use look-up manuals.

The cognitive processes by which Jim and Wu achieve the *same behavioral output* are radically different. Jim used simple matching, while Wu used intelligent grasp of meanings. If Wu is the foil, Jim as a computer is being contrasted with Wu as a person.

However, the original thought experiment leaves open the possibility that it is a brain, say Wu's, that is the implicit foil. The cognitive processes by which Jim as computer and Wu's brain achieve the same behavioral output may be very similar. One might want to say that the concepts of 'understanding' and 'not understanding' are misapplied when the entities in question are not persons but brains or other parts of persons. Does it follow from Searle's premises that a whole system, of which Jim is simulating the brain, could not be properly said to understand?

Searle, not surprisingly, has been unmoved by this objection. However, there are plenty of responses to Searle's rejection of the brain-as-foil objection to his original thesis. For example, Copeland (1998) simply points out that the fact that because a part of a system cannot be said to understand it does not follow that the whole system of which it is a part cannot be said to understand.

What can be learned from the original thought experiment with the two possible foils, Wu the person and Wu's brain, made explicit? A computer which passes the Turing test is in the same position as Jim, that is, it produces what look like answers to the questions represented by the inputs. It does so entirely mechanically. Just like Jim, it does so by associating the physical entities representing questions with those representing answers from the equivalent of look-up tables. There are no grounds for thinking that it understands the ideographs, that is, that it attributes meaning to them. This disposes of the force of the Turing test. No computer that operates in this manner and passes a Turing Test in Chinese could be declared to be a competent speaker of Chinese, or possess any other cognitive skill, on the basis of behavioral criteria alone. Searle calls the illusion of understanding produced by the performance of Jim and the equivalent computer 'as-if intentionality', as opposed to the 'intrinsic intentionality' of signs as understood.

Unlike Jim, Wu understands the ideographs. For him they have that seemingly mysterious extra property of 'intrinsic or genuine intentionality'. Both Jim and Wu respond with ideographs, which, according to the outsiders, are correct answers to the questions they posed. Does either the original argument or the extended version with explicit foils show that a brain could not be a computer? The thought experiment shows us that a computer cannot be a stand-in for a *person*. It does not show that Jim as computer could not be a stand-in for someone's *brain*.

If Searle hopes to show that a GOFAI computer could not be an adequate model of a human brain, the level of comparison implicit in the thought experiment is wrong. It does not show that brains cannot be computing outputs that both the person whose brain it is and the people with whom he/she is interacting take to have intentionality. Jim (and his computer substitute, say R2D2) should be compared not with Wu but with the brain of Wu. Wu's *brain* does not need to understand the ideographs, or to attribute intentionality to them. It responds mechanically. Indeed, as Coulter (1979) has argued, it is a gross fallacy to personify the brain. A computer could be an adequate model of a competent speaker's brain while failing as a model of a competent speaker.

The difference between a machine and a person as a performer of cognitive tasks lies in the nature of the whole person, the social context and so on. Indeed, one can take this criticism a step further. No one who is thinking is aware of the intentionality of the material states of his/her brain. Nor are they not aware of them either. The concept of 'awareness of a meaning' has no application to brains. Similarly it has no application to computers.

This brings out deep-lying presuppositions in Searle's way of extending the scope of the concept of intentionality to include material entities other than perceived signs. Searle asserts that some brain states, of which a person is unaware as such, must possess intentionality in one who genuinely thinks, understands and so on. He makes this quite explicit. Here is what he says, in an exposition of the implausible idea that there can be unconscious intentional states:

> But our unconscious mental states are not like … words and pictures in [a] … filing cabinet, still in their pristine original form; rather they are like the words

and pictures in the computer when they are not on the screen. Such mental states have a totally different, nonmental, nonconscious form, but they are still unconscious *mental* states, capable of acting causally in ways similar to conscious mental states, even though at the particular time they are unconscious there is nothing there except neurobiological states and processes describable in purely neurobiological terms.

(Searle, 1998: 86)

According to the original account of intentionality, neurobiological states do not have intentionality. No one is using them as meaningful signs. Intentionality is a contextually based attribute of signs in use. Neurobiological states cannot be *mental* states. This observation is not a report of a discovery, but it expresses a feature of the grammar of our language.

Searle's proposal changes the concept of intentionality. In effect, he is proposing a new grammar for psychology, as if he were simply defending what we already have. It involves not only a new way of conceiving of neurological phenomena but also a new way of conceiving of conscious experience. Searle's argument hinges on the claim that neurological states can be causes in the same way as conscious states can be causes. Therefore they must be ascribed the main feature of conscious states, intentionality. This extension of the scope of the Causal Picture (Searle, 1998: 64–5) is doubly objectionable. An agent consciously using meaningful symbols according to local rules and conventions to accomplish some project is not a causal process among the symbols! Intentional activities are not causal. Neurological processes are causal. Causality was put forward as a common feature that would carry intentionality with it from conscious symbol management to neurological phenomena. However, the bridge is not linked to the left bank. So there can be no conceptual traffic across it.

Our brains do not understand. They do not assign or contemplate meanings. There are only electrical and chemical processes in brain activity which would have no meaning except in so far as they are the workings of cognitive tools that *people* use to think with. Intentionality is a property of the signs that we, as whole people, take notice of, read, write, manipulate in various ways. Such signs have their natural location in *public places* and are only later appropriated by individuals to use in private cognitive procedures, like doing sums 'in one's head'. The unknown workings of someone's brain are not part of that person's private procedures. Where is the argument for the radical presupposition of this proposal? If we accepted it, the very conceptual system that Searle relies upon for a common understanding of what he writes would be undercut.

Tools take on a life of their own only in fairy stories. Remember in *Fantasia* when Mickey Mouse as the sorcerer's apprentice sets the brooms in motion by themselves? In the real world a broom is nothing until *someone* pushes it. Here is the comparison laid out explicitly:

1   *GOFAI computer:* meaningful sign → keystroke (via compiler) → a material state of a register (no intentionality survives).

2   *Human being*: meaningful sign → perception → a material state of the brain (no intentionality survives).

Let us pause to reflect on the discussion. Are we trying to answer a scientific question? Then we should do an experiment. It has been done (Harré and Wang, 1999). It gave just the answer one knew it would. It is a necessary truth that unless one knows a language one cannot write sentences written in that language. Are we trying to resolve a conceptual issue? Then we resort to analysis of concepts.

The issue is clearly conceptual. Should we call what a computer does 'thinking'? If the comparison is between whole persons and computers the answer is clearly 'No'. If the comparison is between computers and brains the answer is also 'No'. This is because neither computers nor brains can properly be said to think. However, a brain is a part of a person, who can think. There is nothing in the arguments we have studied that forbids us from using computing machines as models of brains. This move makes good sense when we take brains as tools used by persons for various tasks. However, it is the persons who think!

Individualistic presuppositions

It is important to realize that Searle's thought experiment and many of the responses to it presuppose *individualism* in matters of language and psychology. Whatever cognition is, it must be something that is located in individual human beings. In our role as philosophers of psychology we must bring this presupposition into the open light of day and examine it. Cognition is the management of meanings, and meanings have an irreducible social or collective dimension. The presupposition of semantic individualism must be a philosophical thesis that can be dealt with only by conceptual analysis. Is it coherent? What are the necessary conditions for a mark to be meaningful?

1   No sign could have a meaning in isolation from all other signs in a symbol system.
2   No sign could have a meaning for an isolated human being, independent of the current material and social context and the history of the uses of that sign.

Intentionality is a mark of real cognition. A material entity that serves as a meaningful sign is taken, by those who use it, as pointing beyond itself to a thing, an action, a thought and so on. The intentionality of a sign is not a material property of the thing that is the sign bearer. It is not *any* property of the sign object. It consists of our sense of how it might be used in a certain cultural frame or way of life. It is important to get the 'whole context' objection right. Only persons-in-context can be said to understand, or have any other cognitive attributes and skills. Intentionality is a property not of a single isolated sign but of a sign in a well established context of practices with which people accomplish cognitive tasks.

Global aspects of linguistic meaning

In an influential study of the powers and limits of computing machines as sources of models of cognition Winograd and Flores (1986) pointed out that there are three features of linguistic meaning that are not plausibly represented in a GOFAI model of cognition, that is, one in which each sign is independently represented by a unique state of the material system. These are contextuality, historicity and indexicality. Could the local and historical context relative to which the sign is taken to have a use be represented in the cognitive system of the person who so understands it? If an attempt were made to incorporate this information in a GOFAI machine by means of representations of the totality of the items necessary to represent all possible contexts, input one by one, it would require a huge amount of time and a 'memory' of unattainable proportions.

Contextuality

The word 'ball', for example, takes on all sorts of different meanings in different contexts, forming a field of family resemblances. There are tennis balls, billiard balls, balls of wool, the ball of the thumb, formal balls, ball gowns, ball joints and so on. There is no necessary closure to this network of similarities and differences in use. Each use, and an indefinitely large pattern of uses yet to be made and which once were made, are cognitively significant in their variety nonetheless. If the necessary ancillary information were itemized for input into a GOFAI computer, how many trillions of bits would be required? The task of representing the totality of contexts recognizable by any cognitively competent human being in the registers of the memory banks of a GOFAI machine is staggering in its scope and complexity. Could this ever be part of the furnishings of an individual mind? Of course not. It exists as myriad affordances of the environment.

Historicity

The use of a significant sign at any one moment in the history of a language or other significant symbolic practice and at any moment in the life of the individual who uses it depends on what has gone before. This is no less true of the others who grasp its significance, each in his/her own way. Think of a word like 'cup' or the word for any other intentionally rich material thing, such as 'flag' or 'horse'. The current way it can be used is a sediment from decades or even centuries of previous uses. The intentionality of the cross of Christianity is not only highly contextual but is enriched with millennia of usage. Again, the task of representing all this in a GOFAI machine or the individual mind it purports to model beggars the imagination.

123

Indexicality

When a word or other significant sign is used, it carries with it certain unique aspects of the individual who uses it and the concrete situation in which it is used. For example, the use of word 'I' indexes what is said with the spatial location, moral standing and other personal aspects of the speaker at the moment of speaking. There are trillions of speakers and trillions of situations in which they speak. How could the totality of the indexical loadings of just the personal pronouns be represented in a GOFAI machine? The implication of the Winograd and Flores comments is clear: human cognitive practices and machine processing of computable functions representing these practices are incommensurable in orders of magnitude, if in nothing else.

 learning point   **The problem of intentionality**

Psychological phenomena display meaning, intentionality and normativity, conformity to standards. This sets limits to the kind of machine that could serve as a model for human cognition.

1   The question of intentionality

    a) Inputting a meaningful sign creates a meaningless physical state in the machine. Is the representation of a meaningful sign in a state of the human brain equally meaningless?

    b) Searle's 'Chinese room' argument is meant to show that a 'thinking device', the material states of which have no meaning, can pass the Turing test.

    c) Only persons can understand meanings. Therefore the argument shows only that a computing machine is not a good model of a person. However, it could be a good model of a person's brain.

    d) Searle's assertion that brain states of thinking beings have intentionality elides the Causal and Agentive Pictures. The argument proves only that the mechanical simulations of cognition require no intentionality. Machines could model the human brain thinking. What is wrong is the thesis of one-to-one representations.

2   The impossibility of representing the meaning of each sign by a unique material symbol independent of context, etc. Meaning involves:

    a) Contextuality.

    b) Indexicality.

    c) Historicity.

The representation of normativity

An expert system is a set of rules and conditions for its possible applications. When represented as a program and run on a computer the machine can simulate the cognitive performance of experts. For example, there are diagnostic programs that can output the name of a disease when given the description of some symptoms. The rules are meant to ensure that the output is correct, that is, meets certain standards as set by the relevant community. Everyone is some sort of expert. We do know how to do many things correctly.

In the technical world of knowledge engineering the simulation is required only to produce the correct output from some given input. It is not required that the intervening process should simulate the human cognitive process, conscious or not.

In cognitive psychology we need to consider whether, when input and output are correctly simulated, it is legitimate to infer that the intervening processes in the machine simulates the cognitive processes carried out by a human being acting in conformity with relevant standards of correctness and propriety. The key move in the case of explicit instructions is the transformation of a rule from a normative or mandatory statement in the imperative mood into a line in a program that is realized as a non-normative causal process in the machine.

Problems with a rule-based psychology

The loss of normativity

When a rule is input into a machine as part of a program it becomes a setting of a register that functions causally, in accordance with the laws of electromagnetism. The act of inputting a representation of a rule changes the electrical state of a register or registers. However, rules in real life are not causes of the human behavior that conforms to them. There may be a myriad different causes of conforming behavior. Rules do not determine what *happens* in the future. They determine what *should* happen. Unlike causes that necessitate their effects, *ceteris paribus*, all else being equal, rules can be rejected, ignored and changed. When people shape their thoughts and actions in conformity to rules it is presupposed that the rule has not been rescinded or forgotten.

If a rule is represented by an instruction in a program then it is transformed *ontologically*. It is no longer a norm but a cause. When a representation of the content of a rule is input into a machine the normative force is lost in the transformation. Only people conform to or violate norms. Brains, and computing machines, do what they do. To assess the possibility of simulating the normative aspects of cognition we must look more closely into the way rules, conventions, customs and habits serve as the bearers of norms in everyday life.

The status of rules in psychology

Human behavior, both practical and cognitive, is dominated by norms, standards of correctness. Not any way of sawing wood, or any way of enumerating a flock of sheep, will do. It is tempting then to think of rules as having a very important explanatory role for understanding how indeed we do manage to live within the constraints of norms. Rule following may come to be seen as *the* archetypal cognitive procedure. However, there are great difficulties in this easy generalization from the psychology of following instructions to the psychology of having good habits. There are two broad ways that the word 'rule' is useful in making sense of human actions.

1   People pay attention to a rule as an explicit instruction and do what they think it says to do in the circumstances, as they understand them. Rules, thus understood, are not the causes of a person's behavior. Rules fix what is to count as correct or proper in the circumstances. They guide action but do not fix what is to happen. Nevertheless, someone who wants to do things correctly would be wise to consult the relevant rule and to follow it. Rules have an important part to play in the way people manage some of their actions.

2   A person may be so trained in proper behavior as to act as if he or she was obeying a rule, though what has been done is habitual, done without thinking what is the correct action to take or conclusion to draw. A useful phrase for describing this kind of conformity might be 'acting in accordance with a rule'. The habit may once have been acquired by following an explicit instruction repeatedly until it faded from consciousness. Or – and this is important in psychology – it may be that the habitual behavior has been picked up in some other way, by imitation of a role model, for example. Yet that way of thinking or acting is still subject to standards of correctness and propriety. In such a case, a psychologist or a linguist may try to write down the norms that seemed to be implicit in the behavior as explicit rules.

Ryle (1947) drew out another implication of the distinction between following a rule and acting in accordance with a rule. There is, he notices, a strong tendency to assume that when behavior is assessable by reference to standards of correctness or propriety, and it is not produced by following explicit instructions consciously, there must be a hidden and unconscious version of explicit rule following going on. However, it would be wrong to go on to assume that in such a case a person would be unconsciously following a rule in the same way as he or she would have followed it consciously. One might slip into this mistake if one persisted in treating rules as if they were causes of the behavior that conformed to them. People use rules. Rules do not use people!

Unconscious versions of what is necessarily conscious cannot be used to create models of hypothetical processes supposedly occurring in the realm of the unobserved or the unobservable. What determines whether a rule has been followed is how far a person's actions meet the criteria of correctness that the rule would express if formulated explicitly. It is not determined by how one's conforming behavior comes about. There are all sorts of ways that a person can implement a rule, some involving explicit attention to an instruction, others simply acting as one has been trained to act without any particular thought in mind. The mechanism of acting in accordance with a rule may well be wholly material. The tools of conformity work that way!

The frame problem

Human beings are able to apply rules successfully in all sorts of incompletely specified circumstances. How is a computational model to simulate this commonplace human capacity? We must keep in mind that a computational model is an *abstract* representation of whatever process it models. This aspect of the difficulty with modeling actual human cognition has been called the 'frame problem'. Since no GOFAI machine could possibly hold representations of all possible contexts for the application of some set of norms, how are compromises to be reached? Setting up such a compromise is 'specifying a frame', a relatively small and finite information pack. Boden (1988) has pointed out that we are never in a frame-free situation. Some array of concepts must be in use in order to begin any human project, not least for identifying what we perceive in the local environment.

Marvin Minksy (1975) offered something like this definition of a frame:

A frame is a hierarchical structure of rules or 'frame axioms' the lowest level of which consists of slots into which names and individual descriptions can be inserted.

The 'frame axioms' are the rules for the correct performance of some task.

A universal all-purpose frame could not be input to a GOFAI computer item by item, together with the rules for its decomposition into situation-dependent mini-frames. Too many data would be required, and each item of data is itself frame-sensitive. In practice, computer programmers construct restricted frames, as abstract representations of a cognitive system. Thus there is the British birthday party frame, with slots for presents and for persons of various sorts. One of the frame axioms specifies that the number of candles on the cake should be the same as the age of the celebrant. What if the celebrant is eighty-five? Another frame axiom specifies that everyone should sing 'Happy birthday to you, dear Marvin,' and so on. No frame can be prepared in advance for every contingency.

Some of us have puzzled over the problem of how to get the tiger, the goat and the cabbage across the river when they can be transported only one at a time. If the boatman takes the tiger first, the goat eats the cabbage. If he takes the cabbage, the tiger eats the goat. If he takes the goat, he has to take either the cabbage or the tiger on the third trip. Trouble will ensue on the opposite bank while he goes back to get the last one. So long as the frame excludes a peg and a rope, there is no solution.

Not only are too many data required for computation to be possible, but also most of the relevant data at any one time simply may not exist. How much of what really happened in Montrose, a small town in Pennsylvania, is actually available for input when some issue arises that could be referred to an 'expert system'? Not much. For example, in a notorious murder case we can see the role of the frame. In 1976 a man out skeet shooting with a friend was killed by gunshot wounds near Montrose. Was his companion guilty of murdering him? The cognitive frame for applying the rules of a judicial trial or a coroner's court included then as now a slot for forensic evidence, such as the angle of entry of the fatal charge of shot. The body of the dead man had been buried without any attempt to determine this aspect of the matter. In the absence of that information, the coroner found the death accidental. Finally, after twenty years, the body was exhumed, and the slot filled. With the new evidence in place a verdict of murder against the dead man's companion was reached. In this case there was no doubt, given the database available at the time, which rules to apply and which to suspend.

However, there will, in general, be more than one way of updating a database as a situation unfolds. Each way involves the abandonment of a different frame axiom. We would have to decide using considerations that were not in the frame which revision to choose. Consider the case of Jim and the bagel. Frame axiom X: a bagel bought at t will be edible at $t + 1$. Frame axiom Y: a person hungry at t will be hungry at $t + 2$ unless he/she has eaten. We learn that Jim is hungry at t and buys a bagel. He bites it at $t + 1$. Which of axioms X or Y do we abandon if all we know is that Jim is hungry at $t + 2$?

Remember Brook Shields's aphorism? Spit out everything that tastes nice! Here are three possibilities. Jim has an insatiable appetite for bagels. In that case axiom Y must be set aside. Jim is an anorexic and follows the Brook Shields principle. Jim bites but does not eat the bagel. This leaves both frame axioms standing. The third possibility that later emerges is that a disgruntled employee at the bagel factory put soap powder in the dough. *This* bagel, though bought at t, is not edible at $t + 1$. Therefore we set aside axiom X.

What does this fable tell us about cognitive frames? Whatever frame axioms one settles on, something unexpected may appear 'out of the blue' and render the frame inadequate. There is no conceivable way that a frame rich enough in content to cover all possible eventualities could be input into a GOFAI computer, even if we could assemble the data, item by item.

Charniak and McDermott (1985) suggest that the frame problem differs greatly in severity from case to case. If inputting new data does not substantially alter the frame, as it did in the case of Jim and the bagel, we can proceed as if the frame were complete. In all real cases we make an empirical compromise, a working approximation to a stable universal frame. In the context of human psychology this is not an adequate theoretical solution. We make inferences unhesitatingly in conditions of minimal information. Moreover, that is because we can survey the context for whatever items of information we need. Cognition is not confined to the pre-existing resources of an individual mind.

There is no solution to the frame problem. The problem is not the computational model of cognition as such. It is the kinds of computational procedures in which we are modeling the application of rules and conventions. These examples show that the point of view in which standards of correctness, norms and so on are represented explicitly by frame axioms is surely flawed as a general background within which to construct models of human cognition.

The frame problem arises in part from the persistence of the presupposition of individualism. It is presupposed that all the data necessary for the performance of a cognitive task must be represented in the machine, item by item, to be processed in the CPU as required. Obviously, no real machine could possibly hold all that would be required to perform a von Neumann-type computation for all the cases a human being may run across and which he or she manages to cope with. However, if we could devise a machine that worked not in the GOFAI manner but globally, then, perhaps, the frame problem, as we have been studying it, might not arise.

If we want to hang on to the general outlines of the computational model, we need to find another kind of computing machine. It must be one which will carry out the operations we need to perform in carrying on cognitive activities, say reasoning, remembering and deciding. However, it must do so without *using* representations of rules in any way. In particular it should be capable of performing the required computational tasks without having individual rules or individual meaningful signs represented materially in particular states of the machine, for example as the bit strings in a group of registers.

---

learning point   ## Can normativity be represented?

1   The kinds and roles of rules:

   a)   Generally a written expression of a norm. Used to express immanent or implicit norms in explicit, usually written form.

   b)   Can be used as an explicit instruction – sometimes a simple imperative: 'Do this.' More usually a conditional imperative: 'If the situation is thus and so, do this (think this) and so on.' This kind of rule represents an expert's skill.

   c)   In neither case a nor case b do rules cause conforming behavior. This is because they fix not will happen in the future but what would count as the correct thing to happen.

   d)   Implicit rules are not unobserved versions of explicit rules, nor is acting in accordance with a rule an unconscious version of following a rule. Analyses of action patterns should be teleological, that is, goal-directed.

2   Rule to program instruction to bit string deletes normativity:

   a)   In a von Neumann machine 'norms' constraining the performance of discursive tasks would be input as instructions in a program, and explicitly represented in states of the machine. They would function as physical causes of changes in physical states of the machine. They would thus lose their imperative and future-directed role.

(continued)

b) How much information is required to make the application of a rule unambiguous? An indefinitely large amount. This raises the 'frame' problem.

c) A frame is a set of frame axioms, or rules of procedure, associated with 'slots' for specific situation descriptions.

d) Since to input a frame 'for all seasons' an impossible amount of data would have to be represented item by item in the machine. The 'bagel' thought experiment shows that in principle every frame is vulnerable to unexpected new data. Charniak and McDermott suggest empirical compromises as cases test frame axioms.

Conclusion

Before we can assess the strengths and weaknesses of the First Cognitive Revolution we must pause to take stock. From a philosophical point of view the 'cognitive science' project, looked at globally, is on the right lines. It does conform to the requirements of scientific realism. Methodologically it fits the well established pattern of research programs in physics and chemistry. Phenomena are identified and classified. Empirical generalizations are made on the basis of experiment and observation. Models of possible generative mechanisms are constructed. Where are the weaknesses?

Psychological phenomena

There are problems with the identification and classification of psychological phenomena. The development of an adequate account of the nature and typology of psychological phenomena has been ignored or sidestepped. We will look briefly at some examples of this failing, drawn from both practitioners and theoreticians. Some research programs have simply made use of commonsense categories. In Chapter 5 we saw how carelessly some of these were interpreted by Churchland in presenting a supposed ontology of folk psychology. Other programs have been based on novel psychological concepts, only loosely linked with the working categories of ordinary language. The troubles are both ontological (what sorts of existence do psychological phenomena have?) and taxonomic (what kinds of phenomena are there?).

Searle's theoretical psychology presupposed an important ontological thesis: that psychological phenomena are attributes of individual people. However, there is plenty of evidence to suggest that much that we take to be psychological exists in the interactions between people. For example, remembering is not only something that individuals do but also an interpersonal conversational activity, involving several people (Middleton and Edwards, 1990). To abstract individual acts of recollection as the exclusive domain of the psychology of remembering is sloppy. Of equal importance in real life are the many ways we think about the future. We hope, wish, want, plan, anticipate and so on. What little research has been done in this area has been almost entirely concerned with probabilistic predictions. What is missing from cognitive psychology is the careful and detailed study of the discursive procedures by which people actually carry out cognitive projects, such as deciding, remembering, classifying and so on. In cases where this sort of research has been done, for instance Rosch's (1973) studies of how people actually classify things, there is an obvious gap between what people do and how a GOFAI computer could be used to perform a task that falls within the same abstract characterization.

In Chapter 8 we shall return to this issue. Some misinterpretations of psychological phenomena can be put down to the subtle influence of the Causal Picture that is presupposed in the way that empirical studies are presented. Others are to be explained by the persistence of the presuppositions of Individualism.

These misinterpretations have an important and paradoxical influence on ontological matters. Adopting the Causal Picture deletes the active person from the ontology of psychology. The individual human being is reduced to nothing more than the place where impersonal causes bring about impersonal effects. This leads us to the question of the best way to interpret artificial intelligence models.

Models and their interpretations

There are also problems with the ontology of the mechanisms which artificial intelligence models are meant to allow us to identify. Several difficulties with the computational model of thinking have been highlighted in this chapter. Some of the presuppositions in the program initiated by Turing's original conjecture have turned out to be problematic. Remember that the scientific program involves a three-stage transition from an abstract artificial intelligence representation of an information-processing system to a model of a concrete mechanism capable of performing the necessary operations to hypotheses about possible brain structures and processes.

The original artificial intelligence models presupposed that bodies of knowledge could be itemized and that each item would be represented by a unique material state of any mechanism that would realize the relevant abstract model of the cognitive processing being studied. This presupposition is explicit in Newell and Simon's symbol system hypothesis. In Chapter 9, we will see that this and other presuppositions of GOFAI computing models must be rejected. Not only are they incompatible with observable psychological phenomena, but they are also incompatible with much that has been learned about how the brain works.

The very idea of a mental mechanism poses a deeper threat to a truly scientific psychology. Unless we are careful, the active person will be deleted from our ontology a second time! We lack an adequate metaphor for expressing the role of the human brain in human cognition. Such a metaphor must allow for the preservation of the materiality of the mechanisms of cognition, which are the material realizations of some artificial intelligence model or other. They must also allow for the ineliminability of human agency. We can take heart from the fact that the physical sciences also make use of ineliminable agencies. Physics rests on an ontology of charges and their fields. Psychology must be grounded somehow in an ontology of active people and their skills. This is the project of Parts III and IV.

---

self-test   Study questions

Chapter 4 Psychology as the science of mental substances

1   What was Descartes's ontology?

2   Why did he think mind was distinct from body?

3   What did he use his doubting for?

4   Why is *cogito ergo sum* fallacious?

5   What was Descartes's mental taxonomy?

6   What was Locke's ontology?

7   Give examples of ideas of sensation and ideas of reflection.

8   Perception was one major category for Locke. What was the other?

9   Give examples of simple ideas and of complex ideas.

10   Distinguish ideas of primary from ideas of secondary qualities.

11   What role did Hartley give to 'vibrations'?

12   How did Hartley link mental and material aspects of a human being?

13   How did Hume distinguish impressions and ideas?

14   What were the three Principles of Association for Hume?

15   How did he reduce them to two?

16   What role did Kant give to schemata in experience?

17   How did Kant justify postulating the transcendental ego?

Reading

Robinson (1995) chapter 7.

Chapter 5 Psychology as a science of material substances

1   What are the three versions of materialism?
2   What is ontological materialism?
3   In what way did Hobbes's materialism echo Newtonian physics?
4   What is methodological materialism?
5   Why is it important to correlate kinds of mental and material phenomena?
6   What is conceptual materialism?
7   What is the main thesis of eliminative materialism?
8   What is theory-ladenness?
9   Give two objections to the eliminative materialist program.
10 Why must the 'person' concept be preserved in any scientific psychology?
11 What is ethology?
12 What were Aristotle's four levels of being?
13 How do animals function as self-movers?
14 What were Aristotle's requirements for a complete scientific explanation?
15 What is the basic principle of evolutionary psychology?
16 Describe the path from genetic endowment to cognitive practice.
17 Give two examples of studies which throw doubt on exclusively genetic explanations of cognitive capacities.
18 What does the discovery of the unexpectedly small number of genes in the human genome have to do with psychology?

Reading
Robinson (1995) chapter 9.

Chapter 6 The beginnings of cognitive science

1   What did Bruner mean by a 'Judas eye' experiment?
2   What did the coin sizing experiment show?
3   What did the word recognition experiment show?

(study questions continued overleaf)

4   What did the reverse-colored playing cards experiment show?

5   What did the Bruner group infer from these and other experiments about the processes of cognition?

6   Are unobservable cognitive processes like observed ones?

7   Are they like neurophysiological processes?

8   How would artificial intelligence models help us to understand cognition?

9   What is a TOTE machine?

10   How does a system interpretation of a TOTE machine differ from a computer interpretation?

11   Distinguish the demands on artificial intelligence as engineering from artificial intelligence as psychology?

12   What was Turing's principle that he proposed for defining artificial intelligence as psychology?

13   What is a computable function?

14   Illustrate with a simple example from logic.

15   What is an abstract Turing machine?

16   What is binary notation?

17   What is a register?

18   What is a bit string?

19   What is a compiler?

20   What is Newell's symbol system hypothesis?

21   What is multiple realizability?

22   What is von Neumann architecture?

23   What is the principle of representation?

24   What is the Turing test?

25   Could a chimp pass it?

26   Would a computer passing the Turing test tell us *how* people think?

27   Compare the use of a computing machine to simulate cognition with its use to explain cognition.

28   What is intentionality?

29   Describe the 'Chinese room' thought experiment.

self-test   Study questions continued

30   Does it prove that a computer could not be an adequate model for a person?

31   Does it prove that a computer could not be an adequate model for a person's brain?

32   How does Searle's implicit 'foil' weaken his argument?

33   Why do we think meaning is a global phenomenon?

34   What do we mean by the contextuality, the historicity and the indexicality of meanings?

35   Distinguish following a rule from acting according to a rule.

36   Are rules causes of conforming behavior?

37   What is a 'frame'?

38   What is the 'frame problem'?

39   Discuss the Charniak and McDermott proposal to test frame axioms empirically.

Reading

Copeland (1998) chapters 1, 3, 4, and 6.

Towards a scientific psychology

The demise of behaviorism was followed by various attempts to create a realist cognitive psychology. The First Cognitive Revolution failed for two main reasons. It was unsystematic in the analysis of psychological phenomena, relying too much on the surviving methodology of naïve positivistic experimental methods. The version of artificial intelligence it took up was implausible as an analytical model for psychological phenomena and as an explanatory model for the means of their production.

According to the version of cognitive psychology we are developing in this course the mental realm includes both private and public phenomena. It is nothing but a flow of private and public patterns of symbols created and managed by human actors according to local norms and conventions. Basing psychology on this insight requires the study and preservation of the psychological concepts of ordinary languages as they are used in the everyday lives of ordinary people. They must be part of the basis of scientific psychology. They define the broad domains of cognitive tasks, such as remembering, deciding, calculating, classifying and so on. Using the available symbolic resources, people undertake cognitive tasks. The concept of 'skill' can be used to link individuals with the matrix of interpersonal symbolic and practical interactions.

Though the study of language as a symbolic tool for cognitive tasks will play a prominent part in Part III, the thesis that only the use of language *is* thinking is much too narrow. Creating and managing private images, drawing pictures, making models and other forms of public performance are among the cognitive skills that human beings deploy.

The vehicle of cognition, whatever it is, must be meaningful. The distinguishing mark of all that is meaningful is intentionality. The final step in completing our understanding of this feature of the symbolic vehicles of cognition will be to dispose of the last remnants of the Cartesian point of view that still linger in the writings of some philosophers apropos of cognitive psychology. This is the thesis that there are both intentional symbols and mental states. We shall use a combination of philosophical analysis and Ockham's razor[1] to dispose of this domain of redundant entities. We must get rid of the metaphorical use of the word 'mental' to refer to material states and processes relevant to thinking, feeling, perceiving and acting.

Looking at the phenomena of psychology dynamically, as attributes of the unfolding of orderly patterns of meaningful action, opens up the possibility of there being other models for explaining the orderly progression of events than the cause–effect relationship borrowed from a superficial conception of the physical sciences. For instance, many episodes can be understood as shaped by the necessity of conforming to the conventions of a particular narrative, according to the story lines that are recognized in the local traditions. This is something like a compass needle conforming to the local structure of the magnetic field. There are many other possibilities.

When we examine the patterns of thought, feeling and action closely there seem to be four main groups of rules, customs and conventions involved in their formation. Each group can be identified by the class of entities presupposed in the uses of its constituent rules and conventions. Following Wittgenstein, we will call such groups of norms 'grammars'. A Soul-based grammar, a Person-based grammar, an Organism-based grammar and a Molecule-based grammar are all in active use in the West, though not by everyone on every occasion. The four titles reflect the ontological presuppositions each embodies. Souls, Persons, Organisms and Molecules are basic or unanalysable sources of activity in these four ways of describing human life.

In Chapter 7 we shall see how the unity of a scientific psychology can be achieved, despite the diversity of the four grammars. There are two ways of linking our knowledge of patterns of meanings with what we know about the neurophysiology and anatomy of the human organism. The most important link between psychological phenomena and the brain and central nervous system is the Task/Tool metaphor (T/T). People bring their cognitive projects to fruition, more or less satisfactorily, by means of material mechanisms, including their brains and other bodily organs.

The second link is the Taxonomic Priority Principle (TPP). We pick out organic and molecular items relevant to meaningful psychological phenomena by the use of criteria drawn from the use of the Person grammar in managing the symbolic exchanges with which people carry out cognitive tasks in everyday life.

Using the Taxonomic Priority and Task/Tool Principles together, we can identify the molecular mechanisms by means of which people deal with cognitive problems, such as remembering events, answering questions, solving equations, classifying rocks and so on. A tool is defined relative to the tasks it can be used to perform. By means of task/tool we can incorporate the materiality of human beings into psychology without reducing psychological phenomena from meaningful acts to material causes and their effects.

Chapter 8 takes up the task of illustrating how typical psychological phenomena are analysed in the terms of meanings and norms of correctness. We return to mainstream psychology to see how much of the work of psychologists can be reinterpreted in discursive terms and rescued as contributions to the hybrid discipline that we have sketched in Chapter 7. Some misleading terminology must be tidied up before we proceed. The misuse of the terms 'instrument', 'experiment' and 'measurement' needs to be put right. While psychology legitimately makes use of 'apparatus', working models of aspects of psychological phenomena, there can be no place for 'instruments' or 'measurements', except as dangerously stretched and misleading metaphors.

Three case studies of the reinterpretation of studies of psychological phenomena originally presented in causal terms are offered as exemplars of how psychological phenomena should be thought of. Close attention to the phenomena allows us to see that *attitudes* cannot be hidden causes of behavior. They are properties of the *expression* of beliefs and opinions. Nor does the concept 'theory of mind' fare any better. Fortunately the results of both fields of mainstream research can be reinterpreted to make sense in the discursive mode. As reinterpreted, they can be taken up into discursive psychology. The third example, research into the origin and role of the sense of self, has been a major project for discursive psychologists. Studies of the uses of the first person have been used to enquire deeply into how individual people in different cultural and historical situations express their uniqueness as persons. In all three cases – attitudes, theory of mind and the sense of self – the psychological phenomena appear as attributes of the flow of intentional actions produced by a person or persons engaged in the performance of various cognitive tasks.

The scientific realist paradigm bids us look for a deep explanation of the phenomena revealed by the analytical phase of our studies. We must not make the mistake of inventing a hidden realm of mental processes and states to explain the observable realm of thinking, feeling and acting. Ryle (1947) and Wittgenstein (1953) drew attention to this fundamental error. To go beyond the realm of meanings and rules, we need to find inhomogeneous foundations, groundings of human cognitive skills in something that is not a skill nor any of the products of skilled action, like a thought or its expression in a proposition. The task/tool metaphor is the key to progress.

How are we to pass from a task specified in terms of the management of meaning to a tool the workings of which must be described in organic, causal terms? The answer seems to lie in the development of abstract computational *models* of the processes of meaning creation. In certain circumstances they can be interpreted as hypotheses about possible processes and structures in the brain and nervous system. One does not need to presuppose that the brain is a computer to use the technology of artificial intelligence to open up possibilities of neuro-scientific research into brain anatomy and physiology.

In Chapter 9 we will follow the most recent developments of artificial intelligence very closely. The First Cognitive Revolution stalled on the simplistic computational model drawn from the way the standard computer worked. In that picture the brain as cognitive tool is a computer and it runs programs much as the von Neumann version of the Turing machine runs its programs. There were supposed to be representations of data and rules in specific locations, in something like the binary code. There is assumed to be one or more central processing modules. This picture has turned out to be way off target. Nothing much like it can be detected in the human organism. Brain scans show distributed sites of activity for unitary cognitive processes. Brain micro-anatomy has shown how at least some of the 100,000,000,000 neurons in the system are connected into nets. Happily for the prospects of a scientific realist psychology, a new-style artificial intelligence model has appeared, parallel distributed processing or connectionism. In this model of the brain there are no mental states, nor are there item-by-item representations of anything required in this approach to cognitive activities. Knowledge and skill are grounded in the overall patterns of connections in very extensive neural nets. In some cases, as we shall see, work with artificial neural nets has already shown that there are grounds for optimism, that at last a truly scientific psychology is in prospect.

Note

1   In the fourteenth century the philosopher William of Ockham enunciated the famous principle that we should never multiply entities beyond necessity.

Grammar and cognition

In Part II we made the acquaintance of several attempts to develop a psychology that emulates the natural sciences. None proved satisfactory. Sciences develop at least as much by abandoning old metaphors and adopting new ones as by the accumulation of empirical data. Indeed, the significance of a body of data will usually depend upon the system of metaphors with which it is interpreted. Darwin's famous metaphor of 'natural selection' would be a contradiction in terms if taken literally. As a metaphor expressing a powerful model of the process of evolution it not only framed the theory of organic evolution but also determined how the fossil record was to be interpreted. In this chapter we begin the development of such a metaphor for a scientific psychology. Since it expresses the main source of analytical and explanatory models, the working tools of sciences, at the same time we shall be firming up our grasp of the necessary ontology, the catalog of what we take to exist in the domain of cognition.

The overall project of creating an adequate cognitive psychology is built on the principle that when people are thinking they are actively engaged in carrying out cognitive tasks according to local standards of good work. The generic model or source of all forms of cognition is the cognitive task performed with symbolic tools. These first order tools are created and managed by the use of second order neurological tools, the organs of the brain and central nervous system. In this chapter we begin the detailed study of the symbolic systems through which cognitive tasks are defined and carried out.

Cognitive phenomena, the domain of cognitive psychology, are the topic of discursive psychology. This catch phrase, now in current use (Edwards and Potter, 1992), expresses one powerful working model for analysing and categorizing the processes of the performance of cognitive tasks. Thinking, remembering, deciding and so on not only often take the form of conversations, but when carried out in other symbolic media than language the cognitive processes are nevertheless conversation-like. They are structured by meaning relations and can be seen to aspire to normative standards of correctness and propriety.

Symbols and their meanings

Signs, symbols, and intentionality

The symbols people use to perform cognitive tasks are of many different kinds. Some are public, such as conventional marks on paper, pictorial models and so on. Others are private, such as mental images, the words with which one talks to oneself, and so on. The material vehicles of meaningful acts can be called 'signs'. When considered with respect to their meaning they can be called 'symbols'. Ferdinand de Saussure (1916) provided a simple way to characterize an entity as a sign. When is a red light a sign? It must appear along with other similar entities in various sequences. On each of its appearances its presence must be understood as excluding one or more other such entities. Thus a red light is a traffic sign. It appears in sequences of colored lights. Each time it appears it excludes green and amber.

However, what does it mean? As a symbol a red light means 'Stop'. It has that seemingly mysterious quality, intentionality. We have already encountered this concept. For a sign to be used as an intentional symbol it must be part of the means by which a people carry out all sorts of tasks, according to local conventions and customs. This simple-sounding resolution of the age-old problem of the meaning of 'meaning' comes from Wittgenstein (1953: paras 1–31). It is, of course, circular. A sign is a meaningful symbol as far as people use it for performing cognitive tasks. Cognitive tasks are those jobs that people work at by using signs as meaningful symbols. Tasks and the symbolic tools by which they are accomplished mutually define one another. Cognition is no exception.

The task/tool circle is true of every human practice. A tennis racquet is a tool for playing tennis. Tennis is the game that, among other things, is played with tennis racquets. This is just the kind of circularity that one finds when the concepts one encounters are basic and definitive of a certain practice. Having procedural knowledge of the practice, how to do it whatever it is, brings along with it an understanding of the uses to which the relevant means are to be put. Nothing more fundamental is required.

The 'mind behind the mind' fallacy

Someone may complain about this treatment of meaningfulness. Surely there must be something deeper that explains the intentionality of symbols? This makes it look as if intentionality or meaningfulness is a property somewhat like color or warmth. There is something deeper that explains the warmth of a freshly brewed cup of coffee, namely the unobservable motion of its constituent molecules. Mislocating intentionality as a property of the sign has led two otherwise deeply opposed philosophers of psychology to commit the same mistake. Fodor (1979) and Searle (1983) have both proposed accounts of intentionality in terms of mental states, committing versions of the mind behind the mind fallacy. In addition to meaningful symbols, signs with a use in a practice, these philosophers have insisted that there are also mental states. The doctrine has been well summed up by Horst (1996: 43).

> [For] Searle (1983) intentional and semantic properties of symbols are to be explained in terms of the semantic and intentional properties of mental states … Fodor's view is quite the reverse: namely, that it is the semantic and intentional properties of mental states which are to be explained, and they are to be explained in terms of the intentional and semantic properties of symbols – specifically, the symbols that serve as the objects of propositional attitudes.

The phrase 'propositional attitude' refers to alleged cognitive states such as 'believing …'. The idea that people have propositional attitudes to the content of some proposition is all part of a kind of revival of the Lockean ontology of thinking as the shuffling around of mental entities.

There is so much wrong with the Lockean program for a psychological science that we will not pause to engage in polemics. Suffice it to say that Wittgenstein's account of meaningfulness in terms of human practices needs no grounding in hypotheses invoking a level of mental activity behind the practical actions of people thinking. There are no mental states other than people's subjective experiences. As Ockham wisely taught us: do not multiply entities beyond necessity. Only a mistaken presupposition that intentionality is like color, and needs to be accounted for by reference to some deeper property of cognitive systems, could lead one to the hypothesis of 'mental states'.

Before we leave the topic it is well to look over what the concept of 'mental state' may be used to refer to. One possibility is that a mental state is just a material state of a person's brain and central nervous system that is described in mentalistic terms. One might metaphorically describe a brain in a certain state as 'thinking'. Of course, brains do not think. Only persons can be so described. This kind of talk is best avoided. Searle seems to have used the expression 'mental state' in this metaphorical sense, leading him into the strange claim that brain states of which the possessor is unaware have intentionality. Another possibility is that the phrase 'mental state' might be used to refer to the abstract state of an imaginary Turing machine performing computations the outcome of which mimics the outcome of a person thinking. The state is not material, since that Turing machine could be realized in many different material set-ups. However, this state is an abstraction, a feature of a model in use by a psychologist still struggling to make the GOFAI stage of artificial intelligence viable as a theoretical basis for cognitive psychology.

'Mental state' as either a metaphor or as an abstraction has little to offer cognitive science but a source of confusion.

The central role of language

Though I have emphasized the breadth of the range of symbolic means that we must attend to in understanding how we perform cognitive tasks, language remains the most important. It is both an exemplar of discursive processes and a model for understanding those procedures that are not strictly linguistic. It will be wise to look closely at the part played by language as a vehicle of thought. Two matters seem important at this juncture. The first is the relation between the resources of language and the limits of what can be thought. The second is the role of language in making the private experiences of individual people available to others in a public communication.

Language and the limits of the thinkable

It hardly seems controversial to claim that people use symbolic systems of various kinds as instruments of thought. However, many philosophers and psychologists have believed that thought exists independently of the symbolic forms in which it is clothed and by means of which it is expressed. For example, a distinction between 'thought' and the linguistic forms in which it is represented was prominent in the seventeenth and eighteenth centuries. Thomas Hobbes held that there were sequences of ideas and that there were also sequences of words. By a kind of one-to-one mapping the latter were matched to the former. 'Words so connected as that they become organs of our thought, are called SPEECH, of which every part is a name [of a thing or of a thought]' (1651 [1953]: 15). Thinking is not always privately talking to oneself, Sometimes a cognitive act, such as deciding which path to take through the woods, is achieved by manipulating symbols of other kinds, such as images and mental pictures. Sometimes the symbols have a material embodiment in compasses and maps.

Instead of trying to give a general answer to the general question 'Is thinking inherently linguistic?' it seems wise to consider some particular ways in which language and thought are related, without making any assumptions about other media of cognition. The key insight is that language, though of huge importance, is not the only medium of cognition. Let us remind ourselves of the basis of the distinction central to the very idea of cognitive psychology, between things which have significance only in themselves and those things that have the remarkable property of intentionality, pointing beyond themselves. Discursive psychology is based on the principle that whatever cognitive media there are – for instance, the non-linguistic practice of sketching a map to convey to a visitor how to find one's apartment – is cognitive just in so far as it can be seen to be intentional and normative. The visitor's sketch is not just a pattern of lines on paper. It is also a representation of the neighboring terrain. Host and visitor alike share the presupposition that the sketch is accurate, within the demands of the task.

Edward Sapir (1966) and Bejamin Lee Whorf (1979) are often credited with the thesis that forms of thought are determined by language. Their thesis has been understood as something like this: what one can think is what one can say. However, this extreme position cannot be found in the writings of either man. Instead, as Lakoff (1987) has pointed out, Sapir and Whorf share a more interesting and less controversial thesis, that distinctions which become embedded in grammar limit or constrain the forms of thought which are *readily* available to the user of the language in question. Put this way, the Sapir–Whorf hypothesis would have seemed quite commonsensical to Wittgenstein, for whom the frames within which we formulate thoughts are none other than taken-for-granted grammars. In the discussion to follow I shall be assuming that the Sapir–Whorf hypothesis, as I have presented it here, is generally acceptable.

It has sometimes been objected that the Sapir–Whorf hypothesis, even in the modest form, is still too strong. It would seem to imply that the users of different languages not only think in different ways, but also perhaps could think only in the way their mother tongue favors. If we can find some way, however clumsy, in another language for expressing a concept or judgment that is elegantly or economically expressed in the language of the culture that is its natural home, then we will have shown that thought is not rigidly constrained by language. There may, then, be only one common human psychology expressed more or less elegantly in different languages. This is not a matter that can be decided by armchair reflection.

Language as the medium of public expression of private experience

If we are to be able to make a study of public language use as a method of investigating psychological phenomena, some of which are private, we must have a suitable account of the relation of the public activities of speaking and other symbolic acts to the private activities and states they express. The notion of 'expression' will serve as the basis of our account, restoring the role it had in nineteenth-century psychology (Danziger, 1997). A simple extension of Wittgenstein's famous Private Language Argument opens the way to a general distinction between using language to describe our private experience and using it to express that experience. This distinction will serve to give general support to the discursive method of exploring both private and public cognitive acts.

Language use is not only public, as in conversation, producing an interpersonal realm of meanings. There is also a private realm of human experience, and there are private uses of symbolic systems that play a key part in its production. How are the features of that realm to be studied by psychologists and philosophers?

The distinction between expression and description is an important ingredient in the famous Private Language Argument (Wittgenstein, 1953, paras 240–315). Wittgenstein is discussing the general question whether a language could exist if the only way meaning could be established was by pointing to exemplars. The learner's attention is drawn to examples of what a word is used to refer to. This idea seems reasonable when the meaning of words for large public objects like palaces or elephants are being taught. However, could it work if the exemplars were strictly private, such as bodily feelings? If by inwardly pointing to such feelings a person could learn words, a strictly private language would be possible. However, if the exemplars were strictly private, they could not be used to teach anyone else the use of the relevant words. They could not even serve as a stable basis for the speaker's own practice. How do we learn words for private feelings if we cannot learn them by pointing to public examples?

The process of developing a vocabulary for private feelings begins, Wittgenstein suggests, with natural expressions of pain, joy and so on. As a child develops psychologically and socially it learns to substitute simple vocalizations and finally verbal formulas for natural expressions. As a substitute for laughing and dancing around, the words 'I'm so happy' can be used to express happiness. The tendency to say such things becomes part of what it means to be happy. When people sincerely say they are happy, they do have private feelings to express. However, the relation between the verbal act and the feeling is not that of description to object described. If it were, the words and the objects they describe would have to be independent of one another, since descriptions can be wrong. However, if the words express feelings, just as laughing and singing may, then, *ceteris paribus*, they are part of a whole, a complex of feelings and behavioral tendencies no part of which can be left out of what it is to be happy.

The domain of psychology: the act–action distinction

Can we find a general principle by means of which the stream of human activity could be partitioned in the most psychologically illuminating way? It seems natural to adopt the act–action distinction as a way of displaying the structure of cognitive processes. Actions are what people do intentionally. Acts are the meanings of actions. A nod is an action which, in the appropriate circumstances, can mean that one agrees with what has been proposed. In other circumstances the very same action can mean that one is indifferent to the outcome. Acts are relative to contexts and story lines. In the garden of Gethsemane a kiss is a betrayal. In greeting the Pope it is a mark of submission and respect.

Having partitioned a stream of activity into a sequence of elements, the question of how the elements are related must be taken up. Relations between meanings and standards of correctness are relevant to this problem. For example, some act–action patterns are the result of a person deliberately following a rule. 'If you cannot remember something right away, think about something else and it will come to you.' Sometimes act–action patterns are matters of habit. Once upon a time people solved arithmetical problems without calling up the rules.

The possibility of a scientific psychology presupposes three principles:

1   Human beings actively engage in both public and private discourse, streams of meaningful acts.
2   People express themselves by the use of both verbal and non-verbal acts.
3   Public and private, verbal and non-verbal acts fall within the same general system of categories.

To be acceptable, even to be intelligible, people's cognitive acts must conform to local standards of propriety and correctness. This is the basis of 'discursive psychology'.

The choice of 'discourse' as the leading metaphor of cognitive psychology expresses the ontological principle that the flow of intentional actions *is* the very 'stuff of mind'. All sorts of practices fall under this heading. Some are linguistic, some are not. All are intentional, that is, all are meaningful, and all are subject to standards of correctness, propriety and so on. The medium in which cognitive activities are being carried on, linguistic or non-linguistic, will determine the choice of particular analytical and explanatory models for the conduct of research.

According to the 'discursive' point of view, as sketched above, psychology is primarily the study of processes – streams of human actions and interactions. These can be understood in terms of their meanings for the actors and interactors and the norms and traditions that are generally accepted. Many of these streams of meaningful actions make sense in terms of narratives, story lines well known in the culture. Within this general scheme conversation is the most useful, but not the only, model for analysing such streams of action. Adopting this model for a research program invites the researchers to treat all that people do, collectively and individually, privately and publicly, as if it were a kind of conversation.

This leads directly to the study of what people must know and what skills they must possess to be able to produce the required actions meaningful as acts. Complementary to each mode of collective action there must a repertoire of individual skills and dispositions, knowledge of how to do things.

The final step in a psychological study of some cognitive procedure, say remembering or classifying, is the proposal of a 'grammar' or grammars expressing the norms that seem to be relevant to what people are doing. There are both tacit and explicit grammars. In order to use any explicit technique one must make use of a repertoire of tacit knowledge. When such knowledge is formulated explicitly the use of that knowledge as an explicit guide to thought and action will depend on yet another corpus of tacit knowledge. What was explicit in one context may be tacit in another. Cognitive psychology must record explicit knowledge and bring to light whatever is presupposed in making use of it.

The fact that acts are created by the uptake by others of the intentions of actors, a fact registered in the act–action distinction, is of very great importance to the human sciences. Cognitive psychology is concerned with how actors produce intentional actions in the light of how they interpret the actions of others as acts. Psychological phenomena are, I have emphasized, attributes of the flow of actions interpreted as acts, that is, as meaningful in accordance with the ways meanings are assigned in the local culture. Actions, however, are produced by individuals. Cognitive sociology, or social psychology, is the study of acts, the joint product of an intentional action and an interpretative act. Cognitive psychology is the study of how individuals come to bring about meaningful actions in contexts that are themselves meaningful.

The grammars of everyday life

The whole of human life is enmeshed in loosely linked and fuzzy-edged standards of correctness and propriety. For the most part such standards are presupposed in the way we think and act. It is the business of psychologists, sociologists, linguists and other students of human affairs to bring these presuppositions to light. They can be *expressed* for scientific purposes in terms of systems and clusters of rules. We have adopted Wittgenstein's term 'grammar' to refer to useful ways of grouping such sets of rules into semi-coherent systems. Managing a part of one's life by deliberately following explicit rules happens from time to time. However, we must not slip into presuming that when we are ordinarily conforming to locally valid standards in the use of signs and the management of symbolic procedures we are following rules unconsciously. For the most part the results of research into the norms of cognitive procedures are descriptions of good and bad habits.

Contemporary Anglo-American patterns of thinking, feeling and acting seem to be shaped by four main grammars.

A *Soul or S grammar* expresses what is presupposed in ways of thinking and acting which make use of the principle that each person has an immaterial soul, inhabiting, but not identical with, the material body. Not so long ago this grammar was in common use. The basic categories of active beings recognized in this grammar were God and souls. Among the main classificatory categories of act–action were 'sin', 'temptation', 'confession' and 'redemption'.

S grammar, as expressing an acceptable and unquestioned way of shaping one's thoughts and actions, directly through following rules and indirectly in good habits, is now confined to certain rather restricted groups of people. For example, members of the Mormon Church, in Utah, use this grammar both in the management of their actions and in commenting on the actions of others. One notices, however, that the terminology is still in widespread used for rhetorical purposes, for example in the speeches of candidates in the election for the US presidency. As far as I can see it plays no role at all in the foundations of contemporary cognitive science.

A *Person or P grammar* can be used to express what is presupposed when we treat embodied persons as the basic particulars and originating sources of activity. It is expressed in ways of doing things that we see everywhere in everyday life. It is widely used to comment on the actions of oneself and others. Among some of the specialized dialects of this generic grammar are the idioms of the courtroom, Freudian psychotherapy and so on.

A main feature of P grammars is the way that responsibility is dealt with. This is particularly important for a philosophy of psychology. In the transition from infancy to maturity a being that has native agentive powers matures to take growing responsibility for what it does. This is expressed not only in actions but also in the uses of language. The P grammar is presupposed in remembering. To have remembered something is to have recollected it correctly. Only people remember, not brains. To say 'I remember …' is to take responsibility for the authenticity of the report. The P grammar is presupposed in playing tennis. The exchange of shots is constrained by conventions of meaning: 'On the line is in.' The contest is also constrained by rules of procedure: 'Change ends after four games.' Scores accrue to people. People play shots, good and bad. The players are taken to be responsible for what they do. A huge number of tacit conventions are also involved. The winning player hurls his/her sweatbands into the crowd, for instance.

An *Organism or O grammar* is being used more and more to express aspects of human life that seem to be common to *Homo sapiens* and other higher animals. The basic powerful particulars, the active beings, are organisms. It has many similarities to the Aristotelian approach to understanding human life that we looked at in Chapter 5. Higher animals appear to be agents acting to achieve some end. Yet, except in rare cases, animals do not act intentionally in the full sense that would bring into play the grammar of attributions of responsibility. Responsibility talk addressed to family pets is surely metaphorical. When addressed to certain primates, such as domesticated chimpanzees, it may have a deeper significance, widening the scope of the domain of moral agents. We also use responsibility grammar for talking about, though not usually to, neonates. Babies act for an end but surely not for a purpose. The O grammar expresses those aspects of human life that seem to fall outside the domain of well trained habit and the following of explicit rules. The rapid development of the biological sciences, particularly genetics, has led to an expansion of the scope of the O grammar as a means of classifying and explaining more and more human activities. We shall need to discuss some of these proposals in detail.

A *Molecular or M grammar*, based on molecules and molecular clusters as the basic particulars and originating sources of activity, is also in current use. Among the discourses shaped by M grammar are human physiology and molecular biology. Discourse framed in this grammar includes such attributions of agency to molecules as the power (alleged) of melatonin molecules to put one to sleep by inducing a change in brain rhythms, and the power ascribed to excess hydrochloric acid to cause heartburn, in the sense of discharges in the pain receptors. Reference is more likely to be made to molecules when acceptable cognitive skills have broken down. Defective production of neurotransmitters in old age is one example of the use of the M grammar in relation to a cognitive process.

The S and P grammars express semantic and conventional necessities. Explanations of the way sequences of act–actions unfold may be based on meanings. You prefix your instructions for finding the way with 'I think we should go under the bridge.' I proceed with caution. I read that gerbils are herbivorous, so I do not feed them any meat. The score is forty–thirty in the fifth set, and McEnroe serves an ace. The umpire says, 'Game, set and match.' These are all kinds and degrees of semantic or logical necessities.

The O and M grammars express natural necessities. Explanations of the way some patterns of human behavior unfold are based on empirical laws and hypotheses about the workings of material mechanisms. Twins tend to have similar personalities. Lithium tends to reduce the violence of mood swings in the manic/depressive disorder. Language abilities are grounded in Wernicke's and Broca's areas of the brain. These are all kinds and degrees of natural necessities.

We have a loose cluster of grammars that express the standards of proper acts and actions for the human domain, the S grammar, the P grammar, the O grammar and the M grammar. The S grammar and P grammar express the powers of active human being to use habits and conventions as tools to accomplish their projects. The O grammar and the M grammar express the power of organic mechanisms in the genesis of human behavior.

Only the S grammar can be dispensed with. In practice the P grammar, the O grammar, and the M grammar fit together into hierarchies, complementing one another. We will look very closely at how they are brought into a coherent and unified hybrid psychology.

In the introduction to Part II, the Causal Picture and the Agentive Picture were presented as essential ingredients of psychology. Neither could be reduced to the other. The Causal Picture requires the use of the O grammar and the M grammar. The Agentive Picture requires the use of the P grammar.

The study of coughing, 'bexology', illustrates how the two pictures complement one another. You are at the opera, and Luciano Pavarotti is about the launch into 'Nessun dorma' in the last act of *Turandot*. You feel the bronchial tickle that precedes a cough. It is immensely difficult to override the bodily machinery to hold it back. Only a counter-cause will do. Perhaps you have taken the precaution of bringing some 'Fisherman's Friends'. To give an account of this event one would turn to the O and the M grammars. On another occasion you are chatting to a friend on the campus. Your friend is regaling you with the latest scurrilous gossip about the dean. You look up and there is the dean coming up behind your friend. You cough warningly. In this case you deliberately make use of the very same bodily mechanism that was almost uncontrollable in the opera house. To account for semantic coughs one invokes the P grammar. A similar analysis can be found in Button et al. (1995).

The intentional stance

Some fifteen years ago a somewhat similar suggestion to our one plus two grammars was made by D. C. Dennett (1987). He called his threesome 'stances'. A brief look at the similarities and differences between Dennett's 'stances' and Wittgenstein's 'grammars' will help to make the role of the latter yet clearer.

Dennett declares that his 'book is about how to talk about the mind' (Dennett, 1987: 1). Of course, we are now sensitive to the way that, unless the author makes an explicit disclaimer, such a declaration presupposes that there is a mind as a something, which exists independently of talk and other uses of symbolic systems. In effect, Dennett's proposal turns out to be a way of talking about mental activities, which do not necessarily presuppose any Cartesian supports in mind stuff.

Anticipating much of the line of this course, Dennett remarks that whatever we are doing, be it psychology or digging ditches, there is no way to avoid philosophical presuppositions. He asks what it is that organizes our capacity to be so good at understanding other people. The answer lies in the fact that we can predict each other's behavior. We can do that because we adopt 'the intentional stance' to one another. To adopt this stance is to treat 'the object whose behavior you want to predict as a rational agent with beliefs and desires … exhibiting what Bretano called intentionality' (Dennett, 1987: 15). By coming to a conclusion about what an agent ought to do we can predict what an agent will do.

Taking the intentional stance sounds remarkably like choosing to use the P or Person grammar in describing and critically discussing how we manage our public and private lives. However, there are some differences worth remarking. For a start, the P grammar has a much wider range of uses than in predicting what other people may do. Furthermore, according to the discursive point of view, thinking and acting intentionally is not a manifestation of mentality. It *is* mentality. The intentional stance is what we each take to ourselves as well as to others.

We have focused on meanings and norms, while Dennett focuses on desires and beliefs. This is not a trivial difference. The idea that individual beliefs and desires are the raw material of inferences as to what people will do is simplistic. Much of what people do is what is required of them by their current material and social circumstances. There is very little room in most people's lives for the realization of the pattern 'This is what I want; this is what I believe will achieve it; so this is what I will do.' Dennett's human being is not only a psychological individual but also managing life in a much more self-aware way than most of us achieve.

Complementary to the intentional stance are the physical stance and the design stance. In taking the physical stance to some object one tries to discover its material constitution. This allows one to use the laws of physics and chemistry to predict what it will do in this or that circumstance. This is similar to the way we sometimes find it useful to construe certain aspects of our lives by the use of the M or Molecular grammar. Adopting the design stance involves acting on the assumption that the object was designed to behave in a certain way. Therefore, it will so behave in the appropriate circumstances. This is not unlike what happens when one construes one's life by using the O or Organism grammar.

Certain aspects of human lives are highlighted by the adoption of each of these stances. However, Dennett treats the three as if they were, so to say, on the same level ontologically, that is, with respect to the categories of beings the existence of which is presupposed in adopting each stance. Molecules and organisms exist independently of discourses, though what we pick out from the array of material existents to fill our categories will be determined by the categories we possess. Mental phenomena are quite different. We have learned to see them not as attributes of a mental substance. They are nothing but aspects of the flow of joint action in accordance with local norms of correctness and propriety. Those relevant to cognitive psychology are properties of discourse.

Skill

The P grammar is both an expression of the implicit rules and conventions according to which people carry out cognitive and practical tasks and an important device for performing the appropriate act–actions explicitly and knowingly. What exactly is the status of 'implicit rules and conventions'? They do not exist in a hidden realm of unobservable cognitive processes as molecules exist in a hidden realm of unobservable physical processes. The concept of 'skill' needs to be imported into psychology to complete the account of psychology as the management of meaning. In acting skillfully a person picks out relevant aspects of his or her external and internal environment. What that person then does is subject to standards of correctness and propriety. A person acquires skills by training and practice. To a skilled person correct action is 'second nature'.

However, just like the friend who consciously made use of the bronchial cough mechanism for a discursive purpose, so from time to time people pay attention to how well they are using their skills. Sometimes they 'work on them', going back to some earlier stage in their lives, when the skill was being acquired.

How can the P grammar be both a resource for description of and commentary upon action and a guide to action? It is possible only because it has become second nature. It is *immanent* in skills and good habits.

Meta-discourses or 'human sciences'

Since scientific psychology is itself the product of the cognitive activities of human beings it must be applicable to itself. Human sciences, according to our point of view, must include discourses about discourses. If the cognitive performances of ordinary life are shaped by implicit commitment to the P, O and M grammars, these are the organizing principles of the folk psychology that ordinary people use to manage their lives. We could call them 'primary discourses'. What then of the grammars that shape the thought patterns and practices of psychologists researching the cognitive activities of ordinary people going about their ordinary daily business?

When we examine examples of contemporary psychological research we find that there are broadly speaking two sets of explanatory concepts in use:

1   Most phenomena are analysed into *cause-effect pairs* (the Causal Picture).
2   A few phenomena are analysed into *rule-governed sequences of meanings* (the Agentive Picture).

A psychological problem is usually identified by the use of the concepts drawn from taxonomies of meanings and rules, from our ordinary vernacular. Subsequent research programs tend to be couched in terms of causal concepts. However, there are no mental causes and effects, according to the discursive point of view. They are an illusion produced by using causal *concepts* to redescribe what are actually discursive phenomena. Causal concepts are appropriate only for describing and explaining events and processes in the material world. They belong in discourses using the O and M grammars. By the same argument, the use of concepts from the meanings and rules repertoire should be restricted to discourses using the P grammar. Mosquitoes act purposively but not intentionally, and so do babies. Acids act causally but neither purposively nor intentionally. If we are talking about meanings and the performance of acts, there is no place for causes, and if we are talking about molecules there is no place for reasons.

I believe that most of academic psychology as a secondary discourse is shaped by the same trio of grammars as shapes the primary discourse, namely P, O and M grammars. Psychologies, in their historical and contemporary variety, are among the secondary genres. Some favor the cluster of P grammars, and so value folk-psychological explanations and analyses (Smedslund, 1988). Others favor the O grammar and so emphasize sociobiology and ethology (Wilson, 1998), while yet others favor the M grammar and neuropsychology, looking for explanations of this or that feature of human life in terms of neurotransmitters and the like (Churchland, 1986).

Seen thus, there is the possibility of tertiary discourse genres, shaped by the same P, O and M grammars. Among these is the psychology of psychology. This is no fantasy. For example, Potter and Wetherell (1987) examine the psychological character of psychologists' discourses about psychological phenomena. Freud's use of cocaine may call for an M grammar discussion.

The S grammars that involve notions like 'soul' and 'spirit' do not play an explicit role in psychology as building principles of scientific discourses. In other times and places they have been very important. Descartes's psychology of the self as a 'mental substance', which also doubles as the immortal soul, is just such a grammar. However, the S grammar does play a covert role in contemporary scientific studies of human life. Why are such thinkers as Francis Crick so passionately devoted to finding a proof of materialism? I believe it is because they fear the continuing influence of religion on our ways of thinking about people and our practices for dealing with them. We can trace this negative influence back into the eighteenth century, when the philosophers of the Enlightenment, such as Voltaire, were so hot against the established Church.

As we have come to see it the task of psychology is to produce a discourse about human thinking, feeling and acting that has certain attributes, those of the kinds of discourses we are accustomed to call 'the sciences'. The problems that have beset psychology in the last hundred years can be put down, in large part, to setting about this admirable task with a false picture of the established sciences. In this course we have already acquired a good knowledge of how physics is actually done. Now we have to bring that knowledge to the task of abstracting, from the many false starts revealed in the history of psychology, the right way to bring the project to fruition.

At the same time, we must not lose sight of the fact that ordinary people face the same task every day of their lives – how to make sense of what people, including themselves, think, feel, perceive and do. How are we to keep our feet firmly on the solid ground of everyday psychological knowledge and skills while building a superstructure of explanatory models that anchors our psychological discourse in the solid ground of good scientific practice and the neural mechanisms of the embodied person?

There is a further complexity that cannot be ignored in concrete research. This is the differences in the degree of access to cognitive resources available to different people, and the differences in the rights of others to use this or that resource. Some of these differences and distinctions are very well known. Some have been researched in a relatively new branch of social psychology, 'position-ing theory' (van Langenhove and Harré, 1999).

Positioning: the moral dimension

New Paradigm research in social psychology has shown that there are subtle and contextually sensitive presuppositions about the distributions of rights and duties to perform certain categories of acts. These implicitly constrain rights of access to the materials needed to carry out cognitive projects, be they in ordinary life or in psychological research programs.

These rights to access and to use discursive resources differ from person to person, and for any one person, from time to time. The term 'position' has been used to refer to those momentary clusters of rights and duties to think, act and speak in certain ways that are evident in the flux of everyday life. A position is linked with the kinds of acts that a person in that position can be 'seen' or 'heard' to perform by the use of meaningful signs. Positions and permissible repertoires of act–actions are linked to the story line, the conventional narrative, that the people so positioned, are in the process of living out. In a trial the various partici-pants are formally positioned with respect to what sorts of speech acts they can legitimately be heard to perform. The judge may refuse to allow what someone says to be 'heard'. It must be struck from the record. A witness is so positioned that he or she is not permitted to draw inferences from the matters of fact reported. This pattern of position/speech act/story line is all but ubiquitous in human affairs.

In one respect our studies of cognitive practices and the tools we use to carry them out are necessarily abstracted from the domain of concrete human activities. We are abstracting from the fluid and shifting positions that people occupy, resist, impose on others, refuse to take up and so on. Our interest is in what people do and how they do it when they are authorized or take themselves to be authorized to do it. Of course, disputing about whether or not oneself or some other person is authorized, that is positioned in a certain way, is sometimes an exercise of reason and subject to the conditions of well grounded and well rounded thought. But whether a claiming or disclaiming of a position is adequate or not is dependent on the particular content of what is under dispute, the status of the disputants and the larger social context.

The ontology of persons

We must pause to take a closer look at the ontology of the P or Person grammar. Let us set out the parallel between the ontology of physics and the ontology of cognitive science, as it is revealed in the P grammar expression presuppositions.

1   In physics there are charges and poles, their fields and the motions that are the observable products of the interaction of their causal powers.

2   In cognitive psychology we have persons, their skills and capacities, and the meaningful actions that are the observable products of their mutual activities.

Thus far we have a nice parallel. However, the P grammar ontology is more complex.

1   Persons are not only originating actors. They are also aware of things and events in the material environment and of things and events within their own bodies. Not only are people aware of these material domains, but they are also aware of the centered structure of these domains. Each person experiences the environment and his/her own body as centered on a vantage point, so the story goes, from which each person perceives the world. For each person there is just one such field of objects and events perceived, with just one center. Kant called this vantage point the 'transcendental unity of apperception'.

2   The products of the activity of charges and poles are motions or incipient motions. Motions have magnitude and direction, relative to some frame of reference. The products of the activity of people are intentional actions, which have meanings as acts, relative to some local interpretative scheme. For the most part intentional actions are interpreted as acts in a field of people, sharing a project and a P grammar to plan and discuss it, if need be.

The concept of person, which serves us as the ontological anchor of our system, has much in common with William Stern's 'personalism'. Stern defines 'person' as follows: 'The "person" is an individual, unique whole, striving towards goals, self-contained and yet open to the world; capable of having experience' (Stern, 1938 [1939]: 70).[1] Stern comments that 'except for the criterion of "experiencing," which was purposely placed at the end, the specifications throughout are *psychophysically neutral*. Into the totality of the person are woven both his physical and psychical aspects' (ibid.). This is very close to the idea of 'embodied person' as we are using it in our studies. Furthermore, persons for Stern are essentially active.

> A living being is of such a character that its total *nature* is continually being actualized through its activity while likewise remaining a whole in its incessant intercourse with its environment.
>
> (Stern, 1938 [1939]: 71)

> The person is a totality, that is, a *unitas multiplex*. ... All the multiplicity included in the person ... is *integral* to the totality; ... it is the *consonance* of multiplicity with the personal whole and of the person with the world that makes human life possible.
>
> (Stern, 1938 [1939]: 73)

In other words, the biological, experiential and norm-regarding attributes of a person are the necessary characteristics of one entity, without any of which it would not exist as such. That entity is logically prior to and not the mere aggregate of these three sets of characteristics. Stern's ontology requires persons to be viewed as *sources* of activity: 'the person is not here regarded as a mere go-between or passive theatre of psychophysical events, but as the true generator and carrier, governor and regulator' (Stern, 1938: 85). The body is among the instruments a person can use for realizing projects.

Despite its forward-looking stance we come from Stern's account with a certain disappointment – personal being is given. How do persons come to be? We are not concerned in this course with development psychology but a brief sketch of the work of Lev Vygotsky is in point.

According to Vygotsky (1962), every higher cognitive function exists twice over, once in the social environment of a developing human being and then as a competence or cognitive skill to be exercised by that being. The mediation between social environment and individual person is achieved by a kind of psychological symbiosis. An infant's attempts at skilled performance, be they motor or intellectual, are supplemented by someone more skilled. At this point the skill is, as Vygotsky says, in the zone of proximal development. The infant takes up these supplementary supports into its personal repertoire of meaningful actions, and so competence or skill is acquired. An infant never appears in the social world as a wholly incompetent member of the family, since its individual deficits are made up for by the actions of others. Infants live as component parts of dyads and triads. These little groups perform cognitive and motor acts.

Persons are members of a world of persons.

'Mind–body' ties: three links between P, O and M discourses

We are now in a position to deal with one of the most persistent problems in the philosophy of psychology – traditionally formulated as the relation between mind and body. We seem forced to admit the truth of two incompatible ways of describing the activities of human beings.

When the P grammar is used, people appear as embodied actors performing intentional acts constrained by rules, customs and conventions. When the O and M grammars are used, people appear as complex organisms subject to material causality. Mental and material phenomena seem to be radically different in kind. Thoughts are weightless, free of the power of gravity. Limbs are locked in the gravitational field of the earth. Meaningless and meaningful signs can have similar dimensions and weigh the same.

Nevertheless, mental processes, such as deciding to throw a ball, seem to lead to material processes, the hand and arm moving in such a way as to project the ball into something like the trajectory the thrower intends. Injuries to the body seem to be the cause of painful sensations. Molecules of salicylic acid, aspirin, seem to be effective in eliminating some pain. And so on, through a huge catalogue of ways that the mental aspects of a person's being are inter-related with the material aspects. Mental and material phenomena seem to be causally related to one another. If they are radically different in kind, how can such causal relations possibly exist?

The situation seems irresolvable. It is easy to see how philosophers of psychology could be driven to adopt one or other extreme solution. If there are only material phenomena, there is no fundamental problem. If there are only discursive phenomena, there is no fundamental problem either. However, repeatedly, both ways of thinking about what people do seem to be forced upon us.

Could a way be found for people to have both within a *scientific* psychology?

Rethinking the problem

The project of setting up a hybrid science requires the symbol using capacities of human beings to be brought into a unified scheme with the organic aspects of members of the species *Homo sapiens*. This demands the dissolution of the mind–body problem. Can it be set aside as an illusion, based on a mistaken presupposition?

We can see how much cognitive science is in need of a unifying metaphor from the following quotations taken from some recent numbers of the leading journals in the field. One finds at least four ways of referring to the relation between activities described in the P grammar and processes and states of the brain described in the M grammar.

1   *Anthropomorphic: the brain personified*

'The *ability* of the right frontal lobe may be unique in integrating cognitive and affective information …'.

(*Brain* (1999) **122** p. 657)

'… part of the brain that *helps people* recognize themselves in a picture'.

(Attributed to Dr. J. Keenan, Beth Israel Medical Center, *The London Times*, 1999)

2   *Causal: Molecules to Mind*

'… ecstasy *affects* blood flow as well as *mood*'.

(*New Scientist* (2001) 2306, p. 19)

'… the right hemisphere is important in the *activation and maintenance* of peripheral meaning associations between words …'.

(*Cortex* (2001) 39/3, p. 341)

3   *Causal: Mind to Molecules*

'… [differentiating] those brain regions in the larger network of activation that are involved in langauge processing on the sentence level from those *activated by* text level processes'.

(*Cognitive Brain Research* (2001) 11/3 p. 337)

4   *Agnostic*

'... brain areas that *mediate* these talents [language and abstract thought]' and
'... human abilities *arise* in parts of the cortex'.

(*New Scientist* (2001) 2306, p. 7)

The point of presenting these quotations is not to criticize the authors of these passages. Rather, they illustrate the problem of finding a coherent and fruitful way of creating a common discourse in the face of the seemingly incompatible 'grammars' that are needed to describe the cognitive activities of human beings, thinking, remembering, managing meanings and so on. The next step is to try to find an acceptable way or ways of synthesizing the two branches of cognitive psychology into a unity.

The trick upon which the possibility of a unified cognitive science depends is to shift the focus from entities to discourses. We have already encountered the metaphor or leading idea with which the unification of the whole field of psychologically relevant discourses is to be accomplished, the metaphor of cognitive tasks and neural tools. It fits in neatly with a more traditional unifying principle: that relevant organs, material states and processes are picked out by association with discursive entities, states and processes, by the use of pre-existing cognitive criteria.

Having shifted the focus of our enquiries from the insoluble puzzle about how two wholly disjointed substances could interact, and avoiding the complementary pitfall of the attempt to build a human science on the basis of one or other of these alleged substances exclusively, we can turn to examine ways in which the Person-based discourse, the Organism-based discourse and the Molecule-based discourse are related to one another. There are at least two ways in which links are in fact established between the grammars that dominate the discourses of the Western form of life. There is the task/tool metaphor by which tasks defined in terms of the P discourse are accomplished by the use of tools described in terms of the O and M discourses. Skills and capacities defined in the P discourse are grounded in structures, states and processes described in O and M discourse terms. The second link comes about through the way that classificatory systems applicable to the entities, states and processes describable in the O and M discourses are dependent on classifications of entities, events and processes which are identified in the first instance as belonging to types defined in the P discourse.

The task/tool link

The idea that cognitive tasks often require the use of material tools will be developed in detail in Part IV. The first step in this sketch is to introduce the metaphor of 'brain as tool'. Consider the way human beings carry out certain cognitive tasks, such as adding up a bill. We are accustomed to think of a pocket calculator as a tool for doing sums. However, since that gadget is a prosthetic device, accomplishing cognitive tasks formerly performed by our brain, it seems entirely appropriate to apply the same concept to the brain, or a relevant region of it, when we are engaged in performing the cognitive task without using a prosthesis. A certain electronic device is a 'calculator' only in relation to the task it is used to perform.

Material tasks also engage persons as agents. There too we make use of material tools. Some of these are prostheses for body parts that are not neurological. For digging, we need spades. They are prostheses for hands, to which, in the absence of spades, we are obliged to have recourse, even now. Pieces of iron are 'spades' only in relation to the task they are devised to perform.

There are some tools that far outstrip their prosthetic ancestors, for both cognitive and material tasks. Bulldozers are spades of a sort, but of another order altogether when the task in hand is shifting earth. The same is true of computing machines when the task in hand is arithmetical or the reliable storage of vast amounts of data. How much better they are than an abacus or an inventory inscribed in cuneiform on clay tablets.

Finally there are cognitive tasks for which we use cognitive or symbolic tools, for instance reasoning carried on with propositions. At this point the simple task (P grammar)/tool (M grammar) scheme seems to be in need of further development. To produce a statement, expressing a proposition, which is to serve as a tool in the task of solving a problem, is to engage in a task using a material tool, one's brain. Here we seem to have the use of a tool to produce a tool. This, too, is a metaphor with a familiar place in industry. We shall explore this metaphor somewhat further in what follows.

What advantages does the task/tool metaphor have over ways of expressing the role of O and M entities and states as enabling conditions for P activities?[2] People do not generally talk of their brains as tools. However, the point of introducing a metaphor is to extend the power of the existing language to cope with new insights and situations. Boundaries that seem to be impenetrable need to be examined. The metaphor of body parts as tools seems unproblematic in such a piece of advice as 'If you can't find a trowel, use your hand to scoop out a hole to plant the seedling.' The idea of 'tool and task' seems already to be fully formed in the common injunction to someone stuck in some problem: 'Use your loaf!' meaning 'Use your head [brains].' 'Brain as a tool' is the scientifically innovative or creative concept that comes from the extensions of the 'Use your ...' metaphor, inviting us to look on our brains in a new way. Philosophical justification can be found in the prosthesis argument, set out above. Since calculator, electronic organizer and even one's pocket diary are tools for cognitive tasks, though there are cognitive skills needed to use them, we can also use our brains as prostheses for prostheses, stand-ins for 'extrinsic' cognitive tools. One can try, by reflection, to remember the appointments recorded in a mislaid diary. The brain or one of its modules is functionally equivalent to something that it is not at all controversial to classify as a tool.

Could we find a place for the program of artificial intelligence in the psychology inspired by the Second Cognitive Revolution? The adoption of the task/tool metaphor offers a natural way in which the technology of building machines to perform cognitive tasks can be integrated into a comprehensive psychology.

According to discursive psychology mentality is, for the most part, best construed as symbolic manipulations that are both intentional and normative. The models constructed by 'knowledge engineers' are analogs of cognitive processes. Programs are written which, when run on a computing machine, lead to states of the machine that can be construed by a human operator as answers to cognitive problems. Successful projects of this kind can serve a double purpose in psychology. The programs can be used as sources of hypotheses about the formal grammars of task setting, rule accessing and expressive activities generally. This application develops naturally from the demands of devising a program to simulate some human activity. An essential intermediate step is writing a hypothetical set of rules the following of which would lead to the required result. In this model it would be a state of the machine that could be read as 'an answer' to 'a question'.

In adopting the task/tool metaphor as the basis of a scientific psychology it would be natural to construe neural mechanisms as tools for performing mental tasks. Successful projects in artificial intelligence can also be recruited to the project of cognitive science, as the source of schematic representations of the material properties of the tools used in discursively defined projects. Since many of these tools are material systems found at various levels in the brain, the artificial intelligence models can, in some cases, serve as the source of important and perhaps testable hypotheses about brain architecture and brain functions. In Part IV we shall be following two case studies in which the dual role of artificial intelligence will prove the key to applying the task/tool metaphor.

In the light of our understanding of scientific method, how are we to construe the task/tool metaphor? It is clearly serving as a supertype, controlling a type hierarchy from which the various models for theorizing about human action can be drawn in a systematic fashion.

The Taxonomic Priority Principle

This thesis expresses the basic principle of the classificatory technique by which neural states, structures and processes are identified as relevant to cognitive processes. By the use of the Taxonomic Priority Principle (TPP) the proper tools can be picked out from among all the available material things as just those relevant for the tasks in hand. The molecular bases of memory, for instance, can be identified only if they are picked out in relation to acts of remembering performed by the people whose brain states and processes are being investigated. Similarly, we can identify certain features of people's brains as abnormalities only if we have a way of identifying abnormal kinds of speech or conduct. Unless we could identify cases of people having word-finding problems we could never identify a tangle of plaques as the relevant abnormality for Alzheimer's condition, nor could we look for damage to the immune system as the relevant abnormality for chronic fatigue syndrome.

In general, the criteria of identity for states, processes and structures of the P discourse exercise 'taxonomic dominance' over the criteria of identity for neural states and processes relevant to psychology, that is, for the O and M discourses. Relevant neural states and processes are picked out by attention to the cognitive states and processes that are occurring along with them. This is the Taxonomic Priority Principle. It has the effect of making the relation between mental states and processes and the relevant brain states and processes a necessary relation. It is conceptual, not empirical. This is an important point that needs spelling out. If the relation were empirical, items from each 'side' of it would have to be able to be picked out independently of the way items on the other side were identified. Then research might reveal that there was a correlation between them. In medicine there are plenty of examples of this kind of discovery. For instance, we identify coffee drinking according to certain criteria, and we identify Parkinson's disease by another and different set of criteria. These sets of criteria have nothing to do with each other. Research has established a very good correlation between coffee drinking and a low incidence of developing Parkinson's disease. However, if we use a PET scan to pick out the parts of the brain that are activated when someone is reading, the criteria for identifying those parts include the criteria for knowing whether someone is reading. It is a matter of logic that these are parts of the brain known as a 'reading machine'. This way of picking things out has been called 'top-down' classification.

There are ways in which such taxonomic relations, once established, are protected against disturbance. The most important has a central role in the establishment of empirical research projects in neuroscience. Here is how it works. Suppose we do an experiment on a subject, say carry out a PET scan of the participant's brain, while he or she is performing some cognitive task, say calculating. The Taxonomic Priority Principle allows us to identify what is revealed in the PET scan as among the relevant locations for the neural processes used for calculating. Imagine that we repeat the experiment on the same subject on another occasion and find a different neural process seemingly showing up in the PET scan. Do we abandon the thesis? No. We save it by the hypothesis that there is a so far unobserved neural process in common to both occasions. We set about trying to find it. The case is somewhat different if we repeat the experiment on a different subject and get a different result. In that case we tend to partition the population into two groups, for each of which the Taxonomic Priority Principle holds. For example, the finding that men and women read with different parts of their brain is not permitted to upset the principle. The problem is resolved by partitioning the human population into two groups by gender with respect to the skill of reading as defined in terms drawn from the P grammar.[3] Thus we have men readers and women readers as two P discourse categories, each with its relevant but different brain mechanisms.

Finally, we must be clear on the difference between the role of the task/tool metaphor as a supertype for model making and the Taxonomic Priority Principle. The latter is a conceptual principle, constraining the way that concepts in the three grammars *must be* construed so that the project of a unified psychological science can be achieved.

So far we have looked at the task/tool metaphor in a rather informal way. However, the introduction of the theory of science as model making allows us to give a much more precise characterization of the role that task/tool could play in the development of cognitive science. We have seen it as one of the ways by which the three grammars can be united into a cognitive system or paradigm of the management of practical and theoretical research in cognitive psychology, taken as a whole.

Psychology as a hybrid science

Having looked at the ways in which the P, O and M grammars can be bound together into a comprehensive conceptual system fit to serve as the basis of a science, the next step is to turn to the kind of science that will thereby be made possible.

Since doing psychology is a human activity, the same principles should apply to it, as to any other pattern of meaningful actions that realizes well established story lines. If psychology is a cluster of narrations, what are the relevant grammars? It would surely be unacceptable to most psychologists to describe their professional activities in the O and M grammar. Only if presented in the frame of the P grammar could credit be claimed for a successful research project, since only in a frame in which the concept of 'person' picks out the basic active particulars does the concept of responsibility have a place, and hence the concept of credit.

There is, in a sense, only one stream of action. As described in the P grammar it displays such phenomena as 'emotions', 'attitudes', 'memories', 'items of knowledge', 'performance of athletic feats' and so on. Using the metaphor of a stream, we might think of these phenomena as eddies, whirlpools, froth and waves in the continuous flow of meaningful action that dries up only on the brain death of the actor. Some are ephemeral and others more enduring.

In setting up an empirical science one begins by distinguishing the kinds of beings with which the study is concerned. A science starts with rudimentary classification schemes, simple type hierarchies. As the science matures, these develop in all sorts of ways. Since they express the kinds of beings with which the science is concerned, from a philosophical point of view, we have called them 'ontologies'.

The basic particulars

The prime directive for developing an ontology for an empirical science is: *seek the sources of activity*. They will be the basic or fundamental powerful particulars of the ontology.

It seems that the basic type hierarchy that has evolved in psychology in the course of the Second Cognitive Revolution has two main branches, one material and one discursive.

The first branch consists of the agents that produce material processes, in the environment and in the bodies of organisms. The active basic particulars are molecular clusters of a huge variety of types. For work on this branch we have recourse to a discourse style shaped by the M or molecular grammar. The mode of action of M entities is causal and deterministic.

The second branch consists of the agents to which we assign goal-seeking capacities, and for our purposes the basic active particulars are predominantly whole organisms. For this branch, we have recourse to the O or Organism grammar. The mode of action of O entities is teleological, in the manner discussed so subtly by Aristotle.

The third branch consists of the agents that produce patterns of symbols, that is, of meaningful signs. The active beings are embodied persons as intentional agents. For work in this branch we have recourse to the P or Person grammar. The mode of action of P entities is intentional, that is, by recourse to meanings and rules in the carrying through of projects.

As singular sources of action and the embodied centers of perceptual fields, people are centers of discursive activity. It is important to realize that, according to this ontology, when considered in relation to discursive activities, people are not *psychologically* complex. They produce complex private, public intentional, ever changing, and evolving structures of discursive acts. Those that are private we are inclined to call mental, thoughts and feelings, but *qua* intentional acts they differ not at all from public acts, except in so far as the interactor whose uptake completes the action as a meaningful act is, in the case of private acts, oneself. We produce our own minds, just as we produce conversations, tennis matches, orchestral performances, ditch digging and so on with others.

There are no hidden thought processes, feelings and perceptions of actions in the P domain, according to the point of view being developed here. The program of scientific realism is not to be fulfilled by postulating an imperceptible realm of unobservable *mental* mechanisms, as Freud did in introducing the unconscious *mind*. Scientific Realism in psychology is achieved by making use of the task/tool metaphor in proposing neural mechanisms as among the tools that people use for accomplishing their P grammar tasks. The workings, *but not the roles*, of these tools are described and explained in the M and O grammars. However, the M and O domains are tightly woven together in that O processes are routinely accounted for by recourse to hypotheses about hidden molecular processes. Since at least some M processes are observable in principle, the proposal of a hidden mechanism explanation of how tools work can often lead to a research program in an effort to verify the verisimilitude of the working model of the mechanisms on which the hypothesis depends.

Neither branch of the dual ontology can colonize the other. Human beings in the molecular ontology are machines with no moral attributes. Brains in the person ontology are tools for use in tasks set discursively. The task/tool metaphor will be developed more extensively in Part IV, when we study two real research programs. It is just the typology we need to bridge the distinction between bodily organs as structured molecular clusters and people, particularly in those cases in which the molecular clusters are parts of the bodies of those people, such as brains and hands.

Individualism and collectivism

The fact that some cognitive processes are both public and jointly conducted by more than one person, usually in a conversational interaction, raises the question of what sorts of collectives are capable of cognition. There are two main kinds of grouping that appear as referents in psychological discourses. There are structured collectives, like families and other institutions, which are self-maintaining groups, held together by real relations. Then there are taxonomic or purely notional collectives, logical constructs tied together because the individual members share some common properties. The members of taxonomic collectives are so rarely bound into a system by any real relations that we can safely neglect the possibility. It should be obvious that only structured collectives can be the sites of group cognition. We find joint public cognitive processes in the life courses of families, research groups, sports teams and so on. Only to these does P grammar analysis in terms of rules and intentional actions apply.

To illustrate the difference between an individualistic and static conception of psychology as the study of mental states and a discursive and dynamic conception of psychology as the study of intentional interactions, a discovery about older people's capacity to remember is very much to the point (Dixon, 1996). To remember something is to produce a representation of a past event in some form – verbal, pictorial, auditory and so on. Memorial acts are necessarily intentional in that the act refers beyond itself, in this case to something in the past. A putative memorial act is an act of remembering only if it is a reasonably correct representation of its purported target. Remembering is not only intentional but also normative. How is norm conformity established in remembering? Only in exceptional cases is it achieved forensically by finding concrete evidence of what happened. In everyday life, certification of memory is by negotiation, a discursive process among interested parties (Kreckel, 1981). Laboratory studies, in which evidential material is routinely and securely preserved as part of the experiment, able to be recovered intact and used to check the accuracy of recollections, are relevant to only a tiny proportion of everyday memorial acts.

Individual older people do not perform as well in laboratory tests of memory skills as younger people when both groups are tested individually. However, when older people are taking part in conversations about the past their capacity to remember is as good as that of young people when they are engaging in such conversations.

Why is Dixon's research so significant? Claims about the psychology of memory and aging, certifiable as 'scientific', not only affect other inhabitants of the laboratory and the readership of journals of gerontology. They leak out into the lay world, affecting the attitudes of the social services and employers to the capacities of older people. They also affect the confidence of older people in their own skills and abilities. The bald claim that older people do not remember as well as younger people is not only false, it is immoral!

(learning point) **Discursive psychology: the presuppositions**

The concept of a grammar (Wittgenstein)

1   An open set of rules and conventions that expresses the standards of correct use for symbols and intentional actions.
2   Each grammar is identified by the basic kinds of individuals its use presupposes.
3   In current use there are four main grammars:
   a)   S or Soul grammar.
   b)   P or Person grammar.

   (These grammars include rules for the use of moral concepts.)

   c)   O or Organism grammar.
   d)   M or Molecular grammar.

   (These grammars do not include rules for the use of moral concepts.) For our purposes we will be concentrating on P, O, and M grammars for contemporary psychology.

Positioning theory

Not everyone has equal access to or the right to use this or that grammar, or fragment of grammar. A cluster of rights, obligations and duties in the discursive domain is called a 'position'. Positions are related both to story lines and the acts that are the meanings of intentional actions.

The interrelationship of the four grammars

1   Hybrid psychology:

   a)   We should delete S grammar from our repertoire.
   b)   We should develop a comprehensive way of relating the brain and nervous system to the discursive acts of the conversational model of cognition.

      i)   *Task/Tool metaphor.* Tasks are defined in terms of meanings and rules of correct use of symbols and intentional actions. These are first order tools. Second order tools are identified by Taxonomic Priority Principle as those bodily parts, and prostheses, used by someone to perform the required tasks. (Tools work according to the laws and models of the natural sciences.) Examples: playing tennis, digging a ditch, remembering one's mother's birthday, solving a problem.
      ii)   *Taxonomic Priority Principle.* The criteria of identity for relevant entities in the brain and nervous system (O grammar) include the meanings and rules of symbol using (P grammar). Example: PET scans of a person performing a symbolic task to look for brain region excitation.

Conclusion

According to the outlook of the Second Cognitive Revolution, psychology is to be construed as the study of certain kinds of processes, streams of human actions and interactions to which a certain range of models or metaphors can be applied. The stream of events that is the product of human activity can be described in various ways. Each descriptive mode or 'grammar' highlights different features of the stream and leads us to partition it in different ways. Those phenomena we ordinarily take to be psychological, such as memories, the sense of self, attitudes, self-esteem, emotions and so on, are like eddies and standing waves on and in the stream of personal and interpersonal action.

The three dominant grammars in current use for describing and explaining what human beings do are the person or P grammar, the organism or O grammar and the molecular or M grammar. These titles emphasize the basic particulars that are characteristic of each way of examining the stream of human activity: persons, organisms and molecules. The P grammar includes the rules/meaning relation as the organizing principle of the P-type analysis of every same stream of activity. The O grammar includes a basic teleology that may or not be associated with cognition. The M grammar includes cause–effect relations as the organizing principles of a third way of analysing the stream of activity.

How could three grammars each describe the same stream of activity? If there are three grammars, in what sense is the stream of activity the same? The key to this conundrum is the distinction used throughout this chapter between actions, material processes intended by those who produce them, and acts, the meanings of actions to those who understand them. Analysed according to the cause–effect principle, the stream of activity consists of material events explicable in terms of the working of neural and other mechanisms. As analysed according to the rules/meaning principle the stream of activity consists of intentional actions explicable in terms of projects and rules. In general there is no one-to-one mapping from the individual events picked out by the M partition of the stream onto the actions picked out by the P partition. However, there is a firm tie between the kinds of things people do and the mechanisms they use to do them.

It is to the study of the stream of action that psychology is, or should be, primarily directed, according to the point of view of discursive psychology. It is to the flow of actions that a certain hierarchy of metaphors and corresponding models applies, and only to that flow. The P grammar metaphor of life as conversation will be illustrated in Part IV, in the worked examples of prominent research programs. Part of the point of using remembering and classifying as examples of hybrid psychology in action is to illustrate the contrast between imposing an M grammar on the phenomena, with its built-in preference for causal relations, and making use of the more natural P grammar, with its preference for meanings and rules as explanatory concepts.

Since it is people who produce the stream of actions, both individually and jointly, and both publicly and privately, there is a secondary study of no less importance. It is directed to working out what people must know and the skills they must have acquired to be able to take part in the intentional and normative activities of everyday life. The way people have to be able to cope with the whole gamut of human life cannot be accommodated under one grammar any more than the events they take part in can. Unlike classical physics, in which a single type hierarchy comprehends the ontology of all the beings in its domain, and thus requires only one comprehensive grammar, psychology is irreducibly hybrid. Human beings are present to the world and to each other in three forms: as persons, as organisms and as complex clusters of molecules. None of the grammars grounded in these ontologies can be dispensed with, and none can be extended to comprehend the others without incoherence.

Notes

1   Translation by Michael Bamberg from the original edition.
2   My understanding of the task/tool metaphor was greatly advanced in discussions with Bennett Helm and John Deigh.
3   This point became clear to me during a discussion with Kevin Weinfurt.

Cognitive science: the analytical phase

Cognitive tasks and symbolic tools

According to discursive psychologists, cognitive tasks are accomplished by the skillful use of symbols. The conversational model directs our attention particularly to linguistic performance. For example, to consider the pros and cons of a decision is to engage in a kind of debate, which may literally take the form of a conversation. Cognitive projects like remembering, deciding, expressing disapproval, coming to an opinion, are often accomplished linguistically, or by symbolic activities that are language-like. However, there are many kinds of symbols in use for carrying through cognitive tasks other than words. Scientific thinking often involves thought experiments, performed in the mind with imaginary apparatus. Many technical cognitive tasks are done by the use of graphs and diagrams. These symbolic devices are first order tools. People use them for accomplishing their cognitive projects.

Cognitive tasks and first and second order tools

The basis of hybrid psychology as cognitive science is the principle that symbolic/linguistic skills are materially grounded in brain structures and neural processes. These are the second order tools with which we carry out tasks with the first order tools of symbolic repertoires. Bodily organs are material tools. People use them for all sorts of tasks, some cognitive and some practical. As we found in the last chapter, the tool metaphor is both complex and hierarchical. Some cognitive tasks are carried out by the use of an appropriate symbolism, as when we carry out a calculation by writing out the arithmetical steps as a pattern of numerals. The same applies when we manage to reassure someone of our intentions by repeating a promise even more vehemently than when we first gave it, and so on. Symbols are a kind of toolkit. We use our neural equipment as tools to manipulate symbolic tools.

From whence do these toolkits come? The properly shaped brain develops as a cognitive toolkit by explicit training regimes. More important, however, is the role of psychological symbiosis emphasized by Vygotsky (1962). He demonstrated the way the efforts of a novice to carry out some task are complemented by contributions from someone more skilled. The novice imitates these contributions and so becomes capable of doing the job by him/herself. For the most part symbolisms have their origins in collective practices. They are maintained and passed on as traditions, slowly changing from epoch to epoch.

The hybrid science principle again

To be able to accomplish cognitive tasks with symbolic or first order tools we must be using second order tools, our brains and hands, in performing the routine moves with which the higher order task is accomplished. I cannot add 15,679 to 34,598 unless I can add 9 to 8 to make 17. To perform the latter task I use my brain, while for the former I use my hand to write down the elementary formulas as tools to accomplish the more complex task.

If language and language-like systems were major instruments in many human activities, particularly those we generally regard as psychological, studying their uses would be a way of studying these activities, in a concrete fashion. This would be especially so if, though private, such activities had public expression in language or something language-like. While the causal metaphysics reigns in neural studies, the meaning/rule metaphysics reigns in symbolic studies.

Misled by a mythical version of the methodology of the physical sciences, psychologists have carried out all sorts of research projects into important aspects of cognition, framed in the Causal Picture. The first part of this chapter will be devoted to illustrating how to recover the results of these experiments within the Agentive Picture, by careful redescription and reinterpretation. We will learn how to translate from a misleading cause/effect presentation to a more plausible meaning/rule interpretation.

Reinterpreting experiments

Instruments, experiments and measurement in physics

Physicists make use of two broad kinds of laboratory apparatus. Psychologists have borrowed the terminology of the physics laboratory to describe the devices they use in empirical studies. We need to decide to which of the two main categories the so-called 'instruments' of psychology belong. This is of the greatest importance, since the ways they are each related to the domain they are used to investigate are very different.

There are devices that change their state under the causal influence of some changing property of the environment in a way which varies systematically with changes in the environment. For example, a thermometer measures the degree of heat in its immediate environment because the length of the mercury column is causally related to the level of molecular energy in its surroundings. The same principle governs the use of the barometer, the hygrometer, the voltmeter and many other instruments. Let us call a piece of equipment of this kind an 'instrument'.

There are also devices that are material analogs or models of some real physical system. For example, a gas discharge tube is a model of the upper atmosphere and the current in it is an analog of the solar wind. The glow in the tube is an analog of the aurora borealis. A calorimeter with a mixture of ice and salt can be treated as an analog of the sea in winter, and so on. Let us call this kind of equipment 'apparatus'.

Only the first kind of device can yield measurements. They are simply read off the changing state of the instrument. The height of the mercury is a consistent effect of the molecular state of the hot liquid. So we say the temperature *of the air* is 22° C, though what we observe is the length of the mercury column. The relation of the measured to the measurer is causal and deterministic.

Devices of the second kind have all sorts of important uses. However, no measurement can be derived from a property of the model. The relation between device and reality is analogy, not causality. We can say that the freezing point of the sea is −4° C on the basis of the behavior of the saline solution in the calorimeter. It may be a good estimate but it is not a *measurement* of a property of the sea. It is an inference by analogy from a property of the model to a property of the subject of the model. We can use the calorimeter model to explain why ice floats on the surface of the sea, leaving liquid water below.

Instruments, experiments and measurements in psychology

Psychologists use expressions like 'instrument', 'experiment' and 'measurement', which are almost certainly borrowed from the physical sciences. Could they mean the same thing as physicists mean by the use of these words? Since there are at least two kinds of experimental equipment used in physics, instruments and apparatus, with very different logics, we may find that, while psychologists could not be using one of these kinds, they might be using something that conforms to the logic of the other. That is indeed just what we find. Unfortunately, most psychologists are seriously confused about these matters. They tend to interpret the study of set-ups corresponding to apparatus, which are actually models or analogs of that which they help us to investigate, as if they were measuring instruments, the properties of which are effects of causally efficacious states of that which is measured.

Psychologists use the word 'instrument' for such devices as questionnaires and checklists. 'Subject' answers questions or checks off items. The experimenter performs statistical analyses of the answers. If this were an instrument of the same type as those used in physics, the answers should vary systematically with some varying property of the subject. The relevant property that varies should be varying in that subject, and causing a variation in the properties of the instrument.

Are questionnaires really instruments like thermometers? To answer this one must pay close attention to what is going on when someone provides written or spoken answers, marks a checklist or indicates a point on a Lickert multi-point scale. The participant is answering questions posed by the psychologist. This joint activity is a kind of formal conversation. As such, a questionnaire is a *model* of an informal conversation. The answers to the questionnaire are not caused by some mysterious unobservable property of the person answering it. The results of using a questionnaire as an 'instrument' in a psychological investigation are not measurements at all. They are logically parallel to the results of using an apparatus as a model or simulation of a real-world set-up and reasoning analogically from the one to the other.

The point of the experiment can be understood only by examining the analogy between the questionnaire as formal conversation and an ordinary discussion of the same topic. The results of the whole procedure, particularly the bringing out of correlations between types of questions and types of answers, are neither more nor less than expressions of narrative conventions and semantic rules governing the kind of conversation modeled.

Interpreting empirical studies in terms of concepts like 'instrument' and 'measurement' presupposes a causal metaphysics. Reinterpreting such studies in terms of concepts like 'model' and 'simulation' presupposes a meanings/rules metaphysics. Let us now look closely at an example in which the reinterpretation enables us to recover interesting and cognitively significant results from what otherwise would have to be dismissed as nonsense.

Transposing an experiment from the causal to the agentive frame

Can the results of investigations mistakenly interpreted as 'measurements obtained by using an instrument' in an 'experiment' be recovered and reinterpreted in a way that would make sense? In a study reported by Long et al. (1994) the people involved, already cast in a passive role by being called 'subjects', were asked to take part in two kinds of conversation. One was called 'brainstorming', an informal conversational format, and the other was more formal. There were two versions of the formal conversational format. In one, participants answered questions about themselves and the groups to which they belonged. In the other, the conversational task was to evaluate the results of the brainstorming sessions. Both formal conversations took the form of answering questionnaires. The results of the analysis of these conversations were called 'intercorrelations of self-esteem measures' (ibid.: 319).

The metaphysical presupposition of the uses of the term 'measurement' must have been that there was a hidden state in each of the participants, their self-esteem, which caused them to answer the questions in certain ways, different answers caused by different degrees of self-esteem. (In physics a gas thermometer and a mercury thermometer can yield results that are intercorrelated as a measure of the hidden state of the gas, namely its internal energy.) However, if we think for a moment about the content of the 'self-esteem' experiment, it should be quite clear that this could not possibly be the right description of the results. The 'data' were actually contributions to three overlapping conversations, concerning the opinions the conversants had about themselves and about other people.

The first involved such conversation openers as the Texas Social Behavior Inventory, and replies were constrained by using the usual n point scales. The second conversation was on environmental issues. The third required the people who took part to rate the solutions proffered in the second conversation on various discursive criteria such as clever, witty, etc. The third conversation was presented as a measure of 'collective self-esteem'. There were two formal conversations, more or less about an informal conversation, which were compared by the 'experimenters'.

Despite the causal rhetoric implicit in the use of expressions like 'inter-correlations', and in the use of terms like 'predictors', 'influence' and so on, a glance at the results of the analysis makes it quite clear that what was actually brought out were semantic rules and discursive conventions. These express some of the local conventions for talking about oneself and about one's fellows and their relation to people in other groups. In short, the answers to the questionnaires are not effects of high and low states of Personal and Collective self-esteem (for which the scientistic formula-like abbreviations PSE and CSE were used). They are displays of the implicit knowledge of rules and conventions required for carrying on such conversations. They could not be effects of some internal property of the minds of the participants. Even if there were such a property, it could not have been accessed by the use of a questionnaire. A questionnaire is not an instrument. It is a piece of apparatus, enabling the investigators to set up a working model of the process being studied.

The causal language continued into the presentation of the results (ibid.: 326). 'Where CSE does produce those differentiation effects [namely, talking about one's own crowd differently from talking about another crowd], encouraged by the comparative context, this is clearly stronger for low CSE than for the high CSE, which is the exact reverse of the pattern for PSE.' Since both CSE and PSE are not mental states of different people but collections of discourse conventions, all the experimenters can possibly be doing is trying to see the differences between two ways of speaking, each appropriate to its subject matter. The expression 'comparative context' simply refers to the kinds of story line to which the authors of these discourse fragments were required to conform to produce a meta-meta-discourse - a publishable psychology paper.

The sad thing about this example, and the hundreds like it that find their way into print, is that while they can be made sense of in the discursive frame, the choice of an inappropriate causal rhetoric not only obscures the real results but encourages an attitude to other people that is deeply worrying. One's fellow human beings are not automata, their behavior driven by such alleged mental states as high and low PSE and CSE, but fellow contributors to the human conversation. The 120 people (referred to as 'males' and 'females', as if they were animals) deserve better than this from those they helped in their researches and so in their careers.

Conversational dispositions and skills are grounded in material states of the brain, not in anything psychological. Nor does knowledge and conversational skill vary in one person, as heat varies in one sample of water. Presumably, *different* participants give *different* answers to the questionnaire. Therefore, even if there were an unobservable mental state that was being measured, it would be like length or height, which varies from object to object but is invariant in each. The statistical analysis of the results of using questionnaires is not like the statistical corrections to the result of making many physical measurements of the same property, say the temperature of molten sodium. It is not about variations in the properties of individuals at all, but about distributions of properties in a population. It is not, and never could be, a measure of a property that inheres in one person.

Thus when Argyle (1987) did a study of happiness by asking people to fill in questionnaires about their lives, he was accessing the stories people tell about their lives. So what he was getting from analysing them was a mix of semantic rules for the use of the word 'happy' and the conventions for telling autobiographical stories to a stranger – story lines, in short.

Reinterpreting a statistical analysis in the agentive frame

I want to drive home the point made in the last section by turning to the problem of the interpretation of statistical analyses of the answers given to the questions posed in questionnaires and interviews. I shall use as an example an excellent doctoral study of how responsibility for one's emotions is assigned to one by other people and by oneself. It is the work of Matthew Spackman (1998).

Having obtained answers to his questionnaires, Spackman subjected these to a standard multivariate analysis. It led to him to identify certain 'predictor variables' for ascriptions of responsibility for one's emotions. *Mentions of* intended actions, feelings and thoughts correlated positively with the *attribution of responsibility* for the emotion to the person who displayed it, as did mentions of awareness of such feelings and actions. On the other hand, mentions of the intensity and the appropriateness of the emotion correlated negatively. If it was thought that one intended to shout at someone, and that one was aware of that intention, then one was held responsible for the emotion. If the emotion was intense, when one was really mad at someone, or inappropriate, irritated by some trivial error, one was not held to have been responsible. These are correlations between aspects of a conversation between Dr Spackman and the participants in his study, namely *between what was mentioned by the participants* (Spackman, 1998: 48). How are these correlations to be interpreted?

A correlation can turn up for three reasons. It may be because the correlated items are linked by a causal relation, there being some mechanism that produces the one when triggered by the other. For example, one may wince when subjected to a 'Chinese burn'. It may be that one of the items is part of the meaning of the other. For example, flying is never mentioned when talking about kiwis, since a kiwi is defined as a flightless bird. Finally, it may be that there are narrative conventions that require that if one sort of thing is said then another sort should follow it. If one refuses an invitation one must give a reason. In which categories do Spackman's correlations fall?

Clearly the first two are semantic. What it means to be responsible is to know what one is doing and to intend it. So is the third, since the implication of qualifying the emotion as 'intense' is that the emotion display is out of the control of the person. It is part of the meaning of the concept of responsibility that one cannot be held responsible for what one cannot help. Inappropriateness is more uncertain, but it seems not to be semantically related to responsibility. Rather it seems to highlight a narrative convention, that anecdotes about emotions should make sense. That seems to entail that contextually inappropriate emotions are meaningless, and so could not be relevant to attributions of responsibility.

Spackman's results are wholly explicable within the framework of meanings, rules, conventions and story lines. Moreover, that makes them very interesting indeed. They reveal how we use the concept of responsibility and how we are supposed to tell stories about episodes in which issues about responsibility for emotions can be or have been raised.

Causal interpretations as rhetoric

Much contemporary psychology is written in causal language, as if it were an M discourse. However, a close look at the methods adopted in many research programs shows that this is an inappropriate grammar. It must be interpreted not as a substantive frame, alternative to the meaning/rule frame, but as a rhetorical device adopted to give a certain air of prestige to the report. Why can this be said with such certainty? Because the actual method of research involves the participants giving commentaries on the narratives with which the 'experimenter' presents them. It may also involve a participant trying to find the right words to describe him or herself, and so on. These are all narrative matters, of how a story should be told. They are analysed by the researcher, usually along with other discursive material. Despite the fact that questionnaires and checklists and so on are *called* 'instruments', and the answers that are given to them are called 'data', and the results of analysing these discourses are called 'measurements', they are nothing of the sort, *if those words mean what they mean in physics*. If they do not mean what they mean in physics it would be well for the researchers who use them to enlighten us as to what they do mean. It can hardly fail to turn out that they are names for discourse categories.

We are in the world in which everything we say must be framed within the P grammar. We are describing what people did or were required to do in a certain context, not what they were caused to do. Any necessity in the pattern of action of the participants can have only two sources: the social set-up of the experiment and/or the semantic, syntactic and pragmatic rules for using symbols in the appropriate way. While many psychologists think they are doing mainstream psychology and conforming to the scientistic paradigm, they are actually doing something different but quite respectable, namely some small-scale discourse analysis. What they present as causal laws are none other than discourse conventions. They are narratologists, despite themselves.

Two worked examples

Drawing such dramatic conclusions from a theoretical analysis of the nature of the scientific method, itself a loose conglomeration of techniques, needs support from some worked examples. I shall offer three case studies to substantiate the discursive turn as the route to a paradigm for psychological research that really does emulate the methods used in experimental physics. Two have been chosen to illustrate the fallacy of misappropriate uses of the causal frame in two regions of the domain of the P grammar. The third is a sketch of the way discursive methods can be used to penetrate a range of psychological phenomena that, until recently, have been outside the scope of psychology altogether.

Attitudes: the causal interpretation

In ascribing an attitude to someone, am I attributing a permanent mental state to that person or commenting on the way that person performs certain discursive acts?

Presented within the causal frame of the recent tradition, attitudes are treated as if they played the role of unobservable causes of observable behavioral effects. Having this attitude causes this behavior. Anti-intellectualism or philistinism is an attitude and showing contempt for high culture is one of its effects. Here is an example of the attribution of just this attitude. However, we shall see that the cause–effect metaphysics cannot possibly be the right interpretation of the metaphysical status of whatever it is that the word 'attitude' is supposed to pick out.

> What was it that made so many of us detest Margaret Thatcher, though in many ways still admire her. Partly it was her deep philistinism, amounting not just to a failure to understand, but a positive hatred of culture, learning, and civilization.
>
> (Warnock, 2000)

Here we have a quite straightforward citation of an attitude, philistinism, as a correlate of certain patterns of behavior, in which Lady Thatcher displays her hatred of learning and culture. Notice that the author of this powerful condemnation uses the phrase 'amounting to' to express the thought that philistinism just consists of those displays. There is no suggestion that there is some hidden cognitive state, 'philistinism', causally responsible for what Lady Thatcher shows in what she says and does. An attitude is evident in a display. It describes a kind of display. It cannot be cited as a cause of a display, any more than being pasta can be cited as the cause of the constitution of spaghetti.

Sources of the 'hidden cause' interpretation of 'attitude'

To understand how this mythical type of mental state came to be part of the ontology of mainstream psychology a look at the history of the uses of the word 'attitude' is most instructive. We are fortunate in having available a brilliant study of the history of psychological terminologies, Danziger (1997).

As Danziger tells the story, the concept of 'attitude' was first used to describe the way a person appeared in public, especially the positioning of the body. The link between bodily posture and psychological state was established through the thesis that public bodily postures (attitudes) expressed private thoughts and feelings. Expression was not causation. In this important respect, we find that early understandings of how the private and the public aspects of human psychology were linked were very much as Wittgenstein saw them in his later psychological writings. Groaning is not caused by pain, but expresses it. The tendency to groan and the unpleasant feeling are aspects of a single psychological whole. Leaning back against the bar in a Wild West saloon expresses wary contempt.

In recent decades the all-pervading metaphysics of causality has overlaid the original expressive relation between the private and the public. Commenting on the current metaphysics, Danziger remarks:

> The link between the two domains is [purportedly] causal. Dispositions like motives, attitudes, and personality characteristics are conceived of as causing 'behavior', much as a gas under pressure might cause the movement of a cylinder.
>
> (Danziger, 1997: 138)

The full oddity of this metaphysical shift will come out only when we turn to the methodological innovations that accompanied it. It seems to have come with the development of a method of attitude 'measurement', derived more or less directly from market research. This was the now almost ubiquitous questionnaire method of enquiry, misaligned with the use of instruments in the physical sciences.

The search for a methodology led directly to market research as the source of a working psychology. Opinions, that which was expressed in the answers that people gave to questionnaires, were, it was assumed, the outward and visible expression of inner and invisible mental entities, attitudes which caused the questions to be answered in specific ways:

> [of] getting agree/disagree responses, usually from groups of students, to opinion statements that intercorrelated sufficiently to form what was called a 'scale'. The use of several, statistically linked, opinion statements distinguished attitude 'scaling' from opinion polling. ... [the aim was to measure] supposedly universal attributes of the hypothetical entities underlying surface opinions.
>
> (Danziger, 1997: 151)

To make this step, to shift attitudes from expressive displays to causes of behavior, the metaphysics had to be more clearly made out, and attitudes located as attributes of individual people.

> 'attitude' is more than simply a dispositional term. It is taken as referring to an actually existing state of affairs inside the individual ... Underpinning its use,

there is a whole metaphysic of unobservable but real and distinct entities that push and direct the person from within. This image gives plausibility to the idea that attitudes can be *measured*. ... When discussing the change from the original, expressive use of 'attitude' to its psychological use, we noted that this involved a splitting of the older unity between an inner state and its outward expression.

(Danziger, 1997: 145)

This splitting was not the result of an empirical discovery. It came about through the shift from a normative metaphysics of meaningful action to a causal metaphysics of behavior. And that, as Danziger shows both in this book and in his earlier classic, *Constructing the Psychological Subject* (1990), was driven by social forces independently of any theoretical arguments that might have backed it up. From a scientific point of view, it was quite gratuitous.

Here we have the same sequence of seemingly innocent steps that lead from a well founded concept for an important aspect of people in action to a gratuitous and unsupported innovation.

The metaphysics of the contemporary attitude is clearly stated by Olson and Zanna (1993: 131). They say that 'the utility of the attitude concept rests on the assumption that attitudes influence behaviors'. Since there could be no such influence, the conclusion must be that the concept has no utility. If we find that one form of expression of an attitude is correlated with another form of expression of the same attitude we have not proved that a common inner state exists. All we have discovered is either a semantic rule expressing synonymy between two forms of expression, or a narrative convention for a self-justifying story. To try to revive the causal story by inserting 'specific behavioral intentions' as the causes of 'specific behaviors' will not work, since the same argument applies.

The famous study of attitudes to educational achievement by Stevenson et al. (1993) revealed that American parents were very satisfied with the education their children were getting. Of course, this correlates with 'presenting a positive attitude'. This is a powerful discursive rule or narrative convention in the United States, that shapes how one talks about things that matter to one. It is then simply a semantic consequence of this rule that American parents say they are satisfied with the education provision. The one cannot fail to be a predictor variable for the other, since they are internally related as components of the same concept. We can infer nothing whatever about the quality of the education offered at primary schools in the United States from this research.

'Expressing an attitude to ...' is one way of describing how people evaluate other people, social practices and even brands of coffee. It is a discursive category. Explanations of how evaluations vary have to be based on the narrative conventions for telling stories of various kinds, including answering questionnaires for psychologists.

But what sort of attributes? Here is an analogous case that should make the matter very clear. Tigers and lions are felines. The category of 'feline' is classificatory. It would obviously be a mistake to invoke an unobservable property of this lion, its felineness, in explanation of why it was carnivorous, purred when contented and so on. In the same way, an attitude word is classificatory. It is a collective name for a variety of semantically related ways of making favorable and unfavorable comments on some practice.

Theory of mind

This popular phrase has been used a great deal in writing up research into the development of cognitive skills by infants and children, and even appears in the presentations of some animal studies.[1] The phrase was probably first used by Premack and Woodruff over twenty years ago.

> In saying that an individual has a theory of mind, we mean that an individual imputes mental states to himself [*sic*] and to others (either as conspecifics or to other species as well). A system of inferences of this kind is properly viewed as a theory, first because such states are not directly observable, and second, because the system can be used to make predictions about the behavior of other organisms.
>
> (Premack and Woodruff, 1978: 515)

Humphrey made the tie with language as the bearer of the 'theory of mind' explicit.

> There is, as far as I know, no language in the world that does not have what is deemed an appropriate vocabulary for talking about the objects of reflexive consciousness, and there are no people in the world who do not quickly make free use of this vocabulary.
>
> (Humphrey, 1984: 3)

Where do the concepts expressed by the vocabularies and grammars of different languages come from? The commonsense account would be that these systems are passed on through the generations, changing in the process of transmission. We have to acknowledge that real language/culture systems seem to have very diverse explanatory systems built into them. 'Why did he/she do that?' may call for an answer citing anything from the voices of ancestral spirits to a neurotic compulsion to have a good reason.

Some of the possibilities look a bit like causal explanations, but others do not. The crucial question is deeper. What uses do people actually make of such words as 'believe', 'want', 'hope for' and so on? Are they imputing mental states to others when they use them, and, even more important, are people imputing mental states to themselves when they use them reflexively?

Let us look at a case: someone bends down and scrabbles round under her chair. I say, 'Why are you bending down like that?' She says, 'I think [believe] my pen has fallen down there, and I want [desire] to get it.' Is that a causal explanation? Clearly not. It is used to make the bending down intelligible and warrantable, meaningful and proper. The same narrative job could have been done in other equally convincing ways. 'I dropped my pen, and I need it to take a note,' 'I'm always losing things, and that pen has a sentimental value,' and so on. If these are rival causal explanations, they must sustain the query: which one is correct? Real and rival causal explanations, say of malaria (plasmodia or marsh gas), cannot both be true. However, all the desire/belief explanations I have just given could be true together. Their job in our cognitive economy is not parallel to that of describing hidden causes in scientific explanations.

Wellman's (1990) interpretation of the belief/desire vocabulary is more sophisticated than that of Premack and Woodruff in that he takes both to be what we have called 'grammars'. They are systems of concepts that fix ontologies, that is, what we take to exist in a domain and, at the same time, also fix explanatory formats. Unfortunately he too trips over the same rough patch that brought Skinner down. He takes the explanatory formats that can be constructed with such concepts as beliefs and desires to be causal. This is just the misunderstanding of the everyday uses of English and other languages that Wittgenstein so carefully dissected and to some extent freed us from.

Learning a theory of mind is not learning about unobservable entities and processes that bring about the phenomena we can observe. It is not like learning about electric fields, anions, and cations, as the hidden mechanisms referred to in a theory of electrolysis. Learning a theory of mind is no more but no less than acquiring mastery of certain discursive conventions for making what people do intelligible and warrantable, including the things I do myself. 'Why do I always choose the Tin Roof Fudge Pie?' 'Because I like it.' That sounds a bit as if I were reminding myself of some inner state, a liking for Tin Roof Fudge Pie, which causes my voice to utter the words 'I'll try some of your Tin Roof Fudge Pie.' However closer attention to this event shows that the various components that this way of talking seems to single out, such as the words, the anticipatory images as one goes into the Victorian Restaurant in Montrose PA, the taste, and so on, make up a unity. If any of these components were absent, it could not be said that R.H. likes Tin Roof Fudge Pie. To like it is not to be in some inner state but to be disposed to do any of this entire complex of things. To make sense of all this for someone puzzled by the way I keep finding reasons to make a detour through Montrose PA, I need to have a repertoire of 'explanatory' concepts at hand. Mastery of this sort of skill is to have a 'theory of mind'. However, we can now see how unfortunate a metaphor it has turned out to be. It soon set people looking for the psychological analogs of the anions and cations that figure in the explanations of electrolysis, which was indeed a theory of electrical conduction in solutions.

More needs to be said about cases in which I use mentalistic talk to make sense of someone else's actions, to display them as intelligible and warrantable. What would count as getting it right? On the naive reading, the test would be whether there really were just such unobservables as are referred to in the 'theory'. The ionic account of electrical conduction in solutions is tested by a search for free ions migrating through the liquid, from the positive to the negative pole and vice versa. But an account of someone's actions in terms of beliefs and desires is good only in so far as it anticipates one of the possible accounts that the other person would give when asked to explain these actions.

'Explaining' is used for two rather different discursive activities. It can refer to a procedure for making what is to be explained intelligible. If I ask you to explain the American constitution I want an exegesis so that Thomas Jefferson's masterpiece becomes intelligible. However, if I ask you to explain the spread of Hong Kong B influenza, I expect you to refer to unobservable entities, viruses, the nature and behavior of which explain the epidemic. 'Theory of mind' concepts play a role in explanations of the first kind, not of the second. We learn to use a certain vocabulary in making what other people do intelligible and warrantable, and for presenting my own acts in a similar defensible way. However, it is a gratuitous piece of philosophizing to interpret words like 'belief', 'attitude' and so on as referring to mental entities, the stuff of a theory of mind.

Grammar as a research tool

If the phenomena of human psychology are aspects of the public and private flow of the discursive activities, act–actions, one would expect to find studies not only of the different levels of phenomena into which that flow can be partitioned but also of the principles by which the relevant components of the flux are ordered. We have seen that attempts at using the cause–effect principle fail. Taking the conversation model seriously would suggest that 'grammar' may not only serve as a metaphor for a wide range of ordering principles but also have a literal role in the psychologically relevant analysis of what people do. In this section I shall be drawing on recent studies in the grammar of personal pronouns as a way of throwing light on the expression of a person's sense of self, of the singularity and uniqueness of one's personal being.

The psychology of selfhood

A more difficult cluster of problems than those we have touched on so far concerns the psychological aspects of personhood, particularly the sense of personal singularity and uniqueness that is a ubiquitous feature of human consciousness. The criteria for making judgments on the identity of other people have been a focus of interest for philosophers since the writings of Descartes became well known in the seventeenth century. How far do these criteria help us to understand the sense a person has of his or her own singularity and uniqueness? This can be a problem for developmental psychology. How is the sense of personal identity acquired? It can be a problem for gerontology. How does the sense of personal identity decay and is sometimes wholly or partially lost? It is important for psychopathology, since a baseline is needed from which to define and identify troublesome deviations.

Broadly speaking, the issue can be sharpened to this. Is one's sense of one's own singularity based on an empirical discovery that one is in fact a unique individual? Alternatively, is it a standing condition of being a person at all? It makes sense to say that one has discovered that the Joe we knew at elementary school and the Joseph we see thirty years later presenting himself as a candidate for the presidency are the same person. However, does it make sense to say that one has discovered that the person one was yesterday is the same person as one is today? If the first question makes sense and the second question does not this suggests that while the identity of other persons is a matter of fact, the identity of oneself is a standing condition of personhood, without which one would not be the person one is.

Why is there a problem? Why not undertake a search for the private self that is at the core of the public person by turning one's attention 'inwards' to examine one's private experience? In philosophy, phenomenologists, especially Husserl, tried to tackle the problem of the nature of personhood through attention to how singularity of self is experienced by a human being. He did not succeed in bringing this investigation to a satisfactory closure, since he seems to have held radically different views at different times. At one time he argued that the self as an inner entity, the real core of personhood, is not available to phenomenological investigation, a subtle kind of introspection. In later works he seems to suggest that there is such an experience as attending to one's 'self', an experience of the core of individual being.

This vacillation is not surprising, since we find the same sort of thing in earlier periods of philosophy and psychology. Hume, for example, denies that one can have an *experience* of one's self. Introspection can yield nothing but streams of experiences. The being which one seeks is the very being that is doing the seeking. Therefore it can never be discovered by introspection. Here is Hume's famous exposition of the point:

> For my part, when I enter most intimately into what I call *myself*, I always stumble on some particular perception or other, of heat or cold, light or shade, love or hatred, pain or pleasure. I never catch *myself* at any time without a perception, and never can observe anything but a perception.
>
> (Hume, 1748: Book 1, section 4)

Later, Samuel Butler was to resolve the debate of that epoch by making the very modern point that the singularity of self is presupposed in every human thought and action. Locke's suggestion that the self is the string of memories a person has about him or herself cannot be the last word, since the very concept of memory presupposes a person to whom the experiences picked out as memories occurred.

I owe the following metaphor to Albert Mosley. Just as the sun is the gravitational center of the solar system, so persons are the embodied centers of the little worlds that each and every one perceives. The sun acts from its center of gravity. That is an abstract point in the sun's sphere, a mere location. There is no 'gravitational entity' inside the sun which would account for the gravitational action of our star. Persons seem to themselves to be the center of their fields of perception, both inside and outside their own bodies. These are just locations, geometrical points. There is no entity there to account for the power the person has to perceive. There is just the embodied person.

Philosophers have a word for the process of gratuitously turning abstractions into material beings: 'reification'. This is just what we are tempted to do in this case. There is an abstraction, a geometrical center of the pattern of observations we can make of the environment and of our own bodies. To take this for an entity, a 'self', is reification, creating an entity where there is merely a location.

Some uses of the word 'self'

In the P grammar 'person' is the basic category of being. Persons are the ultimate agents. In the domain of this grammar, persons are singular beings with no hidden mental architecture or cognitive structures. Introspectively a person can pay attention to private experiences and to whatever aspect of mental architecture is presented consciously. People perform public and private meaningful acts. To think of the private experiences of a person, of their own acts, as *a mind* is another gratuitous reification, turning a flow of experiences into a thing. People are characterized cognitively only by dispositions, propensities and powers. They are singled out for most purposes by the uniqueness of their bodies as material beings in space and time. How is this to be connected with the experiences that individual people have of themselves as singular beings? Research begins with a study of the means by which a sense of personal uniqueness is *expressed*.

The word 'self' has a variety of uses in the P grammar. In general, it is used to pick out what is singular or unique about a person. There are two very widespread uses on which I shall focus. There is the self as perceiver. In everyday discourse it is persons who are said to see, feel, smell and hear things. If we examine the material world beyond the boundaries of the body, as each of us perceives it, we find one embodied person at the vertex or pole of an array of material things. Moreover, when we turn our attention to our own bodies we also find a polarized structure. Our experience of our own limbs, organs and so on is ordered as if it were centered on the very same being, the person, who is at the center of the first perceptual field, the things in the material environment. We talk about our body states and parts, as they are perceived, as if the very same person perceives them as perceives the ordinary furniture of the world. However, as I have emphasized above, with all the authority of David Hume behind me, no *thing* can be discovered at the center of the field of what is perceived when I turn my attention to myself, try as I may.

Now we have a tension. The person as a thing among things is embodied and located in ordinary space. However, the person as occupying a point of view within the body is not embodied, nor is it located in the spatial field of the body in the same way as the embodied person is located in the spatial field of ordinary things. The former has a fixed point in the body field, while the latter has a trajectory of locations within the thing field. The self-as-perceiver is not the whole person, since it is no more than the reification of the point of view from which the body that is integral with the whole person and the material environment is centered.

How could we make any further progress in understanding our sense of personal uniqueness and singularity? How do we come to have it? Can we lose it? How is it expressed? The discourses of personhood involve the uses of certain classes of words, above all personal names and personal pronouns. In particular, it may be worth taking a very close look at the way the word 'I' and functionally equivalent expressions are actually used. Though we cannot make much progress by trying to study the private and elusive experience of self, we can certainly begin to study the public and overt expression of selfhood in certain linguistic practices.

We have already mastered the distinction between expression and description in getting to know Wittgenstein's account of how it is possible to learn a publicly meaningful vocabulary for conducting conversations about private experiences. The principle that lies behind the discursive analysis of the psychology of selfhood is that the vocabulary of personhood is expressive, not descriptive. Words like proper names and personal pronouns are not used in descriptions of the sense of identity but to express it.

The 'selfhood' that is to be expressed

What are the main features of the sense one has of one's own singularity and uniqueness, that is, that one is only one being, and that there are no others exactly the same? There seem to be two such features, which, though connected, are very different from one another.

There is the spatio-temporal centering of one's fields of perception, including one's material surroundings and the state, condition and parts of one's own body. This phenomenon is surely an aspect of one's singular and unique embodiment, which appears in one's sense of having a continuous trajectory through the material world, different from anyone else's. Then there is the ever-changing totality of one's beliefs about oneself. No one else has a set of beliefs exactly like these, even at the same moment in the history of the world.

In ordinary everyday English the word 'self' is used for both aspects of personhood. While the sense of the singularity of one's selfhood as the one who perceives the world from a certain location in space and time is a standing condition for being a person at all, one's beliefs about oneself are or purport to be factual. They could be discussed in a critical way with another person who had also formed an opinion about the attributes of the person in question. There is no specially privileged point of view from which a person has absolute authority on his or her own attributes. However, the same is not true of the perceptual centering of experience. That is indeed experienced only by the perceiver, and is singular and unique to each one of us. How could it possibly be studied? How could the ways these various aspects of selfhood tie into one another be a topic for an empirical investigation?

I return yet again to the description/expression distinction to show how such an investigation can be opened up. It is to myself as an embodied person that I ascribe beliefs, skills, memories, dispositions, height, weight, and so on, when I am asked questions about myself. 'I' is used to pick out the entity that is being described. Of course, the reference is contextually sensitive, since its function is to draw our attention to the *speaker* as a person. But in telling what I can see, hear, touch and so on, it is not the whole person to which attention is drawn but to the point of view in space and time from which that person perceives the world. This is not an entity but an abstract location in space and time. It is not like a mountain, but like the latitude and longitude of that mountain.

The uses of 'I'

People have proper names or some equivalent unique appellations such as a Social Security number. However, 'I' seems to be *the* 'self' word. It does important work in displaying and expressing the sense of self. By studying first-person grammar we can get a grasp of the seemingly elusive 'self'. The grammar of first person expressions is quite unlike that of the third person. One can come to know to whom 'he' or 'she' refers by tracking back or forward through a sequence of pronouns until one reaches an ordinary referring expression like a proper name or definite description. 'Young George Washington picked up *his* axe and *he* chopped down the cherry tree.' The role of first person is to index the content and social force of an utterance with some attribute of the speaker ('I') or the relevant speaker reference class ('we'). One knows the person in relation to whom 'I' is used only by knowing who the speaker is. Two main attributes of the speaker are relevant to the role of the first person.

'I' indexes the factual content of a description of some aspect of the material world or report of some state of the speaker's body with the spatial location of the speaker. This location is grammatically expressed, but not grammatically created. It is just a fact about a speaker that he or she is at that moment in a certain location in an array of other material things.

'I' also indexes the social and moral 'force' of an utterance with the moral standing, reliability, trustworthiness and so on of the speaker. This force is in large part grammatically created, since to use the word 'I' is to make a commitment to whatever it is that is said or implied by what is said.

In this grammar we find a clue to some aspects of the self, the sense one has of one's singularity and uniqueness as a person. While the place-defining role of 'I' seems to be universal in that all languages we know of use the first person for this purpose, the commitment role varies widely. It depends on the degree to which there are institutions of verbal commitment recognized in a society, and on the degree to which acts of commitment are personal or collective (Mühlhäusler and Harré, 1990).

learning point **From a causal to a normative metaphysics**

Words and other symbols are first order tools, while brains and hands are second order tools for people to accomplish tasks.

1 Instruments and apparatus:

   a) Physicists use *instruments* to measure the properties of material objects and *apparatus* to model them.

   b) Psychologists' research equipment can only be apparatus, that is, models of discursive phenomena as psychological processes.

2 Examples of reworking of psychological research:

   a) Self-esteem cannot be a hidden mental cause of answering questions in a certain manner. It can be only a set of culturally specific narrative conventions.

   b) Most statistical correlations in psychology express semantic rules, not causal tendencies.

   c) Causal language is used for rhetorical purposes, to conform to conventions of writing psychology.

3 Two detailed studies of discursive analysis:

   a) Attitudes:

      i) Hidden cause interpretations

      ii) As attributes of public performances.

   b) Theory of mind:
The accounts of how people understand people, including themselves, reify private and public cognitive processes as hidden mental entities.

4 Grammar as a research tool:

   a) The psychology of selfhood.

      i) Self is unobservable.

      ii) A hidden entity or geometrical point?

   b) 'Self' is used both for the center of a perceptual field and for personal attributes.

   c) 'Self' includes uniqueness of embodiment and uniqueness of personal attributes.

   d) The pronoun 'I' is an indexical.

      i) It indexes content with the location of the speaker.

      ii) It indexes social and moral force of an utterance with the moral standing of the speaker.

      iii) First person pronouns express a sense of self rather than refer to an inner core of being.

   e) Learning a language and other symbolic devices and shaping a mind are two aspects of the same developmental process.

Conclusion

The use of cognitive/discursive words like 'self-esteem' to refer to hypo-thetical entities that seem to be needed to complete a cognitive account of some psychological phenomenon that fits the scientific realist pattern needs to be looked at closely. How are these words actually being used? Is their use an indication that the psychologist who uses them believes that there are unobserved cognitive entities causing a person to act and speak in certain ways? It seems not. We shall come across other examples of mis-placed reification in which there are presumed to be unobserved cognitive processes going on, of the same type as observed ones, which are taken to be responsible for what people do and say. The implausibility of pre-supposing the existence of imperceptible mental processes should alert us to the possibility that the words that seem to refer to unconscious acts of cognition, such as 'implicit memory', are best seen as metaphors. Close attention shows us that they are actually used for describing neural activities that are relevant to the overt, observable cognitive activities that they are introduced to explain. In this chapter we have learned how to eliminate bogus mental entities from the ontology of psychology in favor of public and private symbolic acts and the powers and dispositions of individuals to perform them skillfully.

The hybrid nature of psychology as both a cultural and a material science appears in its meta-discourses that make use of all three grammars, the Personal, the Organismic and the Molecular. This means that a great deal of the vocabulary that we have drawn from ordinary language is routinely used in a literal sense for the discursive acts of everyday life. It is also used in a metaphorical sense for the material tools through which our cognitive and material tasks are routinely accomplished.

The technical question to be answered in trying to interpret the results of existing research and to develop programs of study to carry cog-nitive science further is this: *to what type hierarchy do the referents of seemingly common words belong in this or that context: is it mental/discursive or material/neurological?* If the words are used literally, the entities and processes to which they refer are mental/discursive, to be studied within the frame of the P grammar. If they are used metaphorically, the processes in question could be material/neurological, to be studied within the frame of the O and M grammars. As we have learned in this chapter, the mistaken adherence to a cause/effect metaphysical scheme has led psychologists into using common psychological words or their close technical relatives to refer to hypothetical but unobservable *mental* entities and processes.

Which should one prefer? The robust reality of discourse and its neurological machinery contrast sharply with the shadowy character of hypothetical mental processes, which are not sustained by any actual sym-bol system. Playing with cognitive unobservables invites a return to a closet Cartesianism. Indeed, that is exactly what one finds in consulting the liter-ature. Surely we have had enough of this kind of mysterymongering! There is no mental substance. Matter, arranged in appropriate forms, can sustain both causal and semantic structures.

If we read the uses of the mentalistic vocabulary as metaphor, we have an admirable example of scientific model building, in which the model that one is led to by the metaphor is a subtype in a type hierarchy that includes other observable neural activities as subtypes.

Finally, it seems as if a great deal of psychological research can be recovered from oblivion simply by replacing the causal frame by normative readings. Perhaps there is enough material locked up in 'technically' opaque rhetorics to fuel a grand undertaking, the recovery of a scientific understanding of important aspects of our culture. That would indeed be something worth doing.

Note

1   I owe notice of these useful quotations to Changsin Lee (1998).

Connectionism and the brain

Why, given the disappointments with the GOFAI project as psychology, should we continue to try to develop artificial intelligence models of cognition and the tools by which cognitive tasks are carried out? Why not jump straight from discursive analysis of act–action sequences to neurological hypotheses? There are three reasons for continuing to pursue this research program:

1   Our discussions have confirmed the commonsense principle that the relevant states and processes in the human nervous system, especially the brain, possess neither intentionality nor normativity. They just *are.* Artificial intelligence modeling gives us a technique for creating abstract representations of mechanisms that can perform analogues of the processes in the brain without requiring representations of specific content.[1]

2   Scanning techniques provide neuropsychologists with information about the location of cognitive processing but very little knowledge of the processes themselves. Furthermore, since the brain regions that are thus identified are relatively very large, containing hundreds of thousands, sometimes millions, of neurons, the disparity of scale means that some other technique must be employed to follow the processes that are going on when people are using their brains as cognitive tools. The connectionist turn in artificial intelligence is particularly well suited to that role, as we shall see. There are many similar situations in the physical sciences. Experiment disclosed the molar gas laws, such as Boyle's relation between pressure P and volume V of a confined sample of gas ($PV = K$). However, the molecular model was required in order to make this law and others like it intelligible.

3   Psychology may be like optics. The geometrical optics of light ray propagation gives physicists a very good idea of where optical phenomena occur. Nevertheless a succession of models of the processes involved has led to deeper knowledge of the fine grain of what light is and the way it behaves. First came the particle model, which was followed by the wave model, only to be superseded

eventually by the photon model. In the same way PET scans can give us knowledge of the location of the necessary cognitive tools. We have had a succession of models of the processes going on at those locations. First, there were the pneumatic models of Descartes, then the telephone exchange, then GOFAI as a development of system theory, and finally we have connectionism, the model to be described in this chapter.

In considering in more detail how computational *models* are related to the real people using their real brains to manage their real lives that these models represent, we must remind ourselves of the basic distinction between abstract and concrete 'Turing machines', introduced in Chapter 6. A concrete Turing machine is some version of the gadget with an endless moving tape and a reading and writing head that has become the archetypal blueprint for any material mechanism that could realize the set of computational rules that Turing proved could evaluate any computable function. Von Neumann's version of this machine marks the end point of a certain line of development in modeling cognition 'mechanically'. By an abstract Turing machine I mean the set of rules that expresses the methodology for evaluating all possible computable functions.

The psychological applications of computational modeling depend on the viability of using some version of the concrete Turing machine as a model of the way the human brain is structured and performs those diverse operations that, when they are manifested, we call 'thinking'. The role of the abstract Turing machine in psychology is quite indeterminate, once one takes model making seriously as the main methodology of a cognitive science that is aimed at founding the psychology of cognition in people's use of their brains as thinking machines. That the manifested form of some cognitive process, expressed discursively, can be mapped on to a computational procedure governed by the rules of the abstract Turing machine tells us almost nothing of relevance to the psychology of cognition.

The great advance in cognitive science that connectionism offers is ontological. Connectionist models, or neural nets, made up of interconnected artificial neurons, are metaphysically plausible. There are real nets of real interconnected neurons in the brain and nervous system. The question we can now pose is this. 'How far do the "neural nets" of connectionist architectures map on to the neural nets revealed by brain anatomists, when the outputs of each are analogous?' The suggestion that there may be registers, programs, compilers and the like in the brain is neurological nonsense. That period of artificial intelligence as a source of cognitive science is, in essence, behavioristic. Therefore it does not begin to count as a real *science* of cognition. The old artificial intelligence models were simply metaphors reflecting a certain analysis of cognitive displays or behavior. We will see this vividly illustrated in our study of remembering in Chapter 11.

McCullough and Pitts (1943) proved many years ago that a 'neural net' can compute all the functions that a concrete Turing machine can compute. Another way of putting this result is to say that both Turing's machine and a neural net are realizations of the abstract Turing machine, the set of rules that Turing laid down for all computable functions. That would leave neural nets and von Neumann machines more or less level pegging as analogs of the brain and nervous system, even if we accepted the thesis that thinking is computational. The psychological application of computational models must be controlled by the ontological demand that the mechanism in which those rules are realized must be a plausible model of a real brain structure. Let us turn to look closely at the architecture of idealized connectionist systems to prepare for a comparison with the structures of arrays of cells in, at least, some parts of the brain.

section one

What is a connectionist system?

The basic concepts we need to explain 'connectionist systems' are 'neural net' and 'parallel distributed processing', or PDP for short. Sometimes the connectionist family of models is referred to as PDP devices. The point of the phrase 'parallel distributed processing' is to draw attention to the fact that the steps in the simulation of a cognitive process are not taken sequentially as they would be in a von Neumann machine. Many are taking place simultaneously. They are combined by virtue of the structure of the connections in the net. This has an enormously important theoretical and practical consequence. Items of information are not stored as such at specific sites. Indeed, the very expression 'items of information' is misleading when applied to parallel distributed processing. Taken strictly, the concept of 'representation' has no application in connectionism. Though some authors use the term, it can be only a metaphor. The term is probably best avoided, since the implications are quite misleading. There are no representations of items in the net. We *could* say that a body of knowledge is represented in the whole net, though it hardly seems helpful to do so.

Neurons and nets

If the computing mechanism is an artificial neural net it must run by parallel distributed processing, several artificial neurons processing inputs at the same time. If the mechanism runs by parallel distributed processing it must take the form of a network of interconnected neurons, each processing the inputs it receives from others and activating connections with others.

We need the concept of a neuron before we can set out the system in detail. There are both artificial and real neurons to be taken account of. This is the key to the metaphysics of connectionism that makes it the most plausible source of models for a genuine cognitive science. An account of thinking as abstractly modeled in a net the nodes of which are artificial neurons can be transformed into a scientific explanation of thinking just in so far as artificial neurons can be related to real nerve cells and their patterned arrangement in real brains in real people.

The real neuron

A real neuron consists of a cell body with a number of dendrites, nerve fibers conveying nervous impulses into the cell body. The cell body is extended into an axon which links up with the dendrites from other cells at synapses (see Figure 9.1). While neural impulses are electrical within the axon and the dendrites, the axon/dendrite links are chemical, mediated by neurotransmitters (see Figure 9.2). There are a huge variety of versions of this basic layout to be observed in different parts of the nervous system and in different organisms. Nevertheless the basic layout is universal, and from the point of view of modeling a real fragment of the brain and nervous system in a system of artificial neurons the general layout is all that usually needs to be taken into account.

The transmission of pulses along a nerve fiber comes about by the differential migration of sodium and potassium ions at successive locations along the nerve fiber. There are specific channels in the cell membrane for the passage of sodium ions and others for the passage of potassium ions. These channels can open and close. Initially the cell has a resting potential, across the cell membrane. This is caused by the continuous migration of sodium and potassium ions into and out of the cell. In the resting condition three sodium ions migrate out for every two potassium ions that flow in. The net effect is a small net negative potential across the cell membrane. The first step is the depolarization of an initial location on the nerve cell, brought about by the influence of the other neurons connected to it. Stimulation by influences from other neurons causes a small change in the surface membrane of the cell. At a certain threshold the sodium channels open and there is an inrush of positively charged sodium ions. The

Figure 9.1
Basic structure of
real nerve cell

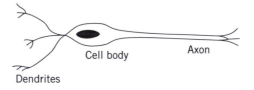

Cell body   Axon

Dendrites

Figure 9.2
Synapse in detail

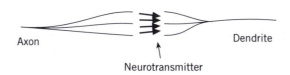

Axon   Dendrite

Neurotransmitter

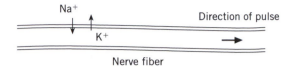

Figure 9.3

Migration of
sodium and
potassium ions

potential across the cell membrane becomes momentarily large and positive. This is called the 'action potential'. Almost immediately the sodium channels close and potassium channels open. Positively charged potassium ions flow out, reducing the potential difference between the outside and the inside of the cell to its original resting value (see Figure 9.3). That region of the cell body is said to be repolarized. The process is repeated at the adjacent part of the nerve fiber. This results in a relatively large potential difference between the inside and the outside of the nerve fiber at the next location in the neural fiber. Thus a wave of action potential passes along the nerve fiber.

It is important to realize that there is no longitudinal movement of electrically charged ions along the nerve fiber.

Real neurons transmit and emit electrical impulses discontinuously. There is a threshold level of excitation that must be reached for the neuron to 'fire'. This is the threshold that must be reached for the process of depolarization to begin.

Real neural nets

A net of real neurons is formed by linkages between dendrites and axons. Real neural nets can be two or three-dimensional. We need to set up a terminology for distinguishing artificial intelligence 'neural' nets from real networks of cells in the brain and nervous system. I shall call the former 'model nets' and the latter 'real nets'. The expression 'neural net' was long ago hi-jacked by those who thought that the invention of connectionist modeling brought the problems of developing a fruitful way of analysing real neural structures to an end. Of course it hasn't. I use the term 'neural net' to specify the supertype for connectionist modeling. 'Model net' and 'real net' are among the subtypes.

The artificial neuron

An artificial neuron is an elementary processing unit with multiple input channels and one or more output channels. These channels are connections to and from other artificial neurons or nodes. Inputs can be excitatory, that is, tending to bring about firing, or inhibitory, that is, tending to inhibit firing (see Figure 9.4). 'Bring about' and 'inhibit' are metaphors that give an intuitive sense to the positive or negative value of the strength of components of the input. The positive or negative strength of an input is the product of the activity of the neuron and the 'weight' of the connection. This product is called the 'strength' of the connection.

Figure 9.4
Structure of an
artificial neuron

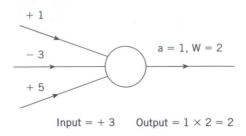

Input = + 3   Output = 1 × 2 = 2

If the weight is positive the impulse is excitatory. If it is negative the impulse is inhibitory. The total input is simply the arithmetical sum of the strengths of each of the input 'dendrites' or connections. There is a mathematical relation, the activation function, with which the output activity can be found from the total input.

There are several activity functions in use in connectionist modeling. The simplest computes the arithmetical sum of the weighted inputs, then compares this sum with the pre-set value of a threshold, in the same units. If it exceeds the threshold, it 'fires'. 'Firing' is emitting a signal at a certain activity level. When this is multiplied by the weight of the connection, we get the strength with which the impulse is transmitted to the next neuron or neurons in the array (Figure 9.5). Other activity functions have been tried out, for example the sigmoid function pictured in Figure 9.6.

Any 'surplus' strength in input over the minimum required to activate the neuron's output mechanism is lost as information.

Figure 9.5
Threshold function

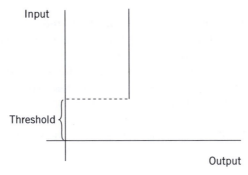

Figure 9.6
Sigmoid function

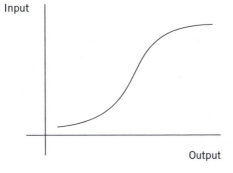

Input surface

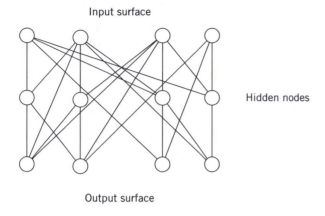

Figure 9.7
Connectionist
neural net

Hidden nodes

Output surface

Artificial neural nets

An artificial neural net or model net is a two-dimensional interconnected set of artificial neurons (see Figure 9.7). The simplest artificial net is one in which all neurons or nodes are connected to all others. The connections are such that an output of one neuron is an input to another. A 'connection' is any link between one artificial neuron or node and another. The connections link the nodes into a net. It is evident that many neurons are processing inputs simultaneously, in parallel. Such a net has edges. The choice of edge in which to input 'information' and the choice of which will display the final output of the net is important for the setting up of the system. When an input edge is provided with a set of input values the edge is said to be 'clamped'. The signals emitted by the output edge will be called simply 'output'.

There are various refinements in net structure that are not of great importance for our studies. For example, the total output signal could be split up into several different components, so that there could be several connections through which the activity of a neuron entered into the operation of the whole network.

To train a model net the nodes at the input edge are clamped in an on/off pattern, for example representing the binary symbol for 'Fido'. Suppose the net is to serve as a classifier. Does it do work which could be called 'classifying this creature' correctly? Does it output 'dog'? If not – and that is the most likely outcome of the first trial – the net must be trained. That involves going through the net and adjusting the weights of the connections, over and over again, until the final output is that which is required. The net now *holds* the information that Fido is a dog.[2]

From real net to a model net

This mode of action of artificial neurons or nodes is analogous to the mode of action of the real nerve cells that constitute the brain and nervous system of organisms, including *Homo sapiens*. In addition, there is a thoroughgoing recipro-city between the connectionist layout of the model net and the real anatomical structure of groups of neurons in several parts of the brain. This relationship makes it possible to implement the general ontological constraint on the invent-ing of model nets and connectionist hypotheses as representations of real nets. A model and its possible real subject, observable or unobservable should be subtypes of the same supertype. Without that relationship any serious cognitive *science* would be impossible.

The mapping from real network to model net, and model net to real net, fol-lows a simple rule: each synapse linking a dendrite with an axon in a real net is represented by a connection between one artificial neuron or node and another, in the corresponding artificial net. (See Figure 9.8, derived from McLeod et al., 1998: 53, figure 3.1.)

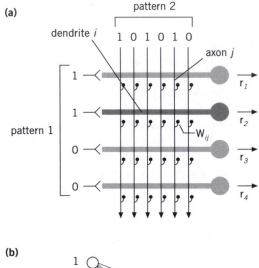

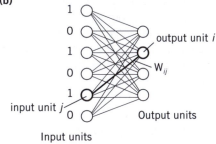

Figure 9.8 From real net to model net. (a) The network as it might appear in the nervous system with axons synapsing on to dendrites of cells r_1 to r_4. (b) The network in the conventional connectionist format with an input presented to one set of units (indexed by *j*) producing an output on another set indexed by *i*. (From P. McLeod, K. Plunkett and E.T. Rolls, *Introduction to Connectionist Modelling of Cognitive Processes*, 1998, by courtesy of Oxford University Press)

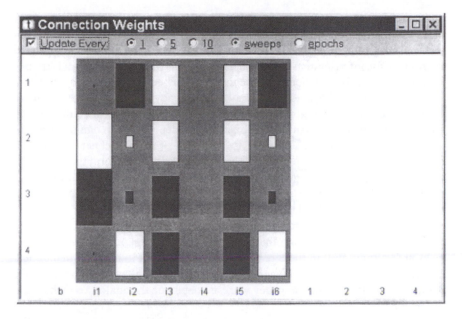

Figure 9.9 Hinton diagram of the pattern associator. (From P. McLeod, K. Plunkett and E.T. Rolls, *Introduction to Connectionist Modelling of Cognitive Processes*, 1998, by courtesy of Oxford University Press)

In both real and model nets there are usually many neurons between the input and output surfaces. These are referred to as the 'hidden layers' of the net. Knowledge engineers have developed a standard way of representing the state of the connections among the hidden nodes of model nets (Figure 9.9). Hinton diagrams represent the strengths of connections, that is, the product of the activity of the relevant node and the weight of a connection in accordance with the following conventions:

1   The area of the rectangle representing a connection is proportional to the strength of that connection.
2   White rectangles represent positive strengths and black represent negative strengths.

A Hinton diagram is generated automatically by the program that simulates the model net. It is a convenient way of examining the effect of a training program on the fine structure of a model net.

Model nets as research tools

The question of the verisimilitude of a model net as a representation of a real network of neurons can be raised only if the results of running tests of the ability of the input/output patterns of the model to simulate the inputs to and outputs from the corresponding real neural nets are favorable. Given the plausibility of the general modeling relation between artificial and real nets, behavioral analogies give us grounds for inferring real structural analogies between a real net and its connectionist model. Neuroscientists have the task of checking out the analogy.

The testing of behavioral analogies has already begun for such cognitive performances as classifying, remembering, pronouncing written or printed words and a number of others. An artificial net can model a certain cognitive process when activated and, at the same time, the structure of the model net is an analog of the structure of the real neural tool that is being used to perform that cognitive task. This suggests that there should be conformity between the structure of the model net and the results of anatomical studies of the fine structure of those parts of the brain implicated by the use of the Taxonomic Priority Principle as the sites of cognition. PET scan techniques for picking out activation centers can be used to identify regions of the brain that seem to be serving as tools for the cognitive tasks under study. Within these regions, we would expect to find real neural nets or something functionally equivalent to them. We need to have in mind the main features of model nets and how they work as we pursue the analogy on which the model is based.

For example, suppose a net outputs the code for 'Mary' when we input the code for 'Brian's sister'. The whole net holds the 'information' that Mary is Brian's sister. However, the relational concept 'sister' is nowhere represented in the cognitive system. Similarly, if the input edge is clamped to represent '2' we can train the net to output '4'; inputting '3', we get '9' as output and so on. Then the net would, as a whole, hold the relation '… is the square of …' though that relation is not represented anywhere in the cognitive system.

It is also true that a net trained to give the correct answer to the question 'Who is Mary's brother?' could, without further training, give the correct answer to other questions on unrelated subjects. This is because there is nothing but a mass of abstract connections in the net. There are no representations of specific rules. There is no representation of the content of the items of knowledge which the net structure models. This capacity is called 'superpositional storage'. This is not perhaps a well chosen expression, but it is in current use.

In Chapter 11 we will encounter the phenomenon of *knowing how* to do something when it is not presupposed that a knowledgeable and skillful person could recite the relevant rules explicitly. This is called 'procedural memory'. Connectionism can serve, one hopes, both as an abstract model of cognition and as a possible iconic model of the brain mechanism, which serves as the tool by which people perform the tasks that they know how to do, in this sense. Connectionism fits the concept of procedural memory very well.

The flow of activity in the standard model net is from the clamped edge to the output edge. This layout is called 'feed forward'. There are net architectures in which connections are such that the activity states of nodes later in the progression feed back some of their output to nodes earlier in the net. In most model nets each node processes inputs in a deterministic manner. There are probabilis-

tic versions of nets that output values only according to a certain probability function. These are called Boltzman nets. We shall not be tackling them in this course.
Their structure and properties can be followed in Bechtel and Abrahamsen (1991:
97–9).

Worked example

Let us imagine that we have modeled a small portion of the brain in a model net
with six input nodes and four output nodes. This net is very simple (taken from
McLeod et al., 1998: chapter 3). It does not contain layers of hidden nodes. It will
look something like Figure 9.10. Let us suppose that it is part of the brain that
people use for remembering. We want to train it to recall the date of the American
Revolution. Let us suppose that a binary representation of the words 'American
Revolution' is '111010'. We clamp the input surface with this configuration of
'on' and 'off' neurons. We want the output to display the configuration '1100',
which we imagine represents the correct answer, '1776'.

We can do this by hand for such a simple net. Let us further suppose that
the activity of each neuron is 1, and that the weights of connections are either
1 or 0. To construct a 'weight matrix', columns represent input nodes and rows
represent output nodes. Figure 9.11 is the untrained weight matrix of this component of the 'memory machine'. The weight of each of the connections is zero.
Each cell represents a connection. Cell 'a' represents the connection I_4/O_2. The
number in each cell represents the weight of that connection. The rows respectively represent O_1, O_2, O_3, O_4.

We clamp the input surface with **111010** and keep adjusting the pattern of
weights. Eventually we reach the configuration in Figure 9.12. The strength of
each connection is the product of the activity of the input cell, taken to be '1' for
this example, and the weight of the connection. The first row represents the
strengths of the inputs to output node O_1, the second row the inputs to node O_2
and so on. The total input to each output node is just the sum of the strengths of

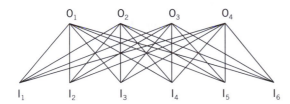

$O_1 \quad O_2 \quad O_3 \quad O_4$

$I_1 \quad I_2 \quad I_3 \quad I_4 \quad I_5 \quad I_6$

Figure 9.10
Untrained net

I_1	I_2	I_3	I_4	I_5	I_6
0	0	0	0	0	0
0	0	0	0 a	0	0
0	0	0	0	0	0
0	0	0	0	0	0

Figure 9.11
Untrained weight
matrix

199

Figure 9.12
Weights in a
trained net

1	1	1	0	1	0	Total input	Output configuration
1	0	1	0	1	0	3	1
1	0	1	0	1	0	3	1
0	0	0	0	0	0	0	0
0	0	0	0	0	0	0	0

the relevant input connections. The final set of four nodes has a threshold set at +2, firing (that is, switching *on*, taking the value '1') only when the input is +2 or greater. The output surface will then display a configuration of *on* and *off* nodes that represents the code **1100**. The net is now trained. It will look something like Figure 9.12. This net, with the weights as above, will always give the right answer to the question 'In what year did the American Revolution take place?' But nowhere in the net are there any data represented as such. Rather the knowledge that 'it' possesses is distributed over the whole structure.

Strokes and other lesions

The characteristic feature of the GOFAI period of artificial intelligence simulation of cognition was the inputting of rules into the material system as the program. Each rule has a definite site and an unambiguous expression in some symbolic system, usually binary. There are no rules in the connectionist mechanisms. There is no program represented in the machine.

An important consequence of this, particularly relevant to the question of the realism of the connectionist modeling project, is 'graceful degradation'. A net will still give a close approximation to the output it has been trained for even when a few nodes are destroyed or connections disrupted. In a von Neumann machine any failure in the system is catastrophic, as all of us who have had 'crashes' on our PCs well know. Brains suffer graceful degradation. Only if someone has a massive stroke is the cognitive power of the system severely compromised. Alzheimer's condition gradually worsens over many years and may remain on a plateau for decades. If brains are made of nets of nets, then the modeling of any organ of cognition from within the brain, such as the hippocampus, by means of an artificial net or nets must have a certain initial plausibility for the reason of graceful degradation alone.

Problems with the brain structure :: model net analogy

The crucial role of neurotransmitters

The synaptic connections between dendrites and axons, which are mapped on to connections in our working models, are mediated chemically. Neurotransmitters are secreted by the source fiber and taken up by the target fiber. Disturbances in the chemistry of these processes can have dramatic effects on the functioning of the nervous system.

There are a great many different chemical molecules serving as neuro-transmitters. Acetylcholine, noradrenaline, dopamine and seratonin are the most common, together with a class of molecules called 'neuropeptides', of which the endorphins (pain suppressors) are the best known. The vital role of these sub-stances can be seen in such conditions as Parkinson's disease, in which an inadequate supply of dopamine interferes with the neural mechanisms involved in facial expressions, bodily movement and posture. Disturbances in the chemistry of the brain disrupt the smooth working of the real neural net. Some molecules block the uptake of certain neurotransmitters, by occupying the site to which the neurotransmitter molecule would normally attach itself.

In short, there is a rich sea of chemical activity without which the net-works of brain cells would not function. In the models we have been considering this aspect of neuroscience is set aside, as if the linkages or connections across synapses were simply electrical, 'making a good contact'. Medical science tends to drive neuroscience, so it is not surprising that most of the research into the role of neurotransmitters has been into the effects of transmitter malfunction.

In the relevant model nets one can create analogs of these malfunctions, either by knocking out a node or by changing the input/output function, perhaps to simulate random firing even when the threshold input has been achieved.

Are the organs of the brain neural nets?

In some regions of the brain the anatomical structure is very net-like, for example in the hippocampus. However, in other regions it is not like a PDP net. If this observation is correct there will be *natural* limitations on the power of the connec-tionist model approach to establish the basic principles of a scientific psychology.

It may even be the case that cognitive psychology will have to rest content with having reached the 'discursive psychology' level for some psychological functions which involve no such simple task-to-tool relation that has made work on remembering exemplary of the new approach. As we shall see, progress towards creating a properly scientific account of the cognitive skills involved in classifying is very limited, while research into remembering and the tools people use to accomplish recollective tasks has flourished.

People learn 'the same thing' in many different ways, unlike artificial nets

The training sessions to which a model net is subjected are initiated from out-side the net. Someone, a teacher, has to realize that the output is *not correct*. Then the teacher initiates the sweeps that run through modifying the weights of connections until the output is 'correct'. However, human beings can and do engage in self-instruction. People can realize that the answers they come up with are sometimes wrong. They can correct misapprehensions by trial and error, under their own control, so to speak. This does not seem to be a particularly deep or fundamental difficulty. It is not hard to imagine a system of nets, the task for some being to monitor output from others, according to various criteria.

---

learning point **Connectionism and parallel distributed processing**

1   Real and artificial neurons:

  a)   A real neuron has dendrites (input) and axon (output).
  b)   Axon of neuron 1 is connected to dendrite of neuron 2 via a synapse.
  c)   Each synapse is represented by a link or connection between two artificial neurons.
  d)   An artificial neuron has multiple input connections and a single output, which is input to another artificial neuron.

2   Net structures:

  a)   A neural net is a multi-layered array of artificial neurons, connected with one another.
  b)   The input array of neurons is a surface, as is the output array. The intermediate layers are 'hidden'.
  c)   Fixing the input surface as a pattern of on/off nodal states 'clamps' it.
  d)   Influences are propagated through the net until it reaches equilibrium and there is a stable output.
  e)   This is a feed-forward process.

3   Processing at neurons:

  a)   The total input to a neuron is the arithmetic sum of the activity values of each input.
  b)   A neuron will fire only when the input has a certain value, or will fire according to a certain function.
  c)   There are several possible activity functions determining the output of a node, given a certain input.

4   Strengths of connections:

  a)   A neuron emits a signal at a certain level of *activity*.
  b)   The connection as activated has a certain *weight*.
  c)   The strength of the input to the next neuron is *activity* × *weight*.

(continued)

5 Training a net:

    a) If the output is not as required, e.g. 'trout' is classified as 'mammal', the net must be trained, that is, the weights of the connections changed.

    b) Changes are made until the output is as desired.

6 Strengths and limitations of model nets:

    a) Strokes and lesions can be modeled. Model nets can still function correctly with some neurons knocked out.

    b) Neurotransmitters are essential to synaptic transmission. They do have explicit analogs in model nets.

    c) Some parts of the brain are not obviously net-like in fine grain structure.

    d) There are many ways of learning 'the same thing' in real life.

    e) In some cases, such as hippocampal function, the brain may literally be a neural net.

    f) Nowhere in the net models do we have representations. One of the most telling objections to mapping cognitive activities on to brain processes can be circumvented.

section two

The brain as an organ for performing cognitive tasks

Just as the hand is an organ for grasping, and the eye for seeing, the brain is an organ for thinking. How do we know? There are two quite different ways of investigating this hypothesis. One is negative, drawing conclusions from what someone cannot do when some part of the brain is damaged. The other is positive, identifying which parts of the brain are activated when a certain task is being performed. In neither case has technology revealed the workings of the brain in detail. However, there is no doubting the interest of the broad results that have been obtained.

As in any biological study there is an anatomical aspect, the architecture of the brain as a structure of interconnected parts. There is the 'gross anatomy' of the brain, in which we pick out and name major features that are visible to ordinary perception. Then there is the micro-anatomy of the parts of the gross anatomy, studies made by microscopic examination at the level of the brain cell or neuron. In this course we shall go into no more gross anatomical detail than we need in order to specify the location of the processes that are made 'visible' by the scanning methods we will survey.

There is also a process aspect, the physiology of the brain as a living organ. The new scanning technologies have revealed the sites of the neurophysiology of the active brain in a good deal of detail. Thinking is a process. Neuroscientists must look for processes when they explore the way brains work when people use them as thinking tools.

There have been some surprises. The traditional anatomical maps of the brain displayed a number of clearly identifiable and seemingly separate parts, with bundles of nerve fibers connecting them into larger clusters. It seems obvious that neuroscientists should take almost for granted that specific cognitive, experiential, perceptual and motor functions should be located in this or that anatomically distinct part of the brain. The organ of vision, it would seem, is the eye and the visual cortex. Yet brain scans show very clearly that several other parts of the brain are active when a person is looking at something. There is certainly a great deal of unfinished business in the localizing of function.

For example, for many years neuropsychologists took it for granted that the neural basis of linguistic skills lay in Wernicke's and Broca's areas in the left temporal lobe. Damage to these regions of adult brains was reliably correlated with deficiencies in linguistic performance. Now an extraordinary discovery has been made.[3] Very young children, in whom these areas are severely damaged, nevertheless go on to acquire nearly normal linguistic skills. Why is language learning channeled to these areas in the normal processes of the development of linguistic skills, when it could have been grounded elsewhere?

The anatomy of the human brain

Though there are technologies that reveal the inner structures of the brains of living persons, they have been developed mainly for medical purposes. In the case of brain anatomy the fine detail one finds in 'atlases' of the brain come from post-mortem dissections of brains removed from the bodies they once were used to control. Anatomical images of living brains reveal the location of blood clots (haematomas) characteristic of strokes, and of tumors. These images are invaluable for the management of diseases of and damage to the brain. They are rather coarse-grained.

The major anatomical features of the brain relevant to those aspects of cognitive psychology studied in this course are highlighted in Figure 9.13. Only the areas relevant to the issues raised in Part IV have been emphasized. There are many excellent 'atlases' of the brain.

The physiology of the human brain

Thinking, acting and so on are skilled performances. According to the Hybrid Psychology methodology the brain is the main tool that people use to perform

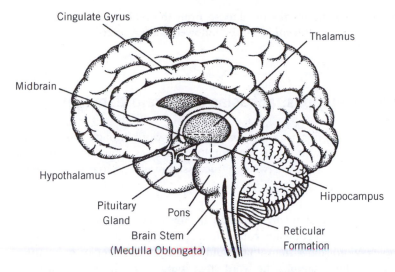

Figure 9.13 A median section of the brain showing the location of the hippocampus. (From R.M. Restak, *Brainscapes*, 1995, by courtesy of Hyperion Press, New York)

them. A performance is a process, a sequence of steps which, taken together, accomplish the task in hand. The workings of the brain as tool ought to be found in the processes that are occurring when cognitive work is being done. Anatomy is not irrelevant, of course, since the first step in testing connectionist models must be to try to identify the location in the brain where the relevant neural activity is going on. There are three main techniques.

1   When a person is unable to perform certain cognitive or motor tasks it is sometimes possible to identify the part of the brain that is damaged. The damage may be due to an accident or a stroke or the slow accumulation of minor faults. I will call this 'deficit reasoning'.

2   The whole brain of a living person is electrically active. Some of the activity can be detected as rhythmic pulses or waves. The amplitude and frequency of these waves differ during different states of consciousness and during different cognitive tasks. For example, during sleep a characteristic pattern appears, different from that displayed by the brain of the person who is awake.

3   There are several techniques, each depending on a specific technology, by means of which the state of the brain of a living person can be studied while that person is performing various tasks, including thinking. One way, pioneered by Penfield (1975), is the electrical stimulation of different parts of the brain while the person is conscious, and relating this to what that person then reports experiencing. The most important, for our purposes, is a technique by which chemical activity at different sites in the brain can be directly monitored. When a part of the brain is active, energy is required. It

is supplied by the uptake of glucose from the blood. The location and degree of glucose utilization can be followed and presented in an image of the living brain.

Negative correlations: aphasias and brain damage

The best way to follow this pattern of reasoning is to work through two examples of negative reasoning, from loss of function to hypotheses about the positive role of organs of the brain. Here are two very successful research projects, employing negative inference.

1   One study, brought to my attention by my colleague Chandan Vaidya, made use of a phenomenon called 'font-specific priming'. The task was to complete word stems, stems that could be completed by ten or more different words. For example, the word stem 'pun ...' could be completed as 'punctual', 'punitive', 'punt' and so on. The participants were 'primed' by being shown completion possibilities, half in the same font as the word stem and half in a different font. One would expect word stems in the same font as the priming word to be completed with that word better than chance. Simplifying somewhat, it turned out that, against a control group suffering from amnesia due to injury to certain parts of the brain who displayed the priming effect, one participant, with a different brain injury from the controls, did not display 'font-specific priming'. This person had right-occipital lobe damage. The experimenters reported their results in the following form: 'Patient M.S. failed to exhibit font-specific priming, despite preserved declarative memory. *Therefore*, perceptual specificity in visual priming depends on visual processes mediated by the right occipital lobe rather than the medial temporal; and diencephalic regions involved in declarative memory [defective in the amnesiac controls]'.[4] (Vaidya et al., 1998).

2   I owe to Stephen Sabat another very striking example. In a dark room a spot of light seems to move. If a participant leans sideways the motion effect increases. However, if someone who has lost sensation on one side is asked to lean in that direction, the increase in motion does not occur. We would naturally infer from this that the auto-kinetic effect involves both visual and kinesthetic perceptual systems.

Both cases are inferences by negation. If a person is unable to perform a certain cognitive or perceptual activity and, relative to those who can, suffers from the some injury or deficit to the nervous system, we infer that the uninjured structure or process is involved in the normal cognitive or perceptual activity.

The problem with this research technique is subtle. It depends on the distinction between necessary and sufficient conditions. It must be pointed out that such experiments or observations establish at best that something is a necessary condition for a certain activity to be possible. It does not show that it is a sufficient condition, or even that it is an important or particularly salient part of the conditions for an adequate performance. There can be injury to all sorts of different features of the brain and deficits in its normal activities. Any, some or all could be correlated with loss of cognitive-discursive powers. However, which of these features and functions is, so to say, doing the work, from the point of view of the neuropsychologist, is not easily deduced from the absence of this or that necessary condition. Without gasoline the car will not run, but the gas tank is not the part that is 'doing the work' of propulsion.

Positive correlations: scanning technology

There are a number of technologies for examining the living brain. Several are relevant to the project of a hybrid psychology. One, however, stands out, as a useful exemplar for illustrating the strengths and limitations of direct observation of brain processes. This is the technique of positron emission tomography, or PET. It can be used to monitor the all-important process of glucose uptake. It can thus reveal the parts of the brain that are active during the performance of different tasks. Not only do PET scans show us 'where the action is', but they also reveal how much glucose is being taken up, and so offer a measure of the level of neural activity at different places in the brain during cognitive work.

The basic physics of positron emission tomography

There are four main ideas that one needs to grasp to understand how PET scanning works:

1   It is possible to insert radioactive atoms into the relevant chemical compounds and to locate them by the radioactive emissions from the decay of the radioactive atom or 'label'.
2   Radioactive fluorine atoms can be inserted into a compound that is very similar to glucose and is taken up in a way similar to the uptake of glucose.
3   When a fluorine atom decays it emits a positron, a particle similar to an electron but with a positive charge. When a positron meets an electron they annihilate one another with the emission of two gammas rays in opposite directions.
4   By surrounding the human subject with detectors, pairs of gamma rays can be registered and their trajectories and point of origin readily worked out.

Putting these four principles together, we have a technique for locating and measuring the uptake of glucose at various sites in the brain of a participant who is performing some cognitive task while inside the machine. There are two key facts that make this technology viable. The compound that includes the radioactive fluorine 'label' behaves very similarly to glucose. The way glucose behaves is easily deduced from what is learned about how the glucose analog behaves. The positron that is emitted as the inserted fluorine atom decays travels a very short distance before it meets an electron and vanishes in a puff of gamma rays! Since the apparatus enables us to know very precisely where the annihilation took place, the location of the original fluorine atom can be fairly accurately deduced.

How does the glucose analog get into the subject's brain? By being fed into his or her blood system.

We now understand what the 'positron emission' means. Now for the other technical term, 'tomography'. This term refers to the process of creating an overall image of the state of the subject's brain from the results of detecting the locations of a great many pairs of gamma rays. This has to be done by a suitably programmed computer. In the end, we can enjoy amazingly detailed pictures of the distribution of neural activity in the brain of someone performing a cognitive task.

There are two points to note when we examine these pictures. The first is the large size and small number, relative to the size and number of brain cells, of the areas where activity is taking place. In evaluating the results of PET scans we must keep in mind that there are 100 billion brain cells, interlinked in networks of great complexity! A PET scan may show a dozen sites, of varying dimensions and level of activity. The second point, of even greater importance theoretically, is the wide spread of the many locations activated when an *experientially unified* cognitive process is going on. Certainly some areas seem to be more important than others in the workings of the brain as the main cognitive tool. Nevertheless, the activation of the minor areas seems to be necessary too. This makes the La Mettrie idea of exceptionless correlations even less attractive as a way of establishing a general conceptual link between the discursive story and the neurological story. If anything, it favors the principle upon which a realist cognitive science ought to be based, the task/tool metaphor.

Localization of function is improved by the use of the 'subtraction' principle.

The subtraction principle

In order to pick out the regions involved in the performance of some cognitive task it is necessary to 'subtract' representations of the neural activity of the resting or cognitively inactive brain. 'The resting state is the experimental state where the subject is not required to perform any specific act but, nevertheless, much ongoing neuronal activity is occurring' (Duara, 1990: 6). The subtraction principle must be applied with care. Different regions of the brain may have different 'baseline' or resting levels of glucose uptake, indicating different levels of resting activity. The same region of the brain can show different resting levels at different times.

Subtracting the resting levels of activity from the total activity displayed when a task is being performed gives the neuropsychologist a fair picture of the level and distribution of neural activity to be put down to the task alone.

Limitations of the inferences from positive correlations

The examples of studies in cognitive science that follow in Chapters 10 and 11 make use of artificial intelligence models, in particular of the modeling relation between artificial and real neural nets. The real nets contain millions of cells, each of which is activated in a specific way as a node in a net. The best PET scan picks out active sites in the brain, the most sharply delineated of which contain many thousands of real neurons. Even with the most sophisticated technology, we are many orders of magnitude short of the ability to study the workings of the individual components of real neural nets.

Is this a reason for despairing of ever creating an adequate psychology along scientific realist lines? Surely not. The cognitive scientist is in much the same position as the physicist intent on finding out the inner workings of atoms. Individual electrons in individual atoms cannot be traced, nor can individual quarks in individual protons. Models are tested by the experimental results they make intelligible, and by their ontological plausibility. This, we know, derives from the type hierarchy in which they have a place. In the detailed worked examples to follow we shall see how the very same methodology can be put to work in assessing the adequacy of the complex pattern of reasoning upon which a well founded cognitive science depends. From an analysis of tasks we derive an abstract model by the use of the principles of artificial intelligence simulation. In turn that model can be given a concrete interpretation by the technique of transforming artificial neural nets into hypothetical real neural nets that we learned in Section 1 of this chapter. With the help of PET scans we can locate whole nets. Since the connectionist version of artificial intelligence is built on the principle that it is *whole nets* that are trained to yield a certain output from a given input, the fact that our technology does not permit the study of the neurophysiology of the brain cell by cell need not be something to be depressed about.

---

learning point **Artificial nets and real brains**

1   Problems with the net/brain analogy:

   a)   Neurotransmitters play an important role: they can be modeled only in input/ output functions.

   b)   Hippocampus is net-like but other regions are not obviously so.

   c)   People learn 'the same thing' in many different ways.

2   The brain as an organ:

   a)   Complex anatomy of regions and pathways, with some localization of function. *Note* the paradox of juvenile and adult effects of damage to Broca's and Wernicke's areas.

(continued)

b) Techniques of investigation: identifying anatomical regions active during cognitive task performance.

   i) Negative correlations: functional deficit and brain damage.
   ii) Positive correlations: glucose take-up during task performance. Use of PET scan techniques.

c) Limitations of scanning techniques as psychology

Conclusion

In the next two chapters we will follow two examples of the implementation of the research program for a psychology-in-full in detail. We will begin with the discursive analysis of remembering as a human practice. Then we will set out the cognitive psychologists' categories of types of remembering, followed by an account of the models that they have developed. These are not candidates for analogs of real mechanisms, since they are based on categories drawn from everyday practices of remembering and various refinements and developments thereof. The next step will be to revise these models by transforming them, in so far as that is possible, into artificial intelligence form as connectionist mechanisms. Finally these models will be used to develop hypotheses about the role of anatomical structures in the brain, particularly the hippocampus, as material realizations of the models and their net structures.

This will be followed by a study of practices of classifying and categorizing. This example is important, since it is very easy to see where a GOFAI model tempted artificial intelligence specialists into a premature modeling attempt. Work by cognitive psychologists, developing out of discursively oriented research into actual classifying procedures and practices, showed that the models were seriously defective. By shifting from GOFAI to PDP or connectionist models a start can be made in developing more plausible neurophysiological hypotheses as to the mechanisms that we use for performing these tasks.

Using these examples, we will examine the results of brain studies in relation to the final step, that is, to the possibility of interpreting an artificial neural net as a realist model of an actual brain structure. In so far as this can be achieved, we will have completed a scientific study of two of the most important cognitive skills, remembering and classifying. The pattern of analysis that runs through a discursive analysis to an artificial intelligence abstract representation of the meaning/rule analysis to its reinterpretation as a model of neural structure and functioning will have been illustrated in two real cases. The success of these sketches offers us a good reason for taking this pattern as the most promising start yet to the realization of the dream of a scientific psychology.

Notes

1   A quick survey of three years' issues of the influential journal *Cognitive Science* revealed a predominance of connectionist models. Few, however, involved explicit links with possible brain architecture and processes.

2   The word 'holds' is to be preferred for describing the state of a trained net. 'Stores' retains some of the flavor of the representational account of how knowledge exists in a thinking machine, artificial or organic.

3   It was mentioned by a speaker at Georgetown University, spring semester, 2001. I have not been able to confirm it.

4   My emphasis.

---

self-test **Study questions**

Chapter 7 Grammar and cognition

1   What is the difference between signs and symbols?

2   Must mental states be invoked to explain the intentionality of symbols?

3   What is the Sapir–Whorf hypothesis?

4   What is the Private Language Argument?

5   What is the act–action distinction?

6   Why is the concept of 'skill' needed for cognitive psychology?

7   What is the S grammar?

8   What is the P grammar?

9   What is the O grammar?

10   What is the M grammar?

11   How do Dennett's three stances fit in with the idea of distinct 'working' grammars?

12   Compare the pattern of causal explanations with that of meaning explanations.

13   What is a 'position'?

14   What are the main features of the concept of 'person'?

15   What is the task/tool metaphor in cognitive science?

16   How does it link grammars?

17   What is the Taxonomic Priority Principle?

(study questions continued overleaf)

18   How does it link grammars?

19   Compare individualist and collectivist approaches to psychology.

Reading

Edwards (1997), chapter 1; Dennett (1987), chapters 1–3.

Chapter 8 Cognitive science: the analytical phase

1   What is the distinction between first and second order cognitive tools?

2   What is an instrument used for in physics?

3   How is it related to what it is used to measure?

4   What are typically called 'instruments' in psychology?

5   How are they related to psychological reality?

6   Illustrate the process of transposing research results from a causal to a discursive frame.

7   How can statistical results be interpreted in a discursive frame?

8   Does it make sense to assume that attitudes are causes of behavior?

9   What is the actual content of 'theory of mind' hypotheses?

10   What are the two main senses of 'explanation'?

11   Can the self be studied by introspection?

12   How is the English word 'self' actually used?

13   How is the English pronoun 'I' actually used?

Reading

Radden (1996), chapters 1–2.

Chapter 9 Connectionism and the brain

1   What is a parallel distributed processing?

2   Why is this layout called 'connectionist'?

3   What is the structure of a real neuron?

4   What is the structure of an artificial neuron?

5   What is an activation function?

6   What is activity?

7   What is meant by the 'weight of a connection'?

8   How are real neural nets related to artificial neural nets?

9   What does 'clamping' mean?

10   What is graceful degradation?

11   How is a net trained?

12   What is a Hinton diagram?

13   What are the advantages of connectionist layouts as models for neuropsychology?

14   What are the disadvantages?

15   What is the 'brain as tool' hypothesis?

16   Give an example of negative inference in neuropsychology.

17   Give an example of positive inference in neuropsychology.

18   What is the basic physics of PET scans?

19   What is the subtraction principle?

Reading

A relatively elementary but very clear account of connectionist modeling can be found in Copeland (1998), chapter 10. Students with a special interest in more of the details of connectionist modeling are referred to McLeod et al. (1998), chapters 1–4. We shall be using material from this text in Part IV.

Cognitive science in action

Part III completes our studies of the components of a research program in psychology that could qualify as genuinely scientific, according to the ideals of the natural sciences. It is time to apply all this to some worked examples. The three chapters that comprise this part illustrate the hybrid research paradigm in detail. Each concerns a major aspect of human cognitive practices and skills.

Our studies in the philosophy of science have highlighted the two main phases in building a science in any domain.

A comprehensive yet flexible classification system must be available to bring order to the phenomena of interest. To facilitate this part of the project we may need to make use of analytical models.

Once patterns among types of phenomena have been picked out, they are in need of explanation. The format for providing an explanation is no different in cognitive psychology from what it is in physics. We must be able to represent the processes through which phenomena in the domain of interest are produced. Explanations are based on empirically adequate and ontologically plausible representations or models of the underlying structures and processes through which phenomena come to be. Ontology is important in both phases of research.

1   What sort of being inhabits the domain of the phenomena? In psychology these are public and private *acts*, that is, meaningful performances by human agents.
2   What supertype should be chosen to fix the type hierarchy from which models of the explanatory domain are created?

In psychology we are faced with a fundamental problem of coherence between the type hierarchies with which we classify cognitive phenomena and the type hierarchies from which models of generative processes are drawn. Unity can be achieved without any reduction of thoughts to things by making good use of the master model for the whole of cognitive science, the task/tool metaphor. Cognitive tasks are discursive while cognitive tools are neural, or prostheses for neural, tools.

Cognitive activities are symbolic, managed by rules, conventions and customs that have their source in the activities of people in social groups. Individuals appropriate local cultural resources, acquiring the skills each needs to live successfully in whatever environment they may find themselves. There are all sorts of tools to be used for cognitive tasks. Psychology is the science of the use of material tools that are parts of human bodies. Cognitive tasks are performed, very often, by specialized organs, the brain and central nervous system.

Step 1 The phenomena

Research must begin with an analysis of the performance of the cognitive practice that has been chosen as the topic of interest. Practices such as 'remembering', 'classifying', 'reasoning' or 'calculating' must be followed from initial situation to completion. All sorts of tasks are comprehended under each of these supertypes. Studies of cognitive phenomena, 'on the hoof' so to say, yield catalogs of meanings and task-related standards of correctness and propriety.

The results of such studies can be *expressed* as a set of rules. These fall into two main types. For some tasks there are explicit rules or instructions that must be followed attentively if the task is to be carried out correctly. For some tasks, we rely on our previous training and the good habits we have acquired. To describe this kind of task performance in terms of rules is a useful metaphor. There is no such thing as unconscious rule following. In each category we find constitutive rules defining the practice and regulative rules expressing the local standards for the acceptability of the required performances.

The methods for this stage of research have been developed in discursive psychology. In some circumstances there is a limited role for experiment-like investigations that can enlarge the field of phenomena. However, care must be taken to avoid slipping into misleading causal language for describing the results of such investigations.

The task of cognitive psychology will be to create working models of the cognitive processes by which the patterns of meaningful actions identified in Step 1 are produced. Some cognitive processes are carried out publicly through the medium of language. Conversational analysis will provide analytical models of these processes. In these cases the source and the subject of the model are the same. Some cognitive processes are private and individual. The Vygotskian principle tells us that they are derived from public and collective conversational performances. Hence the obvious source for explanatory models of such processes is again conversation. In these cases the source and the subject of the model are different in some respects. The source is public conversation; the subject is private ratiocination.

Thinking is a symbolic activity, whether it is performed privately or publicly. For example, we remember by creating symbolic representations of the past. However, the means or tools by which we manipulate symbols are material. Some are internal to our bodies, like our brains. Others are external, like pencils and calculators. Some psychologists are interested in modeling how the tools work, others in modeling symbolic processes *per se.*

Step 2 The explanations

How can we build the necessary bridge from our knowledge of cognitive tasks to hypotheses about the tools by which we perform them? In this course we have followed the development of one increasingly plausible and fruitful route. We can use artificial intelligence simulations both as abstract expressions of systems of cultural rules and as the hypotheses about brain structures and processes that would implement them. These yield hypotheses to be offered as invitations to neurophysiologists to look for the real neural mechanisms to which these models, if they meet the joint criteria of empirical adequacy and ontological plausibility, are supposed to be analogous.

Artificial intelligence projects, properly interpreted, are exemplars of how psychology as 'the hybrid science' should be pursued. Programs represent sets of rules for the performance of cognitive or material tasks, extracted from an analysis of acceptable practice. The computational system represents the material groundings for the dispositions, skills and so on implied by the ability of the person to perform the cognitive and material tasks correctly. That can serve as a model for well grounded hypotheses about how the brain and nervous system work as tools for these and other tasks.

Why do we need an intermediary set of models drawn from artificial intelligence? Could we not go directly from cognitive phenomena to states of and processes in the nervous system? Unfortunately there are two major reasons why this will not do.

For the most part the processes by which people carry out cognitive tasks are unobservable. They are not available to conscious introspection, or to neurological research. Even if the difficulties of observation were to be overcome, there is a startling diversity of scale between the two domains that are to be united by the task/tool metaphor and the Taxonomic Priority Principle. PET scans, as we have studied them in the last chapter, reveal very coarse-grained features of the active brain. The activated regions probably contain hundreds of thousands, even millions of neurons. The processes that serve as cognitive tools are to be found in patterns of activation of dendritic and axonic nets at a scale many orders of magnitude more fine-grained than anything revealed by current methods of investigation. This is exactly the situation in the natural sciences. This is just the point at which a science of psychology should open up by the development of powerful and plausible models of the unknown and unobservable processes going on in the second order tools by which people bring about the phenomena in question.

Here is another example of 'scale disparity' in a research program. We have extremely fine-grained and detailed knowledge of human anatomy and physiology. The explanation of adult bodily traits by reference to inheritance of parental characteristics was initially developed by the application of Mendel's laws to sequences of patterns of observable characteristics, generation by generation. Those laws are very simple. However, in the observable processes of cell division, essential in the building of bodies, the unit is the chromosome. For example, male and female, as somatic categories, were explained by reference to observable distributions of X and Y chromosomes. The fine structure of the twenty-odd chromosomes in which the thousands and thousands of genes presupposed by Mendel's laws were physically located was unobservable. To match the fine grain of anatomical and physiological studies at the descriptive phase of human biology, Watson and Crick constructed a model of the unobservable fine structure of chromosomes. This was their famous 'double helix', built out of four organic bases, and representing the genome.

The situation is the same in cognitive science. Discursive analysis gives us very fine-grained and detailed analyses of cognitive processes. PET scans and other procedures give us very coarse-grained analyses of the relevant brain mechanisms, just as coarse-grained as were the chromosomes. Only by developing fine-grain models of the neural networks can we begin to resolve the 'scale disparity' in cognitive psychology. That requires the modeling techniques of artificial intelligence, in particular the innovatory modeling of brain processes in artificial neural nets.

Human life is molecular, biological and symbolic. To describe the whole gamut of human activities, at least three kinds of discourse are required. There must be a discourse in which persons are featured as the active authors of streams of symbolic activities. There must be a discourse in which human beings appear as organisms interacting with each other and with the environment. There must be a discourse in which the molecular structures of neural and prosthetic tools are modeled.

Psychology, as one among the discourses of humanity, will surely take at least three forms. There must be a discourse of persons in symbolic interaction, both public and private. There must be a biological discourse of organisms and their behavior. To complete the scientific study of cognition there must be a discourse concerning the molecular constituents of the relevant aspects and organs of the human body. None of these discourses can replace either or both of the others without doing irreparable harm to the project of psychology itself. In practice the three discourses are linked in several ways. In Part III we explored the three discourses in some detail, and contrasted and compared the ways they can be linked into cognitive psychology, the hybrid science.

Now, in Part IV, we will follow the realization of our methodological project in two research programs, the study of remembering and the study of classifying. In the last chapter we will look at some of the ways that cognition can go wrong. The same pattern of identifying cognitive acts and forming hypotheses about the state of the relevant neural tools is evident in the field of psychopathology.

All this is made possible by the adoption and use of the two main principles through which the domain of symbols and the domain of neurons can be unified. The taxonomic priority principle allows us to identify the active regions revealed by the use of PET scans and other non-invasive techniques as the sites of the brain processes a thinking person is using to accomplish the cognitive tasks in hand. Regions are not classified anatomically, but functionally. In developing the technique of connectionist modeling to try to represent the fine structure of neural tools used for cognitive tasks, we need the task/tool metaphor to establish the functional unification of discourse analysis with brain studies to complete the hybrid science.

The sources of rules, conventions and customs are to be found in culture and history. The origins of neural mechanisms, the tools of cognition, are to be found in the Darwinian evolution of the human body in an environment increasingly dominated by cultural forces. However, though the origins of second order cognitive tools, organs in the brain, are natural, there is evidence that they are shaped by cultural forces to an extent we are only just beginning to understand. Studies of the cognitive differences between separated monozygotic twins are one promising line of research into the relative influences of genetic programs and cultural environments on the physical form of brain structures. Less well known, but equally important theoretically, have been studies of the effect on brain structure and organization of different ways of representing language. Tsunida (1972) showed, many years ago, differences between the brains of Japanese and Westerners that can plausibly be explained by differences in the ways that Japanese and English are written. It has been suggested that changes in the distribution of cells in the hippocampus come about through intensive learning of detailed topographical knowledge.

The memory machine

Thinking about the past is a cognitive skill of the utmost practical importance. In this chapter[1] we shall follow the development of a scientific study
of remembering to illustrate the methods of cognitive science in some
detail. A scientific study of the phenomena of some domain, be it subatomic physics or the psychology of remembering, requires the following:

1   An open set of categories, for classifying the phenomena that fall
    into the domain of interest. Some boundary criteria are needed
    to mark off those phenomena that fall into the domain from those
    that do not. Such a boundary will inevitably be fuzzy and often con-
    tested. A psychological domain laid out in a scientific taxonomy
    must remain pegged at certain points to the everyday working
    categories that ordinary people use to manage the relevant phe-
    nomena. Unless we can meet this requirement, we are in danger of
    losing touch with the phenomena themselves. A preliminary study
    of the everyday practices that we call 'remembering', 'recalling',
    'reminiscing' and so on is necessary to fix the domain of phenom-
    ena we are trying to understand. By tracing out the rules for the uses
    of the relevant words we will have an overview of what people pick
    out with this vocabulary.
2   We need models to represent the domain of observable phenomena
    and the unobservable processes by which those phenomena are
    brought into being, change, perish, relate to one another and so on.
    Analytical models are needed to simplify and abstract from the
    complexity and fuzziness of the phenomena as they occur in real
    life. With the help of the working concepts of our growing and
    improving taxonomy we can carry out the essential first stage in
    psychological research. Here we can exploit the conversational
    model, looking for the meanings of what people do and the norms
    that frame what they do in standards of correctness, propriety and
    so on. Other analytical models will prove of value from time to time.

For the final stage of a scientific research program we need explanatory
models to represent and to stand in for the working processes of the

second order neurological tools people use to carry out the relevant cognitive tasks.

The sources of both kinds of models are a matter of concern. The sources of analytical models need not be ontologically plausible. They need provide only scaffolding for analysing and classifying phenomena. However, the sources of explanatory models must be constrained by ontological plausibility. In the physical sciences their function is to stand in for unobservables. Scientific method requires them to be analogs of possible beings that may inhabit the world beyond the limits of observation. The situation is not quite the same in cognitive science. The explanatory models stand in for the way that neural tools work. The concepts for describing processes and structures in the brain are not found in the classificatory categories of the descriptive phase of research. There we use meanings and rules. However, in cognitive science, models of the workings of second order cognitive tools in the brain and nervous system refer to states and processes that can, in principle, be observed. However, brain processes are studied by methods other than those by means of which psychological phenomena are observed.

Psychology majors will almost certainly have taken a course on the subject of 'Memory', covering many of the topics introduced here. The material in this chapter is meant to be detailed enough to serve as an illustration of the structure of a complete research program in cognitive science. It is not a mini-course on the psychology of memory. The layout of the chapter shadows that of the recommended co-textbook, Cohen et al. (1993). The task/tool metaphor on which this course is based applies nicely to their research program as well. It supports their distinction between systematic research into the practices of everyday remembering and the construction of artificial intelligence models powerful enough to provide strong hypotheses about the nature and modes of working of neural structures in the human brain, the main tool of cognition.

The practices of remembering have socio-cultural origins. The tools of remembering have natural, Darwinian origins.

section one

The vernacular vocabulary of remembering

We will begin with a brief study of the words we use to talk about various practices that involve thinking about the past. Once we have established the topic in the world of everyday English speakers, we will turn to a sketch of some of the terminologies and distinctions that psychologists have distilled out of their commonsense categorizing of kinds and cases of remembering. We will then follow the enlargement of the semantic field of concept of 'remembering' to include phenomena that do not usually fall into that category.

What can be remembered?

The lexicon of words for referring to recalling the past are nearly all prefixed with 're-', suggesting that in remembering people are doing something they have done already. We have re-member, re-call, re-collect, re-minisce, re-live, re-cover and more. To remember the past is not to repeat it as such. To remember something from the past is, in all sorts of possible ways, a reworking of the original experience of some event, state of affairs and so on, public or private, *in some symbolic form.*

A claim to remember can be sustained by the production of a correct description or picture of the relevant past event or state of affairs, and defeated by the failure to do this. What is the difference between someone saying 'The tree was blown down in April' and 'I remember that the tree was blown down in April'? In many cases the phrase 'I remember ...' serves to express a claim to be an authority on some past matter. The implicit claim to authority may need backing up. 'Well, I was there' or 'I saw it go down' may often clinch the matter. What follows the past-directed, authority-claiming prefix is usually introduced with 'that'. 'I remember *that* the tree was blown over in April.' The act of recollection takes the form of a statement describing whatever is alleged to have occurred when a memory is given public expression. The cognitive process involved is often called 'recollection' or 'recall' as well as simply 'remembering'.

This form of words is also used to claim that one has an ability or skill acquired at some time in the past. 'Remember' is used to claim the permanent possession of manual and intellectual abilities and skills. We say that we remember *how* to open the safe, cut a parallel groove with a tenon saw, solve a second order differential equation and so on. The claim may be challenged. Backing it up often requires a demonstration of the ability in question. Why do we use the verb 'to remember' in this case? It covers skills and abilities that are not native endowments. One can remember only what one has once learned how to do, still knows, and has not forgotten. 'I remember how to walk' sounds odd, while 'I remember how to paddle a canoe' does not. Nevertheless, there are occasions on which such questions as 'Have you forgotten how to walk?' do have a use, for instance after someone has been bedridden for months.

The main uses of the word 'know' fit nicely with these two major uses of 'remember'. We show that we 'know that' something is the case or that such-and-such an event happened, and so on, by recalling it in the form of a statement. We could equally well have said that we 'remember that' such and such event happened. In exercising a skill we show that we 'know how to do something' or we could say that we show that we 'remember how to do something'. Learning, knowing and remembering are strongly conceptually related. In learning we acquire certain skills and abilities, certain bodies of knowledge that are relatively permanent. In remembering we make use of those skills and find public and sometimes private expression of what we have learned.

In both 'remembering that' and 'remembering how' the past is invoked, explicitly in the one case and implicitly in the other. In neither case is the past revived as such. The past is inaccessible. There is no time travel. What has happened, what once existed and so on has gone for good. What is at issue are *representations or consequences* of something that happened in the past. In common parlance we talk freely about having access to the past, but that we never have. At best, we encounter or conjure up traces or representations of the past.

The verb 'to remember' in the past and future tenses

Second and third person uses of the past tense of the verb 'to remember' are just descriptions of what someone other than the speaker did in the past. The past tenses of first person remembering verbs obey a different logic from the present tense uses. In the present tense they are used to make defeasible claims. In the past tense they are just like second and third person uses. They are used to report successful and unsuccessful attempts to recall a fact or to display a skill. The future-tensed expressions have various uses, depending on context and content. For example, 'Yes, I will remember to put the cat out' is a promise or reassurance as well as a prediction of what I will do. However, 'If I tie a knot in my handkerchief I will remember to buy more bread' seems to be a simple prediction only. The responsibility for a reminder has been passed from the speaker to something else.

Remembering as an achievement

To remember something is to recollect it correctly. It follows that remembering is an achievement. One may try, for example, to remember someone's birth date, and just fail. In everyday life, we routinely make use of a distinction between 'trying to remember' and 'remembering'. This distinction is used for both the recall of facts (someone's name, a date and so on) and the display of rusty skills (tying a reef knot, using a search engine and so on). The distinction between trying and achieving is central to our everyday concepts of remembering. If someone has come out with a claim to remember something the crucial question of its correctness, accuracy and so on can always be raised.

'Knowing', like 'remembering', is a success word. If one's claim to remember some event turns out to have been wrong, one just did not remember it. If one claims to know some matter of fact, and one has it wrong, one did not know it. If one cannot perform some skilled activity that one claims to know how to do, one simply did not know how to do it. Logically one cannot know wrongly, any more than one can remember what did not happen and what one did not learn.

Ryle (1947) has explored the distinction between trying and succeeding. He distinguishes task verbs, like 'running' and 'trying', from achievement verbs like 'winning' and 'noticing'. An achievement is not a process and has no temporal duration, only a temporal moment. Generally speaking, 'remembering' in the sense of 'recalling' is an achievement verb. Such phrases as 'trying to remember', 'searching my memory for …' and so on are task verbs. Displaying a learned skill or ability sometimes follows the task/achievement pattern. 'Eventually I got the knot tied' is like that. However, reminiscing at length about the events of yesteryear is a continuous activity. Nevertheless, it must incorporate certain achievements. In a nostalgic discussion of schooldays I recall the time we lost the rugby match.

We do not usually recollect the experiencing of the event remembered as another event. Usually we claim to remember the unfortunate incident at the vicar's tea party rather than the event of the experiencing of the incident. Sometimes though, the very experiencing of the event may itself be memorable.

The problem of authentication

A claim to have remembered something requires the content of the claim, in whatever medium, to be more or less correct. A recollection must represent some past state of affairs *successfully*. Just what 'successfully' means in the context of remembering is a difficult problem, largely because the commonsense criterion of comparing the content of the recollection with what it purports to represent cannot usually be applied. In most cases in real life there are no records or traces of what occurred against which to test the verisimilitude of what we claim happened.

Most real happenings leave no trace. This fact is not represented in the classical psychology of remembering based on Ebbinghaus-type experimentation.[2] In many laboratory-based studies the question of the temporal stability of the stimulus materials, of their existence unchanged throughout the experiment, is never raised. That the experimenter has 'the past' in hand is just taken for granted. An array of nonsense syllables that one might use in an experiment to test the '7 +/– 2' rule can be permanently recorded on a tape or a video loop. It would be wildly eccentric seriously to dispute the presupposition that the data on the loop used in the experiment are the same as the data on the very same loop used to assess the results of an experiment. However, in real remembering there are usually few, if any, stable material traces of the past. Whatever traces there are can always be challenged. Recall the trouble over DNA in the O.J. Simpson trial. Was the glove his? And so on.

This point is very important for the scientific study of remembering as a cognitive practice. Just to take an experiment at random: here we have a description of an experiment done by Postman and Phillips many years ago.

> subjects are presented with a list of unrelated words and asked to recall as many as possible in any order they wish. … when recall is immediate, there is a tendency for the last few items to be very well recalled, the so-called recency effect. After a brief filled delay, however, the recency effect disappears.
>
> (As reported in Baddeley, 1998: 38b)

Notice that it is taken for granted that the material has survived unchanged from the moment at which it was presented to the participants to the moment at which they recall 'it'. Try the experiment again, but this time let the stimulus materials be the various items you had for dinner two weeks ago! Or almost anything else that one may be required to remember in some everyday context. In real life we usually assess the accuracy of recall by comparing the content of one act of remembering with that of another. Reliable material records are very rare.

It is in the nature of time that we cannot experience either the event recollected or the then contemporaneous experiencing of it a second time. Remembering is a new experience, usually, though not always, in another medium, of that which was once experienced. All *acts* of remembering are, at least in principle, claims to have recovered some aspect of the past by conceiving a representation or description of it. Given the usual lack of concrete evidence, the opinions of other people influence our accepting of this or that thought or utterance or drawing as a reasonably correct representation of the past. Since there is rarely any accessible material evidence of what happened in the past, remembering as an everyday practice is as much a social as a personal activity. In the absence of forensic evidence – and even that can be disputed in a court of law – one can have recourse to the (unreliable) recollections of other people who are thought to have been in a position to have some authority as to what happened.

Quite often an attempt to recover the past through arriving at an accurate and defensible representation requires a dialog in which more than one person is involved. Remembering is often conducted discursively, through claims and counter-claims as to the reality of some aspect of the past with which the people involved were or could have been directly and personally involved. This will lead us into the fascinating topic of collective remembering pioneered in the work of Middleton and Edwards (1990) and Dixon (1996).

section two

Remembering as a topic for cognitive psychology

Glenberg is quoted in Garnham (1997) as answering the question 'What is memory for?' with the general and anodyne comment that it is 'in the service of perception and action in a three-dimensional environment'. However, everything in the cognitive equipment of a healthy and whole-minded person exists in that service. We need to frame our scientific studies of remembering and forgetting in a much more detailed catalog of *tasks and tools*. For example: 'What do people use the relevant parts of their brains, biologically inbuilt equipment, or their electronic organizers, shop-bought memory machines, for in everyday life?' This question has quite diverse answers. 'For keeping appointments, for finding the way home, for remembering one's mother's birthday, for ordering lunch in France, for taking part in a quiz show' and so on and so on, including 'for taking part in a psychological experiment'. Having identified the various tasks comprehended under the umbrella concept of 'remembering', including its metaphorical extensions in knowledge-engineering contexts, the next step may seem to be to simply pick out the neural tools that are being used in carrying out these tasks. Unfortunately, matters are not so simple.

We learned in Chapter 9 that between the cognitive phenomenon, characterized by meanings and rules of correctness, and the neural tools by means of which a competent person performs cognitive tasks, we must insert an artificial intelligence model. The complexity of the phenomena revealed by discursive analysis and the relatively coarse-grained character of the results of brain scan studies means that the work of matching the diverse structures of task and tool to one another requires an intermediary. Areas identified by PET scans may contain huge numbers of brain cells in reticulated arrays, the structure of which is intimately bound up with their function.

Attempts to go from the way acts of remembering are performed to the way neural tools work have not been successful except in so far as they have involved the construction of informal artificial intelligence models to bring the phenomena and the explanatory hypotheses into co-ordination. We will find very instructive examples of such models in the current cognitive psychology of 'memory'. It is not just a matter of the relative detail with which phenomena and neural mechanisms are known. An intermediary is also a logical necessity. It is necessitated by the simple fact that remembering is a *normative* discursive practice, while neural activity is causal and material.

Neisser's paradox and the Ebbinghaus paradigm

Modeling, the heart of cognitive science, as it is of any scientific enterprise, is constrained by two external relations. It is constrained by what we know about public conduct and procedures and skilled performance on the one hand, and by neurological possibilities on the other. Ulrich Neisser (1976: 2) first brought this point to prominence. He presented a paradox: 'If X is an important or interesting feature of human behavior, then X has rarely been studied by psychologists.' This insight led Neisser to the concept of 'ecological validity', that is, the requirement that the results of laboratory research should be generalizable to the patterns of ordinary life. In the case of research on 'memory' in recent times the distancing of the laboratory version of remembering from the matters that people recall, reminisce about and so on can be laid at the door of Ebbinghaus.

Most laboratory studies of remembering follow, in some measure, the original methods of Ebbinghaus. He studied the memorial capacities of individual people acting individually. He presented his subjects, often just one subject, himself, with material to be remembered. At some later time, the duration depending on the aim of the experiment and the type of material presented, the subject was asked to recall what had been seen or heard. Ebbinghaus was interested in the relationship between the material presented and the material recalled. For instance, he looked into the proportion of the original material that was recalled after lapses of time, in various circumstances. He followed this up by trying to find out how the proportion changed with time.

In our terms, Ebbinghaus's research program can be seen as an exploration of how the memory machine works in the abstract. To eliminate all the effects of meaning on the basic processes of learning and recall he created a special kind of material for his experiments, 'all possible syllables of a certain sort were constructed' he says. '... (Ebbinghaus, 1885 [1987]: 22). '... these syllables were mixed together and then drawn out by chance and used to construct series of [nonsense syllables] of different lengths ...' His project was to find out by experiment how many repetitions were necessary to learn sequences of syllables of different lengths. Having carried that part of the project through, he turned to study the effects of the elapse of time on how readily sequences of various lengths could be relearned. Using statistical averages, he describes his method as follows: 'when I [himself as subject] memorized series of syllables of a certain length to the point of their first possible reproduction, the times or the numbers of repetitions necessarily differed greatly from each other, but the mean values had the character of genuine constants' (Ebbinghaus, 1885 [1987]: 52).

This set-up is not much like the sort of remembering tasks that one is faced with in everyday life! Laboratory work in the study of remembering, using Ebbinghausian methods, is hopelessly compromised from the start *if it purports to be an investigation of people remembering things*. Should the lack of Neisser's ecological validity force us to reject the results of Ebbinghaus's experiments as useless artifacts of the laboratory method? Not if we are working in the task/tool framework. Conceived within the project of building artificial intelligence models of the tools people use for carrying out tasks of remembering, laboratory studies take on a different appearance. Ebbinghausian experiments are studies of the capacities of neural tools, in abstract and idealized conditions. We need to know what the inbuilt memory machines are capable of in the unreal conditions of the laboratory if we are to understand how they are used in the very different conditions of the real world.

The solution to Neisser's paradox is neither to reject Ebbinghausian experiments out of hand and demand instant ecological validity nor to insist on bringing all psychological phenomena into the 'laboratory'. The upshot of implementing such a policy would be to abandon the scientific project altogether. We would become bogged down in intolerable complexity. The solution is to find a conceptual system that will comprehend both methods of enquiry, each assigned its proper role. The task/tool way of looking at cognitive psychology provides just such a comprehensive conceptual system. Neural mechanisms are the 'natural' tools for certain cognitive tasks. Ebbinghaus-type experiments can be used to explore the capacities of memory machines in the abstract.

Important though it is to know what the human memory machine will do in the abstract, the psychology of remembering is broader. It must include how people use memory machines in real life, when the Ebbinghausian conditions for the assessment of correctness of recall often cannot be met at all. Of course, there must be criteria for correct recall in use, otherwise the complex pattern of criticism and correction could not be put to use, nor could memory be distinguished from fantasy.

The problem of the workings of memory machines

At first sight it would seem as if identifying instances of remembering, and noting what was happening in the brain and nervous system when someone performed one of them, would be enough to allow us to pick out the neural toolkit with which we carry out everyday remembering tasks. There are many structures and processes that occur in the human brain and nervous system, but only certain regions are seen to be active when someone is exercising the power of recall. The tools for remembering must be among those parts of the nervous system we are endowed with by Darwinian selection.

However, the seemingly simple step from an analysis of remembering practices to a cognitive science of remembering, involving the mechanisms by which remembering is achieved, is much more difficult than one might suppose at first sight. In this chapter we explore some important suggestions as to the ways it might be accomplished, and assess the progress that has been made so far in this work. We will also identify certain blind alleys that once looked promising but have turned out to be dead ends.

We will need to consult the neurophysiology and neuroanatomy of those organs in the brain that we use for remembering. However, to be able to understand how they work, we need to draw on knowledge engineering, in particular the artificial intelligence techniques of connectionist modeling. We will see how by bringing these two specialist branches of knowledge together the transition from common understanding through cognitive psychology to models of memory machines can be achieved. The final step to an understanding of certain neural systems as naturally occurring memory machines may at last be achieved.

A full psychology of remembering must include studies of the nature and role of various non-natural devices. We now use a great many prosthetic devices like agendas, electronic organizers and knots tied in handkerchiefs. These serve as ancillary equipment for performing some of the same range of memorial tasks as used, once upon a time, to be the preserve of the human brain alone. Not only are they of interest in their own right, but it is also possible – indeed, likely – that how they work can throw light on how natural, organic memory machines work.

Generic models: representation and retention

Another general problem must be addressed in setting up a scientific treatment of the phenomenon of remembering. It concerns the choice of generic model, the supertype shaping our working type hierarchy, within which to frame theories and research projects in the cognitive psychology of remembering. We start with the correct principle that whatever characterizes the diversity of type of material to be remembered, be it facts, meanings or ways of doing things, must also character-ize what is recalled when it is recalled. However, it does not follow that whatever characterizes what is remembered and what is recalled must also characterize the way this ability is maintained in the remembering system between the moments of acquisition and recall. The plural noun 'memories' leads one rather easily into thinking that to remember something is to have some mental item retained some-where 'in the mind'. Nearly a century ago Ogden and Richards (1934) coined the word 'engram' to describe material traces that played the same role in a materialist psychology of recollection as 'memories' played in a mentalistic one.

To help us understand this difficult point it will be helpful to introduce a dis-tinction between two possible forms a general account of the ability to remember could take. The 'representation' thesis runs something like this: remembering something consists in being in a permanent mental or material state that corres-ponds to the event as it was originally experienced or a routine as it was originally learned. Remembering is simply bringing out a conscious representation of that state or a display of the behavioral routine. According to this thesis, there is a three-way pattern of correspondences. One runs from past event as experienced to a persisting representation 'in the mind'. The other runs from the persisting representation to a present display. The cognitive psychology of remembering is shot through with the metaphor of 'storage'. Items, it is said, are stored here and there in the system. Indeed, it seems often to be presupposed that they are held in material form in actual locations in the brain and central nervous system.

Alternatively, one could hold to the 'retention' thesis. In the past a person acquired the ability to produce a representation of the original experience or a re-run of the original routine on a later occasion, without any existential implications about how the ability was maintained. There may be no material representations of particular events or specific steps in a routine in the brain and nervous system. Yet the whole system may be able to perform as required.

The distinction between representing the past and retaining the ability to recover a version of the past is by no means merely verbal. Metaphors are vehicles for models. We have learned how to analyse models in use in a scientific discipline into a supertype and its dependent subtypes. The metaphor of 'storage' carries with it a dominant supertype, controlling many subsidiary models created for par-ticular cases. Recalling our studies of the basic concepts of artificial intelligence, it is easy to see that the storage metaphor is a natural ally of the thesis that cog-nition is computation in a generally GOFAI mechanism. In our desktop hard-ware there are, literally, representations of input as filled registers in the body of the machine. The metaphor of remembering as the acquisition and retention of an ability is a natural ally of the thesis that cognition occurs in neural nets with no specific locations for item-by-item representations.

The research program summarized

Recalling our general discussion in earlier chapters of what is required for a genuinely scientific program of research, we note that there are five stages to a complete treatment of a phenomenon like remembering. In the first stage, it involves an analysis of the practice as it is carried out in everyday life, including studies of analogous phenomena in cultures other than our own. With this material in hand (often simply assumed or taken for granted by psychologists) we can begin to identify different kinds of remembering, some by content, some by function and some by other criteria that emerge in the effort to construct a taxonomy. We may come to notice psychological phenomena that had previously escaped our attention.

At this point, the task/tool metaphor comes into play. It directs the attention of the researcher to the tools by which people conduct memorial tasks. The tools that have interested most psychologists are 'natural', the organs of thought, located in the brain and nervous system. Some psychologists have constructed processing models of what look at first like possible mechanisms of remembering. We will look closely at the nature of some these, using Baddeley's inventions as a leading example. In fact many of these models are merely ways of expressing the results of observations and experiments, and only very loosely indebted to concepts drawn from knowledge engineering.

Before the step to neural investigations can be made, models of memory machines must be thoroughly refined and developed in detail, as artificial intelligence models. From what we have learned so far, it is likely that only connectionist models will prove to be adequate both to express the phenomena and to represent the neural tools by which people carry out the tasks of everyday remembering. Only then will we have that guarantee of existential plausibility that makes it worth looking into the brain for analogs of the structures and the processes that characterize working connectionist models. Only then can there be a confluence between neural studies and the study of the cognitive phenomena in question.

S.E. Hampson has put the matter very well: 'Fortunately, the development of connectionist science has provided the behavior-analytic community with an opportunity to forge those all-important links with those involved in the study of neurophysiology [and anatomy].'

After constructing an artificial intelligence simulation of the information-processing structures of abstract memory machines that would serve as tools for various varieties of remembering, the next task is to provide a model for neurophysiological testing. Such a model must fit the known features of the discursive performances involved in remembering on the one side, so to say, and the possibilities of neural functioning on the other.

In discussing the current scene I will generally prefer the term 'remembering', with its connotations of process and activity, to the word 'memory'. Whether the latter is used generically or as a noun purportedly referring to some continuing state of a person's mind, it carries unacceptable substantival implications. Most of the authors to be discussed tend to use the noun, even though they usually mean to refer to a cognitive *process*.

In all the sciences, knowledge is presented in a complicated pattern of metaphors and analogies. This has the enormous advantage of encouraging creative thinking. At times it has the disadvantage that unwanted aspects of the sources of metaphors or analogies creep into the application of the metaphorical usage. Physicists are more alert to this problem than are psychologists. One of the skills we must acquire in developing our understanding of cognitive psychology is sensitivity to the limits of the working metaphors. Such metaphors are necessary to the scientific standing of the field yet remain problematic. They are both growing points and sources of danger.

section three

Cognitive psychology of remembering, phase one: a descriptive taxonomy

We begin our survey of the cognitive psychology of remembering with a scheme for classifying types of remembering, including some recently proposed categories. It will quickly become apparent that there is a wide variety of considerations and criteria in use in distinguishing kinds of remembering, each of which has value in particular contexts. Many acts of remembering could be classified under more than one heading.

It would seem to be obvious that the ways we remember visual, auditory and tactile experiences must be different from the ways that we remember meanings, stories, recipes and so on. These must be different again from the way we remember the way home, knowing which way to turn at each junction when we reach it, though we could neither visualize the route nor give adequate instructions to a visitor beforehand. While there is something in these commonsense distinctions, a hundred years of studies of how and what people remember have led to a variety of classificatory categories, each having a certain utility in an appropriate context. I believe we can say definitively that some proposals are certainly mistaken and others still in need of clarification, while others look like being here to stay.

Two preliminary observations are in order to understand the significance of the various taxonomies. First of all the entities and structures referred in these classification systems are *abstract* entities and processes. The question of whether they have real-world analogs is in many cases still open. Secondly, there is the pervasive metaphor of remembering as storing, and of memory as a *store* or *stores*. Along with that image goes the metaphor of memories as discrete items of knowledge. In the course of this survey we will come to see that the metaphor of remembering as storing is more misleading than helpful. We will replace it by another: the metaphor of remembering as acquiring an ability to perform certain tasks.

The distinction between individual and collective remembering is now well established. The majority of studies of the domain of memory phenomena have been conducted with individual participants. The memorial processes investigated have been sited in individual people and, for the most part, have not been consciously monitored by either the participants themselves or by the psychologists conducting the studies. In collective remembering the process of creating a representation of the past can be followed explicitly. The distinction between collective and individual remembering is the broadest of the classificatory categories to be used in this study.

Collective remembering

There are two major categories of collective remembering. In one class of cases the remembering activities consist essentially of a conversation between members of a small group. It may be a family (Kreckel, 1981). It may be a couple (Dixon, 1996). It may be a group of casual acquaintances (Middleton and Edwards, 1990). In the course of the conversation, various proposals are put forward. Some are ratified and some are rejected. The upshot is a socially constructed representation of the past event, of the alleged item of knowledge and so on that was the focus of the conversation.

This work has shown how important are rights in the formation of agreed versions of the past. Kreckel, and Middleton and Edwards, have shown that there are unequal distributions of power and authority to adjudicate a dispute as to the verisimilitude of a remembering claim put forward by one of the participants.

There are now well established differences between how successful people are when remembering collectively and the same people remembering individually. This is of great importance in the gerontology of remembering. Dixon, and others, have shown that while the individual's capacity in remembering declines with age, collective remembering by pairs of old folk is as effective as collective remembering by matched pairs of younger folk.

The second major category of remembering collectively is institutional and national remembering. The past of a nation, for example, is re-presented to the citizens in all sorts of ways. For example, there are annual memorial ceremonials, such as the two minutes' silence on 11 November with which the British remind themselves of the end of the First World War. There are May Day celebrations in many countries. There is Presidents' Day in the United States. Schwartz (1990: 81–107) studied some of the processes by which the relevant media produce collective memories.

Memorials and museums are prime examples of media for collective remembering. So far, these modes of memory have not been given the attention they deserve. For example, I know of no studies of the preliminary decision making and planning that go into setting up a museum exhibition.

Individual remembering

Let us begin with a catalogue of standard distinctions in modes and types of remembering. The final step will be to set them out in a type hierarchy.

Short-term and long-term remembering

The distinction between short-term and long-term 'memory' was once fundamental to the psychology of remembering. The high point of the metaphor of 'short and long-term stores' was many decades ago. One sees it pervading the work reported in Atkinson and Shiffrin (1968), for example. It is implicit in George Miller's famous formula for the limits of short-term remembering: that the item should consist of seven plus or minus two elements, whatever they might be. Though cognitive psychologists recently have more or less dropped the distinction in its simple form, the concept of a distinctive short-term memory capacity is the basis of some very important research and consequential model building. It has been important for verbal learning, especially when the learning of verbal material has been divorced from discursive contexts. It is very closely tied to the 'store' metaphor, in that it pictures representations of current happenings as cognitive units, 'memories', thought of as *items* stored in short-term memory. Long-term memory consisted of some short-term memory items which have been transferred elsewhere in the system to a long-term store or stores. However, this picture of stores and the transfer of items between them no longer commands unquestioned assent. It is now thought to be a mistake to assume that there is a long-term memory *system*, which functions like the short-term one. Indeed, the very idea of *items* of information is now becoming outmoded in cutting-edge memory studies.

Why has the concept of 'long-term memory' lost favor? It is partly due to the realization that there may be several memory systems, of different types and working in different ways. Remembering something for a long time may not be the result of the transfer of material from one 'store' to another essentially similar 'place'.

Declarative and procedural remembering

The term 'declarative memory' as used in contrast to procedural remembering, covers two subspecies, episodic and semantic memory. Here is how Engelkamp and Zimmer (1994: 1) define *episodic* remembering: '... memory for objects or events we have seen ... speech that we have heard or texts that we have read ... actions that we have performed'. The distinction between episodic remembering, that is, remembering incidents from the past, and semantic remembering, that is, remembering the meanings of words, was made by Tulving (1972). The ability to remember the meanings of symbols does not require recall of the context in which the meaning was first learned. Generally, the context is preserved as either an explicit or an implicit part of what is remembered of an autobiographical episode, whereas in learning and remembering meanings the episodic context is not, in general, remembered. This distinction roughly corresponds to the commonsense distinction between remembering particular events with which one was involved and remembering matters of fact, such as the date of a battle. People rarely remember the moment when they learned that the battle of Hastings occurred in 1066.

Procedural memory comprehends the maintenance of abilities and skills that have been learned at some time in the past. Typically, procedural remembering is evident in remembering how to perform certain tasks, such as proving the Pythagoras theorem or changing a light bulb.

There are two main modes of procedural remembering recognized in psychology: implicit and explicit remembering. This distinction was first proposed in these terms by Graft and Schachter (1985: 501): 'implicit memory is revealed when performance on a task is facilitated in the absence of conscious recollection; explicit memory is revealed when performance on a task requires conscious recollection of previous experience'. In subsequent writings Schachter has refined this definition, particularly as to what is meant by 'conscious recollection'. Despite this clarification, it is not entirely clear what the distinction is. It is easier to understand what may be meant by implicit procedural memory. When the implicit/explicit distinction is used in linguistic contexts it is tied with another phenomenon, 'priming'. The phenomenon of 'priming' can be illustrated in the case in which some item of information given to someone at the beginning of an experiment, and not explicitly recalled, can be seen to have influenced the perception or understanding of some item presented later. In studying the phenomenon of 'priming' it is easy to distinguish experimentally between the two kinds of implicit linguistic memory, semantic, that is, remembered meaning, and lexical, that is, remembered form, simply by using bilingual participants. For example, in semantic priming the speed of recognition of a word is affected by the content of words presented before someone is asked to try to recognize a newly presented word. The form of the words presented earlier also affects recognition rates. This is lexical priming. For a bilingual the semantic priming effect will be independent of the language in which the priming act is performed. Lexical priming will be sensitive to choice of language. 'Horse' and *caballo* are semantically equivalent but lexically distinct.[3] These two words should have the same priming effect for Spanish–English bilinguals but different lexical effects.

In explicit procedural remembering one may have to consciously recall and attend to an instruction or some matter of fact in order to proceed to the next step in some complex practice. For example, I have to remind myself when changing a light bulb that some bulbs screw in but others need a push and a twist. I look at the base of the bulb before I begin to insert it into the socket.

The distinction between procedural remembering on the one hand and semantic *and* episodic memory on the other is not entirely satisfactory in that one could make a case for treating semantic remembering as the exercise of a skill, or even the manifestation of a habit. If we were to follow Wittgenstein's popular conception of meaning as use we would be more inclined to make the basic distinction, that between procedural and episodic remembering, with both the procedural and the declarative category having two sub-categories, semantic and non-semantic abilities and skills, and semantic and non-semantic statements or reports.

We can see this point more clearly by asking, 'How would one find out whether someone knew the meaning of a certain word?' One could ask whether the person could give a verbal account of the meaning, say by citing a synonym or a formal definition. One could also ask the person to make up a sentence including the word in question, to see whether he or she could make correct use of it. Both methods of exploring this question have been used in empirical studies of semantic memory.

In order to guarantee that psychological distinctions and categories, such as those above, have anything to tell us about human cognition we must maintain a link between them and the working categories of the everyday practices of remembering. We do not ordinarily talk about having remembered the uses of words when we are effortlessly engaged in conversation or writing or verbally mediated reflection. However, there are some cases where we do, and these, I believe, are sufficiently important to justify the creation of the psychological categories of semantic remembering, that is, remembering and forgetting as displayed in a verbal skill, and remembering as displayed in a verbal explication. Here are some cases:

1   semi-technical term: 'Do you know the meaning of the word *roux*?' (a paste of oil, water and flour).
2   Proper names: 'I'm sorry. I can't remember your wife's name right now.'
3   Granny: 'I'm sorry, dear, I can't remember the word for that!' (pointing to a teacup).
4   Foreign words: 'Do you remember the French word for "ladle"?'

Prospective and retrospective remembering

This distinction among types of episodic remembering is clear in import, but its implementation in detailed cognitive models seems rather tentative. Retrospective remembering is any exercise of the 'memory machine' to recall something which one has already done intentionally. Remembering is called 'prospective' when the memorial task is to remember to carry out an intended action in the future.

Empirical studies have concentrated on the relationship between prospective and retrospective remembering. The ability to remember things in the past does not seem to be all that is required to remember to do something one has planned or intended to do. This is a very odd result, since common sense would suggest that all that should be required is remembering relevant past actions, for example that one had made up one's mind, publicly declared an intention and so on. Most of the empirical studies have been carried out with participants whose abilities in one or the other or both of these everyday-remembering tasks have been impaired (Burgess and Shallice, 1998). The reasoning is familiar in cognitive neuroscience. If the disturbance of a cognitive function is correlated with damage to a part of the brain, then it is inferred that a similar part in an intact brain was the organ by which the function was implemented.

learning point — ## Remembering: vocabularies and classifications

1 Remembering as an everyday practice:

   a) Linked with concepts of learning and knowing:

      i) Remembering that ...
      ii) Remembering how to ...

   b) 'Remember', like 'know', is a 'success' word:

      i) 'Trying to remember' describes a task.
      ii) 'Remember' is often used to mark an achievement.

   c) Authenticity of recollection is usually determined by coherence between stories. There is rarely any forensic evidence for the events of everyday life.

2 A summary taxonomy of remembering concepts in use in cognitive psychology (Figure 10.1).

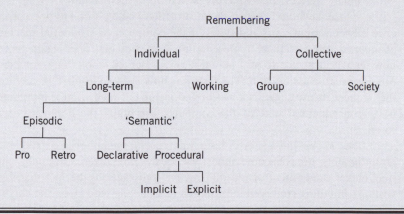

Figure 10.1 Summary taxonomy of 'rememberring' concepts

Cognitive psychology of remembering, phase two: explanation

Some important metaphors

Three main metaphors need to be deconstructed if we are to see clearly how the cognitive models, derived according to the principle by which modules are matched to distinctions of function, that was emphasized above, are to be interpreted. They are 'representation', 'information' and '(en)coding'. Deconstructing a metaphor is not necessarily a criticism of the practice of using it. Science would be nothing without the metaphors by means of which theories are constructed, new concepts are built, models are conceived and their structures worked out. Nevertheless, they are metaphors. When we begin the business of transforming an abstract model, such as Baddeley's 'working memory system', into a plausible artificial intelligence model we must pay close attention to the figures of speech employed. Each of the three has a long history, involving major but superseded theories of how remembering and other cognitive processes occur.

'*Representation*' implies that a kind of simulacrum of the item remembered is stored somewhere in the human person in some form or another. Perhaps it takes the form of a picture for remembering a landscape, or a proposition for remembering what has been said, and so on. Literally, 're-presentation' is to present whatever it is again. The naive sense of the expression reappeared in computer science in the days before neural nets, when it was thought that the compiler, in rendering keyboard input into electrical impulses ordered in accordance with a binary system, created a representation in the machine of what had been put in via the keyboard. When the idea of there being a one-to-one correspondence between input units and states of the computer as a material machine was abandoned, the notion of representation was stretched once again to describe how the whole structure of a neural net 'represented' something, for example a non-Linnaean classification. The term has now been so leached of any meaning that at most its use suggests a weak relationship between what is input and what is the consequential state of the computer, the brain, the nervous system and so on.

'*Information*' has a shorter history as a useful metaphor in cognitive science. Unfortunately, it has become almost vacuously generalized. Originally 'information' meant the content of an 'informative' proposition, the fact that saying or writing something conveyed information to someone who knew the language. In this sense a newspaper or a manual of instructions would contain information.

When Shannon developed his general theory of transmission lines for such systems as telephones he called it, non-metaphorically, 'information theory'. It was concerned with the constraints on the electrical transmission of information.

However, the mathematical treatment of the properties of such lines quickly changed the meaning of the expression 'information' into a metaphor. For example, the 'information content' of a received message, 'b', is the logarithm of the inverse ratio of the probability that the message that was sent was 'a'. The metaphorical use of this term is widespread. Indeed, one might want to say that the same vocable, 'information', is being used for two quite different concepts. For example, in a fairly standard description of the architecture of the hippocampus, thought to be the seat of certain aspects of the neurophysiology of the remembering machine, one finds such expressions as 'during its course through the brain this information [namely the input from perceptual systems] ... is then communicated to the EC' and so on. In one sense there is no *information* in the brain at all. There are only electrical pulses and synaptic chemistry. The people using this metaphor are not misled by it. Only the lay person unfamiliar with neuroscience would draw misleading conclusions. Students, with a foot in both camps, need to be sensitized to both the necessity and the dangers of metaphors in science.

'*Coding*' and 'encoding' are the archaeological deposit of a thoroughly bad theory of interpersonal communication, sometimes ironically referred to as the 'conduit' theory. The theory is as ancient as it is wrongheaded. It is based on a seventeenth-century picture of the process of interpersonal communication. According to this account a thought in someone's mind is encoded in language, then recoded as a pattern of sounds and, in that form, crosses the abyss to another person. The hearer decodes it, first from sounds into words, and then from words into thoughts. The current metaphor of words as tools in use may also have a short shelf life, but it is vastly preferable to the 'words as conduit' story.

So misleading are the metaphors of 'representation' and 'coding' that it would be well to do without them. 'Information' in a new, mathematical sense, is well established, and should mislead no one.

Models for the psychology of remembering

Models play two main roles in scientific research. *Descriptive* or *analytical* models are used to bring order into some domain of phenomena, to simplify the data and to highlight important relationships. Sometimes such models use the data themselves as a source. Sometimes a different source is drawn upon in constructing the model. *Explanatory* models are used to represent the mechanisms and processes that bring about the phenomena we are studying. Such models draw on sources that are taken to be of the same general type as the real mechanisms *may* turn out to be. Since it is very common that we are unable to examine the processes that produce the observable phenomena directly, models are needed that we hope are analogous to the mechanisms and processes we are trying to study.

In the psychology of remembering we find both kinds of models. To illustrate the first kind, the descriptive model, I will set out Baddeley's well known model, or rather group of interrelated models, of the processes of 'working memory'. These models serve to express what we know of the phenomena of this kind of remembering but should not be supposed to have any pretensions to represent actual neural structures or brain mechanisms. To illustrate the second kind of model, used as the basis of explanations, I will set out a powerful neural net model of the hippocampus as a memory machine. In this case the model is presented as a schematic representation of the actual structure and processes that may be occurring in the hippocampus when certain kinds of remembering are occurring.

Neither of these models makes use of the notion of a 'store' of items, or any kind of filing system analog. We must first ask why the 'storage' image as a source of models for remembering is inadequate, if not downright misleading.

The model of remembering as storage

Along with the idea of remembering as storage went two different theories as to the nature of the stored material. According to Atkinson and Shiffrin (1968), each perceptual mode, sight, hearing, touch and so on was the source of its own kind of memory item. Therefore each sensory modality needed its own independent memory 'store' for its own kind of item. This model of the memory machine has come under criticism, notably by Engelkamp and Zimmer (1994).

For some psychologists the 'storage' model included another important idea, the opposite of the multiple stores model proposed by Atkinson and Shiffrin (1968). The single store model was based on the principle that all remembered items, whatever their origins, that is, whatever perceptual mode items had been acquired in, and whatever their content when recalled, were all stored in the same form. Usually this was presumed to be propositional. What were stored were items of knowledge, as information may be stored in a dictionary or an encyclopedia. After all, what was recollected was putative knowledge even if the recollection was incorrect. Once stored, all subsequent cognitive processing of memory items makes use of the same abstract devices, such as hierarchical classification.

The idea is very simple. Is material which was garnered visually 'stored' in one system, independently of auditory material retained in another store, with material garnered verbally in yet another? And so on. Alternatively, are these simply subsystems of a larger integrated memory machine, so that there could be high-level cross-modal influence in learning, remembering and forgetting?

Multimodal theory is based in the idea that each way of acquiring a memory has its own storehouse. Among the main advocates of multimodal remembering are Engelkamp and Zimmer (1994). However, experiments have shown that if one is required to act out the content of the phrase one is being asked to remember one remembers that content better. According to them, even though each source of remembered material has its own store, different subsystems contribute to episodic memory. How seriously should we take the multimodal hypothesis if we are intent on completing our project with a deep understanding of the neural tools for remembering? It is clear that these 'stores' are abstract or hypothetical entities, created by projection back into the memory system as subsystems from sensory, kinesthetic and motor systems. The interaction of the subsystems produces episodic memory. I do not think we have any reason for taking the multimodal hypothesis seriously as a contribution to a scientific realist cognitive psychology.

Engelkamp and Zimmer (1994: 464–5) confess that they derived their subsystems from a blend of functional and content analyses. As they remark, 'the units we chose were determined by our interests in memory for these entities in the real world'. That is, they derived their subsystems as picture nodes, word nodes and motor programs from how people displayed and how they acquired their memories. We have already noticed how fallacious it is to think that material is retained in the memory machine as anything like the events from it is acquired and the way it is later displayed.

If we find that items that have a linguistic origin and those that have a perceptual origin are involved in remembering some complex matter, how is this seeming fusion of material from disparate sources achieved? One answer would be to hypothesize that all remembering is really carried on in only one modality. For example, a case could be made for the claim that all remembering is propositional, the verbal or verbal-like expression of something remembered. If this 'distillation' actually occurs, the modality of the source of something to be remembered, be it visual, auditory, tactile or whatever, is irrelevant. In the end, it is argued, by Pylyshyn (1973) for example, that all information that is retained over time, that is, is remembered, is of the same kind, namely propositional.

Should the general model of memory as storage fall into disrepute the debate between single or multiple storage would just become irrelevant. Indeed, that is what seems to have happened. As we shall see, adopting a neural network model changes all the details too. Within that framework there are neither stores of memories nor memories as elementary units or items that could be stored. According to the connectionist view the 'storage' model no longer has much utility. However, the concept of short-term memory has survived the transition though bereft of the 'store' interpretation.

Baddeley's working memory model

Though the concept of 'short-term remembering' has survived into the present era of memory research, the way this notion is interpreted, and what is involved in the processes, which the phrase comprehends, have been greatly enlarged in detail (Gathercole, 1997). Most of the research has been concerned with linguistic or more generally symbolic material. The main development of the concept has been through the introduction of the idea of 'working memory' (Baddeley, 1998). One's working memory comprehends what one does or can currently draw on immediately in the performance of some task.

In furthering our project of looking for artificial intelligence metaphors of cognitive functioning, Baddeley's working memory theory offers an ideal example. First proposed twenty-five years ago, it continues to be refined in various ways, and remains a paradigm-defining idea. The theory describes a hypothetical memory mechanism. Unless we take care to use our tools of model analysis, acquired in Chapter 3, it may look as if it is a model in the physical science sense, that is, an imaginary mechanism that would perform in a similar way to whatever it is in the real human being that is used to carry out a memory task. For example, the imagined working of the model must produce an analog of the observed phenomenon that short words are recalled more readily than long words. It must also simulate the fact that word-like entities are recalled more readily than pseudo-signs, which are not word-like. An explanatory model in the physicist's sense must be a representation in some medium of a possible organ in the brain and/or nervous system that real persons really use for these linguistic tasks. How close the analogy can be seen to be determines how readily the structure of the model can be projected on to the material systems of the human brain. If the model is actually no richer in content than an abstract representation of the observed data, an analytical model, then it has no surplus content and could not serve as a guide to the real productive mechanisms. It would be like Robert Boyle's 'spring' model of the behavior of confined gases. This model expresses something important about the behavior of gases without at all suggesting that there is an unobserved 'spring' within the gas sample which would explain its behavior.

In coming to understand Baddeley's model and to appreciate its significance for cognitive psychology it is of the greatest importance that its logical character should be clearly appreciated. Is it merely analytical, abstractly summarizing the phenomena, or is it explanatory, a representation of possible mechanisms?

There are three modules in this model of working memory: a central executive, a phonological loop and a visual-spatial sketchpad. Baddeley defines the loop as follows:

> [it] is assumed to comprise two components, a phonological store that is capable of holding speech-based information, and an articulatory control process based on inner speech. Memory traces within the phonological store are assumed to fade and become unretrievable after about one and a half to two seconds. The memory trace can however be refreshed by a process of reading off the trace into the articulatory control process, which then feeds it back into the store, the process underlying sub-vocal rehearsal.
>
> (Baddeley, 1998: 53–3)

Already in this schematic description we see a cluster of diverse metaphors, one for each component of the model. It is also worth remarking that this model is very much a child of the time. It was developed during the dominance of system models in control system engineering in the 1970s. The model is fleshed out with two familiar metaphors, the 'store', and the 'rehearsal'. Since these are metaphors, the qualification that for verbal remembering the rehearsal is sub-vocal is not strictly speaking necessary. These components are abstract entities, not actual material things. Here is a summary of the observations that led Baddeley to construct his system of models.

The first observation is of the many cases in which we must hold on to something we have seen or heard until the completion of the whole object of which it is an initial part. Examples are sentences or melodies. If we could not remember the first words of a sentence by the time we reached its end we would not understand it. Nor could we appreciate a melody if we could hear it only note by note.

The second observation is that we can perform two short-term retention tasks simultaneously. For example, we can be saying a sequence of numbers over to ourselves, and so retaining them, while solving simple cognitive problems, such as whether the sequence AB represents the state of affairs expressed by the statement 'A precedes B'.

The third observation is that when the retention repetition task is made more demanding the cognitive task solutions take longer.

Baddeley inferred that whatever system is being used for retention and recall it must be independent of that which is being used for solving the cognitive tasks. His model represents this conjecture. There is a central executive, tied to the cognitive tasks, and an independent remembering module, the phonological loop, which maintains the recited sequence of numbers correctly. Remembering phonemes facilitates the recitation task. The phonological loop holds a fleeting memory of the relevant sound, which is maintained by hearing the sound again.

What observations does this model represent? First, that erroneously recalled words are phonologically similar to those we recall correctly. It turns out that meaningless noise does not disrupt remembering of verbal material but articulated, language-like sound does do so. Baddeley asserts that long words are harder to recall than short words because we are engaging in subvocal speaking when attempting to remember a word. So sound dominates all else in verbal remembering.

What is the status of the phonological loop as a model? It is clear that it has great value in expressing the main features of the observations and experimental results that Baddeley catalogs in his exposition of the model. It makes no sense to start looking in the brain for phonological loops. It is a descriptive model of great elegance and power, but only a descriptive model.

What is the source of this model? It seems to be subvocal rehearsal, a practice in which we all engage from time to time. The phonological loop is a kind of visual representation of this kind of 'talking to oneself'. It represents such tactics as repeating a phone number to ourselves as we cross the room from where the phone book is to the phone itself.

Baddeley has expanded his system of descriptive or analytical models with a similar 'device' to express the results of studies on the way that verbal tasks interfere with visual tasks. There must be a separate visual system. The model of course does not represent such a system, but the observations that lead one to make such a conjecture. If one is required to carry out a procedure that involves giving a 'Yes/No' answer to a visual problem, then it seems that participants have less difficulty in carrying out both procedures together if they can point to the written words 'Yes' and 'No' rather than having to say them. It suggests that cognition in the visual mode must be separate from the verbal mode. Baddeley's model of a visual sketchpad where such tasks are performed represents these observations and experimental results iconically, that is, in pictorial form. The model helps to make it clear that two visual tasks can be carried on together more readily than a visual and a verbal task can be.

The analytical status of the model is confirmed when we realize that it is not treated as subject to the usual constraints of scientific realism. Its utility for its author does not depend on whether it yields a description of an organ in the real human neural system, a real memorial mechanism that could serve as a tool for carrying out some memorial task. The phonological store, the device, which holds speech-based information, and the device that manages an articulatory control process, need not be taken literally as representations of possible anatomical structures in the brain with their internal neurochemical processes. Baddeley's model is abstract and heuristic. It is part of the means by which what investigators have observed is articulated into a coherent body of knowledge. The fact that the internal processes imagined in the components of the model involve the unsatisfactory metaphor of 'coding' need not tell against the Baddeley model. It is not a candidate for a realist interpretation as part of a neural mechanism.

Though the simple distinction between two 'stores' labeled 'short-term memory' and 'long-term memory' has been generally dropped, some concept like 'long-term memory' must be in play. We do remember some things for a long while. However, the original concept of long-term memory was used within the framework created by the adoption of the 'memory store' metaphor. In the decline of the 'storage' metaphor for how information is retained, the idea of a transfer of material from one store to another has declined with it. In so far as long-term memory was thought of as being of the same nature as short-term memory, the use of the expression to give an account of long-term retention has been abandoned. For instance, once does not find it in Schachter's (1996) popular account of the psychology of remembering. In our treatment we will turn to concepts like 'ability' to express the observational and experimental data that were once comprehended under the category of 'long-term memory', eschewing the 'store' metaphor completely.

Transforming a cognitive model into an artificial intelligence simulation

Physicists generally presume that the models they are trying to build must be representations of possible real-world entities, structures and processes. Psychologists have not always felt constrained in this way. There is no suggestion that Baddeley's phonological loop must be a representation of something loop-like in the real world. When pressed, psychologists tend to defend their heuristic models in terms of the power to make predictions. This is the core assumption of positivism. Realists demand that models should also be plausible as representations of real-world entities. How are we going to advance from Baddeley's positivism to realist scientific theorizing in cognitive psychology? As we shall see, recent proposals for artificial intelligence modeling address this very point.

It would be wrong to take this disparity between physics and psychology as a criticism of psychological model making. Fortunately, psychology is a multi-layered structure. Baddeley's phonological loop and his visual scratchpad are abstract entities tied conceptually to the phenomena they 'account for'. The development of artificial intelligence, and particularly the connectionist or neural net version of it, has provided us with a third layer sandwiched between the abstract and ideal entities of most cognitive models and the real structures of body and brain. The making of abstract cognitive models, drawing on all sorts of metaphors, is an *essential* step in developing cognitive psychology. The disparity of scale between the observed phenomena and the results of live brain scanning is far too great to allow direct mapping in any scientifically respectable sense.

To transform models such as Baddeley's three-component mechanism of short-term remembering from an abstract model to an artificial intelligence simulation, two steps would be needed. The components of the hypothetical mechanisms must be reinterpreted as processing modules, and the processes that are imagined to take place within them must be interpreted as computations on the binary input to a Turing machine, or, in more recent artificial intelligence, as the input/output pattern of a trained neural net. The final step takes us from abstract representations of the cognitive tools as an artificial intelligence simulation to their hypotheses about their physical realization in the structure and processes of some organ in the brain. It should be clear that the 'working memory model' falls short of a representation of anything that could be found in the neurology of an embodied person. Yet, without it, the steps from patterns of experimental and observational data to working models of the brain as cognitive tool would be extraordinarily difficult.

Models are to be judged by their ability to account for empirical 'facts', *and by whether they can be mapped on to a level of reality different from that in which those facts are to be observed.* We have memorial discourses in the realm of observable matters of fact and brain structures and processes drawn from another level of reality than that of public displays of representations of the past. Using our general task/tool metaphor, which should control the whole of cognitive science, we can say that tasks are specified in the discursive realm and tools and their ways of working in the neurological realm. The methodology, which we are studying in this chapter, should enable us to relate the one to the other. The pattern will be more or less the same as that which allows a physicist to relate the aurora borealis we see to the ionized gas molecules we imagine.

Commenting on the recent history of artificial intelligence modeling of cognitive procedures, Hampson has remarked that 'much of the connectionist research conducted during the 1980s was of the demonstration variety. In effect, connectionist scientists were content to develop models that successfully simulated a certain type of behavior … More recently, however, connectionist science has been interested in constraining its models with neurophysiological data. A

connectionist model, it is argued, should not only simulate a particular performance, but should also be designed and operate in accordance with what is known
about neurophysiological structures and processes.'

Worked example: the hippocampus

Learning and memory are integrally interwoven as cognitive processes. We do
not commonly say we remember what we have been genetically endowed with
a propensity to do. There are uses for expressions such as 'remembering how
to smile' but they are appropriate only in unusual circumstances, for example
for someone at last emerging from the shadow of a doomed love affair. The
metaphorical character of such expressions is obvious. It should be no surprise
that learning mechanisms and remembering mechanisms are interwoven in the
structure of the brain.

The hippocampus as a real neural net

What is the role of the hippocampus as an organ in the whole gamut of memory
machines? If a whole organism no longer displays a function, when a part of it
has been damaged, then in the intact organism that part played a role in the performance of the original function. It is generally agreed that the loss of function
in individuals with hippocampal damage is in declarative remembering, but only
for recent incidents of the relevant type. By using the above principle we infer that
the hippocampus is an organ essential to some aspect or stage of declarative
remembering.

The principle upon which cognitive science rests is simply that between a
psychological account of a remembering process and a neural account of the
organ that people use to perform that process there must intervene an artificial
intelligence model, as an abstract representation of the function. There is good
reason to think that only connectionist models will do. Connectionist models are
tied to neural architecture by the synapse/node relationship that is basic to connectionist artificial intelligence. In Chapter 9 we learned how to make the transition between nets and nodes and neurons and synapses. To illustrate this
procedure in a real case we will look briefly at Rolls's account of the hippocampus as a remembering organ.

Rolls (1989) treats the hippocampus as if it were a neural net, that is, as if
it were indeed a connectionist device. There is thoroughgoing mapping between
synapses in a real neural system and nodes in a model net. In the neuro-anatomy
of real neural organs the relationship can work in either direction, from real neural
architecture to net structures, or from net structures to real neural architecture.

In accordance with this analytical scheme there are taken to be three *sets* or
fields of neurons in each of the left and right hippocampus. Each contains
upwards of a million real neurons. The pattern of excitation passes from the
dentate gyrus (see Figure 10.2) successively to two further fields of cells, the

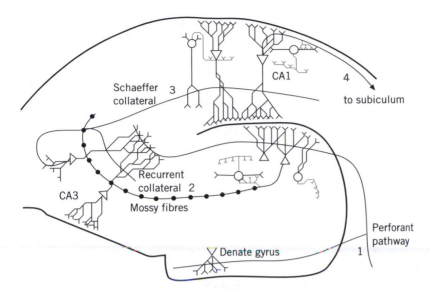

Figure 10.2 Connections within the hippocampus. Input comes through the perforant path (1), which synapses with the dendrites of the dentate granule cells and also with the apical dendrites of the CA3 pyramidal cells. The dentate granule cells project via the mossy fibres (2) to the CA3 pyramidal cells. The recurrent collateral system of the CA3 cells is indicated by the single axon labeled 'Recurrent collateral'. The CA3 pyramidal cells project via the Shaeffer collateral (3) to the CA1 pyramidal cells, which in turn have connections (4) via the subiculum back to other cortical areas. (From P. McLeod, K. Plunkett and E.T. Rolls, *Introduction to Connectionist Modelling of Cognitive Processes*, 1998, by courtesy of Oxford University Press)

whole acting as if it were a sequence of trained nets. The artificial intelligence model becomes the source of anatomical and physiological *hypotheses* about the structure and processes of the hippocampus, and, successively, the relevant parts of the cortex.

Rolls's connectionist model

As in all model making, to fulfill an explanatory role this model of the hippocampus is disciplined by the need for empirical adequacy, that is, it should function as the real thing functions. Empirical adequacy is established, at least at a certain rough-and-ready level, by a standard negative functional argument. 'Hippocampal damage leads to failure to form new episodic memories, but the formation of procedural memories continues' (McLeod et al., 1998: 279). The second demand, ontological plausibility, is met if the model is of the same general type as that of which it is a model. The source must have a place in the same type hierarchy as the subject of the model. The subject is the hippocampus as a mass of neurons. The source, the connectionist architecture for machines capable of simulating cognitive processes usually carried out by a person by using their native equipment, their brain, is a net of artificial neurons. The supertype, 'neural net', encompasses both real and artificial nets as subtypes. If the hippocampus is a subtype of the same supertype as the functionally equivalent connectionist model, it too must be a net of real neurons.

The outline of the connectionist model presented here comes from McLeod et al. (1998: 278–92).

The structure of the hippocampus

This brain organ consists of two major groups of cells, the cornu ammonis and the dentate gyrus. The cornu is differentiated into three parts, CA1, CA2 and CA3. Only CA1 and CA3 are important for the remembering model. Recall how coarse-grained are the regions identified by PET scans. There are more than a million cells in the dentate gyrus, more than 400,000 in the CA1 region and more than 300,000 in the CA3 region.

Input comes from the entorhinal cortex, having its ultimate source in the sensory systems, vision, audition and so on. This feeds into the hippocampus via a collection of axons, the 'perforant pathway', which synapses to cells in the dentate gyrus and to those in the region CA3. The dentate gyrus is linked to CA3, which, in turn, is linked to CA1. From CA1 output feeds back via the subiculum to the entorhinal cortex and from thence to the neocortical regions. This pattern can be followed in the schematic diagram in Figure 10.3 (McLeod et al., 1998: 284, figure 13.4).

The neural connections are complex. For our purposes we need note only that each CA3 cell receives about fifty inputs from the 'mossy fibers', so called because of the number of synapses from them to C3. The C3 cells also receive about 4,000 inputs from the perforant pathway. The axons of CA3 cells branch into 'collaterals', one of which synapses back to the C3 cells. The other inputs go to the cells of region CA1. The sequence, then, is this: entorhinal cortex *to* dentate gyrus *to* CA3 *to* CA1 *and back to the* entorhinal cortex. The connections can be followed in Figure 10.2 (McLeod et al., 1998: 282, figure 13.3).

Bearing mind that the remembering function of the hippocampus is to bring together 'different aspects of an event into a single pattern which can be recalled when cued by some component of the original input' (McLeod et al., 1998: 284). Every time I smell a pig farm I remember, as a child, standing on the boundary fence of the neighboring farm and scratching the back of a large pink pig. The cognitive tool that accomplishes the synthesis of smell, sight and touch is the hippocampus. It returns the product to the neocortex, where it is, no doubt, distributively represented in some other, yet to be discerned, neural net.

The connectionist model

This follows the neuro-anatomy of the hippocampus fairly faithfully. Four neural nets are created, one each for the entorhinal cortex (600 neurons), the dentate

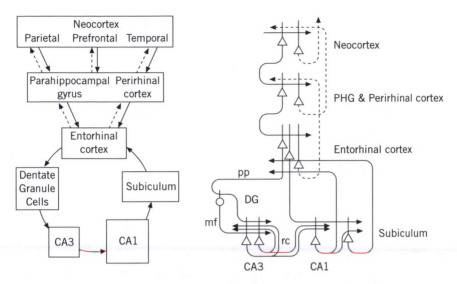

Figure 10.3 Forward connections (solid lines) from areas of cerebral association neocortex via the parahippocampal gyrus and perirhinal cortex, and the entorhinal cortex, to the hippocampus. Back-projections (dashed lines) via the parahippocampal gyrus to the neocortex. *Left*: block diagram. *Right*: more detailed representation of some of the principal excitatory neurons in the pathways. △ represents pyramidal cell bodies. ○ represents dentate granule cells. The thick lines above the cell bodies represent the dendrites, the thinner lines with arrow heads the axons. *DG* dentate granule cells, *mf* mossy fibers, *PHG* parahippocampal gyrus, *pp* perforant path, *rc* recurrent collateral of the CA3 hippocampal pyramidal cells. (From P. McLeod, K. Plunkett and E.T. Rolls, *Introduction to Connectionist Modelling of Cognitive Processes*, 1998, by courtesy of Oxford University Press)

gyrus (1,000 neurons) and the CA1 and CA3 regions of the cornu ammonis (1,000 neurons each). The connections are as shown in Figure 10.4 (McLeod et al., 1998: 287, figure 13.5).

To understand the way the model is constructed an additional concept must be explained, 'sparseness'. The dentate cells send a sparser signal to the C3 cells than the hippocampus receives. The upshot is that the output is less correlated than are the aspects of the input, but it is more sharply categorized. Representations of different events are separated, even if they involve very similar sensory aspects.

The way that a partial clue can serve in the recovery of the whole pattern can be modeled in the net structure of an auto-associator. This way this type of net works is set out in McLeod et al. (1998: chapter 6). See Figure 10.5.

In many respects the model shown in Figure 10.3 is easily legible. The sparseness of the mossy fiber connections with CA3 cells is represented by the proportion of units which become active in response to any input.

The test for the empirical adequacy of the neural net model is simple. The input surface of the net representing the entorhinal cortex was presented with

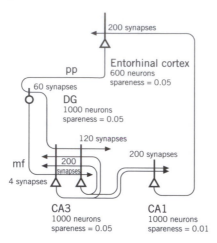

Figure 10.4 A neural network simulation of the hippocampus. The number of units, the number of modifiable connections per unit and the sparseness of each stage of the network are shown. *DG* dentate granule cells, *mf* mossy fibers, *pp* perforant path. (From P. McLeod, K. Plunkett and E.T. Rolls, *Introduction to Connectionist Modelling of Cognitive Processes*, 1998, by courtesy of Oxford University Press)

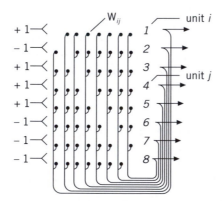

Figure 10.5 An eight-unit auto-associator. (Based on McClelland and Rumelhart, 1985; from P. McLeod, K. Plunkett and E.T. Rolls, *Introduction to Connectionist Modelling of Cognitive Processes*, 1998, by courtesy of Oxford University Press)

random binary sequences. The nets were allowed to stabilize and parts of each of the original input patterns were fed in. What was the consequential firing pattern of the entorhinal nodes? If the correlation between the recalled pattern in the model of the entorhinal cortex and the pattern input is bettered by the correlation between the input partial cue and the retrieved pattern, the net has learned. It has formed the analog of an episodic memory. The results gave very strong support to the empirical adequacy of the model net. Since ontological adequacy had been ensured by the use of the overt structure of the hippocampus as a (partial) source for the model, both desiderata have been satisfied.

We could hardly ask for a better supporting example for the hybrid psychology program and for the strategy of following the realist interpretation of the established sciences as our guide.

---

learning point   ## Models for remembering

1   Models based on the 'store' metaphor are inadequate:

    a)   They require item-by-item representation.
    b)   Multimodal remembering does not fit the storage model very well.

2   *Descriptive models.* Baddeley's working memory model:

    a)   It depends on discoveries about the interference and non-interference of cognitive performances involving different sensory modalities, for example hearing and vision.
    b)   These observations suggest that visual and auditory working remembering are different.
    c)   This is represented by proposing independent remembering tools, such as the phonological loop, which is used for auditory aspects of remembering, which do not interfere with verbal cognitive tasks.

3   *Explanatory models.* Rolls's connectionist model of the hippocampus as a memory tool:

    a)   Anatomy of the hippocampus:

       i)   The hippocampus as threefold structure: DG, CA3 and CA1.
       ii)   It is the tool for forming episodic memories. These can be recalled with partial cues.
       iii)   The regions are linked as input from cortex to DG to CA3 to CA1 to cortex.
       iv)   In the process input is simplified, categorized and unified.

    b)   The connectionist model:

       i)   Four nets corresponding to entorhinal cortex, DG, CA3 and CA1 are set up, connected as in the real hippocampus.
       ii)   The entorhinal net is trained with an input of 100 random binary sequences.
       iii)   It is tested with partial sequences. If the output of the net system is better correlated with the input than the output is with the original input pattern, the net has learned. The experiment was successful.
       iv)   The remembering phenomena are replicated and the model/real system analogy is maintained.

Conclusion

In the first sections of this chapter the everyday and the technical classifications of the main phenomena of remembering were set out and compared. The match was good enough to confirm the cognitive psychology of remembering as remaining true to the phenomena it was originally developed to analyse and explain. The link between prior learning and later remembering is clear in both systems. The relation between knowing and remembering is retained, as well as the important distinction between knowing how and knowing that.

The fact that a person can produce a representation of some event in the past, or display competence in a learned skill, does not entail that there must have been a covert representation lying dormant somewhere in the brain to be activated on demand. The cluster of metaphors around the storage picture is only one possible model source. Baddeley's well known tripartite model of 'working memory' is a neat way of summarizing the results of his studies, but is implausible as the basis of an iconic model of the workings of the relevant organs in the brain.

Abandoning the metaphors of codes, stores and representations opens up the possibility of exploring other sources for models of the cognitive processes of remembering. The work of McLeod et al. exemplifies the hybrid method of cognitive science in a full-scale research program into the psychology of remembering. We use the concepts of artificial intelligence modeling to reach out to the neural processes that must characterize that ubiquitous tool of cognitive work, our brains (Gluck and Myers, 2001). The optimistic note struck in this section may be premature. A quite different model of the brain as cognitive tool has emerged in the work of Suppes and Han (2000). For many years the living brain was studied by the use of EEG equipment. Electrodes were placed around the skull, to detect the electrical field produced by the brain. The strength of this field fluctuated in several overlaying patterns, characteristic of different states of the whole organ, sleeping, waking and so on. With his colleagues, and using more sophisticated analytical techniques than had hitherto been available, Suppes was able to show, using the long neglected EEG methods, that distinct microfluctuations are displayed during the effort to recall particular words. The EEG technique records whole brain phenomena. It is too early yet to say what these discoveries tell us. However, they do suggest a degree of caution in taking the Second Cognitive Revolution for granted.

Notes

1   This chapter owes a great deal to the generous help of my Georgetown colleague, Darlene Howard.
2   Though Ebbinghaus used single participants, usually himself, in his experiments, he pioneered a type of experiment that is still performed. Meaningless

signs are studied and their rate and time of recall are treated as independent variables. Correlations are established between aspects of the material and process of learning and the material as remembered.

3   Key choice is easily demonstrable to have a priming effect in musical experience. For example, the interval C to F in the major is dominant to tonic in the key of F major but tonic to subdominant in the key of C major. The pair of notes is heard differently when the key of F major has been played before they are presented from how they are heard when C major has been previously heard.

The psychology of classifying

Much of the effort put into computer science has been concerned with developing techniques for storing vast amounts of data in an easily accessible form. Such techniques must facilitate the sorting and organizing of bodies of knowledge to fulfill practical needs. We use what we know about the properties and attributes of things, substances, events and processes to assign them to classes, species and types. To do this we need to have a working system of categories. Having classified the beings in some domain, we can draw on the body of knowledge implicit in the classification system to recover detailed descriptions of the beings that have been classified, butterflies, rocks, mental disorders, mushrooms, tennis tournaments or whatever.

Everyday activities depend on the human ability to classify and categorize. Cooks base their procedures on their knowledge of the kinds of ingredients recipes call for. Doctors choose a treatment based on the accepted and standardized classification of symptoms and so on. To do that they must be able to recognize what is before them as belonging to a certain type or kind. How should the exercise of this commonplace human skill be described? What core cognitive processes are involved? How similar are the techniques employed by the experts in one field to those used by those in another? Could the computational techniques developed in setting up diagnostic programs for physicians, for example, be hi-jacked as the basis of a psychology of the human ability to classify butterflies and/or to recognize the grammatical categories of words?

Before we look into the technicalities we need to remind ourselves of the main features of the techniques of classifying as we studied them in Chapter 3, section 1.

The Aristotelian logic of classification

Genus and species

Proposals for classification systems have a long history. Aristotle provided the basis of nearly all proposals for representing a body of knowledge in a handy and accessible form. The beings in some domain of interest were to be grouped into species based upon their common properties. Species were to be grouped into genera, again depending on properties they had in common. Classification in Aristotelian terms was *per genus et differentiae*. The *genus* might be 'pasta', which, being *differentiated* from all other species of pasta by being 'twisted' and 'chopped', gives us the species 'fusilli'. Classification of the stuff in a De Cecco packet *per genus et differentiae* is then achieved by consulting our knowledge of pasta, and its varieties and species. This pasta, being twisted and chopped, not only is but *must* be fusilli. A classification system for pasta, when properly understood, incorporates a body of culinary knowledge.

Properties, which belong to individuals but are not ubiquitous in the species, are called 'accidents'. Common properties, which are not included in the definition of a species, that is, which are not among the necessary and sufficient conditions for membership are called 'propria'. Propria and defining properties can sometimes change places, as more is learned about the domain in question.

Hierarchical classification schemes[1]

The *genus et differentiae* system for classifying the beings in a domain of interest could be expanded to provide a system for storing the entire body of human knowledge. It would have a hierarchical structure of super-genera in a kind of inverted pyramid or tree of knowledge. The Tree of Porphyry was a system for representing all human knowledge, based on Aristotle's logic of classification (Figure 11.1). The Tree of Porphyry is a nice visual presentation of a knowledge system. It is intended to be comprehensive, so there should be a place in it for all kinds of material beings. A diamond is inanimate and material, so it would find

Figure 11.1
A Porphyry Tree

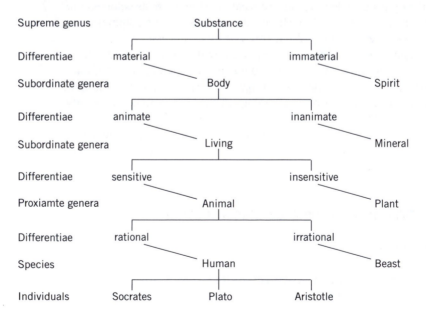

a place in the scheme as a mineral. A worm is irrational, sensitive, animate, and material, so it would find a place as a beast.

This layout makes it very clear that any category 'inherits' all the properties of the categories 'above' it in the tree.

There is no place for individuals in the scheme. In Aristotelian systems classificatory knowledge is confined to the necessary and sufficient attributes of things only as far as they are thought of as members of classes, instances of types or samples of substances. This chapter is concerned with the cognitive psychology of classifying, that is, with knowledge of species, genera and so on. We should remember that much of the knowledge actual people have at their disposal is about individual people, places, historical events and so on.

Linnaean classifications

In the eighteenth century Karl Linnaeus, a Swedish botanist obsessed with revealing the divine order in the natural world, worked out a comprehensive scheme for classifying plants and animals. The organism/species relation and the species/genus relation were based on the same logical pattern. A definition *per genus et differentiae* is a list of properties that an organism must display to be classified as a member of the species in question. Since actual things display a great many attributes, taxonomists need to pick out the most telling with which to define a species. There is a wonderful account of some of the issues involved in making such selections in the scientific biography of Vladimir Nabokov (Johnson and Coates, 1999), who was not only a famous novelist but a lepidopterist of distinction. In this chapter we are concerned only with the cognitive processes that are required, once the key attributes have been settled on.

In making use of Linnaean taxonomies the cognitive process is simple. Are the necessary and sufficient conditions set out in the definition *per species et differentiae* actually displayed by an entity taken as a candidate for inclusion in the species? In a simple computational model, matching registers could simulate such a process.

Captain Ahab is obsessed with a great white sea creature he calls 'Moby Dick'. The crew want to know what it is. Let us suppose that the registers of a GOFAI machine are so set as to represent a knowledge hierarchy in which there is an item representing the necessary and sufficient conditions for something to be a whale. Let us call this machine state 'A'. We represent the main characteristics of Moby Dick as machine state 'B'. The machine could attempt to classify Moby Dick by performing the material realization of the following abstract operations:

1   Match A: A, B
2   Branch: If A matches B then
3   Copy B, in the register left of '*isa* A'
4   Write 'Moby Dick' for 'B' in 'B *isa* whale'.
5   Output: 'Moby Dick is a whale'.

This procedure is wholly attribute-based, comparing the machine representation of one set of properties with that of another.

Is this how people classify things? Are the bodies of knowledge which people draw on to perform classificatory acts actually maintained as hierarchical systems of necessary and sufficient conditions in the cognitive resources of competent individuals?

The expression and representation of bodies of knowledge

According to Sowa (2000), five desiderata should be met by any system that can be used to represent a body of knowledge.

1   There must be a symbol system that maps on to real-world things.
2   Such a system has ontological commitments.
3   A knowledge representational system must include a 'theory', which describes the ways the classified things or substances behave.
4   There must be a medium of efficient computation.
5   There must be a medium for human expression.

At this point it is worth remarking that not only do we expect someone who *knows* about butterflies to *tell* us lots of things but also to be able *do* lots of things. Knowing must encompass both discursive and practical skills, knowing how as well as knowing that.

It would seem as if the fragment of a computational process sketched above could be generalized to any classification operation using a Porphyry Tree or something similar, such as the Linnaean system of botanical and zoological classification. Match, branch and copy operations would be performed repeatedly until the properties of the specimen had been exhausted and the tree had been climbed to its summit. Is that how we human beings do it?

Some problems with knowledge representation in terms of essences

Remember that if we are thinking of progress in cognitive science as involving the simulation of cognitive processes on a GOFAI computer, all that it can do is to compare and change the content of registers. The ultimate question for the cognitive scientist is this: is whatever is proposed in a computational model interpretable as a possible working model of processes that occur in some part of the human brain?

The most obvious and fundamental condition for such a representation is that we must be able to render the type or kind in question in terms of a stable and definite set of properties. For instance, if we want to know whether Mary's little pet is a *lamb* we must compare two sets of properties. One set belongs to the pet, and the other is comprehended in the type <lamb>. What should go into the definition of the species? This question is addressed not to zoologists but to students of everyday life. Would this creature be rejected by ordinary people as a lamb if it never went 'Baa'? I think not, even though we can be fairly sure that all lambs that have ever been do and did actually go 'Baa'. Must its fleece be 'white as snow'? Surely some properties are more central to being a thing of this or that kind than others. How do we carry through the Aristotelian distinction between essence, propria and accident in ordinary life?

Let us suppose that this problem is set aside by making some practical compromise. If it is a woolly ungulate, it is a lamb. By a simple comparison between a suitable representation of the properties actually exhibited by Mary's little pet and the representation of the essential properties in the definition *per genus et differentiae*, we can see whether Mary's little pet is a <woolly ungulate>. If it is, then Mary's little pet is a lamb. So we have used our knowledge of farm animals, suitably represented in the registers in our GOFAI computer, to find out how to classify Mary's pet, hitherto of unknown provenance and nature.

Is that how people actually reason about types and instances? Was something like this going on when Mary's father presented her with the pet? I think we can confidently say 'No'.

Problems with the *genus et differentiae* principle

How do we distinguish essential properties from the propria, those properties which are universal but not used as part of the essence? The distinction seems in many cases to be arbitrary. We do need sometimes to shift properties from one to the other as the rest of our knowledge changes. In one context, say that of creating another Dolly, the first animal clone, the genome might be thought of as the real essence of sheephood. In another context, say dealing with a foot-and-mouth outbreak, the commonsense category of 'sheep' would no doubt be defined by visible appearances alone. Furthermore, if we are dealing with real cases there is rarely a perfect match between the properties of a candidate entity and the essence that defines the type. GOFAI computers do not deal in vague similarities.

Looking at the matter from the side of essences, it seems obvious that many natural classes do not seem to have similarities clear-cut enough to serve as essences. Just try thinking of the essence of what it is to be a mountain or a desert. Similarly, when we take another step in the use of such a body of knowledge and conjecture that the fleece of Mary's little lamb must be white as snow, how do we do that in the light of the fact that we know that there are a few black sheep around? The Tree of Knowledge must have some probabilistic shadowing around the edges of categories as well, and that does not sit well with the strictness of the necessity and sufficiency of the Aristotelian essences.

To complicate the matter still further we must take account of the importance of a fundamental distinction in the kinds of essences that are made use of in the sciences. In chemistry, for instance, we distinguish between what philosophers since Locke have called the nominal and the real essences of material substances. We studied this distinction as it is used in the natural sciences in Chapter

3. It does not follow that people in general think in the same way as scientists trained in Linnaean methods do. The nominal essence of, say, granite, is comprised of all those characteristics that a geologist makes use of in picking out a rock sample as granite, that is, as falling under the term 'granite' and properly so called. These might include its color, its rigidity and hardness, its responses to chemical tests and so on. However, geologists also make use of the concept of the real essence of granite. This would include the structural properties of the molecules of the rock, their chemical composition, and so on. Generally, a real essence is derived from the relevant theory and supported by complicated patterns of reasoning in the management of molecular, atomic and subatomic models. Real essences explain why the set of properties picked out for practical reasons as the nominal essence of a kind or type or species form a stable cluster. The management of borderline cases, the incorporation of new discoveries and the ever-changing landscape of theory itself requires us to take account of a dialectic between the two kinds of essences, new developments in one bringing about adjustments in the other.

It would seem as if our Porphyry Tree of Knowledge must build in a vast edifice of theory as well as the necessary and sufficient conditions for classificatory tasks that we began with. Do people ordinarily make much use of conjectures about real essences to support their everyday classifications? Do you do that when deciding that fuselli is pasta? What about gnocchi? Its real essence is potato? Does that matter? Does it even register in the thoughts of cooks? Or of Mama mia when the family want pasta?

---

learning point   ## Basic principles of knowledge representation

1   The traditional scheme is based on Aristotle's classification *per genus et differentiae*.

   a)   There are necessary and sufficient or essential conditions of group membership.
   b)   Essential properties and propria are common to members of the kind.
   c)   A universal scheme of categories would be hierarchical.
   d)   Linnaean classifications could be performed by a GOFAI machine.

2   Conditions for knowledge representation:

   a)   Five requirements include symbol system, ontological commitments, theoretical bases, a computational medium and a medium of public expression.
   b)   Problems:

     i)   Essences in practice are not necessarily stable or final.
     ii)   Where to draw the line between essential properties and propria is contextual.
     iii)   There is often an imperfect fit between what logic demands and what we do in practice.

Alternative conceptions of a knowledge base

To comply with the requirements of the methodology of cognitive science a research pattern for the psychology classifying must follow a two-stage procedure. The first stage is descriptive and analytical, directed to answering the question: what is the pattern of discursive acts by which classifying, as a symbolic accomplishment, is brought off? The second stage is explanatory and involves the use of artificial intelligence models: What is the nature of the neural tools by which a person carries out an act of classifying something and does it correctly? Behind all this there must be a body of knowledge which, if publicly expressed in a linguistic form, would appear as a hierarchical system of concepts and associated definitions. Following our methodological path from discursive acts to cerebral tools, we begin with the question: how are bodies of knowledge discursively presented? Once this step has been taken we can begin to play with hypotheses about how a formal model of a body of knowledge could be constructed and how it might be embedded in an artificial intelligence model of the process of classifying. To say that a certain machine process is a 'process of classifying' is a metaphor drawn from the discursive expression of the use of a body of knowledge to categorize things, to make inferences about their future behavior and so on.

There are at least three major alternative ways of thinking about the nature of a body of knowledge that are usable as a basis for cognitive procedures including, in particular, classifying.

Rosch and prototypes

One alternative is the idea that a great deal of our knowledge is not represented propositionally but in concrete images, quasi-perceptually rather than quasi-linguistically. This idea has come from research into how people actually classify things. It goes back to studies by Eleanor Rosch (1973; Rosch and Lloyd, 1978). Rosch showed that matching the candidate object to a prototype of the kind or species in question was more important in classifying it than propositional reasoning about how far the properties of the thing in question matched the necessary and sufficient conditions expressing the formal definition of the type.

To cope with the huge variations in the ways a type is exemplified or instantiated in concrete cases we seem to have a prototypical example in mind. If one asks a group of people what they think of when asked whether a previously uncategorized farinaceous food material is 'pasta' they do not report consulting a list of necessary and sufficient conditions and checking the properties of unknown stuff against them. They report thinking of something like 'spaghetti' and comparing it with the problem foodstuff. When asked to decide what sort of creature an arctic tern is my American students use 'robin' as a prototype bird, while Britons make do with 'sparrow'. In many cases we seem to think with prototypes. When asked to classify a cassowary one matches one's image of the problematic creature with the knowledge-bearing image serving as prototype carrier for 'bird'.

Plainly different people are almost certainly going to use different proto-types for the same cognitive task. The whole gamut of these will probably display the usual bell-shaped curve, with 'robin' at the median and 'humming bird' and 'ostrich' at the extremes, if size is our measure of variation. Does this mean that yet another aspect of psychology will have to follow personality studies in aban-doning the ideal of generality for a study of individual cases and an idiographic science? Not necessarily. It may well be that what we all do with our prototypical images is more or less the same. There can be procedural generality, while con-tent is individual and idiosyncratic. It is upon this idea that the developments of artificial intelligence to be described in this chapter ultimately depend.

There is also the matter of the relative salience of features of any working prototype to the outcome of a classificatory task. Following Way (1992), one could say that if the category in question is 'bird' there are several features likely to characterize anyone's prototype: has wings, flies, lays eggs, nests in trees, sings at dawn and so on. In actual classificatory tasks any one of these may be more or less salient, even to irrelevance. For example: kiwis are flightless, larks nest on the ground, swans do not sing, and, on the other tack, alligators lay eggs, bats fly, chimpanzees nest in trees and some frogs sing.

Parrott and Smith (1981) made use of two of these distinctions in dis-cussing how the emotion of embarrassment could be represented. They showed that prototypical representations were markedly more adequate to the phenom-ena. They compared actual and typical cases, and standard Aristotelian with prototype representations.

Wittgenstein and family resemblances

Another proposal comes from Ludwig Wittgenstein. He pointed out (1953: paras. 65, 66) that many common words are used in a great variety of ways. It is a fallacy to assume that there must be a common (hidden) essence to all of them underlying the surface differences, just because the same word is used. Such an assumption can lead to a fruitless and intellectually deceiving hunt for the alleged common core of meaning. We use the word 'number' for a huge variety of mathematical structures. Must they *therefore* have something in common? In psychology, we have similar fields of family resemblances in the use of key words, such as 'thinking'. There are networks of similarities and differences but there is no common essence.

Suppose we have four salient qualities or attributes that seem to be relevant in some domain: A, B, C and D. There are various ways we picture a formal version of family resemblance. If we require a member to have only one of the defining set we have the structure:

Category = A or B or C or D

Thus

Furniture = for sitting (Chair) or for sleeping (Bed) or for storing
(Cupboard) or for eating off (Table)

What do we do about Rugs, Bookcases, Stoves and so on? In real life it is evident that disjunctive classes of family resemblances are indeterminate in several dimensions. This is no surprise. But it does make the simplistic idea of a body of knowledge organized wholly in terms of necessary and sufficient conditions for class membership seem even more unrealistic as a psychological hypothesis in the foundations of cognitive science.

We could develop more subtle family resemblance fields by requiring similarity in two attributes. This leads to the structure:

Category = (A + B) or (A + C) or (A + D) or (B + C) or (B + D) or (C + D)

Oarsman = (Strong + Tall) or (Strong + Skillful) or (Strong + Quick) or (Tall + Skillful) or (Tall + Quick) or (Quick + Strong)

Wittgenstein pointed out that the extremes (A + B) and (C + D) have nothing in common. Yet we can reach the one from the other by series of case-by-case comparisons. We could go on to develop a tighter family resemblance field for this category by grouping the attributes in threes.

There is no doubt that these structures look a great deal more realistic as formal models of how bodies of knowledge could be represented than do Porphyry Trees. The family resemblance idea can be easily melded with the prototype account to give quite a realistic picture of how a body of knowledge may be manifested. However – and here is the problem that confronts the cognitive scientist – how is this form manifested in public procedures for solving cognitive problems and performing cognitive tasks to be grounded in the neural tools that we use to do these jobs, our brains and their cognitive organs?

Determinate and determinable

There is yet another way in which it has been suggested that a body of knowledge could be organized. Instead of genera and species, or kinds and instances, there are determinables and determinates. For example, 'color' is a determinable and 'red' one of its determinates. Generally properties under the same determinable cannot correctly be ascribed to the same subject, while determinates under different determinables can be. 'Cube' is a determinate under the determinable 'shape', allowing the formation of the conjunctive property 'red cube'.

What would a determinable of determinables be like? Remembering that determinates under the same determinable are mutually exclusive, we can see that the whole of our knowledge could not be represented by a system of higher and higher order determinables, such as 'perceptual property' which has 'color', 'shape', 'taste' and so on as its determinates, since these determinables do not exclude one another. Something cannot be both red and blue all over at once but it can be colored and tasty.

This logical relation has not been the basis of any proposal in knowledge engineering, as far as I know. It is discussed by Way (1992) but not developed into a full scheme that could serve as a preliminary model for the whole of a person's body of knowledge.

Problems common to all approaches to knowledge engineering

In order for some proposal for a knowledge ordering scheme to have a role in a cognitive psychology of human practices of knowledge acquisition, maintenance, management, retrieval and application, real features of the way people do use and manage their bodies of knowledge must be found a place. There is a problem about how far a psychology of classification should take account of idiosyncratic features of the ways particular people manage knowledge. That is a problem common to the whole field of cognitive science. Two general features of real cognition are important and refractory. We need to keep them in mind in considering the psychological plausibility of any model at any stage of the progression from discursive analysis through cognitive psychology to artificial intelligence modeling to neurological research, the essential progression from task to tool. These features have to do with the indeterminacy of the key relations that underlie the ordering of items of knowledge. They are the 'open texture' of systems of categories and contextual variation in similarity assessments.

The open-texture problem

Frederick Waismann, philosopher and sometime confidant and amanuensis of Ludwig Wittgenstein, was struck by the fact that real classification systems, such as the periodic table of the chemical elements, were quite capable of absorbing new items of knowledge without generating fatal internal contradictions (Waismann, 1968: 41–3, 95–7). This meant that the relations between the criteria that were used to assign individuals or particular samples to classes, types and groups must be less rigid than strict necessity would demand. The categories and sub-categories, genera and species and so on that are used by us to describe the internal structure of a body of knowledge are, as he said, related in a system of 'open texture'. Is *apteryx* a bird? It is feathered and winged but it has teeth, unlike any modern bird. Is our system of avian knowledge open-textured enough to find it a place, without forcing us to abandon all the rest of the criterial applications of 'beak' in picking out birds from, for instance, bats? Beakiness is open-textured from another angle, since the proto-marsupial, the platypus, has a beak.

Registers loaded with necessary and sufficient criterial properties as the basis of a knowledge system based on the way we post-Aristotelians classify things will never recognize open texture. Is a Spanish *torta de almendros* a cake, as we understand the concept? It does not contain any flour. Can connectionist models for representing the mechanisms by which a body of knowledge is maintained in a human brain be more successful for advancing psychology than GOFAI models?

The similarity problem

The informal mini-program sketched in the first section of this chapter expressed the idea of classification as the making of a material comparison between the states of two registers. This is the way the model would reach a new state that, when rewritten in a human language, would express a similarity judgment. However, similarity judgments made by real people in real situations are much more complex. Anything can be seen in some respect as similar to anything else. However similar things are, they can always be shown to differ in some way. Some properties are more salient than others depending on context. Similarity in height matters in basketball, while differences in weight matter in a tug-of-war. Are two rival sports teams similar to one another? The question cannot be answered unless the sport and so the context of the judgment are specified. Two tug-of-war teams are not being compared sensibly when we assess their similarity in terms of height. They can be sensibly compared only in terms of weight and strength. We need the concept of weighted similarities.

There are several aspects of similarity judgments that seem to make them problematic for GOFAI machines to serve as models for the cerebral tools we use so effortlessly.

Tversky (1977) pointed out that similarity judgments are not symmetrical. 'Politicians are like wolves' does not entail 'Wolves are like politicians'. The subject term of a proposition sets up a frame in which to make sense of the whole statement.

Medin (1989) pointed out the role of an explicit context. White hair and gray hair are similar but both differ from black hair. However, gray clouds and black clouds are similar and both differ from white clouds. Relevance or weightedness for similarities is clearly related to context.

We have already briefly discussed the importance of ranking features in using prototypes as bearers of knowledge.

If we pick groups of features at random, without reference to the prototype in which they feature, we are likely to create categories that are logically impeccable but practically worthless. 'Nuts and bolts' makes sense but it is hard to think of a context in which 'bolts and elephants' would be useful. Nevertheless, both are found on earth, both are larger than atoms, and so on. How much must the memory banks of a GOFAI machine represent, item by item, to be able to weed out the sorts of examples just described? It is becoming increasingly evident that the cognitive scientist must look elsewhere than to computational models and the von Neumann architecture for a model of whatever is the cerebral tool we use for maintaining and managing a store of knowledge.

Limitations of the project so far

Having input what is essentially a representation of a Porphyry Tree into a GOFAI machine, we have a mechanism by which 'isa' relations are determined by comparison between registers. A set of registers {B} is loaded with the code for 'animal' and a set of registers {A} with the code for 'tiger'. If there is a match in {A} for every item in {B} then the machine, using a branching rule, writes 'Tiger *isa* animal'. To make use of this output we must assume that {B} represents the essential requirements for a thing to be an animal.

In our discussions of the results of research by psychologists and philosophers into the way bodies of knowledge are organized and used we found a relatively poor fit between the basics of the highly successful technology of knowledge engineering and informal, everyday human cognition on four major counts:[2]

1   We human beings use prototypes a great deal in consciously dealing with hard cases. We make *isa* assessments by comparing concrete exemplars at almost any level of a Porphyry Tree. Thus, we might decide whether a tiger is an animal by thinking 'animal' through the concrete image of a dog and comparing it point by point with the concrete image of a tiger.

2   We often work with disjunctive taxa, which are the formal versions of family resemblance fields of words, concepts, images, and so on.

3   We are skilled in relativizing similarity judgments to contexts, with hardly a pause.

4   We often make use of the determinable/determinate pattern in the way we organize our knowledge of the relation between different kinds of properties.

All this makes for difficulties in taking the GOFAI version of the computational model of human cognition seriously as the essential bridge between discursive analysis and neurological mechanisms that we use to implement discursive and practical tasks.

Cognitive psychology of classifying: take one

To illustrate the intermediate phase of a full-scale research program into the use of a body of knowledge in classifying things we will follow the treatment by Estes (1994).

A common features index

In discussing the limitations of unqualified similarity comparisons, I gave a simple example of how changing the context changes the judgments we make about similarities among a group of features. Cognitive psychologists have tended to assume that features can be detached from context. The example that illustrated the effect of context depended on assuming that 'white' was detachable psychologically from 'white hair' and 'white cloud'. This is an unrealistic assumption. Nevertheless it is an integral part of the foundations of the account of classifying offered by Estes and others.

The first step in their approach is to incorporate similarity comparisons between features of the things to be classified and similarities between contexts. Adding up similarities does not capture the pattern of thought involved in making similarity judgments. Medin proposed a product rule. The overall similarity co-efficient for a comparison is the product of two sets of coefficients, 1 for a match and some value less than 1 for a mismatch. Contexts can be assessed for similarity in the same way.

A cricket ball is round, red and bigger than an apple. A baseball is round, white and bigger than an apple. How similar are cricket balls to baseballs? Score $1 + 1 = 2$ for similarity and subtract 1 for dissimilarity. Index: $\sigma = +1$. A locust has wings, an exoskeleton and swarms in millions. A bat has wings, an endo-skeleton and hunts alone. How similar are locusts and bats? Score 1 for similarity and subtract 2 for dissimilarity. Index $\sigma = -1$. Cricket balls are more similar to baseballs than locusts are to bats. It is easy to see that how these sums work out will depend on which attributes are chosen. Salience is crucial.

One can see immediately that if this rule and any further elaborations of it are to be of any use in classifying things it must be assumed that our knowledge of types is simply knowledge of an undifferentiated group of independent features. Salience in context and interrelations between them do not play an important part. In real cases features do not always appear in stable and coherent clusters. In many cases, they are identified anew in each act of classifying, perhaps by applying the product rule. Indeed, Estes insists upon this (1994: 21–2).

The similarity assumption

In trying to assess the worth of the Estes proposal we must once again look closely at the pattern of model building, and, in particular, at the source of Estes's model of a mental 'classifying engine'. Is it driven by the need to map the model on to cerebral structures and processes? Is it an abstraction of the methods of classifying things that a lepidopterist might use to classify a new specimen, using the butterfly collections in the vaults of the Natural History Museum? Is it an abstraction of the way a lepidopterist would write up the results of research in a paper for the journal of lepidopterist taxonomy?

It seems to be implicitly directed to the third of these possibilities. Even then, it is not very realistic. It reflects the old idea, promoted by Thorndike (1913), that similarity judgments are based on relative proportions of common elements, whatever it is that is being compared.

Accessing a body of knowledge for Estes goes something like this. A person is presented with an object and asked to classify it – say a botanist comes back with a specimen brought back from afar. Noting the properties of the specimen sets going a cognitive process by which similar patterns that the botanist has encountered before and still remembers are accessed. Then a feature-by-feature comparison is made. Finally, using the product rule, a similarity index is generated. Thus forms the basis of the judgment: 'Your specimen *isa* rare species of elm.' Here is Estes's own sketch of the process he imagines:

> I assume that a perceived stimulus pattern resonates with stored patterns in somewhat the same way that a tone sounded on a musical instrument resonates with a set of tuning forks, activating vectors in the memory array in direct reaction to similarity of the perceived to the stored pattern.
>
> (Estes, 1994: 14)

Where does this picture come from? It seems to be a projection of what people sometimes do in real life in the public world of geological specimens and butterfly collections. It assumes the old 'storage' picture as if types were represented 'in the mind' in the way that specimens might be laid out in a display cabinet.

We must be very clear about the force of these comments. The difficulties do not go to show that the processes Estes, Medin and others have highlighted do not occur. Their account may very well be a powerful analysis of the perceptual and discursive procedures that people use in consciously matching something new to an exemplar. Such a procedure is vividly described in Johnson and Coates's (1999) account of Vladimir Nabokov's work as a lepidopterist, particularly in developing a taxonomy for the group of butterflies known as 'blues'. Nabokov painstakingly dissected the genitals of specimens, building his classification system on similarities and differences between his specimens and those already in the standard collections. He then *fixed on a particular dissected butterfly as the exemplar of the type*. Type decisions are made by comparing new specimens with *this* butterfly corpse.

Finally, it is worth noticing that when Estes does consider a network model so potent is the old encoding idea of learning as representation item by item in the recesses of the mind that his network is not connectionist.

> The basic representational assumption is that a node is entered in the network for each stimulus pattern perceived by the learner ... similarity between an input pattern and the featural description associated with a node is computed exactly as in the exemplar model ...
>
> (Estes, 1994: 75–9)

There are some very odd aspects of this model, apart from its still incorporating representational assumptions. The similarity relation is computed between observed patterns and descriptions of types, that is, between something material and something propositional. There is no hint in Estes's text as to how this might be accomplished. One virtue of Rosch-type treatments is that types as exemplified in concrete prototypes and actual specimens are commensurable. In order for a candidate specimen to be compared with a species description, the specimen would have to be described. In order for that to be done the salience problem would have to be resolved, since any real thing has indefinitely many possible descriptors.

Cognitive psychology of classifying: take two

The Estes–Medin way of constructing a model for classifying is too dependent on a very narrow source and at the same time projects an implausible representational model of stored features into the mind of the classifier, a mental mechanism the neural implementation of which seems impossible. What do we make of the subsidiary model of the tones and tuning forks?

A different and more promising cognitive psychology of classifying has come from researches by Rosch (1973) and others into what people are doing when they are deciding to what type, group, class, or species something belongs. This is promising on the two major counts that matter for cognitive science. The cognitive model is based on a more general and widespread way of classifying than the feature comparison account of Estes and others. Their account does very well for professional lepidopterists but is implausible for sorting the vegetables in the kitchen, and deciding whether this mushroom is perhaps a poisonous toadstool. In that it does not presuppose a feature-by-feature comparison it sits nicely with connectionist simulations of a body of knowledge relevant to deciding '... isa ...' problems.

Rosch's pioneering researches began with a simple problem: which members of a category are treated by people as the most typical? Her original study (Rosch, 1973) used features or attributes of subtypes of a broader category to identify the most typical one. One asks people to write down the features that occur to them when they see the stuff or hear the word for it. Trying this out in a cognitive psychology class, it will be no surprise to the reader to learn that spaghetti came through as the most typical pasta. Rosch found that 'robin' was picked in the United States while I have found 'blackbird' to be the UK choice of bird.

Given the results of this and other studies, perhaps the whole idea of using the procedure of categorizing by computing an index of weighted similarities and differences in feature comparisons is unrealistic as the basis of a cognitive psychology model. That model should lead to a suitable artificial intelligence model which, in its turn, will lead into the processes that are going on when someone uses their own brain as a tool for classifying something. Is deciding whether a stork isa bird really categorizing by attending to features and comparing them with one's preset criterial bird features? It seems to me that Rosch's studies tend towards a very different conclusion – perhaps we need to revive Gestaltist ideas of integral structures and wholeness to make sense of what people actually do in everyday life. How do people usually classify things? Do they compare one entity with another, as a whole, or do they run over a catalog of features? The move into connectionist artificial intelligence would very strongly favor the former. Of course, this does not preclude a feature-by-feature comparison in hard cases. It is more than likely that biologists at certain stages in building a taxonomy work very much as Nabokov did, dissecting the genitals of butterflies and making feature-by-feature comparisons in order to establish species and genera. However, in lepidoptery and botany, actual specimens, not lists of features, are the bearers of species concepts.

Indeed, this step has been taken by cognitive psychologists in moving beyond prototypes as sets of co-occurring features to exemplars. This is explained by Way (1997: 733) as: 'people's representation of *bird* is a loose collection of specific examples of birds encountered'. Way elaborates this account by bringing in the role of memory: 'actual examples are stored in memory and used for comparison in categorization' (1997: 735).

learning point   **Alternative methods of classification**

1   Non-Aristotelian scheme:

   a)   Prototypes as concrete exemplars of types and categories.
   b)   Family resemblance and disjunctive classes, e.g. 'plates'.
   c)   Determinates under a determinable, e.g. 'red' under 'color'.

2   Common problems:

   a)   Open texture of all actual classification systems.
   b)   The 'similarity' problem.
   c)   General weakness of GOFAI models for simulating human ways of classifying.

3   Cognitive psychology of classifying:

   a)   Attempts to bypass the similarity problem: Estes's work.
   b)   Refinements of the prototype/exemplar account: Rosch's work.

Connectionism: the way forward?

It should now be quite clear that a computational theory of how we make use of a body of knowledge expressed in hierarchies of concepts cannot be the basis of a model of real cognitive functioning. For that reason alone it has nothing to offer the cognitive scientist interested in developing plausible models of the structures and way of working of the relevant cerebral tools.

Let us see first how connectionist models would fare in general. We know that such models do very well in linking pairs of items. Clamping the input surface with the coded expression of a word like 'canine', we can train the net to output 'dog'. However, the cognitive process we want to model must deal with 'wolf' as well. How can it do that? As we learned in Chapter 9, one of the most important features of connectionist nets is the possibility of superposition, that is, of being able to use the same set of weights on the one net to perform a variety of jobs.

If human beings do reason mostly by comparing exemplars and prototypes rather than by testing for the satisfaction of necessary and sufficient conditions, there are some obvious advantages of connectionist models. Drawn from Way's excellent discussion of this issue (Way, 1997: 742–5), the following comments illustrate the advantages of connectionism as the model-building technique for cognitive science.

1　Because superposition is possible, a net can 'store' all the information about the exemplars the person has encountered. As the number of exemplars increases, nets extract prototypes in a way that we will follow in detail in the exercise to follow. Therefore connectionist models accommodate both kinds of lepidoptery, namely comparing whole specimens with the criterion specimen and engaging in a weighted feature-by-feature comparison (McLeod et al., 1998: 87–8).

2　Categories do not need to precede prototypes, as they must in the old model. Simply working with a net will yield prototypes. If we are confined to such questions as 'Tell me your idea of a bird' and you say 'Robin,' 'bird' has preceded 'robin'. However, having the prototype, you can do all the classificatory and other cognitive work with birds without extracting the species concept at all.

3　The similarity problem vanishes. Network adjustments gradually home in on the best relationship between concepts, without needing any arbitrary decisions about the salience of any characteristics for making similarity judgments.

4　Networks associate actual features, preserving all co-occurring attributes. The problematic distinction between essences and propria does not need to be made. In simple cases, categorizing is by wholes.

5　Networks do not contain any representations, only connections. In a network trained to recognize birds there is nothing corresponding to bird features. The commonsense but erroneous idea that we decide whether an eagle is a bird by comparing and checking off its features with the list of necessary and sufficient conditions for being a bird simply has no place in the modeling of how one would use one's body of ornithological know-ledge. One sees the whole eagle as birdlike. There is no 'Carnivore? Yes. Predator? Yes. Wings? Yes' stage at all, as if until the third feature test we were still unsure whether it might be a wolf or a crocodile.

Exercise: extracting a prototype

This exercise is drawn from the co-textbook, McLeod et al. (1998: chapter 4). To understand how the net works we must add an additional feature to our basic model net. The nets discussed in Chapter 9 were all simple feed-forward structures with no internal loops. Training consisted in resetting weights throughout the net. This process had its source outside the net, motivated by an examination of the output, to see whether it was as desired. An auto-associator simply reproduces input as output. However, it feeds back whatever output it produces to the input connections. Training consists of changing the connections until the output matches the input. Once trained, the net can hold independent content with the same weighted connections. It exhibits superposition. This type of net does something else of great psychological importance. It extracts a prototype from many diverse individual inputs.

A semi-interpreted auto-associator net

We will set up our model net in the semi-neurological form used by McLeod et al. as well as a simple node and connection model net. This has the advantage, as we saw in Chapter 9, of the net already being interpreted as an iconic model of a possible brain structure (see Figure 10.5). Each dendrite receives an external input, which passes to its unit, the output of which is fed back to all the dendrites in the net. Each dendrite now receives not only an external input but also the sum of the internal inputs fed back from the other units.

How are the weights changed in the learning process? In the model, it will depend on the learning rule chosen for the task in hand. Here is how McLeod et al. describe the rule:

> If the internal input to a given unit is less than the external then the weights of the connections carrying a positive input to the unit are increased, and those carrying a negative input are reduced. If the internal input is greater than the external, vice versa.

> (1998: 74)

You can now follow the calculations on pp. 75–7 of the recommended cotext.

Disadvantages of connectionist models

Just because some of the problems of naive artificial intelligence model building for one of the most important ways we use bodies of knowledge have been resolved, in principle, by adopting the PDP approach, it does not follow that all is now plain sailing. The optimistic note on which the last chapter ended, with the cell nets of the real hippocampus matching up remarkably well to the artificial intelligence models, is not so easy to strike with the psychology of classifying.

1   Learning by back propagation on hundreds of trials, even if conducted at lightning speed by a clever simulation program, is unrealistic psychologically. The 'Eureka! Got it!' experience is very common. Notoriously, the cry does not show that I *have* got it. Understanding is not an event but a standing condition, a disposition. It can be displayed only in correct performances.

2   The number of concepts a net can discriminate depends on the number of output nodes. Since we can discriminate a seemingly indefinite number of concepts, this openness is not easily built in to the form of a net.

3   The original training of the net sets up certain weights and internal patterns in the connections. These naturally restrict the powers of the net, even with superposition. It would have to be retrained every time a new output was required.

4   Amending weighs in retraining may destroy the power of the net to make the original correlations it was first trained to perform. The brain is a cumulative learning machine.

Neuropsychology of classifying

The final step of the progression from discursive analysis through cognitive psychology through artificial intelligence modeling is the bringing to light of the structure and functioning of the cerebral tools used by people to perform the discursive acts with which we began. Where does this branch of neuroscience stand? How far are PDP connectionist models realized in the real neural tools?

The present state of the art is undeveloped. Neuroscientists are a little further forward than the primitive reasoning from lesions and the cognitive deficits they are associated with. PET scans are now available to identify the regions of the brain serving as tools for various cognitive tasks. As we have noticed at several points these regions are neurologically enormous, involving hundreds of thousands, perhaps millions of cells. The identification of distinct nets, successfully achieved for the hippocampus as a memory organ, is a long way from being brought off for cerebral organs that may be being used in carrying out classifying tasks. At this point in the history of the field of cognitive science, we have something to go on, but in the summary to follow, it will be clear that it is actually very little.

What would one like to know? We do make use of different bodies of knowledge for classifying tasks involving different kinds of entities. The literature is a little confusing, since some neuropsychologists have slipped into a perceptual metaphor, using the word 'recognition' when they mean the upshot of an *'isa'* query. In some of the literature, making such judgments is misleadingly described as 'behavior'. Recognizing something and expressing that achievement symbolically, perhaps as a verbal description, are related but different tasks, and neither is behavior! Generally, the literature is full of unnecessary jargon and pseudo-precise terms.

There are plenty of examples of thorough work on the location of brain activation areas during cognitive tasks. I will describe two that will enable us to judge how far along the way this research has progressed. One is a study of the uses of words, drawing on different levels of an extensive Porphyry Tree (Kosslyn et al., 1995), and the other a series of studies of the making of simple categorizing judgments, such as whether something *is an animal* and something else *is a tool* (Cappa et al., 1998: 354–7). The tasks were given to participants in research programs using a PET (positron emission tomography) scanner to pick up which areas of the brain were activated during the performance of these tasks.

In the first study, participants were given a word, written in one condition and spoken in another, and then asked whether it correctly named a picture with which they were subsequently presented. The words were drawn from three logical levels, the common word for an object, say 'shirt', a subordinate level, say 'dress shirt', and a superordinate level, say 'clothing'. Though the results were couched in terms of discursive metaphors, such as 'searching the memory', 'information look-up' and so on, the outcome was clear. Activation occurred only in the left hemispheres (the participants were right-handed). Subtracting from the results of the scanning of the brain during the superordinate task the blood flow that was detected for the standard task, there were two active areas, one in the parietal-temporal junction area and one in Broca's area. For the subordinate terms, there were activated areas in both left and right hemispheres. This program of studies was quite extensive, and showed how various and how far removed from one another were the activated areas not only involved in the same task but also for different versions of the tasks.

The animal and tool categorization study showed that both hemispheres were active during the task involving living things, animals, but activation occurred only in the left hemisphere when participants were categorizing some non-living things, namely tools. These results, and there are lots like them, pose considerable difficulties for any simple development of connectionist modeling for these relatively simple cognitive tasks. Unlike the case of the hippocampus, artificial intelligence modeling and brain studies are still very far apart.

---

learning point   ## Connectionist models of classifying

1   Advantages of neural net models:

   a)   They can store massive amounts of knowledge because of superposition.
   b)   No similarity problem.
   c)   Essence and propria do not need to be distinguished.
   d)   Neural nets do not contain any representations.

2   Exercise: extracting a prototype:

   a)   Constructing a semi-interpreted auto-associator.
   b)   Superposition can be simulated in practice.

3   Disadvantages of neural net models:

   a)   Back propagation requires an unrealistic number of trials.
   b)   Retraining can destroy already effective superpositions.

4   Neuropsychological studies show different brain areas activated when classifying different kinds of beings.

Conclusion

We have found it necessary to distinguish cognitive projects involving classifying into two main groups. There are those used by scientists and those used by lay folk. Both make use of comparisons between concrete exemplars and actual specimens of candidates for entry into a category. Scientific classifications are taken further and expressed in Linnaean schemes in accordance with the Aristotelian principles of *genus et differentiae*.

There are many problems with attempts to adapt the Aristotelian scheme to all classificatory tasks. Similarities must be counted in and dissimilarities counted out, so to speak. Much depends on context and other considerations leading to the idea of weighted similarities as the basis for classifying. The upshot is that a great variety of classificatory schemes must be countenanced, their use depending on the task in hand.

Lay folk use not only prototypes and concrete exemplars but also family resemblance categories in which things are grouped by many different strands of similarity and difference. In some cases, putting determinates under a determinable – for example, red, blue, etc., under color – is used rather than the Aristotelian subsuming species under a genus.

There are some obvious ways that connectionist models, such as the auto-associator, are more satisfactory than GOFAI models based on comparisons of features. However, enough reservations have been brought to light to show that there is much work yet to be done before the hybrid psychology program can be fulfilled for the cognitive psychology of classifying.

Notes

1   A clear and comprehensive survey of systems of categories can be found in Sowa (2000: 5–75).
2   Even taxonomists use prototype thinking in that there are type-bearing specimens in recognized scientific collections. For a good account of this see Johnson and Coates, *Nabokov's Blues* (1999).

chapter twelve

Cognitive disorders

As far as we know, every human society has recognized that some people do not think in the same way as the majority of the fellow members of their tribe. Some do not feel the way other people do in similar situations. Some do not do what other people would do in the same circumstances. For the most part, we simply do not know how the standards of correctness, propriety and rationality for patterns of thought, feeling and action were actually set. It is tempting to think that it must always have been a matter of the customs and practices of the majority setting the standards for all. However, the history of the uses of psychiatry in the former Soviet Union suggests that powerful institutions may have played a role.

What is clear is that there have been great differences in the way variations from common and accepted patterns and practices have been classified. Some, such as epileptic fits, have been admired and respected in certain societies. Others, such as homosexuality, have tended to be treated as deviant and disorderly. Currently we regard epilepsy as a mental ailment and homosexuality as an acceptable deviation from the practices and customs of the majority. Are these shifts brought about by factual discoveries or are they changes in the conceptual systems with which we manage our lives? Clearly there is work for the philosopher to help to sort out these issues.

Philosophers, we learned in Part I, try to bring to light the presuppositions of human practices. In this chapter we shall be studying some of the presuppositions of the practices of psychiatry and clinical psychology.

Philosophical issues are important for this part of our course for two main reasons:

1   We recognize deviant or improper thought patterns against the standards of thinking that are implicit in and presupposed by our cultural practices.
2   There are various patterns of reasoning presupposed in the practice of clinical psychology and psychiatry that we have already encountered in the course.

Both kinds of presupposition need to be brought to mind as we learn to apply the hybrid psychology principles to the study of thought disorders.

In this chapter we are concerned not so much with the presuppositions of people who think in unacceptable ways as with the presuppositions of those who are deputed to deal with such deviations from what is taken to be the proper way to perform cognitive tasks. For example, the diagnosis of multiple personality syndrome as a deviant way of presenting fragments of one's autobiography depends on presuppositions about the proper way to use personal pronouns in reporting episodes in one's life. In dealing with Alzheimer's condition, clinicians, and others who study this problem make use of both the Taxonomic Priority Principle and the task/tool model in inferring that confused speech is the result of brain damage.

We must bear in mind that the discursive approach to psychology works at two levels. Many psychological phenomena are best thought of as aspects or properties of orderly sequences of meaningful acts. Conversation is both an example of a cognitive medium and an analytical model for analysing performances in non-linguistic cognitive media. In Chapter 4 we learned how to tidy up the somewhat messy normative constraints on everyday cognitive practices into four 'grammars', each based on a powerful ontological presupposition. The hybrid science we have seen emerging in contemporary cognitive psychology makes use of presuppositions featuring the human being as a person, as an organism and as a seething mass of molecules. While many lay people still discuss human affairs in religious terms, the medical profession and others charged with dealing with deviant patterns of thinking make use only of the categories of 'persons', 'organisms' and 'molecules' in their discursive practices. In contemporary psychiatry and clinical psychology soul talk has been dropped.

Cognitive psychology, as it figures in psychiatry practice and in the work of clinical psychologists, involves presuppositions as to what are normal and acceptable forms of cognition. These presuppositions are involved in psychiatric classifications of ways of thinking and acting. They are also involved in decisions as to what is to be done about those whose activities deviate from local standards in unacceptable ways.

section one

Presuppositions of psychiatry and clinical psychology

Broadly speaking, we can recognize four loosely defined and fuzzily bounded categories of waywardness in the annals of historically accessible societies: eccentricity, immorality, crime and madness. The boundaries are fuzzy. Here are some examples:

1   In her old age my maternal grandmother used to go into other people's gardens and brazenly take cuttings from plants she coveted. Was this eccentricity or immorality?

2   So that he might acquire the wife of Uriah the Hittite, King David ordered his general, Joab, to set Uriah 'in the forefront of the hottest battle, and retire ye from him, that he may be smitten and die'. Uriah was killed. 'And when the mourning was past, David sent and fetched her [Uriah's widow] and she became his wife.' (II Samuel, 11, 15, and 27.) However we categorize it, 'the thing that David had done displeased the Lord'. Was this act immoral or was it a crime?

3   Fred West sexually violated, tortured and killed more than a dozen young women, including his own daughters. Was Fred West a criminal or was he suffering from a mental disease?

4   During the 1970s one could see, most days, in the center of Oxford, a middle-aged man dressed only in bathing trunks and assorted brightly coloured scarves. The police and the passers-by treated his antics with amused tolerance. One might say that his behavior straddled the boundary between eccentricity and madness.

It is evident that the boundaries between our Western Judeo-Christian categories of unusual ways of behaving are fuzzy. Other cultures have categorized odd ways of thinking and acting differently. Though this chapter is concerned only with cognitive waywardness, the fuzziness of category boundaries is evident in the categorization of feelings and actions as well.

The concept of personal responsibility shapes much of what is said about and to someone who is saying things that are, for some reason, cognitively 'off-key'. The inference from the unacceptability of what someone says or does to the conclusion that the person's state is pathological presupposes not only that what he or she is doing is odd by local standards, but also that this person in these circumstances is not responsible for what is said and done. There is a conceptual tie between pathology and irresponsibility. To classify what someone does as the work of a creative genius, or the result of a stupid mistake, or a criminal act, presupposes that that person in the circumstances in which they did what they did was responsible for it.

The use of the concept of 'disease' as the supertype dominating the way odd ways of thinking are classified is conceptually linked with concepts such as 'treatment', 'cure' and 'recovery'. These conceptual clusters play an important part in the discursive practices that are involved in the so-called 'medicalization' of everyday life. As philosophers we can see that when a cognitive disorder, such as an inability to identify commonplace objects, is medicalized the person displaying it is excused responsibility for that failure. This sort of case seems unproblematic. However, the medicalization of immoral or criminal behavior raises much more troubling philosophical problems.

The link with the concept of 'cure' carries the presupposition that this being is, was or will again be a person. We cannot say that a stone is irresponsible, since it makes no sense to say that it is responsible, either. Diagnosing eccentricity as mental illness presupposes that someone is not responsible for odd ways of thinking. Since the concept of 'illness' is tied up with that of 'cure', we must also presuppose that such a person could once again be responsible for his or her actions.

It is important to remind ourselves that not only the telling of the stories of a life but many of the most characteristic human psychological phenomena are discursive, brought into being as aspects of the public and private use of symbols under all sorts of normative constraints. Remembering (recollecting the past correctly), deciding (making up one's mind to the best effect), reasoning (drawing a conclusion rationally), persuading (getting someone to change their mind) and so on are generally either performed wholly discursively or make use of discourse in important ways. This is the insight that lies behind the recent trend to use discourse analysis as the methodology for taking the first steps towards a thoroughgoing scientific treatment of psychopathology.

The expansion of the domain of psychopathology

From eccentricity to pathology

The trend to 'pathologize' unusual ways of acting has been commented on by many authors. Here is one very clear presentation of the insight.

> In recent times, we have witnessed a marked rise in the discovery of numerous psychopathologies and syndromes. A wide variety of psychological difficulties and problems are now recognized as constituting identifiable symptoms of characteristics of syndromes not previously heard of. Premenstrual syndrome (PMS), battered woman syndrome, and attention deficit hyperactivity disorder [ADHD] are just some of the disorders lately 'discovered' and offered up for public attention. Alongside this increase in the discovery and categorization of these types of problems is a parallel rise in the provision of counseling and therapy.
>
> (Burr and Butt, 2000: 186)[1]

In this chapter we are concerned with what can go wrong with a person's *cognitive* skills. For example, someone may lose some of the capacity for episodic remembering. Granny cannot recall your previous visit. Someone may lose some of the capacity for procedural remembering. An elderly man can no longer tie his shoelaces. Someone may no longer be able to recognize a common object as belonging to a certain category, such as 'cup' or 'telephone'. Someone may lose the capacity to structure sentences grammatically, and so on.

Common sense suggests there is a distinction between muddleheadedness, being a bit flaky and so on and cognitive psychopathology. It is not easy to draw. The trend has been to bring more and more of the former under the latter. For example, with the advent of attention deficit hyperactivity disorder a new 'disease' has appeared in the cognitive domain. Having attained disease status, recognizing the condition is said to be 'diagnosis'. What was once just one of

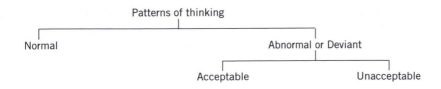

Figure 12.1
Boundary fixing

those 'ways some people are' becomes a topic for psychopathology. There are all sorts of reasons for being exceedingly cautious in accepting the definitions and distinctions of diagnostic manuals, such as *DSM* IV.[2] Nevertheless the category of 'thought disorder' is a useful place for us to start.

In charting the way that psychiatric categories are created and employed we need to take account of a pattern of boundary fixing that can be represented something like Figure 12.1. It does not follow that because a society or culture treats a form of thought or behavior as abnormal that it will also be objected to as unacceptable. A cognitive practice will become a matter for psychiatrists and clinical psychologists just as far as it is both abnormal and unacceptable. Being able to add up columns of figures at sight is abnormal but not unacceptable. Thinking one's wife is a hat is both abnormal and unacceptable (Sacks, 1985).

Story telling and story acting: narratology

The strongest narratological thesis that would link the study of the patterns of story telling to the problem of explaining human action is this: 'Lives are lived according to the same conventions in accordance with which lives are told' (Bruner, 1991). This thesis has profound consequences for the concept of autobiography. It is the fact that an autobiography has both retrospective and prospective dimensions that make autobiographical telling a prime subject for psychological research. Not only do we tell others and ourselves versions of the lives we have led, but also we tell others and ourselves anticipatory stories that express the pattern of those parts of our lives that are yet to be lived. Shakespeare was very good at presenting this aspect of human psychology. His grasp of this phenomenon appears in such famous soliloquies as that of Richard III over the corpse of his predecessor and that of Hamlet attempting to resolve the existential dilemma at the heart of his struggle to find a way to deal with the murder of his father. Should his autobiography end in suicide or in revenge?

At first glance the concept of autobiography could hardly seem more innocent of complications. It is just the story of my life as told by me, from my point of view. Autobiographies may differ in degree of candor and self-absorption, but who is a better authority on what I did and why I did it than myself? However, empirical studies of autobiographical telling quickly disclose all sorts of complexities.

An autobiography is above all a narrative, and in each age narrative genres have their own conventions. Violating these conventions has often been treated as pathological, and a story line deemed unacceptable. Not so long ago there was a man in Oxford who insisted that he was the rightful king of England. He was confined to the Warneford psychiatric hospital. However, of equal interest are cases in which the grammatical forms used for autobiographical story telling are unacceptable. This seems to be the root problem with those who display multiple and incompatible personalities.

Bizarre thought patterns and disordered brains

This course is concerned with the principles of cognitive science, the hybrid discipline that ties together our ability to manage symbol systems with the workings of the brain and nervous system. We have seen how the unification of psychology is achieved by linking the domain of people creating meanings and conforming to norms with the domain of people as organisms composed of molecular structures. The Taxonomic Priority Principle requires that we identify structures and processes in the brain and nervous system by correlating them with cognitive activities classified with the help of discursive categories. The task/tool metaphor requires that the features of the brain and nervous system so identified are looked at in terms of their role in the performance of cognitive tasks. This is complicated by the fact that cognitive skills not only are appropriated from collective cognitive activities in the manner described by Vygotsky (1962) but also are often deployed in joint cognitive activities. All this applies to the identification and study of cognitive activities that are locally set off as deviant and unacceptable, as well as those taken locally to be normal and acceptable.

In setting up the foundations of a scientific psychology we found that there were four 'grammars' in everyday use in Western societies. The S or Soul grammar does not now have a place in psychological science, or in psychiatry and clinical psychology. Cognitive psychology makes use of three basic grammars, the P or Person grammar, the O or Organism grammar, and the M or Molecular grammar. Using the Taxonomic Priority Principle was essential to identify bodily organs that were functionally relevant to cognitive activities, and to pick out from the myriad molecular transformations studied by biochemists just those that were relevant to our understanding how people were able to perform cognitive tasks correctly. By the use of the Taxonomic Priority Principle we can identify defects in the way a person's brain is working from correlations with defective discursive performances, that is, ones that do not meet the local criteria of correctness.

In bringing discursive and neurological studies into a unified hybrid psychology we made use of the principle that, in terms of the P or Person grammar, a person's brain is a (second order) cognitive tool. We nicknamed this principle the task/tool principle. It enables a psychiatrist or clinical psychologist to tie certain kinds of cognitive disorders to characteristic states of the brain. It is a generalized form of the relation between linguistic skills and brain function suggested by Luria (1981). When the cognitive phenomenon in question is picked out as pathological the associated brain state or process inherits the assessment.

The source of standards of correctness must be in the realm to which the P grammar is adapted: people identifying and misidentifying things, puzzling over and solving or failing to solve problems according to local standards of correctness and propriety, and so on. Molecular processes just are – whatever they are. That this or that biochemical process is not what it should be can be judged only by the use of the Taxonomic Priority Principle. Is it correlated with a discursive activity that does not meet the complex pattern of universal and local standards to which 'correct' and meaningful actions must conform? The interplay between cultural standards and categories and neuroscience is well brought out in a survey of studies of the relationship between adolescence and brain development. Spear (2000) shows how aspects of the development of the brain as a cognitive tool tend to sustain the Western distinction between adolescence and puberty.

There is more to be said, from a philosophical point of view. Compare the use of the Taxonomic Priority Principle with other kinds of correlations, say those between the symptoms of a physical illness and the virus infections that cause the symptoms. Each member of the pair 'symptom'/'infection' can be independently identified and instances can be individuated by criteria which are also independent of one another. Furthermore, it is a matter of fact, which might have been otherwise, that this virus causes these symptoms. The parts of the brain relevant to some cognitive skill and the way it is exercised are picked out wholly by reference to criteria derived from observable occasions of the use of the skill. What counts as a 'part of the brain' – say the hippocampus, which we have already studied – is a subtle mix of the shapes and locations of recognizable chunks of neural tissue and functional inferences based on the kind of correlations that appear from the use of PET scans of the brain in use.

That the hippocampus is the site of the transformation of short-term into long-term material basis of remembering is not a matter of fact that could have been otherwise. The criteria for making this identification are derived from observations of people remembering. Had the classification system for observable cognitive activities been different we would have picked out different parts of the brain as the tools by which the cognitive tasks were to be accomplished.

Wittgenstein pointed out that 'grammar' is autonomous, that is, our classification schemes are not wholly derived from what we can perceive. They depend, too, upon the force of what interests us. However, he also remarks that a scheme is of no use if we cannot agree in our judgments as to what is what. 'It is not every sentence-like formation that we know how to do something with, not every technique which has application in our lives' (Wittgenstein, 1953: para. 520).

The presuppositions of psychotherapy

We lay folk have a touching faith in psychiatrists. We believe that they are much concerned with finding out how matters appear to those who consult them. They take seriously reports of private miseries, of fears and anxieties, of voices counselling unwise actions, of impulses to ruin careers by propositioning secretaries or shouting obscenities in public places, of strange bodily feelings and so on. The stories told by the curious characters that haunt the consulting room of the good doctor Oliver Sacks (1985) are intelligible to him. By virtue of his skill as a raconteur they become intelligible to people like you and me. *This* is how it is with the one who sits in the client's chair or lies on the client's couch. 'Tell me ...' is the psychiatrist's characteristic invitation. But what must be presupposed in assuming that the 'mind doctor' understands?

Patients complain of 'chronic fatigue' (CFS). Physical medicine can find no lesions. Are these people malingering? Doctors faced with stories of overwhelming fatigue now tend to believe what they are told. It is acceptable now to believe that the patient really feels utterly banjaxed. It would follow that the fatigue is really debilitating. That means that the patient is exculpated from accusations of malingering. To move from scepticism to belief the patient's utterances must first of all be intelligible to a psychiatrist or clinical psychologist. We can discuss the truth conditions and the deeper significance of what someone says only if there is at least a minimal common ground of shared meaning. The experiences others report are private in the radical sense that they are not telling us about states of affairs visible in the public world.

Why is this problem a matter for cognitive psychology? The cognitive issue is first of all one of classification. What taxonomy is the patient using? And what taxonomy should the psychotherapist use to classify the condition that is reported by the patient? Scientific realists hold that there are real essences behind useful taxonomic categories. Should chronic fatigue syndrome be classified as a psychosocial disorder, a violation of the rules and conventions of proper behavior, or should it be classified as a physical illness like measles? This distinction makes sense only within a realist paradigm. If the condition is physical in origin there must be a relevant unobservable state or process in the brain and nervous system of the patient.

Positioning in this context

The concept of 'positioning' was introduced in Chapter 7 to help us understand the way that conversations and conversation-like interactions unfold. A psychiatric interview is a conversation. Positioning is obviously relevant to how such a conversation develops.

Positioning, as we have learned, is a social process by which each actor in a complex interaction is assigned or takes up a certain limited set of rights and duties with respect to the kinds of speech acts which are acceptable and proper for that person to contribute to the interaction. Positioned as a parent, one can rebuke a child. Positioned as a supplicant, one must accept the decision of the tribunal, and so on. Positioned as a patient, a person concedes expertise and authority to the psychiatrist. Or do they?

Positioning is a dynamic process, and positions are generally ephemeral. Rights and duties to say and do things are established, lost and gained momentarily in the give-and-take of real social interactions. In such-and-such a position certain types of actions were open to one but others were not. Positions can be challenged and reassigned in the course of an episode.

Norms, rules, conventions and customs

In Chapter 7 the concept of 'position' was tied to two other important concepts, *speech act* and *story line*. To take up or to be assigned a position determines the local meaning of what one says and does. A spoken sentence is socially effica-cious as a speech act in ways that often exceed its literal meaning. Relative to how one is positioned one's utterances are taken as the performance of this or that speech act. Episodes of everyday life are usually orderly, and often the source of that order is a cultural pattern of narrative, a story line. Specific positions are always tied in with specific repertoires of speech acts and specific story lines. Change any one member of the interlinked triad and the others change with it. One can see how important acceptances of and challenges to positionings are in psychiatric encounters.

There may be more than one conversation going on, though only one set of sentences has been uttered. The same sentence can express more than one speech act, depending on the positionings assumed by the various people who hear it. It follows too that there may be more than one story line unfolding in the flow of utterances and other potentially meaningful actions.

Classifying phenomena and modeling the unobservable

A project is scientific only as far as a well established system of classificatory concepts, a taxonomy is available, and there is a working type hierarchy for con-structing plausible models of unobservable entities, properties and processes. Ideally, these essential features of a scientific approach to any domain are linked into a coherent overall pattern.

The most important distinction among unacceptable ways of thinking, feel-ing and acting is between psychoses and neuroses. There is a standard distinction in clinical psychology and psychiatry between psychosis and neurosis. Kraepelin dealt with psychoses, such as *dementia praecox*, while Freud dealt with neuroses such as *hysteria*. At this point we encounter the essential step in setting up any science, the building of a rational taxonomy, a system for classifying the phe-nomena in the domain of interest. In the current working taxonomy of psycho-pathologies the distinction is drawn as follows.

A psychosis is a disturbance of thought, feeling or action that derives from a clear-cut physical/biological illness, such as thyroid underactivity. It is also characterized as a mental state involving delusions and hallucinations as well as loss of insight into what one is experiencing. (Paraphrased from Julier, 1983: 509–10.) The criteria for labeling a phenomenon a *psychosis* include actual observables and possible unobservables, fulfilling the basic desiderata for a scientific concept. What the psychotic person says and does shows little or no concern for social and material reality. Associated with this is a strong presumption that there is a malfunction[3] of the brain and/or the central nervous system. Classifying a disorder as a psychosis fits nicely into the hybrid science of cognitive psychology in general. Models to represent unobservable neural phenomena are readily constructed on the basis of what is already known, using the methods discussed in Chapter 9.

'Neuroses are exaggerated forms of normal reactions to stressful events. There is no evidence of any kind of organic brain disorder, patients do not lose touch with external reality ... and the personality is not grossly abnormal' (Mayou, 1983: 425b).

The criteria for labeling a phenomenon a neurosis also include references to both observable and unobservable domains. A neurotic person does not 'lose touch with reality'. However, such people exhibit worries and concerns that are unwarranted by their situation as most people would see it. Explanatory models representing the sources of these troubles are constructed from a type hierarchy of discursive phenomena, such as meanings, rules, conventions and so on.

 Sources of concepts of psychopathology: deviance and unacceptability

1 a) Our cognitive practices are rooted in shared presuppositions.
   b) Psychotherapy, as a cognitive practice within the domain of medicine, has its own presuppositions.

2 In our culture we recognize at least four overlapping and loosely defined kinds of waywardness in general: eccentricity, immorality, criminality and insanity.

3 a) Ways of thinking and acting traditionally included in the first two categories are nowadays often transferred to the fourth.
   b) Abnormality, as locally defined, is not necessarily locally unacceptable.

4 a) Brain malfunctions are defined relative to discursive abnormalities by the use of the Taxonomic Priority Principle (TPP).
   b) The human organism as such does not force any particular boundary between the normal and abnormal on us.
   c) The psychosis/neurosis distinction depends partly on the presence of delusions and partly on well supported hypotheses or direct empirical evidence of brain abnormalities, against a background concept of normality established in general by the Taxonomic Priority Principle.

Defects of discourse

Patterns of thought are available for study when they are presented publicly in their discursive or conversational forms. In this course we shall concentrate on only two such patterns. One will be autobiography and its narrative structures or story lines. The other will be syntactical and semantic disorders of everyday speech in everyday situations. In both cases we are confronted by narratives that are locally unacceptable, but for different reasons.

Non-standard story lines using standard syntax

In the small English city of Gloucester there once lived a couple, Fred and Rosemary West. For more than fifteen years they sexually abused and murdered young women, including their own daughters. What was it like to be Fred or Rosemary West? After his conviction Fred produced a substantial autobiography, some of which was published in the newspapers. The English pronominal system and associated positioning devices allowed him to take all the responsibility for the appalling treatment of the victims upon himself. In Chapter 8 we made a brief study of how the sense of self is both established and expressed by the use of pronouns. The first person indexes what is said with the place occupied by the speaker and the degree of responsibility of that speaker for what is said as well as for what is described in the narrative. The indexicality of place that pronoun usage offers a speaker was used time and again to locate Rosemary far from the times and places of the events in question. The indexicality of responsibility was used time and again to locate the whole agentic power in himself. Fred West used standard grammar to tell the story of a pathological way of life.

Broadly speaking, these preliminary remarks suggest that there could be at least two ways in which autobiographical narratives might display a pathology which one would be inclined to say expressed a pathological form of life. Subscribing to common narrative conventions and, so far as one can judge, employing the grammatical resources of English in the accepted manner, in a certain sense Fred West's autobiography was not pathological. The story he told was horrific. However, it was a story the form of which we can all recognize. Perhaps the disturbing effect of the revelations was due in part to the commonplace and even stereotypical use of pronoun grammar and narrative conventions in their telling. He used these devices to position himself as the agent. The speech acts so performed were quite commonplace. The pathology lay in the narrative.

This case is clearly outside our remit as students of cognitive psychopathology. It did not involve disorders of remembering, or struggles to find the right words to express a thought, or non-standard grammatical usages. Fred West, we may say, was an evil man. We can say this because his narrative has all the hallmarks of routine cognitive competence. He entertained no false beliefs and his use of grammar and the logic that it expresses was just what one would expect from the sanest among us. However, organizing one's thoughts logically may leave room for psychopathology. A much studied case, and one of great importance in the establishment of the boundaries of sanity and madness in the law, was that of Daniel McNaughtan (Robinson, 1996: 163–74).

McNaughtan's cognitive deviation was in his persisting in a manifestly false belief as to his situation in life and the intentions of others towards him. Cognitive competence involves not only the ability to reason with given premises but also an ability to make use of evidence in a way acceptable to the majority of people. McNaughtan, believing that his victim was the Prime Minister, Robert Peel, shot and killed Peel's secretary. That was a mistake, not a delusion. However, McNaughtan had insisted that the government was plotting against him, in the face of incontrovertible evidence that it was not. That McNaughtan's brain was affected in some way was supported by evidence of his suffering from debilitating headaches.

In an earlier and influential case a British court had acquitted James Hadfield of an attempt to murder George III. The counsel for the defence argued that being under a delusion was sufficient to exculpate a defendant in both criminal and civil cases. Furthermore there was clear presumptive evidence of injury to Hadfield's brain as a result of bullet wounds to the head sustained in battle. Citing *Hadfield* as a precedent, the defence in the McNaughtan trial produced medical evidence to support a verdict of 'Not guilty by reason of insanity'. The most effective report came from a certain Dr Winslow (Robinson, 1996: 170). In response to the defending counsel's question as to McNaughtan's state of mind, Winslow said, 'I have not the slightest hesitation in saying that he is insane, and that he committed the offence while afflicted with a delusion, under which he appears to have been labouring for a considerable length of time.'

Here we have the pattern Julier (above) set out that distinguishes psychosis from neurosis. The beliefs that led McNaughtan and Hadfield to their 'criminal' acts were delusions. In both cases there was evidence of injury to the brain. Both men must be classified, according to the Julier criteria, as psychotic. In a sense they are responsible for their actions but not cognitively responsible for the beliefs on which those actions were based. Both cases fit neatly into the framework of hybrid psychology.

Non-standard syntax and standard narrative conventions

Violations of the 'one person per body' rule

There is another kind of pathology of autobiography that one finds in the life stories of people like Miss Beauchamp and Eve White/Black, two well known cases of 'multiple personality disorder'. In their narratives, reported as snippets of autobiography, some of the basic rules of pronominal grammar are violated. The usual framework of personal story telling gives way to other orderings of events and other expressions of personhood than those with which our experience of the stories of everyday life have made us familiar and which we make use of ourselves.

In setting up a scientific paradigm one chooses an ideal type as the exemplar for the kinds of phenomena one believes the field for research covers. The main exemplar for discursive psychology is the conversation in which two or more people carry out some cognitive task in the course of speaking (or sometimes writing) to one another. Real conversations are exceedingly complex phenomena, ordered according to multiple levels of conventions and realizing ever shifting personal intentions, consensual agreements and patterns of mutual positioning with respect to the right to speak and the obligation to listen and/or respond. In the course of conversing people create, maintain, transform and abrogate social relations. In the course of conversing people adjudicate disputes, arrive at decisions, confirm or disconfirm claims to remember. As we saw in Chapter 8, people display a sense of self as a singular responsible being in accordance with which they engage in all these activities. What of the seemingly necessary principle that only one person can be embodied in each human organism? Discourses that seem to violate this principle are treated as pathological. The expression of selfhood in cases of multiple personality disorder, MPD, violates a major presupposition of ordinary discourse, the rules for the use of pronouns in the Person grammar.

We have a sense of ourselves as singularities, as unique and unitary beings. However, when we try to investigate the 'sense of identity' it is not revealed by an introspective search for an ego that lies at the core of each person's individual being. There is nothing upon which we can focus either the outer or the inner eye. When I try to examine my very self, that to which 'I' seems to point, it necessarily eludes me, since it is that self that is doing the examining.

This small but immensely important item of phenomenology has been reported and commented on very frequently. How can we possibly undertake a psychological study of the sense of self, and of deviations from the way any given culture requires selves to be, if the very subject of our investigation is for ever elusive? Wherever would one get the idea that there was more than one person in the body of Miss Beauchamp or of Eve White?

The sense of oneself as a singularity is not an abstraction from what one knows or believes about oneself. It is realized in the display of oneself as one and only one person. The main expressive devices used for this task are ready to hand, in the grammar of the first and second person pronouns in some European languages and their grammatical equivalents in others and other language groups.

Everyone has a multiplicity of potential autobiographies, though few may see the light of day. However, each such story is presented as a *version of the same person's life*. What if someone were to tell such stories as events in the lives of different people? This must surely violate one of the most fundamental presuppositions of the very idea of a scientific psychology, that the P grammar and the O grammar are necessarily linked by the principle that only one person can be embodied in each human organism.

In the case of Eve White, Thigpen and Cleckley (1957) describe two distinctive displays of personality, each involving different moral standards. Eve White and Eve Black do not refer to each other as 'you' from the vantage point of a distinctive 'I'. Their autobiographies are sequential. However, Morton Prince (1905) based his diagnosis of multiple personality disorder on Miss Beauchamp's non-standard pronoun usage. She presented three contemporaneous fragments of life stories, autobiographies, each indexed by the use of 'I'. When commenting on life events from the vantage of point of any one of these she used 'you' and 'she' as the lynchpins of each of the others.

Morton Prince's diagnosis presupposes a standard P grammar, in which the life events of a person are indexed to the same human being by the use of the first person. To use the second and third person to index life events to the same material being implied that there were three persons embodied in a common fleshly shell. In ordinary conversation responsibility for actions and thoughts is taken by whoever uses the pronoun 'I'. It follows that responsibility for life events in the world of Miss Beauchamp was distributed between the three 'persons' her non-standard discursive practice created. At the same time as it violated the one person per body principle it depended on the convention that the use of the first person fixes responsibility indexically to the speaker.

Repudiating responsibility for a crime

In telling a tale in the first person one is committed, everything else being equal, to the indexical forces of the use of the pronoun 'I' and equivalent grammatical devices. Thus a report of what has been seen, heard or touched by me is indexed with the place of my body, the time of my speaking, the position I occupy in the local moral order and, in some cases, with my social position too. The ordinary indexical force of the first person is to take or claim responsibility, positioning the speaker as an agent.

A study of fragments of autobiography offered by convicted and indeed self-confessed murderers (O'Connor, 1994) brought to light a discursive convention that routinely presented the speaker as a patient. This is a rhetorical convention, no doubt, but it is also a first step into pathological discourses. The phrase that carries implication of passivity is 'and then *I caught a charge* ...' The model for this construction is something like 'I caught a cold'. Things you catch are personal states and conditions, all right, but they are, as it were, out there, floating about, and by chance and through no fault of your own you run into them. A killing may be reported as something that happened, in a neutral style that neither takes nor repudiates responsibility. That the police should hold the speaker responsible for it, to the extent of charging and ultimately trying and even condemning him, is something that positions the speaker in a moral order as 'the one who should be held responsible for doing it'.

From the discursive point of view singularities of self are not to be explained as the consequence of the existence of a Cartesian ego, a unique person substance. Rather they are patterns of discourse, the spatio-temporal uniqueness of personal embodiment anchoring expression to person through the indexicality of the personal pronouns. Pathologies of self are both aspects of and expressed in the form of pathologies of discourse. In certain cases at least it seems reasonable to claim that the correction of such pathologies may be achieved by the relearning of locally valid grammars. This seems to have been Morton Prince's (1905) strategy when faced with the pathological grammar of Miss Beachamp's discursive presentation of herself as three different people.

 Psychopathology as improper narration

1   Story lines of the wicked and the mad:

   a)   Fred West as a monster of evil. A standard grammar is used to present a non-standard narrative.
   b)   Hafield and the king; McNaughtan and the Prime Minister: not guilty by reason of insanity. Delusions are exculpatory in sufferers from persistent, abnormal and patently false beliefs.

2   Deviant first person grammars:

   a)   Syntactical violations of the one person per body rule. In cases of multiple personality disorder one embodied being produces more than one autobiography. Each story line is identified by the distribution of first, second and third person pronouns.
   b)   Diffusion of agency in prisoners' talk. Catch phrases express passivity, disclaimers of legal attributions of responsibility.

(section three)

Psychopathology and brain malfunction

Since we are looking at cognitive science from a philosophical point of view, that is, trying to discern the presuppositions of this domain of discourse, it is evident that the Taxonomic Priority Principle is playing a very important role in this important classificatory distinction. The psychosis/neurosis distinction depends on presuppositions about the actual or possible demonstration of neural abnormalities, relative to some benchmark, established by applying the Taxonomic Priority Principle to locally acceptable cognitive patterns. It is not an empirical fact that neuroses and psychoses differ as the accompanying brain functions. It is a conceptual matter, decided *a priori*, and depends upon the Taxonomic Priority Principle.

The account so far has been concerned exclusively with discursive phenomena. We have begun to take the first steps along the path of hybrid psychology, towards a complete treatment of one family of psychopathologies within cognitive science. The very distinction that characterizes the kinds of case we have so far encountered makes the application of the Taxonomic Priority Principle to identify a brain lesion or malfunction that is implicated in there being a defective tool for doing this cognitive work pointless. The brains of a liar, fabulist, spy, serial murderer, sponger, layabout and a dogmatic believer are not damaged. The differences do not lie in the mechanisms of cognition but in what they are asked to process.

The insertion of an old trouble into the Hybrid Psychology framework[4]

Close order studies of the discourse of sufferers in moderate to late stages of Alzheimer's condition demonstrate the degree to which many of their higher order cognitive functions have survived. This is often masked by the deficiencies of current assessment procedures, and by the difficulty of sustaining a conversation in the face of the sufferer's word-finding problems (Sabat, 2001). The relation between the brain damage produced by Alzheimer's condition and the particular kinds of cognitive skills that a close study of Alzheimer discourse shows to be intact is a nice illustration of the use of the negative reasoning pattern described in Chapter 9. Though damage to other areas of the brain may be severe, damage to the frontal lobes is rarely on the same scale. Sabat's studies of the discourse of Alzheimer's sufferers have revealed that the capacity of such people to manage indexical pronouns persists into quite late stages of the disease. This shows that there are intact higher order cognitive functions behind the screen of word-finding difficulties. The task/tool principle would suggest that the variety of indexical functions of the use of the first person matches the variety of functions that the relatively undamaged frontal lobes allow people to accomplish.

Revising the classification scheme and the categorial location of the disease

Alzheimer's condition as a specific way of deviating from usual ways of speaking and acting has been carved out of a more general category, senility. Kitwood (1995: 63–71) describes the socio-economic processes by which 'senility' as a natural condition (the 'seventh age' in Shakespeare's famous catalog), was relabeled 'Alzheimer's *disease*', a pathological condition. Something once part of the human condition 'gets turned into a technicality; a paradox is reduced to a problem … hope is offered to the suffering' (Porter, 1995: 61). This development of the working classification system is reflected in the several categories of 'senile X' that are recognized in *DSM* IV. This process is an essential step in the growth of a fully scientific hybrid psychology. Discourse and its conventions are neither an autonomous domain, nor can they be deleted in favor of neuroscience. Let us follow one such development in some detail.

The discursive analysis of the deviant speech of Alzheimer's condition

Sabat's painstaking work in making a close study of just how people suffering from Alzheimer's condition actually talk, away from the diagnostic interview, has disclosed two striking features.

1   People suffering from Alzheimer's condition seem to have quite 'normal' cognitive projects. They want to express intentions, to refer to past events, to clear up misunderstandings, and, in the case of one of Sabat's most interesting informants, to collaborate in research on Alzheimer's itself. The deficits these people suffer from are clearly in the means of expression, not in what is to be expressed. Given time and patience, the interlocutor can conduct a cognitively normal conversation with Alzheimer sufferers (Sabat, 2001: chapter 5).

2   The sense of self, as we found in Chapter 7, is expressed and in part constituted by the capacity to manage the local pronoun system. First and second person pronouns, and the functionally equivalent verb inflections in many languages, are indexicals. They are used to label or index the content of what is said with the spatial location of the speaker and to qualify the social force of what is said with the speaker's moral standing. Correct pronoun use indicates an intact sense of self (Sabat, 2001: chapter 7).

Engaged in the project of constructing a respectable scientific account of this aspect of cognitive psychology, we need to tie in the results of the discursive analysis to the main tool of cognition, the human brain.

Using the Taxonomic Priority Principle to locate the relevant brain conditions

It is easy to see the essential role of the Taxonomic Priority Principle in a scientific study of Alzheimer's condition. It is one of the rare cases where the physiological conditions are so coarse-grained that, unlike the investigation of memory formation that ties in processes in the hippocampus to analyses of remembering as a discursive practice, no intermediate artificial intelligence model is required to mediate the relation between the two domains.

Post-mortem inferences. How is it known that the build-up of protein in brain cells is the relevant physiological condition that damages the brain as an instrument for the management of word finding, among other skills? Post-mortem examinations of the brains of sufferers from Alzheimer's condition, identified by failure to manage intentional actions, reveal a feature not found in the brains of those who do not suffer from the condition. The brain tissue is congested with alien matter, plaques, which mess up the fine structure of the neural mechanisms involved in the use of cognitive skills.

Recent live brain inferences. Now neuropsychologists reason in reverse. If the plaques could be dissolved perhaps the brain would recover some of the essential structures disrupted by plaque formation. The research program that has emerged is fully in accordance with scientific realism.

Following the realist paradigm, one can infer that the unobservable condition of the living brains of Alzheimer's sufferers must be a subtype of the same supertype as those revealed by post-mortem studies in deceased sufferers.

The next step must be to develop means of observing the hypothetical process of plaque formation in the living brain. A new kind of microscope, the multi-photon machine, enables a close study of living brain tissue to be made, using fluorescent tracers introduced into the tissue, in something like the way that PET scan technology uses radioactive tracers.

Still following the realist paradigm, the most recent reports refer to studies of plaque formation and dissolution, not in human beings, but in a working model of the human nervous system, that of the useful mouse. The production of alien protein, amyloid-beta, the villain of the piece, can be halted and the existing plaques dissolved, in mice, by injecting particular antibodies directly into the brain.

While this is good news for Alzheimer's sufferers, it is a splendid example of the power of the hybrid psychology paradigm.

The creation of a new mental illness: the case of attention deficit hyperactivity disorder

Differences between mental and physical diseases

There is a marked contrast in the stories of how new physical illnesses are discovered, compared with how new mental illnesses are created. In physical medicine there is a subtly shifting but fairly stable conception of biological health. Body temperature cycling daily around a mean, insulin production, strength of bones under stress, and so on, go into this standard. Standards of how fat, how thin, how tall, how short, how muscular and so on people should be are more culturally variable. The observable syndrome of symptoms and disorders we now call AIDS was discernible against the background of the standards of biological health. The fact that the symptoms were largely confined to a certain socially distinct group of men left open the possibility that social and psychological conditions played a major role, by depressing the power of the immune system to resist infection. The alternative was a new disease, one that infected the very immune system that was supposed to defend the body against infection.

Scientific realism calls for both hypotheses to be investigated by the usual technique of model building to represent the currently unobservable sources of the observable condition. This was indeed just what happened. Models of possible sociogenic processes were quickly outflanked by the discovery of a virus that attacked the immune system itself.

What happened in the case of ADHD, attention deficit hyperactivity disorder? How did that become a 'disease'? We can say right away that it was not by the discovery of a hitherto unknown category of existents. It was *created*, not discovered.

The creation process is discursive

We have always had such concepts as 'butterfly mind', 'restlessness' and so on. Until recently these had a place in the domain of the P grammar. They marked some of the variations one would expect to find in any group of people. Children were expected to learn to discipline themselves, to sit still and get on with their work. A certain 'flightiness' was even considered charming. Readers of the 'political' novels of Anthony Trollope will recall the charm of Lady Glencora's somewhat disorderly conversation, and the power with which it endowed her.

In recent years these characteristics, whether charming or irritating, have been reframed in a new discourse. Here are some examples from a popular article (Sims and Black, 2001: 66–7). Describing the trouble that Christine McLanachan went through in dealing with her excessively lively sons, the authors write as follows:

> Since reading an article on the disorder nine years ago, McLanachan has become a self-made expert on both child and adult ADHD. It took two long years, however, before her youngest son was *diagnosed* at the age of eight at Manchester Children's Hospital, then her eldest, aged 11. With *the diagnoses* McLanachan slowly learnt through trial and error how to manage her sons. ... other mothers stepped forward fearing their children *had ADHD*.[5]

Now Christine McLanachan has concluded that she too shared similar traits. Just as Tourette's syndrome has opened out to cover those who display no symptoms, with the introduction of a hereditary hypothesis, so too has ADHD. Reframed in medical terminology, in the United States ADHD is attracting psychopharmacology as the first step to the application of the Taxonomic Priority Principle in the search for a correlated state of the brain and nervous system that psychoactive drugs may affect. So far, none has been found. McLanachan herself, though reported as using the medical word 'treatment', believes that the answer 'is more about management than medication'. In this way she never quite abandons the link with the P grammar.

Notice particularly that there are *two* discursive transformations going on at the meta-level, the level of psychological discourse itself. There is the redescription of what people experience in medical terms, marked in the above excerpts in italics. This leads to the use of such words as 'treating' when discussing how such people should be managed. An implicit connection is also being established with current science. There is a clear implication that there is a genetic component in 'knowing what is wrong with you'.

Contesting a grammar: the case of chronic fatigue syndrome

Chronic fatigue syndrome has been the focus of a good deal of controversy. We can learn much about why the choice of grammar matters in clinical psychology by following some of the twists and turns of this story (Sykes and Campion, 2001, II).

The first reaction of the medical profession to people complaining of excessive tiredness, so excessive that it made their lives a misery, was to interpret it within the P grammar, as something for which, knowingly or unknowingly, the people who complained were ultimately responsible. These people were just too idle to get about their daily routine chores. They should be forced or cajoled into making an effort. This interpretation was strongly supported by biomedical studies that failed to reveal any abnormality in bodily function or any signs of infection. Nor could any traumatic or distressing or over-demanding 'life events' be found in proximity to the onset of the condition. The first round of complaints came from middle-class people in demanding jobs. The syndrome was soon nicknamed 'Yuppie 'flu'.

Sometimes the exhortation program worked. However, in an increasing number of cases the 'Buck up!' advice had little or no effect. Indeed, it sometimes made people worse, at least in their own estimation. Once the complaints were taken seriously as of medical relevance, the next step was to try to find a slot in the existing taxonomy of psychopathology. If there were no observable bodily 'lesions', then using the Taxonomic Priority Principle in reverse, so to speak, we can say with confidence that chronic fatigue syndrome is a *mental illness*. But which mental illness? In some ways the talk of CFS sufferers was similar to those routinely diagnosed as suffering from endogenous depression. This is a psychological condition well established medically, and with a variety of psychopharmacological treatments available.[6]

Unfortunately the use of antidepressants was generally ineffective. The hypothesis of a link from a phenomenological or experiential distress to a malfunction of the brain and nervous system became even more tenuous. To find chronic fatigue syndrome a place in the domain of the O or the M grammar seemed impossible.

A new attempt to find a reinterpretation of chronic fatigue syndrome in an O or M grammar and to abandon or contest the P grammar account has been launched, partly by patient associations in the United Kingdom. The argument is subtle. To understand it we must remind ourselves of the general principles of scientific realism. In the physical sciences, if there is no observable cause of a well defined phenomenon, we construct models to represent possible unobservable causal mechanisms. These are given ontological plausibility by constructing a model that is a subtype of a supertype other subtypes of which are known to exist. Patient groups argued along just these lines without explicitly following the methodologies of chemistry and physics.

There must be a physical cause, they argued, whether it is or whether it is not observable. What sort of condition of the body is likely to be responsible for the overwhelming fatigue that sufferers experience? Then someone realized that the symptoms of organo-phosphate poisoning were very similar to those reported as chronic fatigue syndrome. Sheep farmers suffer from this if they accidentally ingest the fluid used as sheep dip. It is known that the poison causes a certain kind of damage to the body. It does not show up in the presence of antibodies, as would be expected from a viral infection. Suppose that chronic fatigue syndrome is the result of a viral infection incurred some time ago. The antibody markers will have disappeared but the subtle damage to the nervous and immune systems will persist. Here is a new explanatory model the source of which is a well known medical condition with a clearly identified cause. If chronic fatigue syndrome is like this then it is, after all, a physical disease and to be found a place within the domain of the O and M grammars.

There are important advantages to be gained by the relocation of chronic fatigue syndrome. As a physical ailment it is something to be ashamed of no longer. Furthermore, as a physical ailment it would attract home help support from the social services, denied to those who suffer from mental illness.

 The transformation, invention and contesting of mental illnesses

1   From senility to Alzheimer's condition. The concept of 'senility' has been refined in various ways:

  a) Taxonomic refinement leads to Alzheimer's condition as a category of defective cognitive performance.

  b) Using the Taxonomic Priority Principle and recently refined brain studies, the recognition of associated brain damage, interpreted through the task/tool principle can be made.

  c) Using P grammar analysis, the preservation of intact cognitive functions can be demonstrated.

(continued)

2 Creating a disease: the case of ADHD:

a) Narrowing the boundaries of 'normality' leaves room for the use of medicalized descriptions.

b) The Taxonomic Priority Principle suggests brain abnormalities, while the medicalized descriptions suggest the search for a 'cure'.

3 The case of CFS/ME:

a) Created by discursively relocating a debilitating condition: from malingering to mental illness to physical problem.

b) The Taxonomic Priority Principle together with a scientific realist attitude has led to organo-phosphate poisoning as a source for biomedical model.

Conclusion

Our survey of some typical cases of cognitive disorders has brought to light the important role of the Taxonomic Priority Principle (TPP), in linking cognitive disorders with malfunctions of the brain and nervous system. We have learned that the classification of a brain process as faulty or a defect in brain structure as a lesion depends wholly on the prior classification of the cognitive performance of some person as disorderly, non-standard or pathological, relative to local standards of proper and/or rational conduct. This logical relation holds whether the cognitive disorder is recognized in all human cultures we know of, such as florid schizophrenia and senility, or whether it is locally defined, such as multiple personality disorder (MPD), attention deficit hyperactivity disorder (ADHD) and chronic fatigue syndrome (CFS). When 'the chips are down', so to say, psychologists, in their clinical role and as psychiatrists, presuppose the principles of the hybrid cognitive science we have been learning about in this course.

Notes

1   Condensation of the descriptive name into an acronym is a sure sign of the transformation of a life problem into a disease. We will look at chronic fatigue syndrome (CFS) later in the chapter.

2   This acronym stands for the fourth edition of the American *Diagnostic and Statistical Manual* for classifying and diagnosing mental illnesses and disorders.

3   Remember that 'malfunction' is defined by reference to the form and function of the brain and nervous system in people who think, feel and act 'correctly' and 'properly' according to local criteria. We now know that some but not all of these criteria are recognized in (almost) all cultures.

4   I owe a great deal of my understanding of this subject to my colleague, Steven Sabat, whose book (Sabat, 2001) is a model of how psychic disorders should be approached.

5   My emphases.

6   The assumption that there is a neat one-way relationship between the pharmacology and the presumed disease entity has been challenged in the case of depression. Does the efficacy of Prozac define a mental condition or does an existing mental condition yield to treatment with this agent? (Fee, 2000: 74–99).

self-test   Study questions

Chapter 10 The memory machine

1   What are the two main uses of 'remember' in everyday life?

2   How is knowing related to remembering?

3   Why do we treat remembering as an achievement?

4   What was Ebbinghaus's methodology?

5   How are memorial claims ordinarily authenticated?

6   Must a capacity to remember be based on a representation of the past in the mind or the brain?

7   What kinds of collective remembering are there?

8   What is the distinction between short-term and long-term remembering?

9   What is episodic memory?

10   What is procedural memory?

11   Is the semantic/episodic memory distinction clear?

12   What is meant by 'implicit' memory?

13   What is 'priming'?

14   What is the distinction between prospective and retrospective remembering?

15   Why should the concepts of 'representation' and 'coding' be dropped from the psychology of remembering?

16   Is the 'storage' metaphor satisfactory?

17   What is multimodal remembering?

18   What is Baddeley's model of 'working' memory?

19   Describe the role of the phonological loop in Baddeley's model.

(study questions continued overleaf)

20   Describe the role of the visual sketchpad in Baddeley's model.

21   What is the cognitive function of the hippocampus?

22   Describe the basic anatomy of the hippocampus and its connections.

23   Describe the McLeod et al. (1998) connectionist model of the hippocampus.

24   How was the connectionist model tested?

Reading

Cohen et al. (1993): Part I, Part IIa and Part III; McLeod et al. (1998): chapters 1–4 and 13.

Chapter 11 The psychology of classifying

1   What is the basic principle of an Aristotelian classification system?

2   Describe a hierarchical classification scheme.

3   How could classifying *per genus et differentiae* be programmed?

4   What are Sowa's five conditions for a knowledge representation system?

5   Is there a fixed distinction between essential properties and propria?

6   What is a prototype?

7   What is the 'family resemblance' concept of a category?

8   Give some examples of the classification of determinates under a determinable.

9   What is the 'open texture' problem?

10   What is the 'similarity' problem?

11   What is presupposed in Estes's 'resonance' theory of cognitive acts of classifying?

12   How do people use prototypes in everyday life?

13   What are the advantages of connectionist models of classifying?

14   What is an auto-associator?

15   What are the disadvantages of connectionist models of classifying?

16   How is brain activation distributed for different classificatory tasks?

Reading

Way (1992).

Chapter 12 Cognitive disorders

1   Name four ways in which someone's thinking and acting may deviate from acceptable patterns.

2   What goes into the cluster of concepts around 'disease'?

3   What is meant by the 'medicalization' of a condition?

4   What is meant by the 'pathologization' of a way of thinking and acting?

5   Give two examples of the narrowing of the scope of 'normal' thought and behavior.

6   What is the difference between discovering a new physical illness and creating a new mental illness?

7   What is the role of positioning in psychiatric practice?

8   What is a psychosis?

9   What is a neurosis?

10 How can an evil autobiography be distinguished from a psychopathological one?

11 How does the use of a non-standard grammar define a psychiatric problem?

12 How far can non-standard grammatical usage be explained in terms of the rational strategy of refusing responsibility?

13 How has the concept of 'senility' changed?

14 How has the Taxonomic Priority Principle been of value in understanding Alzheimer's condition?

15 What is attention deficit hyperactivity disorder?

16 What is meant by the claim that it has been created 'discursively'?

17 What is chronic fatigue syndrome?

18 How has chronic fatigue syndrome been relocated from a mental to a physical disorder?

Reading
Gillett (1999), chapters 2 and 5.

Epilog

The problem faced by those who would create a science of human thinking, feeling, perceiving and acting, in a mold similar to the natural sciences, boils down to this: how can the tension between the culturally shaped phenomena of psychology be reconciled with the materiality of the human organism?

The difficulty of the problem is compounded by the persistence of a positivist myth of the project of science as the correlation of observables. This goes along with the presupposition of an outmoded philosophical analysis of causality as the regular concomitance of types of phenomena. Causal language slips in almost unnoticed, distorting our apprehension of human life central to which is the flow of meanings. The role of the person, in living relation to others, as an active maker and manager of meanings is lost to sight. Human beings are reduced to no more than sites at which causal correlations occur.

Ironically, physics, simultaneously misunderstood and admired as an exemplar, rests on an ontology of interactive beings, charges and their fields. Psychology does not cease to be scientific by adopting and adapting the Person grammar from the discourses of everyday life. That too rests on an ontology of interactive beings, persons and their cognitive capacities and material powers.

The materiality of the tools of intentional action is as evident in tennis as it is in cognitive psychology. Ballistics helps us understand how Pete Sampras can bring off those backhand passing shots. Yet no one doubts that tennis is a cultural phenomenon. Neuroscience can play a role in helping us to understand how Einstein came to see the relation between time and clocks. However, this revelation is a new juxtaposition of meanings, a conceptual revolution.

The Person grammar is indispensable to a scientific psychology. Only by paying attention to the intentionality and normativity of human thought and action can psychologists properly identify and classify psychological phenomena. Only in terms of the Person grammar concept of 'cognitive tools' can the role of the brain and nervous system in thought and action be understood.

References

Argyle, M. (1987) *The Psychology of Happiness*, London: Methuen.

Aristotle (*c.*385) [1908] *Metaphysics* in *The Works of Aristotle*, VIII, ed. W.D. Ross, Oxford: Oxford University Press.

—— [1928] *Posterior Analytics* in *The Works of Aristotle*, I, ed. W.D. Ross, Oxford: Oxford University Press.

—— [1931] *De anima* in *The Works of Aristotle*, III, ed. W.D. Ross, Oxford: Oxford University Press.

Aronson, J.L. (1991) 'Verisimilitude and type-hierarchies', *Philosophical Topics* 18: 5–16.

Atkinson, R.C. and Shiffrin, R.M.(1968) 'Human memory: a proposed system and its control processes' in K.W. Spence and J.T. Spence (eds) *Psychology of Learning and Motivation* II, New York: Academic Press.

Baddeley, A. (1998) *Human Memory: Theory and Practice*, Boston MA and London: Allyn & Bacon.

Bechtel, W. and Abrahamsen, A. (1991) *Connectionism and the Mind*, Oxford: Blackwell.

Boden, M.A. (1988) *Artificial Intelligence in Psychology*, Cambridge MA: MIT Press.

Bower, B. (1996) 'New data challenge personality gene', *Science News* 50 279.

Boyle, R. (1688) [1965] *The Origin of Forms and Qualities*, ed. T. Birk, Hildersheim: Olms.

Bruner, J. S. (1973) *Beyond the Information Given*, New York: Norton.

—— (1983) *In Search of Mind*, New York: Harper & Row.

—— (1991) 'The narrative construction of reality', *Critical Inquiry* autumn: 1–21.

Burgess, P.W. and Shallice, T. (1998) 'The relationship between prospective and retrospective memory' in M.A. Conway (ed.) *Cognitive Models of Memory*, Hove: Taylor & Francis.

Burr, V. and Butt, T.W. (2000) 'Psychological distress and postmodern thought' in D. Fee (ed.) *Pathology and the Postmodern: Mental Illness, Discourse, and Experience*, London: Sage.

Button, G., Coulter, J., Lee, J.R.E. and Sharrock, W. (1995) *Computers, Minds and Conduct*, Cambridge: Polity Press.

Cappa, S.F., Perani, D., Schnur, T., Terramanti, M. and Fazio, F. (1998) 'The effects of semantic category and knowledge type on lexical-semantic access: a PET study', *Neuroscience* 8: 350–59.

Carpenter, R.H.S. (1998) *Neurophysiology*, London: Edward Arnold.

Cartwright, N. (1999) *The Dappled World*, Cambridge: Cambridge University Press.

Charniak, E. and McDermott, D.V. (1985) *Introduction to Artificial Intelligence*, Reading MA: Addison-Wesley.

Churchland, P.M. (1981) 'Eliminative materialism and the propositional attitudes', *Journal of Philosophy* 2: 67–90.

—— (1984) *Matter and Consciousness*, Cambridge MA: MIT Press.

Cohen, G., Kiss, G. and Le Voi, M. (1993) *Memory: Current Issues*, Buckingham: Open University Press.

Cole, M. (1996) *Cultural Psychology: a Once and Future Discipline*, Cambridge MA: Harvard University Press.

Comte, A. (1830–1842) [1853] *The Positive Phiolosophy of Auguste Comte*, trans. H. Martineau, London: Edward Arnold.

Copeland, J. (1998) [1993] *Artificial Intelligence*, Oxford: Blackwell.

Coulter, J. (1979) 'The brain as agent', *Human Studies* 2 (4): 1–17.

Danziger, K. (1990) *Constructing the Psychological Subject: Historical Origins of Psychological Research*, Cambridge: Cambridge University Press.

—— (1997) *Naming the Mind: how Psychology found its Language*, London and Thousand Oaks CA: Sage.

Darwin, C. (1859) [1964] *On the Origin of Species*, Cambridge MA: Harvard University Press.

Dawkins, R. (1976) *The Selfish Gene*, Oxford: Oxford University Press.

Dennett, D. (1987) *The Intentional Stance*, Cambridge MA: MIT Press.

Descartes, R. (1641) [1984] *Meditations on the First Philosophy*, Meditations Two and Six, pp. 16–23, 50–62, trans. J. Cottingham, R. Stoothoff and D. Murdoch, *The Philosophical Writings of Descartes*, Cambridge: Cambridge University Press.

—— (1649) [1989] *The Passions of the Soul*, trans. S. Voss, Indianapolis IN: Hackett.

Dixon, R.A. (1996) 'Collective memory and aging' in D.J. Herrmann, M.K. Johnson, C.L. McEvoy, C. Hertzog and P. Hertel (eds) *Basic and Applied Memory: Theory in Context*, Mahwah NJ: Erlbaum.

Dolan, R. (1999) 'Feeling the neurobiological self', *Nature* 401: 847–48.

Duara, R. (1990) 'Utilization of PET in research and clinical applications in dementia' in R. Duarna (ed.) *Positron Emission Tomography in Dementia*, New York: John Wiley.

Ebbinghaus, H. (1885) [1987] *Memory: A Contribution to Experimental Psychology*, trans. H.A. Ruger and C.E. Bussenius, New York: Dover Publications.

Edwards, D. (1997) *Discourse and Cognition*, London: Sage.

Edwards D. and Potter, J. (1992) *Discursive Psychology*, London: Sage.

Ellis, J.A. (1996) 'Prospective memory or the realization of delayed intentions' in. M.A. Brandimonte (ed.) *Prospective Memory: Theory and Applications*, Hillsdale NJ: Earlbaum.

Engelkamp, J. and Zimmer, H.D. (1994) *The Human Memory*, Seattle: Hogrefe & Huber.

Estes, W.K. (1994) *Classification and Cognition*, Oxford: Clarendon Press.

Fee, D. (2000) 'The broken dialogue' in D. Fee (ed.) *Pathology and the Postmodern*, London and Thousand Oaks CA: Sage.

Fodor, J.A. (1979) *The Language of Thought*, New York: Crowell.

—— (1994) *The Elm and the Expert*, Cambridge MA: MIT Press.

Galileo, G. (1632) [1914] *Dialogue Concerning the Two Chief World Systems*, trans. Stillman Drake, New York: Dover.

Garnham, A. (1997) 'Representing information in mental models' in M.A. Conway (ed.) *Cognitive Models of Memory*, Cambridge MA: MIT Press.

Gathercole, S.E. (1997) 'Models of verbal short term memory' in M.A. Conway (ed.) *Cognitive Models of Memory*, Cambridge MA: MIT Press.

Gilbert, W. (1600) [1958] *De magnete*, New York: Dover.

Gluck, M.A. and Myers, C.E. (2001) *Gateway to Memory*, Cambridge MA: MIT Press.

Goffman, E. (1969) *The Presentation of Self in Everyday Life*, London: The Penguin Press.

Goodall, J. (1989) *In the Shadow of Man*, London: Weidenfeld & Nicolson.

Graft, P. and Schachter, D.L. (1985) 'Implicit and explicit memory for new associations in normal and amnesic subjects', *Journal of Experimental Psychology* 11: 501–8.

Hanson, N.R. (1958) *Patterns of Discovery*, Cambridge: Cambridge University Press.

Harré, R. and Wang, Han-Ting (1999) 'Setting up a real "Chinese Room": an empirical replication of a famous thought experiment', *Journal of Experimental and Theoretical Artificial Intelligence* 11: 153–4.

Hart, H.L.A. (1963) *Law, Liberty and Morality*, Stanford CA: Stanford University Press.

Hart, H.L.A. and Honoré, T. (1959) *Causation and the Law*, Oxford: Clarendon Press.

Hartley, D. (1749) *Observations on Man*, Bath: Leake & Frederick.

Hempel, C.G. (1953) [1965] *Aspects of Scientific Explanation*, New York: Free Press.

Hobbes, T. (1651) [1953] *Leviathan*, Oxford: Blackwell.

Horst, S.W. (1996) *Symbols, Computation and Intentionality: a Critique of the Computational Theory of Mind*, Berkeley CA: University of California Press.

Hume, D. (1748) [1951] *A Treatise of Human Nature*, Oxford: Clarendon Press.

—— (1777) [1963] *Enquiries Concerning the Human Understanding and Concerning the Principles of Morals*, Oxford: Clarendon Press.

Humphrey, N. (1984) *Consciousness Regained*, Oxford: Oxford University Press.

Johnson, K. and Coates, S.L. (1999) *Nabokov's Blues*, New York: McGraw Hill.

Julier, D. (1983) 'Psychosis' in R. Harré and R. Lamb (eds) *The Blackwell Encyclopedic Dictionary of Psychology*, Oxford: Blackwell.

Kant, I. (1787) [1996] *Critique of Pure Reason*, trans. W.S. Pluhar, Indianapolis IN: Hackett.

Kitwood, T. (1995) 'Dementia' in G.E. Barrios and R. Porter (eds) *A History of Clinical Psychiatry*, London: Athlone Press.

Kosslyn, S.M., Alpert, N.M. and Thompson, W.L. (1995) 'Identifying objects at different levels of hierarchy: a positron emission tomography study', *Human Brain Mapping* 3: 107–32.

Kreckel, M. (1981) *Communicative Acts and Shared Meanings*, London: Academic Press.

Lakoff, G. (1987) *Women, Fire and Dangerous Things*, Chicago: University of Chicago Press.

La Mettrie, J.O. (1749) [1960] *L'Homme Machine*, Princeton NJ: Princeton University Press.

Lee, Changsin, (1998) 'Theory of mind: a critical investigation', Doctoral dissertation: Binghamton University.

Lesch, K-P., Bengel, D., Heils, A., Sabol, S.Z., Greenberg, B.D., Petri, S., Benjamin, J., Müller, C.R., Hamer, D.H. and Murphy, D.C. (1996) 'Association of anxiety-related traits with a polymorphism in the serotonin transporter gene regulatory region', *Science* 274: 1527–31.

Locke, J. (1690) [1974] *An Essay Concerning Human Understanding*, ed. J. Yolton, London: Methuen.

Long, K.M., Spears, R. and Manstead, A.S.R. (1994) 'The influence of personal and collective self-esteem on strategies of social differentiation', *Bulletin of the British Psychological Society* 313–29.

Luria, A. R. (1981) *Language and Cognition,.* New York: J. Wiley.

Lutz, C. (1988) *Unnatural Emotions,* Cambridge: Cambridge University Press.

Mach, E. (1894) [1914] *The Analysis of Sensations,* Chicago: Open Court.

Mayou, R.A. (1983) 'Neurosis' in R. Harré and R. Lamb (eds) *The Blackwell Encyclopedic Dictionary of Psychology,* Oxford: Blackwell.

McClelland, J.L. (1995) 'Constructive memory and memory distortions' in D.L. Schachter (ed.) *Memory Distortions: How Minds, Brains and Societies Reconstruct the Past,* Cambridge MA Harvard University Press.

McCulloch, W.S. and Pitts, W.H. (1943) 'A logical calculus of the ideas immanent in nervous activity', *Bulletin of Mathematical Biophysics* 5: 115–33.

McErlean, J. (2000) *Philosophies of Science,* Belmont CA: Wadsworth.

McKeon, R.P. (1941) *The Basic Works of Aristotle,* New York: Random House.

McLeod, P., Plunkett, K. and Rolls, E.T. (1998) *Introduction to Connectionist Modelling of Cognitive Processes,* Oxford: Oxford University Press.

Medin, D.L. (1989) 'Concepts and conceptual structure', *American Psychologist* 44: 1469–81.

Middleton, D. and Edwards, D. (1990) *Collective Remembering,* London: Sage.

Miller, G.A., Galanter G. and Pribram, K.H. (1967) *Plans and the Structure of Behavior,* New York: Holt Rinehart & Winston.

Minsky, M. (1975) 'A framework for representing knowledge' in P.H. Winston (ed.) *The Psychology of Computer Vision,* New York: McGraw-Hill.

Morgan, M. and Morrison, M.S. (1999) *Models as Mediators,* Cambridge: Cambridge University Press.

Mühlhäusler, P. and Harré, R. (1990) *Pronouns and People,* Oxford: Blackwell.

Neisser, U. (1976) *Cognition and Reality,* San Francisco: Freeman.

Newell, A. and Simon, H.A. (1961) 'The simulation of human thought' in *Current Trends in Psychological Theory,* Pittsburgh PA: Pittsburgh University Press.

—— (1972) *Human Problem Solving,* Englewood Cliffs NJ: Prentice Hall.

Newton, I. (1687) [1990] *Principia Mathematica,* London: Encyclopaedia Britannica.

O'Connor, P. (1994) 'I caught a charge', Doctoral dissertation, Georgetown University.

Ogden, C.K. and Richards, I.A. (1934) *The Meaning of Meaning,* London: Kegan Paul.

Olson, J.M. and Zanna, M.P. (1993) 'Attitudes and attitude change', *Annual Review of Psychology* 44: 117–54.

Parrott, G.W. and Smith, S.F. (1981) 'Embarrassment: Actual vs. typical cases, Classical vs. prototype representations', *Cognition and Emotion* 5: 467–88.

Penfield, W. (1975) *The Mystery of the Mind: a Critical Study of Consciousness and the Human Brain,* Princeton NJ: Princeton University Press.

Popcheptsov, P.P. (1990) *Language and Humour,* Kiev: Vysca Skola.

Popper, K.R. (1961) *The Logic of Scientific Discovery,* New York: Harper & Row.

Porter, R. (1995) 'Dementia' in G.E.Barnes and R. Porter (eds) *A History of Clinical Psychiatry,* London: Athlone Press.

Potter, J. and Wetherell, M. (1987) *Discourse and Social Psychology,* London: Sage.

Premack, D. and Woodruff, G. (1978) 'Does the chimpanzee have a theory of mind?', *The Brain and Behavioral Sciences* 4: 515–29.

Priestley, J. (1777) *Disquisitions Concerning Matter and Spirit,* London.

Prince, M. (1905) *The Dissociation of Personality,* London: Kegan Paul.

Pylyshyn, Z.W. (1973) *Computation and Cognition: Towards a Foundation for Cognitive Science,* Cambridge MA: MIT Press.

Radden, J. (1996) *Divided Minds and Successive Selves*, Cambridge MA: MIT Press.

Reid, T. (1788) [1969] *Essays on the Intellectual Powers of Man*, Cambridge MA: MIT Press.

Robinson, D.N. (1995) *An Intellectual History of Psychology*, London: Arnold.

——— (1996) *Wild Beasts and Idle Humours*, Princeton NJ: Princeton University Press.

Rolls, E.C. (1989) 'The representation and storage of information in neural networks in the primate cerebral cortex and hippocampus' in R. Durbin, C. Miall and G. Mitchison (eds) *The Computing Neuron*, Reading MA: Addison-Wesley.

Rosch, E. (1973) 'Natural categories', *Cognitive Psychology* 4: 328–50.

Rosch, E. and Lloyd, B.B. (1978) *Cognition and Categorization*, New York: Erlbaum.

Ryckman, R.M., Hammer, M., Kazcor, L.M. and Gold, J.A. (1996) 'Construction of a personal development attitude scale', *Journal of Personality Assessment* 66 (2): 324–85.

Ryle, G. (1947) *The Concept of Mind*, London: Hutchinson.

Sabat, S.R. (1998) 'Voices of Alzheimer's disease sufferers: A call for treatment based on personhood', *Journal of Clinical Ethics* 9: 38–51.

——— (2001) *The Experience of Alzheimer's Disease*, Oxford: Blackwell.

Sacks, O. (1985) *The Man who Thought his Wife was a Hat*, London: Duckworth.

Sapir, E. (1966) *Selected Writings*, Berkeley CA: University of California Press.

Saussure, F. de (1916) [1978] *A Course in General Linguistics*, trans. Wade Baskin, Glasgow: Fontana/Collins.

Schachter, D.L. (1993) 'Understanding implicit memory' in G.C. & M. Collins (eds) *Theories of Memory*, Hove and Hillsdale NJ: Erlbaum.

——— (1996) *In Search of Memory*, New York: Basic Books

Searle, J.R. (1980) 'Minds, brains and programs', *Behavioral and Brain Sciences* 3: 417–24.

Searle, J.R. (1983) *Intentionality: An Essay in the Philosophy of Mind*, Cambridge: Cambridge University Press.

Searle, J.R. (1998) *The Construction of Social Reality*, New York: Free Press.

Shammi, P. and Stuss, D.P. (1999) 'Humour appreciation: a role of the right frontal lobe', *Brain* 122: 657–66.

Shotter, J. (1993) *Cultural Politics of Everyday Life*, Toronto: Toronto University Press.

Shweder, R.A. (1998) 'Multiple psychologies: the stance of justification and the "place" of cultural psychology', in *Action, Culture and Symbol: Boesch's Legacy for Productive Synthesis.*

Sims, S. and Black, S. (2001) 'Attention seeker', *Sunday Times* 26 May.

Skinner, B.F. (1974) *About Behaviorism*, New York: Knopf.

Smedslund, J. (1988) *Psychologic*, Berlin: Springer.

Sowa, J.F. (2000) *Knowledge Representation*, Pacific Grove CA: Brooks/Cole.

Spackman, M.P. (1998) 'Folk theories of attribution of responsibility for emotions' Doctoral dissertation: Georgetown University.

Spear, L. (2000) 'The adolescent brain and age-related behavioral manifestations', *Neuroscience and Behavioral Revues* 24: 417–63.

Stern, W. (1938) [1939] *General Psychology from a Personalistic Standpoint*, trans. H.D. Spoerl, New York: Macmillan.

Stevenson, H.W., Chen C. and Lee S.Y. (1993) 'Mathematical achievement in Chinese, Japanese and American children', *Science* 259: 53–8.

Suppes, P. and Han, B. (2000) 'Brain-wave representation of words by superposition of a few sine waves', *Proceedings of the National Academy of Sciences of the USA* 97: 8738–43.

Schwartz, B. (1990) 'Remembering Abraham Lincoln', in D. Middleton and D. Edwards, *Collective Remembering*, London: Sage.

Sykes, R. and Campion, P. (2001) *The Physical and the Mental in Chronic Fatigue Syndrome*, Bristol: Westcare.

Thigpen, C.H. and Cleckley, H.M. (1957) *The Three Faces of Eve*, London: Secker & Warburg.

Thorndike, E.L. (1913) *The Elements of Psychology*, New York: Seiler.

Tinbergen, N. (1968) 'Ethology' in R. Harré (ed.) *Scientific Thought, 1900–1960*, Oxford: Clarendon Press.

Tsunida, T. (1972) *The Japanese Brain*, trans. Yoshinori Oiwa, Tokyo: Taishukan.

Tulving, E. (1972) 'Episodic and semantic memory', in E. Tulving and W. Donaldson (eds) *Organization of Memory*, New York: Academic Press.

Turing, A.M. (1936) 'On computable numbers', *Proceedings of the London Mathematical Society*, Series 2, 42: 230–65.

Turing, A.M. (1950) 'Computing machinery and intelligence', *Mind* new series 59: 433–50.

Tversky, A. (1977) 'Features of similarity', *Psychological Review* 84: 327–52.

Vaidya, C.J., Gabrieli, J.D.E., Verfaellie, M., Fleischman, D. and Askari, N. (1998) 'Font-specific priming following global amnesia and occipital lobe damage', *Neuropsychology* 12: 1–10.

van Langenhove, L. and Harré, R. (1999) *Positioning Theory: Moral Contexts of Intentional Action*, Oxford: Blackwell.

Vollmer, F. (1990) *Essays in Theoretical Psychology*, Oslo: Solom Forlag.

Vygotsky, L.S. (1962) *Thought and Language*, Cambridge MA: MIT Press.

—— (1978) *Mind in Society*, Cambridge MA: Harvard University Press.

Waismann, F. (1968) *How I See Philosophy*, London: Macmillan.

Wallace, W. (1996) *The Modeling of Nature*, Washington DC: The Catholic University of America Press.

Warnock, Baroness M. (2000) *The Times* (London), 3 October.

Watson, J.B. (1930) [1958] *Behaviorism*, Chicago: University of Chicago Press.

Way, E.C. (1992) *Knowledge Representation and Metaphor*, Dordrecht: Kluwer.

—— (1997) 'Connectionism and conceptual structure', *American Behavioral Scientist* 40 (6): 729–53.

Wellman, H.M. (1990) *The Child's Theory of Mind*, Cambridge MA: MIT Press.

Whorf, B.L. (1979) [1934–5] *Language, Thought and Reality*, Cambridge MA: MIT Press.

Wierzbicka, A. (1992) *Semantics, Culture and Cognition*, Oxford: Oxford University Press.

Wilson, E.O. (1998) *Consilience*, Cambridge MA: Harvard University Press.

Winograd, T. and Flores, C.F. (1986) *Understanding Computation and Cognition*, Norwood NJ: Ablex.

Wittgenstein, L. (1953) *Philosophical Investigations*, trans. G.E.M. Anscombe & G.H. Von Wright, Oxford: Blackwell.

—— (1967) *Remarks on the Foundations of Mathematics*, trans. G.E.M. Anscombe, Oxford: Blackwell.

—— (1969) *On Certainty*, ed. G.E.M. Anscombe & G.H. von Wright, Oxford: Blackwell.

—— (1979) [1934–5] *Wittgenstein's Lectures, Cambridge*, ed. A. Ambrose, Chicago: University of Chicago Press.

Wundt, W. (1896) [1977] *Lectures on Human and Animal Psychology*, ed. D.N. Rol, Washington DC: University Publications of America.

Name index

Archimedes 39
Argyle, M. 174
Aristotle 62, 92–94, 255–256
Aronson, J. L. 49

Baddeley, A. 242–243, 245, 252
Bohr, N. 47
Boyle, R. 30, 32, 72, 189
Bruner, J. S. 62, 63, 103–104, 105

Charniak, E. 128
Churchland, P. M. 86–89
Cleckley, H. M. 290
Comte, A. 26
Copeland, J. 119
Crick, F. 218

Danziger, K. 177, 178
Darwin, C. 47, 54, 92, 141
Davy, H. 22
Dawkins, R. 101
De Waal, F. 96
Dennett, D. C. 150–151
Descartes, R. 61, 62, 65–68, 153
Dixon, R. A. 164, 233
Dolan, R. 98

Edwards, D. 233
Einstein, A. 30, 32, 33
Engelkamp, J. 240, 241
Estes, W. K. 266–268

Faraday, M. 13, 18
Flores, C. F. 123
Fodor, J. A. 142
Franklin, B. 46

Galanter, G. 106
Galileo, G. 30, 31, 32, 33, 72
Gardner, A. 96
Gardner, B. 96
Gilbert, W. 13, 24, 65
Goffman, E. 45
Goodall, J. 96
Graft, P. 235

Hadfield, J. 288
Hamilton, A. 11
Hampson, S. E. 231, 245
Han, B. 252
Hartley, D. 65, 71–72, 75, 83
Hempel, C. G. 43
Hobbes, T. 61, 81, 144
Horst, S. W. 143

Hume, D. 25, 26, 27, 65, 72–73, 75, 182
Humphrey, N. 179

Jefferson, T. 10, 181

Kant, I. 11, 12, 36, 73–74, 90
Kreckel, M. 233

La Mettrie, G. O. 19, 61, 64, 83–84, 86, 90, 92
Lakoff, G. 144
Lesch, K.-P. 96
Linnaeus, K. 37, 257
Locke, J. 19, 24, 61, 62, 65, 68–71, 72, 82, 84
Lorentz, K. 95
Luria, A. R. 282

Mach, E. 27
McCulloch, W. S. 190
McDermott, D. V. 128
McLanachan, C. 295
McNaughton, D. 288
Medin, D. L. 265
Middleton, D. 233
Miller, G. A. 62, 106, 108, 234
Minsky, M. 127
Mosley, A. 182
Murphey, D. 96

Nabokov, V. 268
Neisser, U. 227
Newell, A. 115
Newton, I. 24

Ockham, W. 140, 143
Olson, J. M. 178

Parrott, W. G. 262
Penfield, W. 205
Phillips, L. 225
Pitts, W. H. 190
Popper, K. R. 43
Postman, L. 225
Premack, D. 179
Pribram, K. H. 106
Priestley, J. 84
Prince, M. 290, 291
Pylyshyn, Z. W. 241

Reid, T. 11, 12
Rolls, E. C. 246, 247
Rosch, E. 131, 261, 269
Ryle, G. 88, 126, 139, 224

Sabat, S. 292, 293
Sacks, O. 284

Sapir, E. 144
Saussure, F. de 142
Schachter, D. L. 235, 244
Schwartz 233
Searle, J. R. 118–121, 122, 142
Shakespeare W. 59
Shammi, P. 99
Shannon, E. C. 239
Simon, H. A. 115
Skinner, B. F. 28
Smith, S. F. 262
Sowa, J. 258
Spackman, M. 174
Stern, W. 155
Stevenson, H. W. 178
Stuss, D. P. 99
Suppes, P. 252

Thatcher, Lady 176
Theroux, P. 99
Thigpen, C. H. 290
Tinbergen, N. 95
Tolstoy, L. 59
Tsunida, T. 219
Tulving, E. 234
Turing, A. M. 62, 112–114, 190
Tversky, A. 265

Vaidya, C. 206
Venter, C. 102
Von Frisch, 95
Von Neumann, J. 114, 190
Vygotsky, L. S. 7, 8, 156, 170, 282

Wegener, K. 8
Waismann, F. 264
Watson, C. 218
Watson, J. B. 28
Way, E. C. 49, 262, 263, 269, 270
Wellman, H. M. 180
West, F. 287
Whorf, B. L. 144
Wilson, C. T. R. 53
Wilson, E. O. 102
Winograd, T. 123
Wittgenstein, L. 10, 12, 88, 139, 142, 145, 146, 148, 184, 262, 263, 282
Woodruff, G. 179
Wundt, W. 16

Zanna, M. P. 178
Zimmer 240, 241

Subject index

Access to the material world 23, 24
Act/action distinction 146, 147
Actions of the soul 67
Activity functions 194
Agency and passivity 60–61
Agency shown in spontaneity 74
Agentive picture 64, 74, 152
Agents, kinds of 163
Alzheimer's condition 292–294, 297
   and intact sense of self 293
Aphasias and inference by negation 206–207, 210
Aristotle's psychology 92–94, 100
Artificial intelligence in psychology 112, 115, 139, 245
   reasons for development 189
Association of ideas 71, 72, 76
Atomism 13, 14, 17
Attitudes, as hidden causes 176–179, 186
   history of concept of 177
   status of 139

Behaviorism 77, 103
Biopsychology 62
Body and mind according to Descartes 68
Brain anatomy 204, 209
Brain physiology 204–205
Brain, models of 140

Causal picture 63–64, 74, 84, 121, 131, 152, 303
   as rhetoric 175
Chinese Room argument 118–122
Clamping a net edge 195
Classification 8, 36, 221
   Aristotelian logic 255–257, 275
   by scientists and by lay people 274–275
   common features 266–267
   hierarchical systems 37–38, 256

human methods, differences from connectionist models 272
Linnaean and GOFAI models 257–258
methods, human and technological 266
neuropsychological models 273–274
practical matching 268
role of concepts 36–37
similarity problem 265
Coding metaphor queried 239, 252
Cognition as computation 109–111, 116–117
   problems 117
Cognitive psychology, topics 1, 6
Cognitive science, history 1, 19
   topics 1, 5–6, 7
Cognitive skills, acquisition 8
Cognitive tools, first and second order 169–170
Collectivism and psychological phenomena 164
Computational models 190
Computer, compared to brain or to person? 119–120
Computers, do they think? 122
Computing machines 111–112
   in engineering 111
   in psychology 111–112, 113
Consciousness, center of 90

Descartes' psychology 65–68, 75, 76, 153
Description and expression 184, 185
Determinates and determinables 263
Development, Vygotsky's account 156
Deviant cognition, cultural and historical variation 277
Discursive contesting of CFS 296–297, 298
Discursive production of ADHD 295, 298
Discursive psychology 141, 166, 216

Dispositions 88
Dynamism 13, 14, 17

Ebbinghaus research paradigm 227–228, 253n
EEG, revival 252
Emergent properties 82
Epistemology 35
Essences, nominal and real 39–40, 41
Ethology, basic principles 95–96
Evolutionary psychology 96–99, 100–101
Existence proofs 52–53, 54
Experiments reinterpreted 172–174
   in thought 31–32, 33
   indirect 30–32
   manipulations of unobservables 30–31, 32, 33
Explaining, patterns of 8, 42
   two discourse modes 181
Explanations, Aristotelian 94–95
Expression and description 145

Family resemblances in classifying 262–263
Fantasy, cognitive 94
Feed forward systems 198, 202
First Cognitive Revolution 62, 105–109, 137
Folk psychology 87
Frame problem 128–129, 130
   solutions 128–129
Frames and frame axioms 127

Genetics and culture 98–99
   and psychology 96–99, 101
Genus and species 255–256
Goals of animate beings 93, 95
GOFAI models and connectionist models 210
Graceful degradation 200
Grammar, as a group of rules 138, 147

deviant 289–290, 291
molecule based 148, 152, 165, 166
organism based 148, 152, 165, 166
person based 148, 155, 157, 158, 161, 162, 163, 165, 166, 175, 183, 278, 282, 289, 303
soul based 148, 165
Grammars, organism and molecule 149, 151, 156, 158, 162, 163, 165, 187, 278, 282, 289
Grammars, soul and person 149, 151, 165

Hartley's psychology 71–72, 75, 76
Hidden nodes 195, 199
Hinton diagrams 197
Hippocampus, connectionist model 247–249, 251
real net and model net 246–251
Human learning 201–202
Hume's psychology 72–73, 75, 76
Hybrid Psychology 68, 74, 99–100, 162, 165, 167, 170, 187, 217, 282

'I', uses of 185, 186
Idea/Brain state correlations 71–72, 83, 85
Ideas
and impressions 72–73
as mental atoms 69, 75
of primary and of secondary qualities 70–71
kinds of 69–70
simple and complex 70, 72, 75
Individualism
and meaning 122
and psychological phenomena 130, 164
Information metaphor 238–239
Instruments, experiments and measurements in physics 170–171
Instruments, experiments and measurements in psychology 171–172
Intension/extension of classes 39, 41
Intentionality 7, 117, 121, 122, 124, 142, 145, 150
in computing machines 118

'Judas eye' experiments 103–104, 109

Kant's psychology 73–74
Knowledge representation
as essences 258–259
desiderata 258, 260
genus et differentiae 259, 260

Language and thought 144
Laws of nature 55–56
Learning neuroscience words 89
Levels of organic beings 93
Locke's psychology 68–71, 75, 76

Materialism 79, 80, 90–91
conceptual 62, 85–89, 91
eliminative, arguments for 86–88
ethological 80, 92
methodological 61–62, 83–85, 91
neural 80
ontological 61, 63, 81–82, 90
Meaning,
contextuality 123, 124
historicity 123, 124
indexicality 123, 124
Mental disease and physical disease 294
'Mental disease' conceptually related to 'cure' 279–280
Mental states, rejection of 143
Mental substances as persons 66–67, 75
Mental substances 66
Mentalism, types of 61, 63, 65
Mentality 18
Metaphor 22, 35
Method of doubt 66
Methodology 35
Mind/body relations 156–158
Model building, cognitive processes 48–49
Model worlds, apparatus 51, 52
Models and type-hierarchies 50, 54
Models
as guides to practice 53
as plausible representations 51, 131–132
in science, history of 35, 43
analytical (descriptive) use 44–45, 54, 215, 216, 221, 239
explanatory use 45–47, 54, 215, 216, 221–222, 239

modes of assessment 50, 209, 215, 245
role in theories 47, 48
subjects and sources 44, 54, 55, 222
uses of the word 43
Multiple Personality Syndrome 288–290

Narratives conventions and autobiography 281, 291
Natural kinds 21, 55
Natural sciences,
characteristics 6, 35
interpretations 24–25
Neisser's paradox 227
Nets, mapping between real and artificial 196
Neural nets 190
artificial 191, 195, 202
real 193, 202
Neural pulses, transmission 192
Neurons,
artificial 191, 193–194, 202
real, 192, 202
Neurotransmitters 201, 209
Normativity,
loss of 125
problem of 7, 117
representation of 125, 129, 278

Ockham's razor 137
Ontology,
of English psychological vocabulary 88
for psychology 14–15
materialist versions 13–14, 35

Passions of the soul 67
Perception and cognition 104
Personifying the brain fallacy 120
Persons,
ineliminable 89–90
ontology of 154–156
preservation of 61
Stern's treatment of 155–156
PET scanning and positive inferences 207–208, 210
PET scans 161, 218, 283
Philosophy,
as study of presuppositions 2
nature of 9–12, 55
Physicalism 79–80
Positioning
in psychiatry 284–285
moral rights of access to cognitive tools 154, 165

Positivism   2, 25–28, 29, 40, 303
Potential, action   193
Potential, resting   192
Presuppositions,
    conceptual   10, 11, 17
    factual   9, 10, 17
    other terms for   11–12
Priming   235
Private Language Argument   145–146
Prototypes
    in classifying   261–262, 269
    connectionist models for   270–272, 274
Psychological phenomena, types   215
Psychology
    exemplars, natural science   59–60
    scientific   15, 16–17, 153, 218
psychopathology, expansion of the domain   280–281
Psychosis and neurosis   285–286
Public and private   145, 146, 147

Realism   2, 28–29, 30, 33, 40
Region One, world as perceived   20, 23, 33
Region Three, world as imagined   22, 23, 33
Region Two, world as visualized   21, 23, 33
Regions of the human *umwelt*   20, 33, 55
Reification, misplaced   187
Remembering
    authentication   225, 226, 237
    and knowing   223, 224, 237
    descriptive taxonomy   232, 237
    collective   233
    declarative and procedural   234–235

episodic   236
implicit and explicit   235
models of tools   229, 231
multimodal   240–241
prospective and retrospective   236–237
psychological taxonomy   237
short and long-term   234
tasks and tools   227, 228
vernacular   223–226, 237
Representation metaphor queried   238
Representation, and retention   230
Responsibility,
    attributions of   174–175
    repudiation technique   290
Rule, acting in accordance with   126
    following   126
    no unconscious version of   126–127
    in psychology   126, 129, 138, 216, 219

Scanning technology   204, 207–209
Science, requirements for   6, 8–9, 221
Second Cognitive Revolution   63, 166
Self,
    as a location   182, 183
    as unique and unified   184, 289
    sense of   139
Self-esteem experiments   172, 173, 186
Selfhood, psychology of   181–185, 186
Signs and symbols   142
Skill   147, 151–152, 167
Stances, intentional, physical and design   151
Store metaphor rejected   232, 240, 241, 251, 252
Story lines, delusions   288
Story lines, deviant   287

Strengths, of connections   194, 202
Subtraction principle   208
Superpositions in trained nets   198
Symbol System Hypothesis   115
Symbols, types of   7
Synthesis of experience   73

Task/Tool (T/T) metaphor   138, 142, 158–160, 161, 163, 165, 245, 303
Taxonomic Priority Principle (TPP)   138, 160–161, 165, 198, 217, 282, 283, 286, 293–294, 295
Taxonomy   35, 41
Theory of mind   139, 179–181
Theory-ladenness of descriptions   86–87
Thought disorder (discursive waywardness),
    and damaged brain   282
    and taxonomy   284
TOTE machine   107, 109
    interpretations   108
Training a net, example   199, 203
Transcendental unity of apperception   90
Turing machine   113–114, 116, 190
Turing's conjecture   112–113, 116
Type-hierarchies   49

Umwelt   20, 55

Von Neumann architecture   114, 116

Waywardness, categories of   279, 286
Weights, of connections   194, 202
Working memory,
    articulatory store   242
    as analytical model   241
    phonological loop   242